PARK ROW

THE INFLUENCE OF THE PRESS

By the same author:

THE INCREDIBLE IVAR KREUGER

PARK ROW

ALLEN CHURCHILL

NEW YORK RINEHART & COMPANY, INC. TORONTO

Grateful acknowledgment is made to the following authors and publishers for permission to reprint excerpts from their copyrighted works:

CROWN PUBLISHERS, INC., New York, N. Y., for permission to reprint a selection from WHEN DANA WAS THE SUN: A STORY OF PERSONAL JOURNALISM, by Charles J. Rosebault, copyright 1931 by Charles J. Rosebault.

DOUBLEDAY & COMPANY, INC., New York, N. Y., for permission to reprint an excerpt from THE TRIMMED LAMP by O. Henry, copyright 1907 by Doubleday & Co., Inc.

E. P. DUTTON & CO., INC., New York, N. Y., for permission to reprint excerpts from THE LIFE AND GOOD TIMES OF WILLIAM RANDOLPH HEARST by John Tebbel, copyright 1952 by John Tebbel, and from AN ADVENTURE WITH GENIUS: Recollections of Joseph Pulitzer, by Alleyne Ireland, copyright 1914 by E. P. Dutton & Co., Inc.

ISAAC F. MARCOSSON, New York, N. Y., for permission to reprint an excerpt from DAVID GRAHAM PHILLIPS, copyright 1932 by Isaac F. Marcosson.

CHARLES SCRIBNER'S SONS, New York, N. Y., for permission to reprint excerpts from NOTES OF A WAR CORRESPONDENT by Richard Harding Davis (1910); WITH THE ALLIES by Richard Harding Davis, copyright 1914 by Charles Scribner's Sons, 1942 by Hope Harding Davis Kehrig; and RICHARD HARDING DAVIS: HIS DAY by Fairfax Downey (1933).

SIMON AND SCHUSTER, INC., New York, N. Y., for permission to reprint an excerpt from THE STORY OF THE NEW YORK TIMES by Meyer Berger, © 1951 by Meyer Berger.

VANGUARD PRESS, INC., New York, N. Y., for permission to reprint excerpts from MAN OF THE WORLD by Donald Henderson Clarke, copyright 1951 by Donald Henderson Clarke.

36,500
June 1958

Dedicated to
The Newspapermen of Park Row

CONTENTS

PARK ROW

CHAPTER ONE

A Midwesterner Comes to Town

IN the early afternoon of May 10, 1883, a tall, gangling, carelessly dressed, almost knife-thin man, whose flying mop of black hair contrasted oddly with a tuft of reddish beard, emerged from one of the most ornate mansions on Fifth Avenue, in New York. It was a bright spring afternoon but the gangling man descended the steps with extreme caution, as if feeling with his foot for the next step in the dark. On the pavement he moved jerkily forward until stopped by the feel of the open carriage which awaited him. Pulling himself inside, he groped with long, sensitive fingers for the seat cushion before setting his long body down. Then in a voice that was guttural, foreign-accented, but pleasant nonetheless, he ordered the driver, "Take me to Thirty-two Park Row."

The man seated in the carriage was named Joseph Pulitzer. He was plainly myopic, perhaps almost blind, even though perched high on his beak of a nose, and anchored behind prominent ears by the thinnest of wires, was a pair of the tiny, almond-shaped spectacles of the day. Yet not only his obvious myopia made him a conspicuous figure. Equally striking was an extreme nervousness, quickly manifested by an inability to sit still. No contemporary ever bothered to record Pulitzer's progress down Fifth Avenue in the direction of downtown Manhattan on that afternoon in May, 1883, but it is safe to say that, as the driver's whip flicked the horse into action, the man leaned tensely forward with shoulders hitching, giving the impression that his own straining did as much as the horse to move the

3

carriage. From time to time he might—in a characteristic gesture—tightly link the fingers of both hands with a fierce pressure, then suddenly release the hands to run one back over the thin, tight skin of his forehead and back through the flying black hair.

Such spasmodic movements, of course, were not visible to the driver, but it is likely that in time he became conscious of them. For it was another characteristic of the high-strung Pulitzer that he quickly infected those around him with his electric energy. In part, this was because his frail body appeared to house such an excess of energy that it seemed alarmingly close to exploding from violent inner force. This impression was far from misleading. Pulitzer's thin, reedy body had grown too fast in adolescence and never caught up with that sudden, unnatural growth. His chest was almost tubercular, causing him occasionally to spit blood. Behind the tiny spectacles the vision of the warm brown eyes was blurred and daily growing dimmer. The rest of his body seemed to be given over to the possession of screaming nerves trying to drive him in all directions at once.

Even so, he could function exceedingly well. On his arrival in St. Louis shortly after the end of the Civil War, Pulitzer had been little more than a Hungarian-born, Magyar-Jewish immigrant boy, lured to the United States by an adolescent hope that in wartime he could ride a horse in the fighting cavalry. In a short time the keyed-up youth had become the most famous reporter in St. Louis. Soon he was both star reporter and co-owner of the German-language newspaper Westliche Post. Now, at thirty-six, he had prospered even more. He was editor, publisher and owner of the highly successful St. Louis Post-Dispatch.

Of these three titles, by far the most important at the time was that of editor, for this was an era when newspaper editors were important men, ranking in the public mind as high as Presidential aspirants or the robust Shakespearean actors popular in the barnstorming theatre of the day. Where a newspaper editor of the 1950's is valued for an ability to find the level of the public mind, the editor of the Eighties was respected for his ability to rise above it. A contemporary editor was looked up to as a fount of enlightenment and wisdom, a mighty fixture expected to guide public thinking. In this process his name often became better known than the paper he edited. By 1883 the two great New York editors—William Cullen Bryant of the Post and Horace Greeley of the Tribune—were dead. But Greeley's death was so recent that his opinions remained alive. It was still possible to end an argument by reaching a short distance into the past to utter the clinching words, "Greeley said . . ."

In New York, Greeley's mantle of importance had not descended on his successor as editor of the Tribune. Rather it appeared to have fallen over the wide shoulders of Charles Anderson Dana, the balding, heavily whiskered editor of the New York Sun. Dana was a former freethinker slowly turning rank commercialist, but he remained a potent newspaper force in spite of—or perhaps because of—this. Now arguments could be ended by resorting to the resounding phrase, "Dana says . . ."

In St. Louis, where the Post-Dispatch was the outstanding crusading newspaper, an equally telling phrase existed. This was, "Joseph Pulitzer says . . ." And now Joseph Pulitzer, nervously impatient, twitching, semiblind behind spectacles that hardly aided him to see, was being driven down the streets of Manhattan in the direction of Park Row, known the country over as the street on which all the important New York daily newspapers were published.

Pulitzer was taking this ride largely because of a grievous miscalculation on the part of his young and gently reared wife. Kate Pulitzer was the daughter of a remote cousin of Jefferson Davis. Through five years of marriage, she had become increasingly worried about her husband's nervousness and failing sight. She also feared tuberculosis. Pulitzer was the father of three children, but wife and family circle hardly saw him as he labored endlessly to make the Post-Dispatch the foremost newspaper in the Midwest. So it is not surprising that after five years of marriage, Mrs. Pulitzer did not understand her erratic husband—and perhaps never would. In the early spring of 1883, she had finally persuaded him to take the Pulitzer family on a trip to Europe which for him was to be therapeutic. Then Mrs. Pulitzer proceeded to make her mistake. She suggested a ten-day stopover in New York, during which her tense husband could begin unwinding by accompanying her to art museums and on shopping expeditions to the growing number of department stores in the city.

To this Pulitzer cheerfully agreed, since he truly cared for his young wife. But the stay in New York left his tumultuous mind almost wholly unoccupied. Dutifully he squired his wife, but at the same time he could find only the newspapers of the metropolis on which to focus mentally. After only a week he had reached the conclusion that New York newspapers did not serve their city well. He was well aware that New Yorkers themselves considered their press the finest in the country, if not in the world. With the possible exception of Dana's Sun, however, the newspapers of the city seemed quite content to remain in a dignified rut that had become comfortable since the days of the Civil War. To Pulitzer, it seemed that New York, a new type of city, required a new type of journalism. By his standards, New York newspapers, now that he studied them, had become atrophied by their own smugness. He felt sure that the people of the city would welcome a change, if only one were offered.

In this, he was not motivated completely by altruism, though his name has come down to us as the very image of the crusading idealist. Pulitzer was also intensely interested in making money, as some of his close associates have taken pains to point out. One has even written of Pulitzer's inner thoughts during this week in 1883: "A little gumshoeing had sufficed to show him that all New York needed to set its monetary glands flowing was a daily dose of tingling sensations. Such sensations were as plentiful as mushrooms, but were being trampled underfoot unnoticed by the editors of the sedate old-fogy newspapers, who thought a bit of snappy personal repartee on the editorial page was a humdinger and that pictures were degrading, if not actually improper."

As he often said later, one paragraph in the New York newspapers of early May, 1883, particularly annoyed Pulitzer, bringing conviction to his belief that the New York press had grown moribund. This was a hidden item stating that the city planned a public celebration for the opening of the Brooklyn Bridge, which grand occasion was scheduled for May twenty-third. This was the sort of news a Pulitzer paper would blazon to the skies, making full use of the black-and-white line cuts which the other papers considered degrading, at the same time whetting the readers' anticipation further by lively and provocative text. Pulitzer had discovered in St.

Louis how much the public enjoyed excitement and celebration and he knew that New Yorkers had watched the building of their great bridge with almost delirious interest. The story of its opening should be built into a two-week wonder.

Instead of playing up the coming event the existing newspapers had played it down. In those days, no editor had yet conceived the idea of across-the-front-page headlines. Instead, papers invariably presented news in what was called tombstone style. News was set up uniformly in long single columns, each with a one-line heading in bold face, so that the front page of a newspaper looked like so many tombstones in a graveyard. The importance of a story was not told by the amount of spectacular headline type put to use, but rather by the number of indented subheads under the head. Thus, when Abraham Lincoln was assassinated, most papers carried the story under headings like this:

AWFUL EVENT

President Lincoln
Shot by an
Assassin

The Deed Done at Ford's
Theatre Last Night

THE ACT OF A DESPERATE REBEL

The President Still Alive at
Last Accounts

No Hopes Entertained of His
Recovery

Attempted Assassination of
Secretary Seward

DETAILS OF THE DREADFUL TRAGEDY

In 1883 newspapers still used such pretentious and unspecific sub-heads. But what added more monotony to the tombstone make-up was the fact that newspapers of the day were large—almost the size of today's baby blanket. Into all this space was packed tight a desert of minute type, broken only by an occasional discreet tombstone head. No special emphasis was given major stories, nor did much thought appear to go into the general arrangement of the paper. As a later historian has testified: "All newspapers except the Sun got out a daily paper as one fills a garbage can, without discrimination or undue mental effort."

Reading from left to right across the front page of the New York Times on May tenth—and no other paper did better—Pulitzer had found such exciting stories as: THE FUNDING BILL IS PASSED—APPORTIONMENT PROBLEMS—DEATH OF GOVERNOR FOSTER IN OHIO—THE CONTROL OF THE SENATE—RIVER AND HARBOR BILL. True, the Times was aimed at people interested in financial news, just as the Sun specialized in flavorsome writing, and the Herald, which in 1871 had gained world fame by sending Stanley to track down Livingstone, now favored society, sporting and foreign news, flavored with backstairs gossip. But a Pulitzer paper would never appeal to a single kind of reader, as most other New York papers did. It would try to capture the interest of all types. Nor would Pulitzer appeal only to the mind, as was the pattern of the day. A paper of his would present the news honestly, but in such a way as to strike the emotions and heartstrings.

Pulitzer had taken special note of the fact that the important New York newspapers beat the drum for the Republican Party. In St. Louis, he himself had first been a Republican, as such serving on the city's three-man police commission and also in the Missouri legislature. He had been a liberal Republican, favoring the nomination of his fellow newspaperman, Horace Greeley, over U. S. Grant. After Greeley's defeat in the convention, Pulitzer had swung in such a wide arc that soon he was labeled a Republican radical. Inevitably, he had become a Democrat and the Post-Dispatch had put its weight behind that party. In New York, as Pulitzer was well aware, the growing lower and middle classes leaned toward the Democratic Party, and as they did no important newspaper spoke for them.

Pulitzer's mind was rapidly proceeding toward a goal, and needed only a catalyst to reach it. This promptly came from his newspaper contacts in New York. His brother Albert was publisher of a lagging paper called the New York Journal, and Pulitzer himself had for a short time been Washington correspondent of the New York Sun. Thus he had been in New York only a few days before hearing the latest bit of newspaper gossip: that the Wall Street financier Jay Gould was weary of publishing the New York World, a paper which had come to him incidentally as part of a giant stock deal. The World was considered the whitest of white elephants, but it was conveniently Democratic, complete with functioning offices and presses in the ·former Western Union Building at 32 Park Row. Beside the potential of a Pulitzer paper in New York, visits to art museums, department stores, and even vacations in Europe faded into quick nothingness. Pulitzer had sent out feelers to Gould and discovered that the asking price for the World was $346,000. Yet Gould would be satisfied with a down payment of $100,000. Further, Pulitzer believed—correctly—that the additional $246,000 could be made in a short time by his kind of New York World. Shortly after noon on May tenth, he drove up to Gould's mansion with the $100,000. The necessary papers had immediately been signed and now, as proud publisher of the World, he was moving with characteristic haste to take command of his new property.

As he did this, Pulitzer's ideas of livening the World did not go so far as to envision banner headlines, but he did see news stories written with punch, accuracy and pathos, dominated by hard-hitting heads and informative subheads, and occasionally illustrated by line cuts. Yet with all his practical ideas for revamping the New York newspaper scene, his great contribution to journalism would never be to the body of newspapers, but to the spirit. For in their devotion to political parties and entrenched wealth, contemporary newspapers had become the organs of party and individual. "Before Joseph Pulitzer," says his employe and biographer, Don Carlos Seitz, "the nation's newspapers did not act freely, open to any cause. It was Mr. Pulitzer's belief that a newspaper was a public servant, bound by no other considerations than to the community. It was a new and welcome doctrine, first to the public, then to the press itself. He would not pander, he would not compromise, and he made himself heard!"

With all his newsgathering innovations and the controversies that stormed about his head, Pulitzer's contribution to the spirit— or the soul—of journalism remained his greatest achievement, so that forty-eight years later the last editor of the World, sadly writing the paper's obituary, could state: "So far as I am concerned, Joseph Pulitzer was the Great Emancipator of American journalism. He freed the American press from the shackles of party and personal yoke and made it slave to nothing but the truth and the facts."

Pulitzer's destination on the afternoon of May tenth was a romantic place. Informally known as Newspaper Row, it was a short street in lower Manhattan called Park Row—"Just a little street with only one side and no square corners," a guide book of the time calls it. Park Row had no square corners since it ran northeast at a slight angle, beginning at Ann Street, where it branched out from Broadway. It could be called one-sided because on its western side lay only the pleasant grassiness of City Hall Park and the picturesque City Hall building itself. With a centralization remarkable even for those times, Park Row and its immediate vicinity had become the home of every New York daily newspaper. Inevitably it was dubbed New York's Fleet Street—or even America's. The actual newspaper portion of Park Row extended northeast from Broadway and Ann to a tiny triangle at Nassau Street, which featured a statue of Benjamin Franklin and was called Printing House Square. Just north of Printing House Square lay the plaza entrance to the about-to-be-opened Brooklyn Bridge. Beyond this, Park Row extended for another stretch, ending at Chatham Square. On this latter section of Park Row, the new elevated trains had their terminus. No major newspapers were printed on this less famous half of Park Row, but as if sharply to point up the difference from the Newspaper Row portion, this was the center of New York's foreign-language press. A German, several Chinese, and (shortly) a Swedish newspaper had offices there.

Dominating Newspaper Row, as well as the entire lower section of the city, was the nine-story New York Tribune Building, facing

Printing House Square and looking directly across at City Hall. Completed in 1875 at a cost of one million dollars, the Tribune Building was still, in 1883, the largest, tallest building in the growing city. As such, it housed not only the city room, composing room, foundry and cellar presses of the thriving Tribune, but also those of the less prosperous Journal. Since the Journal took up only the second and third floors of the building, and the Tribune slightly more, there even remained ample room for commercial tenants.

But marvelous as the red-stone Tribune Building may have been, its high Clock Tower was far more so. A thin tower rising some 285 feet in the air, with a clock so large that all could see it, the Tribune Tower was the architectural marvel of the city. Beside it and the imposing red-stone Tribune Building, the other newspaper buildings running south to Ann Street looked unprepossessing indeed. All were old and few were more than three stories high. Even so, many of them housed more than a single newspaper.

One of the newsmen then laboring along Newspaper Row was Louis T. Golding, managing editor of a paper called the Commercial Advertiser. "Park Row was lined with newspaper offices," he wrote many years later. "It began at Broadway where the Herald, solidly fixed in its white marble building (as became that giant so arrogant) was its south bastion. Then it ran northeast, to where the brilliantly edited Sun and the Tribune held the north end of the line."

The Herald, the Sun and the Tribune were the giants among contemporary New York newspapers. The others existed because, at a time when profits could be made from mere circulation (big advertisements were all but unknown), it was an easy matter for an editor fired from one of the giants to start up a smaller newspaper of his own. Thus many small and forgotten journals were to be found on the Park Row of the period. Following the Herald, Sun and Tribune in importance came Jay Gould's World, the Journal, the Times (after prosperous years under Henry J. Raymond, now on the way to becoming temporarily "feeble and failing, dead from the neck down"), the Star, the Mail & Express, the Commercial Advertiser, the Daily News, the Evening Telegram, the Press and the Recorder. On adjacent streets, within sound of the clattering presses of Park Row, still other papers had gathered: notably the Evening Post and the Staats Zeitung. The German-language paper would soon locate on the less celebrated stretch of Park Row.

Newspaper Row of the day was populated by redoubtable figures who wrote noble, Shakespeare-tinted prose about routine fires or edited copy with diminishing whiskey bottle close at hand. But if one bond could be said to unite all Park Row newspapermen—as well as newspapermen across the entire country—it was the belief that, in the New York Sun, Park Row possessed a treasure. The Sun was in a shabby six-story building at the corner of Nassau and Frankfort streets, facing Printing House Square and sharing the block with the vastly bigger Tribune Building. To reach the third-floor city room of the Sun—the building had until recently been Tammany Hall—it was necessary to climb a spiral iron staircase which wound its way upward through a gloomy shaft. As in all Park Row newspaper buildings, the walls of the Sun echoed and trembled interminably from the rumble of the presses in the cellar. At the top of the spiral staircase was the sanctum of Charles Anderson Dana, the formidable editor and publisher. Beyond Dana's office a huge loft formed such a conglomeration of all Sun departments that it perpetually resembled a madhouse. Into it charged angry pressmen demanding copy, while copy boys scampered about in answer to furious shouts from editors and reporters.

The hub of this teeming confusion was the city editor's desk, and around it the working reporters sat at inclined tables illuminated at night, and usually during the day, by flickering gaslight, though dim electric light would shortly make an appearance in Park Row city rooms. At the tilted desks the men wrote out their stories in long-hand in pencil, more often than not with hats on heads. This fine newspaper tradition had its roots in early days when it seemed the best method of keeping an expensive beaver from being stolen by some unconscionable visitor to the city room. The scribbling reporters would work from handwritten notes, taken as they covered New York on orders from the city editor. Many of the older reporters were full-bearded, while most younger men wore rich mustaches. Only a few of the younger men would be clean-shaven.

As a group the men in the city room would to our eyes seem

drably dressed in white shirts, dark suits, and stiff celluloid collars. A few would wear bow ties, and one or two affected the dressy ascot. All would have on high laced or high buttoned shoes, for these were the only type of footwear for males of the period. In summer or moments of stress, it was customary to tear off coats and vests, revealing trousers held up by antiseptically white suspenders.

Clouds of smoke from pipes and cigars—but no cigarettes—filled the air. Strategically placed around the scuffed wooden floor were large brass spittoons into which older members of the staff expertly spat tobacco juice from amazing distances. The mechanical sounds of news tickers, telephones, and typewriters were, of course, not to be heard, but shouted conversation, loud profanity and bellowing for the copy boys more than made up for lack of mechanical clatter. The general bedlam, however, completely failed to disturb the Olympian detachment of the editorial writers, who sat a little apart from the rest, musing over the state of the nation or studying copies of the previous edition covered with blue-pencil instructions from the mighty Dana himself.

Out of this seeming disorganization came what was then considered the newspaperman's newspaper. "The Sun sparkled like its name, with humorous stories, pathetic stories, bits of vivid description," one contemporary wrote. Where other American newspapers appeared to be edited for a public on which editors looked with condescension, the Sun was edited to be enjoyed by both press and public. All across the country, editors and reporters reached first for the Sun when piles of exchange newspapers were laid out in the office. City editors tried to ape its pungent treatment of news while the daydreams of reporters were largely devoted to envisioning a summons to work on the paragon paper.

No one then alive would dare deny that the reason for this extreme respect was contained in the person of Charles Anderson Dana himself. Under him the Sun was a newspaper which felt free to keep no opinion to itself. It had just called the humble New York Journal, edited by Albert Pulitzer, a newspaper edited by fools for fools. This unkind thrust, together with the sudden appearance of his dynamic brother on the New York scene, would shortly cause Albert to disappear entirely from Park Row. The Sun main-

tained such high editorial standards that it could neither be criti-
cized nor disregarded. Yet for all its arrogance, it was less the perfect newspaper than a superior anomaly among papers. As Pulitzer
had duly noted—considering it a strong point in his New York favor
—the Sun did not print the news so much as the news around the
news. To Dana, as a history of the Sun has pointed out: "Life was
not a mere procession of elections, legislatures, theatrical perform-
ances, murders and lectures. Life was everything—a new kind of ap-
ple, a crying child on the curb, a policeman's epigram, the exact
weight of a candidate for President, the latest style in whiskers, the
origin of a new slang expression, the idiosyncrasies of the City Hall
clock, a strange fourmaster in the harbor, a vendetta in Mulberry
Bend—everything was fish to the great net of Dana's mind."

Working for the man who saw news in such a way could be bewildering. Dana's criticisms were merciless, for he insisted that every
edition of the Sun be perfect. Reporters were on duty for long periods of time, with the average day of ten to twelve hours often lengthening to fifteen and sometimes twenty-four. There were practically no telephones to make newsgathering easy, and a reporter sent
out on a story was required to return to the office and write it in
longhand himself. After that Dana studied and analyzed the story.
Then he cross-examined the reporter, in case any shadings had
been left out—for it was the relentless man's unique belief that,
in interviews at least, the way a man looked was more important
than what he said. Having successfully passed all this, a reporter
might relax happily for a moment, only to hear himself summoned
once more to Dana's office and fired for using the word *balance*
in the sense of *remainder*, which was just the sort of subtle misuse
that Dana specialized in finding.

For, even more than accuracy, the primary preoccupation of
Dana's mind was grammar and English usage. The awesome man was
fiendishly determined that every edition of the Sun stand as a monument to the ultimate in English. No one ever found a grammatical
error or slipshod phrasing in Dana's Sun. It is said that once a literary
critic on another paper sent Dana samples of his better columns in
the hope of an invitation to join the Sun. Almost immediately the
samples came back and the aspirant searched for some indication

as to how Dana had reacted. Finally he found a black line of ex-
clamatory outrage under two words in one column. The offending
words were *none are.*

At the same time, the Sun could display a sense of humor. To
the vast delight of Park Row, the paper often burlesqued prize features printed by rival journals. For instance, a young reporter named
Selah F. Clarke, later one of the immortal Sun managing editors,
had parodied a series of naughty French stories which a smaller
paper, desperate for circulation, had serialized. In a scene Newspaper Row chortled over for years, Clarke had his heroine display
what was then an improper amount of silk stocking. She then
soothed her abashed young man by cooing, "Do not be ashamed
of me, my love, this is my *wooden* leg."

Dana had a favorite city-room maxim: Be Interesting. Another
edict endlessly drilled into his reporters was: Never Be in a Hurry.
These two adjurations allowed Sun men vast leeway. Encouraged to
write in leisurely, atmospheric fashion, they injected into stories
flowery descriptions of scenery, flights of fancy, and even personal
opinion. The Sun was obviously written by gentlemen—it favored
college men, to the fury of unemployed but experienced reporters
around Park Row. Yet not only were Sun stories written by gentlemen, they were written by gentlemen with plenty of time to create.
The result was that most Sun stories read like essays—or, as one
contemporary put it, "The Sun could evolve a classic out of a dog-
fight, an epic out of a football game, invest a tenement house
eviction with pregnant pathos, or make an account of a fire vibrant
with drama."

So towering was the reputation of the Sun that events in its city
room were repeated all through newspaperdom. Thus the newspaper
world quickly learned that in the city room at Nassau and Spruce
Streets a bewildered cub reporter had plaintively demanded of city
editor John Bogart a definition of news. Bogart pulled on his pipe
for a moment, or perhaps paused to swig from the neck of a bottle
of whiskey. "Son," he finally said, "when a dog bites a man that is
not news, because it happens so often. But if a man bites a dog,
that's news."

To work for Dana of the Sun, with his ceaseless demands for

perfection, brought many problems. Still the Sun—no less than any other newspaper of the day—could on occasion become a place of high romance. In our own time, with dozens and perhaps hundreds of reporters covering major news events, it is almost impossible to conceive of a twenty-year-old reporter being ordered by a managing editor to check a rumor concerning no less a personage than an ex-President of the United States. Yet this is precisely what happened to a fresh-cheeked cub named Charles J. Rosebault in the city room of the Sun. Rosebault, who remained with the Sun to become business manager, never ceased to look back with awe and wonder on that magic night.

> Visualize [he wrote later] the task of the reporter, who was sent out around eleven o'clock one winter's night to investigate a rumor that [ex-President] Grant was dying of Cancer. That was all he had to go on—that and the managing editor's suggestion that a friend of the General lived on lower Fifth Avenue. Grant himself and his family were believed to be out of the city.
> Eleven o'clock in the mid-Eighties was past most people's bedtime, and it was half past when the reporter had found the man's residence. After repeated ringing a head was thrust out of the front door. By good fortune it was the man wanted, and he was not cross over this late summons. But he knew nothing at all about the alleged cancer. He had heard the General was ill—yes, and he seemed to remember that Dr. Fordyce-Baker was his physician.
> Away sped the reporter, on the hunt for a drugstore where he might consult a city directory for the address of the physician. It was in one of the 'Forties, and the only way to get there was to dash across Fifth Avenue and control his nerves while the horse-car slowly rolled on up to Forty-second Street and then to Madison Avenue.
> Fordyce-Baker, a distinguished physician and a courtly English gentleman, was luckily awake and in his library when the reporter arrived. Moreover, he was Grant's doctor and was ready to confirm the rumor. Only, being a devotee of accuracy himself, he insisted that what the Sun proposed to write about this should be the truth, the whole truth and

nothing but the truth. To make sure of this he took his seat at the library table and carefully wrote down the history of Grant's illness, its exact nature and the probability of its duration.

A handsome man, and the embodiment of culture and refinement as he sat in his big leather chair writing carefully, pausing every now and then to ponder. A room of noble proportions, lined with books in mahogany shelves, so cosily warm and cheerful with the crackling logs, and such a contrast to the bitter cold dark streets from which the reporter had just come. But for the young man with the frost-bitten face it was a torture chamber, its only significant furniture the Grandfather clock in the corner, ticking away the vital moments. Already it was after midnight and the Sun office miles away. Will the old codger never finish!

Yes, he is done with writing, he has read it over, but even with the surrender of the precious bit of paper the ordeal is not finished.

"Read it aloud, so that we may be sure you can master my writing," says the physician, smiling amiably. "I write such a wretched hand."

In calmer moments the reporter wondered how he had held back from throttling him. Here was a big news story, a sure beat on all the other papers, and he was being done out of it by a doddering old fossil!

At last! At last! He is out and free again. Little does he reck the biting night as he runs like a hound through slush and ice to the nearest station of the Third Avenue elevated road. His one chance is to catch a train within the next few minutes. He can give no heed to the probabilities that he will come a cropper on the slippery pavement. Panting, thoroughly winded, he forces his tired legs to forget their weariness, his sopping feet to skip like a fairy's as he leaps up the steps to the platform. Thank God! Virtue is rewarded. He lands on the train just as the guard is closing the gate! No sooner in his seat than he has his roll of copy paper on his knee and his numbed fingers are racing the pencil across sheet after sheet. When the train rolls into City Hall station, his article is finished. Again he forces his

stiffened body to the courser's pace, bounding up the two
flights of stairs to the city room. Is he in time, after all?

The omniscient managing editor is standing at the little dumb waiter which carries copy to the composing room,
his omnipresent pipe tipped at an impertinent angle. He has
just sent up the final item.

But there are still a few minutes' grace, and emergency
only stimulates to action. Without moving from his place,
the managing editor dashes off a heading—the reporters did
not write the "heads" in those days—and skims the pages
with a glance. It is all over in a jiffy and the manuscript is
on its way.

"Looks like a beat," the managing editor remarks, with
just a suggestion of satisfaction. . . .

The metropolis through which Pulitzer impatiently drove on
May 10, 1883, was a picturesque town with a population of almost
one and a half million. But though a small city by today's standards,
New York possessed the abundant energies of a city which sensed
itself on the verge of extravagant growth. Under the impact of the
immigrants streaming through the Battery, New York was losing
what has been called its Dickensian flavor. The rich excitement
it offered was apparent even to those who lived there, so that a
writer of the time could picture objectively for those who might
venture from the hinterlands:

New York is the great metropolis to all Americans, the
abiding place of all the marvels that made the fame of ancient Bagdad, the Superb. For the stranger, at least, romance lurks in every doorway and vice, horrible yet fascinating, stalks in all the byways. Life is freer, wickeder, bolder
here than anywhere else. Crowds, the rapid pace, and the
everlasting struggle, whether for supremacy or mere existence, seem to create a different sort of being from those who
amble through life in the smaller town. For the outlander
there is always the thrill of excitement in the very atmosphere of the Colossus.

Old New York families, anxious to avoid contamination by the
European hordes, were moving as far uptown as Forty-second Street,

while small, average family residential districts and shops now dotted almost every section of Manhattan Island. A few of the city's important streets were paved and more boasted bumpy cobblestones, but the majority were merely enlarged yellow-dirt lanes. Horse-drawn streetcars had become a proud feature of the city scene and the marvels of the steam-driven Els were on everyone's lips—which is small wonder, since the seats in the new elevated railway cars were plush and the car interiors were decorated with carved-wood elegance.

New York was obviously experiencing violent growing pains. At the same time it remained a small city, with a real commercial district only below Fourteenth Street, or even Canal. Inevitably, the business center would move uptown, but if this move had already started, it was so slow as to be apparent to almost no one. New York would grow—everyone sensed that. But it would be a long time before it visibly became even the city of Four Million—O. Henry's New York.

The below-Canal-Street importance of the city was the reason for the centralization of newspapers along Park Row. Lacking telephones and rapid transportation, it was necessary for newspapers to remain near City Hall and the criminal courts, on both of which contemporary journalism depended heavily for news. Another reason was nearness to the Bowery, in which wide-open district nearly ninety-five per cent of the city's crime originated—though Hell's Kitchen on the West Side would soon cut into the Bowery's exclusive franchise. Behind the Bowery, and feeding its ruthless demands for new humanity, was the Ghetto district of the lower East Side. Already outrageously overpopulated, with a vivid agglomeration of Irish, Italians, Poles, Russians, Bohemians and other definite national groups, the New York Ghetto was incubating some of the worst slums the world has ever known.

Even then it was a district so unclean, unsanitary and generally appalling that a famous newspaper story of the day began, "Hester Street reeked in its native dirt." One of the few pleasures Ghetto dwellers might expect was a view of the sky, but New York streets of the day were festooned with a thundercloud of crossed telegraph wires, soon to be increased by those of the telephone company. These wires all but shut out the sun and sky, yet there was color in the Ghetto, even if it was a dreadful kind. From 1883 to 1900 conditions in the slums improved only slightly, so that it is possible to quote later writers, who discovered the color, about conditions in 1883. Thus, ten years later, the novelist Stephen Crane could give the feel of an 1883 Ghetto tenement when he wrote:

> They entered a dark region where, from a careening building, a dozen gruesome doorways gave up loads of babies to the street and the gutter. A wind of early autumn raised yellow dust from cobbles and swirled it against a hundred windows. Long streamers of garments fluttered from fire escapes. In all unhandy places there were buckets, brooms, rags and bottles. In the street infants played or fought with other infants or sat stupidly in the way of vehicles. Formidable women, with uncombed hair and disordered dress, gossiped while leaning on railings, or screamed in frantic quarrels. Withered persons in curious postures of submission to something, sat smoking pipes in obscure corners. A thousand odors of cooking food came forth to the street. The building quivered and creaked from the weight of humanity stamping about in its bowels.

No one cared whether Ghetto and Bowery children went to school. Overworked, starved, unhappy parents merely allowed offspring to grow beyond the infancy period, then drove them to find work. If the children failed, they were beaten or cast adrift. This and other terrible conditions figuratively set fire to a young Danish immigrant named Jacob Riis, who, almost on arrival in this country, had been bitten by the newspaper bug. Riis quickly made a name for himself on Park Row by rushing back from his first assignment so fast that at the entrance to his building he knocked the managing editor into a snowdrift. In time, Riis was assigned to cover police headquarters, which he did from a small district office on Mulberry Street, in the heart of the infamous Bend, a center of slums and crime. Riis covered his headquarters assignment notably, solving cases which baffled the police. But, more important, he began writing sketches about life on the Bend which were later expanded into a book called *How the Other Half Lives*. In order to prove that the filth and degradation he described actually existed, Riis made himself a pioneer amateur photographer and snapped indisputable pictures of such slum spots as Bandit's Roost and Bottle Alley. "The New York Ghetto," he concluded, "is not fit for men and women, much less children."

The Ghetto was a district of filth and poverty, where only suicides, epidemics and tenement-house fires worked to cut down the soaring population. By nearness to the gaudy Bowery, it also became a factory of vice and crime. By wandering only a few hundred feet, slum children found themselves on Bowery streets where nearly every building was a saloon, a crooked café, a house of assignation, or a flourishing brothel. To anyone who cared to admit the fact, this brought to New York of 1883—the city so rapidly losing its Dickensian flavor—an atmosphere reminiscent of another Englishman's day. Like the London of Hogarth, the rich in New York were disgustingly rich, while the poor were atrociously poor. Yet, worse than being empty of pockets, New York's poor were devoid of hope. Arriving in the expected land of promise, an immigrant found himself laboring twelve hours a day and getting for it the mighty sum of one dollar. At the same time, a strong class system robbed him of ambition. The poor boy of the time seldom got rich in rags-to-riches fashion. When he did, the feat required such ruthlessness that few could hope to emulate him.

In Hogarth's London, the poor took to gin and guzzled themselves into oblivion. Up to and beyond the turn of the century, New York, lacking a Gin Lane, became a city of beer for the poor. After a wearying day, the average laborer had nothing to do but return to a tenement kitchen perhaps shared by as many as a dozen other families. It was a prospect as hopeless as his day of twelve-hour toil, and the only spark of relief consisted in sending one of the progeny a man knew no way of avoiding to the corner saloon with the family beer can. The emaciated child, often a girl, entering a saloon with an empty beer tin, became a cliché of the period. This, together with the fact that so many working fathers stopped at the corner saloon on payday to drink up a week's wages, later became

a potent and unanswerable weapon in the hands of Prohibition-
ists.

Fathers were not the only members of slum families who worked.
The need to put some kind of food into famished mouths drove
wives and daughters into sweatshops and department stores. In a
store, a girl or woman would get from $2.00 to $4.50 a week, a
sum which could be drastically reduced by fines for so-called mistakes. Jacob Riis tells of a thirteen-year-old girl whose two-dollar
weekly salary was cut by sixty cents for a trivial slip, the sixty cents
promptly going into the pocket of the elderly cashier who imposed
the fine. Girls who clerked in stores could be summarily fired for
minor infractions or on complaints of irascible customers. Even so,
these girls were better off than the ones who worked in East Side
sweatshops. Here the top wage was 60¢ for a twelve-hour day, with
the privilege of taking work home at night. Some sweatshops jammed
hundreds of working women into lofts unheated in winter and
furnace-hot in summer. Others were run by small-time operators
called "sweaters," who used Ghetto living quarters as factories. Traveling up and down on the Second and Third Avenue Els, it was
possible to peer into these apartments, where girls stitched with
flying fingers or bent over the new sewing machines, driven on by the
rasping voice of a male or female boss. Jacob Riis, who devoted a
chapter of *How the Other Half Lives* to the evils of the sweatshop,
describes one such apartment this way:

> Up two flights of dark stairs, three, four, with new
> smells of cabbage, of onions, of frying fish, on every land-
> ing, whirring sewing machines behind closed doors betraying
> what goes on within. . . . Five men and a woman, two
> young girls, not fifteen, and a boy who says unasked that he
> is fifteen, and lies in saying it, are at the machines sewing.
> . . . The floor is littered ankle-deep with half-sewn gar-
> ments. . . . The faces, hands, and arms to the elbows of
> everyone in the room are black with the color of the cloth
> on which they are working. The boy and the woman alone
> look up at our entrance. The girls shoot sidelong glances,
> but at a warning look from the man with the bundle, they
> tread their machines more energetically than ever.

It is hardly surprising that among adults of the poorer classes such conditions produced a deep unhappiness and frustration, which in turn created a desire to lash out and hurt someone. There were only two things a resentful Ghetto grownup could lash out and hurt, and these were children and animals. The man-bites-dog news dictum elucidated in the Sun city room had true pertinence then, for the streets of the city abounded in wretched, abused dogs running wild. A great many of these unhappy animals had hydrophobia, and the sort of human-interest story in which Park Row newspapers then reveled told of little children being bitten by mad dogs and slowly dying.

But mad dogs were only a minor source of heartthrob stories. In the crowded melting-pot tenements—also called human rookeries —drunken fathers beat wives and children, often driving the children from home so that on the eve of any holiday, newspaper reporters could always write about homeless, starving children huddled in doorways. Homeless boys played a special rôle along Park Row. From the Newsboy's Lodging House were recruited the urchins who shouted "Uxtry" up and down the streets of Manhattan.

In the dormitory of the Newsboy's lodging a sign read, "Boys who swear and chew tobacco cannot sleep here," but it is unlikely that this harsh rule was rigidly enforced. Newsboys of the time were a seasoned, precocious breed and—seemingly in other cities more than New York—often became so infected by the excitement of the newspaper game that they grew up to be star reporters. Because of the number of newspapers published along Park Row, and the Extras which over the next twenty-five years were published with increasing vigor, there always seemed to be papers for a boy to tuck under his arm and hawk about town. At all hours of the day and night, groups of newsboys waited on Park Row, in the winter huddling over the grates which let off steam and heat from cellar press rooms. Newsboys were perhaps the lucky ones. For them, benevolent citizens had at least provided a lodging house where a bed and two meals a day cost the convenient sum of eighteen cents. But for each boy who lodged at the Newsboy's home there were dozens, or maybe hundreds, who slept in doorways, tenement house stairs, and on park benches. These homeless waifs were called Street Arabs, and it is said that in the few years of its existence a home called the Duane Street Lodging House had cared for at least a quarter of a million.

Staggering as the number of homeless waifs may seem, the number of girls soliciting on the streets of New York was far more so. As early as 1866, Bishop Simpson of the Methodist-Episcopal church complained from his pulpit that there were more prostitutes than Methodists in the city. The good man was not indulging in exaggeration. By 1883, New York possessed some ten thousand easily available daughters of joy and as the population increased the number rose accordingly. By 1890, there were probably twenty thousand, and four years later, when Dr. Charles H. Parkhurst launched a notable moral crusade, the number was set at twenty-five thousand. During this era newspapers carried veiled advertisements of houses of prostitution and, it was reported with horror, respectable men could not sit in city parks without being accosted so frequently that it became annoying. Some bold girls even spoke to men out promenading with their wives, giving exciting verbal instructions as to where they could be found after the wife was safely tucked in bed.

In 1883, prostitution in New York had fallen into the loose pattern which it maintained until 1900, when the Bowery faded as a thrill center. Girls from the Ghetto usually wandered into the Bowery, where, after a few nights of independence, they were grabbed into houses of prostitution. Later, under the beady eye of a pimp, a Bowery girl would be allowed to patrol the Bowery streets, soliciting the out-of-town rubes who visited the much-publicized place. Commercialized vice in New York was an organized business, carefully protected by police who benefited from it financially. Even with great numbers of Bowery girls eager for the prostitute's life, the vice barons of the time remained unsatisfied. They organized gangs of toughs—so-called "cadets"—who put knockout drops into the drinks of girls in bars, or simply hauled pretty ones off sidewalks. One girl so seized was the daughter of a prominent East Side rabbi, and a great hue and cry arose in newspapers over the fact that a respectable girl could be abducted in broad daylight. But so strong were vice interests that no paper suggested the possibility of getting the girl out of the Bowery brothel in which she had been placed. This was known to be utterly impossible, and the girl was left to her life of shame.

While Ghetto girls easily found their way to the Bowery, uptown girls and those from out of town followed a pattern of operating in the area becoming known as the Tenderloin. Eventually this bright-light district along Sixth Avenue and Broadway, and extending north from Twenty-third Street, would supplant the Bowery as the city's center of sex and gaiety. Girls who worked the Tenderloin also functioned as part of a system. They were called Slaves, and their mode of operation inevitably became known as the Slave System. Though the Tenderloin, too, had its houses of prostitution, its main feature was dance halls where amorous men could meet willing girls. Thus the Tenderloin girl was allowed more freedom to operate than her Bowery sister. But no matter how widely she ranged among the tinseled Tenderloin dance halls, she remained a slave, with a pimp for lord and master.

Travelers from London and Paris, both of which cities possessed quantities of streetwalkers, often commented on the youth and freshness of New York prostitutes. They condescendingly attributed this to lack of moral fibre in a young, uncouth nation. Such, however, was not the reason. Jacob Riis and others have paid tribute to New York working girls of the time and the battle most of them waged against the temptations of prostitution. Rather than a lack of moral fibre, prostitution in New York reduced to a matter of human and economic pressures relentlessly driving young girls into streetwalking. Not the least of these was the hopeless monotony of a working girl's life. Laboring for sixty cents or one dollar a day, from which fines could be extracted, permitted a girl to do little more than eat and sleep, without even the relief of an occasional new, colorful dress or hat. This was only one factor. In the Ghetto and other slum sections, young males had little time for or interest in the amenities of courtship and love. Bitter and unhappy like their parents, they operated by jungle law, with girls as prey. And not only was a girl preyed upon by males, but by police as well. Henry F. Pringle has called the 1883 cop on the beat fat and stupid. More than that, he was venal. Well aware that his superiors, from Chief Inspector William I. Flynn on down, were receiving large sums in pay-offs from madams and over-all vice interests, he had no hesitation about getting his bit by stopping a working girl as she returned from late work in a sweatshop. He would then demand her money and, if she refused, arrest her as a prostitute. After a few such experiences, a girl might think it really easier to walk the streets.

Even harder to resist than such blatant shakedowns were the subtle pressures on young girls. Prostitutes walked the streets of every American city, yet respectable folk of the time refused to admit it. For at least ten years after 1883, no novelist dared mention the existence of prostitutes. From those who finally dared, it is possible to learn that in slum neighborhoods everyone seemed to expect a pretty girl to wind up on the streets. As a working girl walked home at night, the taunts of jungle males and envious older women called her a whore. If a girl put a bright ribbon in her hair, she would be followed by urchins shrieking, "Yer on the turf." In *Maggie: A Girl of the Streets*, the first novel written about a New York prostitute, Stephen Crane pictures Maggie's drunken mother accusing her of being a streetwalker when she is a few minutes late getting home. At last Maggie does fall, and her brother brings the news home. With something like glee, as if he has expected it all along, he says, "Maggie's gone teh D'devil! Dat's what! See!"

With all this, the real villain remains the economics of the times. At least the life of a prostitute seemed to offer some change from a life of bleak monotony, together with some of the male companionship and gaiety that a girl requires. A less well-remembered novelist—David Graham Phillips—has described two girls in a slum neighborhood, stoically enduring the barren poverty, the insults of neighbors and the overtures of lecherous employers. Slowly a tacit understanding grows between them. Neither puts it into words, but instinctively each knows she will go on the streets. One Saturday night they exchange a look and realize the moment has come. Leaving the drab tenement room, they are whores by dawn. But at least, for a short time, they have escaped the relentless monotony of slum lives—or what Stephen Crane calls a "life of hardship and insult."

CHAPTER TWO

The Pulitzer World

JOSEPH PULITZER's explosive first appearance in the city room of the World, on May 10, 1883, has long intoxicated the imaginations of chroniclers of newspaperdom. "The tall young adventurer from the West," writes Don Carlos Seitz, "his language still laden with the accent of a foreign tongue, radiating excitement and diffusing energy, came in like a tornado. He disturbed the sleek routine of the place and soon all was confusion. The old-fashioned staff viewed his coming with tremulous dismay." An actual member of the staff wrote a friend: "I hardly know the office. A cyclone has struck, men are hurrying around. J.P. seems to be everywhere, now arguing with a reporter, now dashing to the composing room. He loves argument. . . ."

But whatever the stunning impact of Pulitzer's arrival in the sedate city room, it was matched by the appearance of the first edition of the new World the morning of May eleventh. The new World cost the lordly sum of two cents, and its circulation on that day was 22,761. Physically it comprised eight type-packed pages, six long columns to a page. Heads on stories were set in discreet Roman capitals, each with two indented subheads. There were four such display—or major—stories that morning, each, to the modern eye, proffered with the utmost mildness. The most dramatic was the story of a New Jersey storm, which was headed THE DEADLY LIGHTNING! Below this the subhead read: Six Lives and One Million Dollars Lost. A hanging in Sing Sing had also paid off journalistically, for as the noose fitted about his neck, the burly, unregenerate murderer had bellowed, "Yer hangin' the wrong man."

Sedate as that first page of the Pulitzer World appears today, it was a thunderbolt in the New York of the time. Typographically the paper offered no innovations, but the emotion Pultizer's driving energy had infused into reporters who wrote of the New Jersey storm and the hanging made reading of an electrifying nature. Regular purchasers of the paper were amazed by the brisk readability of the new paper. So were rival editors, who, from solidly entrenched positions, read the World with a condescension quickly tinged by alarm. Some of this stemmed from the fact that it had become known around Park Row that Pulitzer had sent one of his soon to be famous come-at-once telegrams to John A. Cockerill, until recently managing editor of the Post-Dispatch. Cockerill had reluctantly been severed from the Post-Dispatch after shooting a man in a city-room fracas. But now he was free, since St. Louis police had accepted his story of killing in self-defense. And now this frightening and competent man would be joining Pulitzer in New York!

A square, compact man with a bristling mustache, Cockerill seemed to dwell in a perpetual fury. He had been a drummer boy in 1861-65, and, from the contemporary habit of bestowing titles on any solid citizen who fought in the Civil War, was usually called Colonel Cockerill. On putting down his drum, Cockerill had felt the call of journalism. He became a printer's devil on Ohio newspapers, then joined the staff of the Cincinnati Enquirer. There an older reporter named Lafcadio Hearn always recalled him as "a sort of furious young person."

If Pulitzer's body seemed to contain a dynamo far too violent for its frailty, Cockerill's sturdy energies were better contained. His talents thoroughly complemented those of Pulitzer, whose genius was always for the editorial page. Pulitzer was the angry, crusading, inside-page man whose fighting editorials often led to front-page stories. Cockerill was first and last the front-page man. Even more than Pulitzer, he had been annoyed by the lofty prose style of contemporary journalism, which stemmed from emulation of the New York Sun. In St. Louis, Pulitzer had groped for the right style of hard-hitting news coverage, but until he hired Cockerill as his managing editor, he had not found it.

After telegraphing Colonel Cockerill, Pulitzer had also written out a declaration of intent, which he published on the front page of his first edition. In it, he vigorously declared that the World would be a reform newspaper, a fact which could be dangerous to New York papers which, up to and including the distinguished Sun, were content largely to report and nurture the status quo. But Pulitzer was out to change things, as his declaration attested:

> There is room in this great and growing city for a jour-
> nal that is not only cheap but bright, not only bright but
> large, not only large but truly democratic—dedicated to the
> cause of the people rather than that of purse potentates—
> devoted more to the news of the new than the old world,
> that will expose all fraud and sham, fight all public evils
> and abuses—that will serve and battle for the people with
> earnest sincerity.
>   In that cause and for that end solely the new World is
> hereby enlisted and committed to the attention of the in-
> telligent public.

Pulitzer caused his eminent rivals further alarm by the edi-torials he now began composing for the World. In these he went so far as to push forward boldly as the champion of the middle and lower classes. He did this first by attacking the High Society of the day: "That sordid aristocracy of the ambitious matchmakers who are ready to sell their daughters for barren titles to worthless foreign paupers, and to sacrifice a young girl's self-respect and happiness to the gratification of owning a lordly son-in-law. The New York World believes that such an aristocracy ought to have no place in the republic—that the word ought to be expunged from the American vocabulary."

Then, in a skillful transition, he went on to declare that his newspaper intended to be the organ of a new, true aristocracy: the aristocracy of labor, typified by the man of honest, simple toil who supported his family decently, working with stout arm and strong heart, facing life courageously, maintaining his good name through privations and temptations, and winning from his children both respect and love. This brought heady sensations indeed to the middle- and lower-class New Yorker, accustomed to newspapers aimed everywhere except in his particular direction.

Pulitzer's attack on the so-called aristocracy caused an immediate commotion. But he was smart enough to realize that, much as the common man relished attacks on his social superiors, his wife and daughters enjoyed reading of gold-service dinners and costume balls, and spicy accounts of the many society scandals of the day. Pulitzer's attacks on the moneyed aristocracy caused no diminishing in the complete coverage of social matters, and soon he topped the other Park Row papers by hiring Ward McAllister, nabob of the social Four Hundred, as society editor. Thus his readers could both wax indignant over the activities of the rich and enjoy vicarious social thrills, all for the neat sum of two cents.

By May seventeenth, the redoubtable Colonel Cockerill was in full command of the city room and, with all due credit to Pulitzer's flaming editorial energies, the front page of the World also helped push the paper forward.

Pulitzer and Cockerill were fortunate in having the Brooklyn Bridge open formally on May 24, 1883, a day which was also the birthday of Queen Victoria. Pulitzer was, of course, determined to have the World outdo all other papers in coverage of the spectacular local event. He performed the unprecedented by directing his reporters to write background stories on the bridge beforehand. Thus, on the twenty-fourth, the World covered its entire front page with stories of the building of the Bridge, as well as an account of the actual opening ceremonies, together with a large woodcut of the span.

As if this were not enough, Brooklyn Bridge soon provided another workout for the World staff. Pulitzer's complete and meaty account of the Bridge opening had shown how well his paper could cover a formal event. Six days later, on Decoration Day, happy throngs were promenading the Bridge when rumors began that it was toppling. Panic swept the crowd: as Rudyard Kipling wrote, "the blind terror ran from man to man on the Brooklyn Bridge, and the people crushed each other to death, they knew not why." In the wild stampede a dozen people were killed. Led by Pulitzer and Cockerill, the World staff tore around the corner from Park Row to report this tragedy, thus showing how well the paper could cover an unexpected story. Again the entire front page was devoted to the Bridge, but despite the excitement, the World heads remained single-column width, less than an inch high. Even on the brave new World, journalistic restraint—by our standards—was still the order of the day.

Restrained or not, Pulitzer possessed a newspaper New Yorkers liked. Within three weeks, he announced a fifty per cent increase in circulation. By September it had passed the fifty-thousand mark. Until then its chief rivals in the morning field, the Sun, the Herald, and the Times, had professed haughty indifference to the success of the World.

But on September 18, 1883, the Herald and Times suddenly exposed inner fears by dropping their price to two cents—the Herald from three cents, the Times from four cents. Pulitzer could not conceal his glee. "They have given me the town," he exclaimed, a remark later recalled sadly. In this era newspapers believed in gloating over such triumphs, and in front-page statements, the World clamorously drew attention to the fact that it had caused two major rivals to panic. Pulitzer's considerable achievement was increased by the fact that the Herald, in making its cut, reduced the profit to news dealers from one half to one third of a cent. Until this was adjusted—nearly a year later—news dealers slighted the Herald and its circulation sank to unprecedented depths.

Having made his presence so violently felt by the Herald and Times, Pulitzer now needed to jolt the majestic Sun. This he also succeeded in doing, though it took somewhat over a year. Pulitzer had never expected to match the Sun's superb coverage of news. Indeed, he hardly tried, for a city room with the rule "Never Be in a Hurry" was something totally beyond his comprehension. Since the Sun boasted the finest writers on Newspaper Row, Pulitzer decided that the World could best fight back by finding the best news-gatherers. So while the Sun maintained its vaunted superiority in prose, the World usually provided the news first and printed more of it. This might have remained the main difference between the two papers had not Pulitzer next achieved the dream of every newspaper editor. Almost singlehandedly, he caused the nomination of a candidate for President.

In 1883, the Democrat Grover Cleveland was Governor of the State of New York. Pulitzer, made confident by his quick success with the World, began to think of Cleveland as a possibility for the White House. He first ran an editorial declaring that what the country needed was "Another Cleveland." This was a bit of shameless political double talk: since there was already a Cleveland in charge of a key state, why look for another? The sachems of the Democratic Party shortly saw the point, and in convention Cleveland was nominated. "Mr. Pulitzer," says a contemporary account, "seized upon the situation with avidity and made Mr. Cleveland's candidacy the special property of the World." In November, 1884, Cleveland was elected.

So Pulitzer had in a sense become a President-maker, and it was this enormous coup which allowed him to humble the autocratic Sun. Not only was the Sun a ruggedly Republican organ anyway, but during his tenure as Governor of New York Cleveland had succeeded in personally affronting the mighty Dana. Hence Dana's Sun opposed Cleveland with frantic bitterness. It was Dana who coined the word "Mugwump" out of the Mohican tongue to describe Cleveland and his supporters. Dana's friends urged him to take cognizance of the new strength of the Democrats and protect himself by mitigating his virulent campaign. It did no good, and as far away as Chicago, Daily News columnist Eugene Field wrote a poem lampooning Dana's intransigence. When, after several harrowing days of doubt, Cleveland's election was assured, Dana turned his fury on the World. In this he violated a maxim that should have been among the many hung in the Sun city room: Never Attack a Winner. The triumphant World was in a position to absorb his abuse calmly, and in reply term him Charles Ananias Dana. But the most telling indication of Dana's foolishness was the circulation of the Sun, which for years had proudly been published atop the first column on its editorial page. With the appearance of the World, the Sun first began to slip, but during the Cleveland campaign, circulation fell from 137,000 to 85,000. On June 7, 1886, the Sun's proud listing vanished forever.

As the triumphant months rolled by, Pulitzer saluted the confusion of his rivals by increasing the number of pages in the eight-page World to ten. It has been said that no paper is ever more than a picture of the soul of its editor, and the expanded World shortly came to resemble an X ray of the explosive Pulitzer. His striking editorials churned the mass mind by advocating reforms no one else dared mention. Where most other papers sat back calmly awaiting news, the World went out and made it. Largely this was done by inaugurating crusades for reform through the exposure of graft and villainy in official places. "There is not a crime, there is not a dodge, there is not a trick, there is not a vice which does not live by secrecy," Pulitzer told his staff. "Get these things out in the open, describe them, attack them, ridicule them, and sooner or later public opinion will sweep them away." Following this determined policy, the World lashed out with crusading vigor that hit all around New York and extended even to Washington. Pulitzer insisted that every day the paper should play up some distinctive feature, fight, crusade, public service, or exclusive story. "And why not?" asks Lloyd Morris in the book *Postscript to Yesterday*. "This recipe, over the years, brought him an immense power over the mass mind. It enabled him to indulge his passion to be felt in the strife of public forces and to be heard in the consideration of national affairs. And, quite incidentally, it piled up for him the modest reward of some twenty millions of dollars."

Pulitzer's first great public exposure was aimed at the so-called Boodle Aldermen, bribed to vote a street-railroad franchise. This was followed by other juicy disclosures in a town which had recently —through the efforts of George Jones of the Times—thrown off the shackles of the infamous Tweed Ring. Throughout its long life, the World was indefatigable in pursuing such graft and corruption, yet not all Pulitzer crusades were of the downbeat, graft-exposure variety. The World's almost daily battles are far too numerous to mention, but it was the Pulitzer paper which agitated to have unsightly telegraph and telephone wires placed underground, as well as for the five boroughs to be incorporated into one huge City of New York.

Sometimes results of Pulitzer's endless crusading were strange. One of his most successful campaigns on a national scale came when he forced the Government to sell its bonds direct to the public. In part, the World accomplished this by offering to buy one million dollars' worth the moment the bonds were made available. This was done, and three days later Pulitzer was informed the bonds had already earned him a forty-eight-thousand-dollar profit and would make more if held longer. His reddish beard bristled with fury. "We don't want that sort of money," he shouted. Then he summoned his department heads. "Figure out a way to get rid of the money," he ordered. Various suggestions were advanced, among them that the forty-eight thousand be presented to West Point. A hasty check showed, however, that the military academy could not accept such donations. The suggestions went on until at last silence fell and all eyes turned to the business manager, who so far had remained silent. "Why don't we keep it?" he rumbled. This idea was examined, found practicable, and adopted.

Pulitzer's finest crusading hour perhaps came in 1885, shortly after Cleveland entered the White House. Then a recalcitrant Congress refused to vote funds for a pedestal on which to stand the Statue of Liberty, commissioned by the people of France and nobly executed by the famed sculptor, Auguste Bartholdi. When the World learned of this ungrateful Congressional action, it erupted in editorial indignation, proclaiming a campaign to raise by public subscription the one hundred thousand dollars needed for the pedestal. New Yorkers were touched directly at the sensitive point of civic pride, and daily the World printed such stirring responses as:

I am a wee bit of a girl, yet I am ever so glad I was born in time to contribute my mite to the Pedestal Fund. When I am old enough I will ask my papa and mamma to take me to see the statue, and I will always be proud that I began my career by sending you $1 to aid so good a cause.

The inclosed dollar comes from a party of poor artists who dined in University Place this evening.

Inclosed please find five cents as a poor office boy's mite toward the Pedestal Fund. As being loyal to the Stars and Stripes, I thought even five cents would be acceptable.

Shortly, the entire one hundred thousand reposed in the World coffers, and when the Statue of Liberty arrived, New York's fine pedestal was ready to support it. On the great day, President Cleveland accepted the Statue for this country, the sculptor himself spoke in favor of international amity, and a huge naval and civic celebration followed. Pulitzer was present and no speaker failed to salute the people of New York and their civic-minded newspaper for providing the true basis for the occasion.

One day in 1884, a young man named Walt McDougall left his home in Newark for a trip to New York to learn the fate of a political cartoon he had left for consideration in the offices of the satiric magazine *Puck*. Cherubic, humorous, ebullient, a man whose autobiography would be subtitled The Record of a Blameless Life, McDougall was then one of a small group of men trying to exist as news artists. At the moment, McDougall was Fire Artist for the short-lived Graphic, which meant that he chased the fire engines to major fires and sketched the scenes.

His drawings were seldom used, however, and altogether McDougall's artistic life was an unrewarding one. For newspapers—even the World—seldom used drawn illustrations. The halftone process had not yet been adapted to newspaper printing, and plates had to be converted by the artist into pen-and-ink line drawings before engraving. After this, the plates were prone to smudge, and presses had to be stopped while the ink was laboriously wiped off. This slowed down the printing of highly competitive editions and in general caused expensive delays. It all added up to the fact that newspaper illustrations were infrequently used.

At the *Puck* office that morning, McDougall found that his cartoon, which the magazine would necessarily reduce in size to refine its coarse lines, had not been accepted. With the bulky cardboard under his arm, he found himself in City Hall Park. He had no desire to carry the unwieldy object all day and, since it was a Democratic cartoon, he suddenly conceived the idea of unloading it at the World office. Still, he did not have sufficient nerve to do this in person. "The idea of offering a political cartoon to a daily paper," he later wrote, "seemed so utterly absurd that I thrust the cardboard into the hands of the elevator operator and said, 'Give this to the editor and tell him he can have it if he wants it.'"

Next morning the leader of a blameless life was rudely aroused from artistically late slumbers by one of Pulitzer's come-at-once telegrams. He leaped into his clothes and at the ferry saw a copy of the World displaying his cartoon, exactly the size he had drawn it, across the front page. Dazedly, McDougall arrived at the World office where Colonel Cockerill greeted him enthusiastically and led him into Pulitzer's office. There the publisher added to the general unreality of the occasion by rising to greet him. "Young man," he proclaimed, "in you we have found the man who can make pictures for newspapers! We printed an entire edition of fifty thousand copies of the World without stopping the press to clean the cut. That has never happened in the United States before!"

Slowly it dawned on the bedazzled McDougall that, on being handed his cartoon, Pulitzer and Cockerill had measured it. By a happy accident, it had just spread across the front page of the paper. They had ordered a plate made to exact size and McDougall's coarse, unrefined lines had been strong enough to hold up without smudging through the long press run. The trick with newspaper art, then, was to draw harsh lines, big pictures. . . .

In McDougall, Pulitzer believed he had found a rare jewel, and the fact that other papers immediately hired cartoonists who used heavy lines did nothing to change his mind. On the spot, he offered McDougall fifty dollars a week, a huge contemporary sum for a youth still in his twenties. McDougall happily began drawing cartoons and news pictures, undeterred by the envy of members of the World staff who were jealous of his large salary and the pride with which Pulitzer regarded him. Some staff members even complained to Pulitzer, who, when taxed about the favoritism he showed McDougall, had what for any newspaperman is an unanswerable reply. "He draws circulation," he flatly said.

The fact that his beloved newspaper had become the greatest circulation success New York had ever known, causing his personal bank account to rise well toward the million mark, did not persuade Pulitzer to cease working with his accustomed furious energy. On the contrary, the personal demons pushing him seemed to drive even harder. The vigor he put into the World and the emotional excitement of its news stories may have caused some aristocratic families to banish the paper to the servants' quarters below stairs, but this made no difference. By 1885 the circulation had reached one hundred thousand. This was such an event that a tumultuous celebration was held in City Hall Park. A cannon was fired one hundred times, once for every thousand circulation. The Mayor made a speech and every male member of the staff was presented with a tall silk hat by Pulitzer himself.

For a few favored staff members, there was an even more special gift. A World reporter dispatched to wintry Canada on a story had returned attired in perhaps the first fur-lined overcoat ever worn in New York. Because of Pulitzer's weak chest and generally run-down condition, he always felt cold, and a fur-lined overcoat immediately seemed to him as much a necessity as a luxury. He sent the reporter back to Canada to procure one for him. Then, having opened lines of communication, he ordered such coats for top staff members to commemorate the hundred-thousand circulation.

Pulitzer had also purchased a home at 10 East 55 Street. After acquiring the house next door, he combined the two into a suitable mansion of the period. Here his particular pride was a library of first editions and a collection of paintings and Gobelin tapestries, which he now began to accumulate. But no less than in St. Louis, Kate Pulitzer and the children seldom saw Pulitzer in the midst of his luxurious home surroundings. He still worked through every day, usually until midnight, when the first edition of a morning paper went to press.

One reason for this was that an obsessive fear of libel suits, first apparent on the Post-Dispatch, made him read personally every word that went into the World. Pulitzer still found himself unable to delegate authority, though he had buttressed Colonel Cockerill by hiring the experienced Solomon Solis Carvalho from the Sun as

business manager; Ballard Smith from the Herald to be assistant
managing editor under the Colonel; and William H. Merrill from
the Boston Post to take part of the editorial-writing burden from his
own shoulders. But even with these experts beside him, Pulitzer was
still the man who must do almost everything himself, passionately
calling on all his nerves and emotions, even though the nerves and
emotions showed alarming signs of giving way. "He is pushing his
body in a manner no human being can stand," an increasingly dis-
tressed Kate Pulitzer told friends. Yet Pulitzer would make no con-
cessions to visibly failing health. Ever the perfectionist, he enthusiastically labored to infuse his own dedicated personality into a
newspaper that also displayed a personality. Says Seitz:

> "Forever unsatisfied" described his temperament. He
> was forever unsatisfied, not so much with the results as with
> the thought that if a further effort had been made, a sterner
> command, or greater encouragement given, as the case might
> be, more could have been accomplished.

Pulitzer's unflagging industry actually becomes phenomenal
when viewed with the state of his health. His tall, reedy body, the
guttural accent that never left his English, the small chin, watery
eyes and feverish manner all combined to make him resemble an
intense, scholarly teacher of violin or piano. Physically he tired
quickly, but by calling on some inner nervous force could always
continue a dizzying pace of work. Most of the time he appeared
to operate on nerves alone, and seldom did his abrupt actions seem
to possess any basis in physical strength. They were more like reflex
actions dictated by hysterically taut nerves. Pulitzer's chest was still
weak and he coughed frequently. Yet always the primary difficulty
was his eyes, the destruction of which he had begun when reading
proof by flickering candlelight on the Westliche Post. But with all
these depleting drawbacks, he created a tornado of industry such as
few newspaper offices have ever seen.

To those laboring under him on the World, the word *haste*
seemed the key to Pulitzer. The perpetually dissatisfied man always
wanted to achieve more, and to achieve it faster. He first used to

shout, "Circulation! Big Ideas!" at Colonel Cockerill. Having
achieved both, he shouted, "More Circulation! Bigger Ideas!" His
inner circle of advisers was largely chosen for ability to pluck
grandiose ideas out of the air at conferences. Some of these were
downright ludicrous, but Pulitzer always listened raptly. One such
was produced at a meeting where, with perfect seriousness, a discus-
sion was held about the possibility of erecting on the Jersey mead-
ows a signboard so huge that its lettering could be seen on Mars.
Naturally the sign would advertise the World, but it would also con-
vey to Martians friendly greetings from all citizens of the United
States. This plan was all but adopted when it was punctured by a
cruel realist who asked, "What language shall we print it in?"

When the circulation figure of one hundred thousand had been
left behind, Pulitzer's thoughts not unexpectedly turned to the evening field, where the quietly liberal Evening Post was dominant.
Other evening papers were the Daily News, the Mail and Express,
the Commercial Advertiser, the Evening Telegram, and the newly
begun Evening Sun. In 1887 the Evening World, four pages for a
penny, appeared. Next Pulitzer added a special supplement to the
Sunday World, making this a jumbo edition. Both ventures were
immediately successful, and called further attention to the peculiarities of their creator. For Pulitzer, having ascertained that the two
ventures made money, proceeded to disregard them almost completely. "He cared little for the Evening and Sunday editions beyond expecting them to prosper," a biographer states. "He reserved
all his interest and affection for the Morning edition. The others
were commercial ventures. The Morning contained his soul."

Pulitzer's indifference to the Evening World and the Sunday
Supplement becomes truly astounding when their journalistic excesses are considered. In the early days of the World, Pulitzer had
passed out to the staff cards headed TERSENESS—ACCURACY—TERSENESS.
Below this was a statement of the high code of newspaper ethics by
which the paper was expected to abide. The Morning World always
did, but the Evening World violated newspaper ethics constantly,
as did the Sunday Supplement. When the ice dealers of the town
were embroiled with police over ice sales on Sunday, the Evening
World published an account, giving neither name, date, nor place,

of a mother who had vainly sought to buy a small piece of ice for her sick child. It was an obvious fabrication, wrapped up by this touching scene of the mother's return to the child's bedside:

> "I was kept away, darling. I couldn't get the ice be-
> cause . . ." Suddenly the words died on her lips. She knelt
> by the bed and took a little wasted hand in hers. Then,
> raising her face, she gazed up with dry eyes that yet saw
> nothing and whispered: "Thy will be done, O God! Thou
> knowest best!"
> For the child was dead!

Pulitzer completely disregarded such bottom-of-the-well ethics and slowly the staff came to believe that he never looked at the evening edition, much less at the Sunday, which became even more lurid in its sensationalism. "But why doesn't somebody tell him?" one outraged editor demanded after an exhibition of particularly foul taste on the part of the Sunday. "Because no human tongue could describe what the Sunday Supplement is like," a reporter answered.

In the spring of 1888, Colonel Cockerill entered Pulitzer's office to find the editor-publisher slumped dejectedly in his chair. This was unusual, for Pulitzer customarily bent far forward, poring closely over copy-matter on his desk and in general creating a ferment of industrious confusion. On hearing someone approach, Pulitzer looked up and Cockerill could see that his warm, brown eyes had taken on a peculiar purplish color. Worse, they had the vague, non-focusing look of blindness. Pulitzer confirmed this instantly. "I can't see," he said. "My eyes have given out."

He was hustled from Park Row to the consulting room of an eye specialist who, after several days of examination, declared that sight would return if the eyes were given several months of rest. Other doctors, called in to examine the publisher's overworked body, added notes of foreboding. His failing vision, they stated, was only symptomatic of a failing body. His chest was so weak it was a marvel that he did not have tuberculosis. The extraordinary tension of his nerves exceeded the bounds of medical vocabulary.

Pulitzer's prodigiously self-centered mind allowed him to brush aside most of this, but his blindness could not be denied and he consented to take a vacation of several months in California. Shortly he departed for Monterey, leaving Kate in the mansion to take care of the children. With him went two young men who would act as secretaries, companions and—most important, as it turned out— readers. One of the young men was the son of William H. Merrill, Pulitzer's aide as an editorial writer.

The trip was a failure. Pulitzer's sensitive eyes found that the glare of the California sun hit him like a blow in the face. In vain did young Merrill and his friend try to smoke glasses over candles. Pulitzer cowered indoors, demanding to be read to incessantly, and otherwise amused. A steady barrage of memos dispatched to the World offices showed that, though doctors might threaten and his body shriek in protest, Pulitzer had no intention of taking his mind from the World. Copies of the paper arrived daily, to be read aloud *in toto* by one of the young men. It was a rare edition which did not at some point rouse Pulitzer to boiling anger. With his eyesight gone, other faculties—notably hearing—became more acute. So, seemingly, did his memory. From the depths of his mind he would pull forth such seemingly irrelevant bits of information as the fact that in early November the World circulation always fell. In a furious telegram to the New York office, he demanded to know why. Before a reply could arrive, he wired his own conclusion: the World customarily behaved so ineptly in election campaigns that the public grew disgusted with it. In a confidential wire to S. S. Carvalho he asked if the solution might be to dispense with the experienced services of Ballard Smith. Before this could happen the New York office marshaled its thoughts and replied convincingly that the November drop in circulation was due to the shortening of daylight hours. Circulation always grew, it was pointed out, with the lengthening days of spring.

Instead of resting in California, Pulitzer became more nervous and out of sorts. His eyes improved slowly, but now he began experiencing an extreme sensitivity to heat which would be another of the factors rendering him miserable for the rest of his days. Further, California had not proved to be as remote from New York as the doctors hoped. Pulitzer could easily send telegrams of a length and quantity unknown up to that time. It soon became apparent to his

New York physician, Dr. James E. McLane, that the stricken man was
not resting, but was passing his time in chafing frustration. McLane
wired permission to return, which Pulitzer did by way of St. Louis,
where he paused for a rare shake-up visit to the Post-Dispatch.

Back in New York, he immediately found himself embroiled in
a curious episode on the World. Colonel Cockerill provided this by
deciding to oppose the paper's own Grover Cleveland for the Presidency in 1888. Though the paper's editorials passionately advocated
the Democratic candidate, Cockerill's news columns were slanted
against him. Pulitzer, who considered Cockerill among his few close
friends, decided to practice true freedom of the press and permitted
the situation to continue. But at the end of the campaign he declared
that the controversy had given him an unusual opportunity to evalu-
ate the paper's true worth. "Gentlemen," he informed one editorial
gathering, "we have been getting out a fine political paper. From
now on I want a fine *new*spaper every day."

Pulitzer's eyes may have improved, but his other sufferings increased. He went to the World office daily even though the noises he
once loved—sound of presses, shouts for copy boys, turmoil in the city
room—almost drove him mad. "He came against his doctor's orders,"
Walt McDougall writes, "and aggravated his afflictions by efforts
to attend to details. Only death could repress his energy and insatia-
ble curiosity. His invariable inquiry was, *Why?* I heard it the first day
I knew him, and the last."

Kate Pulitzer, Cockerill and Dr. McLane formed a Greek chorus
in the background of his life, begging him to slow down or give up
altogether. But the raging forces driving him allowed no rest. Inevitably his eyesight began to fade again and visits to new doctors
only brought the same verdict heard so many times before: his nerves
were being shattered by living at top pitch. He was presiding over
the destruction of his own constitution.

Yet even as his nerves commanded him to stop, Pulitzer conceived his most grandiose idea. With the World prosperous and well
organized, his meticulous meddling in its affairs seemed to lose point
and he had time to think of his long dissatisfaction with the newspaper's grubby quarters at 32 Park Row. This quickly led to con-

ception of the highest building in New York as a proper home for the
World. The north corner of Newspaper Row, adjoining the entrance
to Brooklyn Bridge, was for sale and on his forty-first birthday Pulitzer
bought this property for six hundred and thirty thousand dollars.
With the architect, George B. Post, he worked out plans for a structure of sixteen stories, an unheard-of height for the time. To make
the splendid Pulitzer Building seem even higher, a gold dome
topped by a flagpole would curve toward the sky.

On October 10, 1889, the cornerstone of the Pulitzer Building
was laid with four-year-old Joseph Pulitzer, Jr., wielding the trowel.
Governor Hill of New York made the address of the occasion and
Chauncey M. Depew the oration. On December 10, 1890—Pulitzer was at this point superstitiously partial to the number ten—the
gold-domed building was ceremoniously opened, as crowds of fascinated citizens milled around City Hall Park. It is difficult today—indeed, impossible—to conceive of the sensation made by the opening
of this sixteen-story building, which towered by at least six floors over
any other building in the city and even surpassed the Tribune Clock
Tower in height. Most of the citizens gazing in awe at the gold dome
were afraid to go up to the inside of the World tower, though elevator
rides on that jubilant day were free to all. Tough-minded Ballard
Smith, veteran of many rugged news stories, was actually afraid to look
out the windows of the dome and could not summon nerve to do so
for nearly a year. The Reverend Dr. Parkhurst, that notable crusader
against vice, was one of those who dared take the elevator ride to the
top, where he offered doubtful tribute by saying that when looking
out the windows he felt like Christ being tempted by the Devil on
the Mount. Still, it was an unnamed citizen who won ad-lib honors of
the day. Stepping off the elevator on the top floor, he crystallized the
event perfectly by loudly demanding, "Is God in?"

Only the tart New York Sun had sour words. Pulitzer's new
building, it said, looked like a brass-head tack. The other papers covered the opening of the building as an important news story, with the
Times exclaiming, "From the terrifying height of sixteen stories men
below lose stature and become crawling bugs." This coverage by
envious rivals perhaps pleased Pulitzer more than anything for, incredible as it may seem, the older newspapers in New York continued

to treat the World as an arrant upstart. Even while the girders of the building were rising, Charles A. Dana, head bloody but unbowed, had stood watching at a window of the Sun city room with his new publisher, Charles A. Laffan. "It looks serious, Laffan," Dana finally grumbled. "Not at all, not at all," Laffan answered. "Still a mere episode, a mere episode."

But with the gold-domed World Building open and functioning, the World could no longer be considered an episode. Cannon boomed, crowds cheered, and daring souls stepped into the elevator to ride to a height few human beings had ever attained before.

There could be no doubt now. The Pulitzer World was here to stay.

CHAPTER THREE

Mr. Hearst Challenges

So Park Row remained for the next five years. The World continued to retain its eminence, even though the World Building was displaced as New York's tallest skyscraper. In a metropolis growing with such rapidity, no building could remain paramount long, and the success and popularity of the World Building only spurred contemporary architects to greater efforts. Soon it was topped by a twenty-story skyscraper erected for the American Surety Company, on Broadway opposite Trinity Church.

Then, in August, 1895—twelve years after Joseph Pulitzer had made his way downtown by carriage to Park Row—another newspaper owner new to New York made a similar journey. His destination was the Tribune Building, which stood beside the World Building, facing Printing House Square, with only Frankfort Street and the Sun between. Before this building, in which his newly purchased newspaper rented the second and third floors, the newcomer—in a manner which can be visualized by anyone with a clear recollection of the film *Citizen Kane*—descended from his carriage.

He was William Randolph Hearst, and the manner of his arrival on Park Row only pointed up great differences from Pulitzer. For one thing, Hearst was not alone. For another, where Pulitzer had sat impatiently forward, seeming to urge the carriage on by the power of his nerves, Hearst sat comfortably back, savoring every moment of the ride from the Hoffman House on Fifth Avenue at Thirtieth Street. His attire was in further contrast to Pulitzer. Where the publisher of the World often looked like a scarecrow, with clothes carelessly strewn over his scrawny frame, Hearst was expensively and carefully dressed. He had a long, heavy face, an awkward body, and large hands and feet. Though the heaviness of his body betokened mature years, there was a kind of youthfulness about him which may have come from his completely unlined face or from the open, agate innocence of his eyes. Or perhaps it was because he dressed in the best sporting manner of the day: checked suit, hard-brimmed straw hat, heavy gold watch chain across his midriff, disappearing into a vest pocket, to emerge again as a shiny, elaborate watch fob. Under his long chin and around a heavy neck blossomed a bunched ascot tie. For the outrageous color scheme of this and his other ties, biographers would later find only one word: chromatic. In the center of the folds of the chromatic tie nestled, Western style, a tiepin glitteringly fashioned from a twenty-dollar gold piece. On his feet, as he stepped across the pavement of Park Row with a lightness surprising in a man of his bulk, Hearst wore the high shoes that were the only type available to men of the time. But instead of being the clumsy, lace-tied black shoes that most men wore, his were a high-style light brown, featuring fawn tops and mother-of-pearl buttons.

Hearst, at thirty-two, had lately risen from rich-boy wonder to solidly successful young publisher of the San Francisco Examiner. Nearly ten years before, he had been expelled from Harvard and, already determined to be a newspaperman, stopped on the way home to San Francisco for a brief spell as a sub-cub on the New York World. Not a single nugget of information remains concerning this interesting stint, but it apparently served to toughen Hearst's resolve to enter journalism. In San Francisco he began efforts to persuade his strike-it-rich father to fall in with his plans. It took time but when, in 1887, Senator George Hearst became convinced that twenty-four-year-old Willie really wanted a newspaper, he offhandedly presented him with the Examiner, which the Senator had acquired in 1880 for a bad debt.

In the eight years following, Hearst had revolutionized San Francisco journalism. He had been a publisher with an unlimited bank account, bold ideas (albeit borrowed ones), and no visible integrity to inhibit the execution of the bold ideas. Taking his conception of journalism from the New York World, Hearst did not sit back and wait for news, but vigorously set forth to create it, meanwhile loudly informing San Francisco that his was the New Journalism. Hearst reporters were indefatigable in working up new sensations and nurturing the heartthrobs in old ones. But with all this there was a strange emptiness in laboring for Hearst. When reporters came to him after a successful scoop, he was prone to cut short the story of accomplishment with questions about how many papers the story had sold. Ambrose Bierce was Hearst's most celebrated West Coast writer. Bierce disliked Hearst intensely. Even though he labored for him for twenty years, the bitter man always referring condescendingly to "young Mr. Hearst." Bierce, too, resented Hearst's seeming lack of interest in real news and his prime satisfaction in circulation. He also disliked the Hearst method of trumped-up sensations. "The Hearst method," he once said, "has all the reality of masturbation."

Yet Hearst's extravagant, if foundationless, journalism had not been harmful to San Francisco. The press in almost every American city except New York, where the World functioned as a catalyst, was stodgy and in need of revolutionizing. By 1895 Hearst had become immensely successful. His father, who had continued to hope that Willie would tire of publishing, had by now carried his disappointment to the grave. However, any financial support Hearst lost by the Senator's death was amply made up by his mother. Young William had been born a twin, with a brother dying at birth or shortly after. Perhaps for this reason Phoebe Apperson Hearst doted on her lymphatic son. Senator Hearst's will bypassed the son completely, leaving his entire fortune to his widow. Mrs. Hearst immediately presented William Randolph with a sum estimated at between seven and eight million dollars. With this convenient amount, he was able to indulge what had recently become a heart's desire. He wanted to become the foremost editor-publisher in New York, the country's most vigorous and important city.

Now he had just taken the first step that would establish him on Park Row. Through agents he had purchased the New York Journal, that tepid morning daily which the New York Sun had declared was published by fools for fools. With the Journal, in the purchase price of one hundred and eighty thousand dollars, had also come a Ger-

man-language edition called Das Morgen Journal. Young Mr. Hearst
had been unaware of this lingual dividend and when informed of it
uttered one of the few wisecracks that ever fell from his lips. "So I
bought a frankfurter, too," he said.

In the company of Charles M. Palmer, business manager of the
San Francisco Examiner, the sportily dressed young publisher was on
the verge of paying his first visit to the Journal. In the city room each
member of the staff was called forward to shake his hand and exchange a few words with the new owner, who, despite his heavy
frame and loud attire, turned out to be the unlikely possessor of a
soft, high-tenor voice, likened by the gadfly Bierce to the fragrance
of violets made audible. Hearst never became the most popular man
on Park Row and some of the future dislike for him was forecast by
one man in the Journal city room. He kept his recollection of
Hearst's first appearance fresh and later set down: "Mr. Hearst entered the room noiselessly and almost diffidently, a tall young man
with a long horse face, close-set eyes and a peculiar strained smile with
a manner that was a combination of Harvard and a faro-bank look-
out."

It is safe to say that each of the men presented to young Mr.
Hearst expected to be fired on the spot, as was the custom of the day
when papers changed hands. But in each there burned a slight flicker
of hope. For the San Francisco accomplishments of their new employer had been of such a spectacular variety that his habits were well
known in New York. One fact preceding him was that—at this point
in his career, at least—the Westerner seemed to have a peculiar liking
for reporters. He did not smoke and seldom drank himself, and could
rise in terrible wrath when a reporter came back empty-handed from
an assignment. Yet it had been noted that if the reporter explained his
failure by saying he had passed out from overindulgence in drink,
young Mr. Hearst was inclined to excuse him.

Further, he continued, despite all, to lean heavily on his managing editor, Sam Chamberlain, one of the most dandified dressers
and prodigious drinkers ever to grace the newspaper scene. Chamberlain was the son of the picturesquely named Ivory Chamberlain, a
mighty newspaper figure in his day. Sam carried on the traditions of
his father's era by permitting his frequent absences on heroic bend-

ers to bring chaos to the Examiner city room and fury to the business side of the paper. None of this seemed to bother young Mr. Hearst. Once, as Hearst vacationed in Paris, the business side cabled the information that Chamberlain had been in full possession of his faculties only one day during the past month. Back came Hearst's serene reply, "If he is sober one day in thirty that is all I require."

In San Francisco young Mr. Hearst had been indulgent with reporters, and the result had been a lighthearted chapter in American journalism. In transferring his operations across the continent, however, Hearst seemed to be going through a hardening process. What had been an adventure in San Francisco had become a formula by the time it reached New York.

One of the strongest features of the formula, if not *the* strongest, would be to obtain the services of the best men available, no matter what the price. For in his eight years as a San Francisco publisher young Mr. Hearst not only learned a lot about the newspaper game, but no little bit about himself. He was not an innovator, but an imitator—or borrower. What he really wanted from a newspaper was circulation, and he believed this could be achieved by constant printing of sensations. Yet Hearst had learned that he did not possess the gift for dreaming up sensations, nor did he see the need to cultivate such an ability in himself. Why should he, when he owned the money to buy men to think up sensations for him, and when papers like the New York World provided crusading paths to follow? Entering the New York field with millions presented to him without strings by the fondest of mothers, he would import a nucleus of talent from San Francisco. Sam Chamberlain, managing editor; cartoonist Homer Davenport; Winifred Black, who as "Annie Laurie" had become the first of the sob sisters; Charles McEwen, who had defined the ideal Hearst story as producing the "gee-whiz emotion"; and Cosey Noble who, when asked if he was Hearst's city editor, always replied, "I was when I left the office." With these San Francisco talents functioning, he would next begin shopping around New York, offering the best newspapermen in town so much money that they could not possibly refuse.

As he shook hands with the various members of the Journal editorial staff, there was little enthusiasm—and no embarrassment

—in Hearst's manner. These men were getting out a third-rate paper, hence they must be third-raters. As soon as possible he would dispense with their services. Rapidly he polished off the pleasantries with the city-room staff, eager to disengage himself as quickly as possible from the sorry plant and its personnel. His last word was that he would not make the Journal his headquarters, but would as long as possible—and here he must have smiled the faro-bank smile—use the office the Examiner had five years before leased in the World Building. If this did not work out, he would, for a time, conduct his business from the Hoffman House, where for his personal use he had rented an entire floor.

Human nature being what it is, it seems likely that on reaching the Park Row sidewalk the sportily dressed Hearst paused to look upward toward the gold dome of the World Building. This would not merely be a Westerner's tribute to the second-tallest building in New York: any attention given by Hearst to the World at this point would have vastly more significance. New York and its soaring circulation potential had not been the only magnet which drew Hearst relentlessly East. In San Francisco his bravura journalism had been little more than a lurid carbon copy of the World. Hearst's confidence, grown enormously over the successful Examiner years, had been bloated by the millions bestowed by his mother. His true purpose in coming to New York was largely to do battle with the champion Pulitzer. Yet Hearst was never one to struggle toe to toe, making any battle a straightforward test of inspiration, resourcefulness and strength. The man who could quickly impress others as sly and furtive had worked out characteristic plans for the fight with Pulitzer. He would take the Morning World's crusading policies, and combine them with the Evening and Sunday World sensationalism. Where Pulitzer had three successful papers he, Hearst, would adopt the successful features of each and roll them in one. His Journal would appear to be a fighting paper, but it would be a paper whose crusades would be conducted with frenzied excitement. This was a bold challenge to the power of the World, but Hearst knew it was sometimes possible to catch a reigning champion overconfidently off guard. And behind him, always, lay the new millions, together with his own considerable experience in newspaper publishing.

To almost any eyes except those of the knowledgeable William Randolph Hearst, the New York World, as it appeared in August, 1895, would have seemed all but impregnable. The daily circulation of the paper was three hundred and seventy thousand, almost as much as the four other morning papers together. Both the Herald and the Sun sold about one hundred and twenty thousand copies apiece; the Tribune seventy-six thousand; and the increasingly sickly Times seventy-five thousand. In the afternoon field, the Evening World was even more dominant with a readership of over four hundred thousand. Far behind this lagged the Evening Sun and the Evening Telegram with one hundred thousand each. The Evening Post, under the dignified, clear-eyed editorship of Edwin L. Godkin, quietly functioned as the real conscience of the New York press. Yet its circulation was only seventy-five thousand—showing, as has been said, the unpopularity of virtue.

For want of suitable rivals, the two Worlds—Morning and Evening—were all but reduced to competing with each other for scoops. The Sunday World Supplement had its quarters in the golden dome of the World Tower, as did the editorial writers for all Pulitzer papers. The eleventh floor of the building was divided in half to create the bustling city rooms of both Worlds. In every sense the eleventh floor was a proud place—the nirvana of a newspaperman's dreams. It was also a stimulating place to work, for as A. J. Liebling would write in *The New Yorker* sixty years later: "From their city room the men of both Worlds could look over and beyond the North River and out to sea, as well as at Brooklyn, across the only high bridge there was over the East River at the time. All Manhattan was visible at their feet and it only accentuated their cockiness."

Among those employed in the city rooms of the Worlds at the moment Hearst peered upward were a tall, eager, athletic young man named Arthur Brisbane, who as a twenty-year-old correspondent for the New York Sun had covered the Jack the Ripper murders in London, then returned to Park Row to begin one of the more spectacular journalistic careers of all time; a firm-jawed, handsome young man named David Graham Phillips, who would eventually be considered by many the foremost realistic novelist of his era; Maximilian Foster, who would graduate to writing sprightly fiction for the Saturday Eve-

ning Post; Hartley Davis, another embryo short-story writer; Albert
Payson Terhune, built along heavyweight prize-fighter lines, who
would write rugged fiction for adults and books about his superb
collie dogs for the young; Bayard Veiller, who by writing the melodrama *Within the Law* would become the outstanding playwright of
his day; Arthur Greaves, who would become city editor of the reju-
venated New York Times; and Roy L. McArdle, who as "Uncle
Tommyrot" was already writing some of the funniest newspaper material in all journalism.

Also laboring on the eleventh floor were drama critic Alan
Dale, the lady feature writers, Ella Wheeler Wilcox and Marie Man-
ning, as well as a quiet-spoken man named Foster Coates, better
known as "Curser" Coates because his versatility with profanity
matched that of Joseph Pulitzer himself. For despite his ascetic, pro-
fessorish appearance, Pulitzer was one of the most profane men who
ever lived. He had acquired his basic English while serving in the
rough-and-ready Union cavalry, not to mention such later jobs as
Missouri mule-tending. These vigorous surroundings left a mighty im-
print on his vocabulary and men working with him never ceased to
wonder at his amazing virtuosity with profanity. Indeed, cursing had
become such an ingrained part of Pulitzer's vocabulary that he practiced the art of inserting profanity into the middle of other words
for emphasis. The only such gem of his which has come down to us
is "inde-goddamn-pendent." Curser Coates, too, was master of the
art of inserting profanity in the middle of other words. Informed one
day that he must do something, he calmly answered that he was under no obli-goddamn-gation to do so.

Surrounding these talents—or talents to be—as they worked on
the eleventh floor of the World Building, were already a few newfangled typewriters, odd-looking objects with double keyboards, one for
capitals, since the shift lock had yet to be invented. There were also
several hand-crank telephones set against the office walls—the Evening World, for example, boasted one city-room phone and one general office phone with the number Cortlandt 365. All Park Row
offices had rewrite men, but not as we know them today. Now the rewrite man sits at the office end of a telephone, taking down facts and
high lights from a leg-man reporter at the scene. Yesterday's rewrite

man was a trusted and experienced hand who had earned the right to polish the prose of the reporters who had both covered and written their own stories.

A few reporters in any 1895 city room would be working from Associated Press flimsies, written in longhand and rushed by hand from the AP office at Broadway and Dey Street. Others might be consulting similar flimsies from the City Press Association, informally called O'Rourke's, which covered routine sources of city news and sold the results, written in unimaginative style, to Park Row papers. But for the most part each reporter laboriously, in longhand, wrote his own particular assignment. Many authorities contend that the best newspaper stories were written this way. Among those believing this was Arthur Brisbane, who later recalled nostalgically:

> When I was young, a reporter went out and talked with the people he was to write about and came back and wrote his own story. He had plenty of time and he was encouraged to write into his story whatever quality of emotion the story held—humor, pathos, romance, etc. Young men got good training and the news columns sparkled with good writing.

The city editor of the World in 1895 was an accomplished young man named Charles Edward Russell. In time, his disgust with slum conditions, prostitution and graft in New York City turned him into an author-reformer who ran for Governor of New York on the Socialist Party ticket. Yet Russell always looked back proudly on his newspaper days, and firmly believed that the story written by the man who personally got it was ever the best story. To his mind, these were "good stories," and he writes:

> It was inevitable that the period of "good stories" should go down before the many assaults that were made upon it, mostly in the way of evolution. The telephone, for instance, saved time and helped the gathering of news, but it abolished much of the old style of reporter's art. . . . The typewriter greatly improved the legibility of copy and hastened its production but few men can compose on the typewriter in terse, compact, vigorous English—the facility

afforded by the machine is too great. The introduction of
the half-tone and use of the camera gave the newspaper a
more striking interest, but also rendered description, the
finest phase of the reporter's art, comparatively unnecessary.

In another way, the city rooms of Russell's period differed vastly
from the city rooms of today. This was the fact that near the elbow of
almost every editor as he worked was a bottle of whiskey, while the
older reporters also made demands on a close-at-hand bottle for inspiration. "We were not milk addicts," one World editor replied succinctly when questioned about drinking in the city room of his youth.
Yet the atmosphere of the city room of the World, or of any other
contemporary newspaper, was far from abandoned. Rather, it reflected swift, skilled, concentrated effort. The liquor consumed in
city rooms was not for the purpose of intoxication. It was a reporter's
privilege to get drunk in off hours, while the drink consumed during
work acted—like chewing tobacco—as a solace and a means of maintaining a hard, steady, up-to-the-deadline pace.

Together with the inalienable right to stoke lagging inspiration
with alcohol, there also went a terrible uncertainty in Park Row city
rooms. This period was, of course, long before the days of the Newspaper Guild. Payday on the World came on Thursday and nearly
every week blue dismissal slips would be found in several envelopes.
Indeed, such paydays were once likened to a giant bowling ball
hurtling through the city room, each week knocking down a few ten-
pins—that is, reporters.

One young man in the World city room, Albert Payson Terhune,
was a fortunate fellow whose family sent him abroad when he reached
college age. On his return, he sold an article to *Harper's*. Solely to get
experience for further articles, he decided to take a job for a short
time on a newspaper. He was hired by the Evening World at
fifteen dollars a week—"such an incredible quantity of cash to receive
every week that I had a feeling of wealth which has never been mine
before or since." He remained on the World nearly twenty years.
When he joined the staff in 1894, the top reporter's weekly salary was
thirty-five dollars—"a Monte Cristo wage" it seemed to Terhune. By
1898, he himself was earning that magnificent sum. By 1899, he had

achieved forty. In 1905, he was making only forty-seven fifty. Then his city-room star began to rise. He was sent out on stories requiring athletic prowess, and shortly was making eighty dollars. Soon after, he began to edit as well as write, and quit the World while making eight thousand a year. But all through this, he writes, "On Thursdays I had to brace myself lest the T pigeonhole should have a bright blue envelope debarring me from the privilege of doing $2 work for 75¢."

It was typical of the Park Row reporter that such matters did not depress him unduly. Or perhaps the lures of the newspaper game made security appear secondary. The right to drink on the job, plus a certain roughness of spirit now departed from the news world, even brought an occasional aura of high jinks to city rooms. Practical jokes were in order and sometimes a whole staff got involved in their ramifications.

One cause of informality was that city rooms were then host to a forgotten breed called free-lance reporters. At the World, a heavy-set, ponderous young man named Theodore Dreiser was one of these. Each Park Row newspaper had a basic staff of reporters but since big stories might break at any moment, beginners and itinerant newsmen were encouraged to hang around the city rooms. If sent out on a story, such a man would be paid at space rates of three to six dollars a column, depending on the prosperity of the paper. The Commercial Advertiser paid $4.32, and no reporter who earned this sum ever knew what the mysterious thirty-two cents stood for. Space rates kept many a newspaperman alive during apprenticeship or hard times, but they also pointed up an employment peculiarity of the times. An especially energetic and aggressive reporter working on space rates might make as much as fifty to sixty dollars a week, and in only a few years an inspired young Post reporter named Lincoln Steffens would take home the vast weekly sum of seventy dollars. Newspaper salaries of the time began at twenty-five dollars and for the average reporter usually ended at forty. Free lances who made more would hastily be honored by a place on the regular payroll at twenty-five.

But whatever their problems of personal finance, the reporters lounging around Park Row city rooms made a picturesque group, exceedingly appreciative of any diversion. One of Pulitzer's early gestures had been to hire Bill Nye, the Will Rogers of the day, to write a

column of chuckles and laughs. Soon the bucolic Nye was a cherished
fixture of Newspaper Row, much admired for his ability as a dead-
pan humorist. When Arthur Conan Doyle, the creator of Sherlock
Holmes, made a visit to this country, Nye strolled into the city room
where an admiring group stood around a compact, stuffy-looking Englishman. The humorist promptly took over the conversation by informing the group that the author of Sherlock Holmes must be in
New York City. For, said Nye, he had just been walking along a
street and had seen a man hanging a sign which said Riordan R.
Riordan, Attorney at Law. An Englishman had also stood watching
the sign-hanging, and finally said to the lawyer, "May I ask, sir, what
your middle initial stands for?" Told that the middle R also stood for
Riordan, the Englishman stated, "Then, sir, I should judge that you
are Irish." Which, concluded Nye, was precisely how he knew Sherlock Holmes was in town, for who else would have such astounding
perspicacity? The Englishman in the World office—who was, of
course, Conan Doyle—did not particularly relish the loud response to
this joke. But it is said that in later visits he became more conditioned
to barbaric American humor.

Visiting Englishmen were responsible for much Park Row humor.
An English artist of the time was Archie Gunn, a talented young man
later to be highly appreciated for his drawing of a nude girl lolling on
a bed and saying into a telephone, "No, I have nothing on today."
On his first visit to this country in 1895, Gunn made the grand tour of
Park Row city rooms, then announced to his new friends that he
thought he would stroll out to the Falls. Not a face changed expression, and no voice warned, as he cheerfully set off uptown. At Forty-
second Street, the slightly weary artist paused to ask a policeman the
distance to the Falls. "What Falls?" the policeman growled. "Niagara
Falls," Gunn answered brightly, adding that he hoped it would be possible to borrow a gun along the way so that he might shoot buffalo
around Buffalo. Told that Niagara Falls was some five hundred miles
distant, Gunn reluctantly turned back toward Park Row. But even
then New York had a way of never disappointing anyone. The city
was testing its first underground pipes and as Gunn reached Thirty-
fourth Street a manhole cover shot howling into the air, landing
with a fearsome clatter just a few feet from him. At Houston Street,

the same thing happened, and once again at Canal. Back on Newspaper Row, the young artist stated that his walk to Niagara had been
more ruggedly exciting than anything he expected.

Though the city rooms of the two Worlds, Morning and Evening,
appeared to be full of robust talents which brought circulation and
confidence to the Pulitzer newspapers, there still were factors working in William Randolph Hearst's favor in any challenge he might
make to the supremacy of the World. The robust talents and high
circulations were, as Hearst well knew, only outward indications of
the condition of the papers. Beneath this surface, the World did not
seem quite so unassailable.

There was even one powerful, special factor working for Hearst.
On the day in August, 1895, when Hearst may have stood looking at
the World Building, Joseph Pulitzer was not occupying his office in
the golden dome. Nor had Pulitzer been there more than a few times
in the years since the mighty structure bearing his name had been
built. On the day its cornerstone had been laid by his four-year-old
son, Pulitzer was in Weisbaden. On the glorious day the building
opened, he was at sea bound for England on a White Star liner with
cabins on all sides kept empty at his expense, while a rope carpet over
the deck outside muffled all sounds of promenaders near his cabin.
As much as humanly possible, he was crossing the ocean undisturbed
by a sound.

For in challenging Pulitzer Hearst was opening war on a blind
man. After the years of abusing his eyes, Pulitzer had finally lost his
vision: or perhaps worse, since his left eye contained a slight suffusion
which allowed sight so dim that it served as a greater strain and irrita-
tion than if he had been wholly in blackness. But his right eye was
totally blind, and sightlessness had turned an already peculiar man
into that most peculiar of individuals—an absentee publisher.

After guiding the two-and-a-half-million-dollar Pulitzer Building
to the architect's drawing board in 1889, Pulitzer had gone to Europe in the hope that doctors there would contradict the verdict of
his American physicians. Kate Pulitzer accompanied him, as did Dr.
McLane, to make the nucleus of the entourages which, constantly
growing in size, would from then on travel with him wherever he

went. In London, Sir Andrew Clarke first examined him and emphatically seconded the New York doctors who said that Pulitzer must take an absolute rest from work. Pulitzer indignantly stormed off to Paris, where Doctors Charcot, Brown-Sequard, Dupuy, Bouchard, de Wecker, Lambolt and Mayer, in separate consultations, repeated the same verdict.

Pulitzer still nursed dreams and proceeded to Berlin where the world-famous eye doctor, Hermann Pagenstecher, also concurred. However, he made the constructive suggestion that a trip around the world might bring relief. Pulitzer responded enthusiastically, for the sound of water lapping against the sides of ships was one of the few sounds in the world he found truly soothing. Accordingly, he boarded ship for a leisurely trip home by way of Greece, Constantinople, India and Japan. With him, as well as Kate and Dr. McLane, went the first of a lifetime stream of young English gentleman secretaries, since Pulitzer also found the gentle tones of well-educated Englishmen sweet to his ears. No ordinary young man would ever do as a Pulitzer secretary and this original one was Claude Ponsonby, son of the famed Lord Ponsonby. But though Pulitzer was surrounded by the beginnings of his later entourage, he still insisted on doing everything himself—exactly as he had on Park Row. Thus, after embarking on his round-the-world trip, he bombarded his Park Row staff with such detailed cables that by the time the boat reached the Aegean, he held the reins of the World as surely as if he were in New York. His doctors had particularly warned of hardening of the arteries in his brain, any one of which might rupture at any time. He was not to bend over to tie his shoes, and the wash-basin in his cabin had been lifted to chin-level. Also important was that he avoid excitement and agitation. Yet as the ship left Greece to point toward Constantinople, Pulitzer had achieved mental ferment over conditions on Park Row. Midway to Constantinople a cable was handed to him which annoyed him still further, though his New York staff later declared it was of an unimportant nature. As the ship drew close to the dock of Constantinople, Pulitzer stood at the rail, while Ponsonby described in detail the scene which to the publisher was little more than a bright blur. Then Pulitzer unexpectedly turned to Ponsonby and said, "How suddenly it has got dark." Ponsonby hesitated, then replied, "It's not dark yet." "It is to me," Pulitzer said.

Immediately, all was consternation. Pulitzer had gone blind, his mental agitation having caused a detachment of the retina which broke the machinery of the eyes. It seemed advisable to return to Europe at once and the party embarked immediately on a boat for Naples. En route, it became apparent that loss of sight had increased a thousandfold Pulitzer's sensitivity to sound, already hideously acute. The throbbing of the ship's engines caused him new agony and the noise of people walking the deck near his cabin made him scream. The slightest noise seemed to bring on nervous paroxysms and, writes one biographer, "All his life thereafter was spent in evading noises, though with unerring ill luck he invariably managed to be at the center of whatever clatter abounded. Extreme debility and depression were natural concomitants of this condition."

Pulitzer's extraordinary ill luck in this direction was promptly demonstrated in Naples, where on doctor's orders the fiendishly tortured man was shut in a dark room and told he must remain there for at least a week. Nearly all the discomforts of his remaining twenty-four years were quickly brought to bear on the invalid lying in the dark. He could not work, though his mind cried to do so. He could not see. Then all at once the blessed silence of the room was shattered by all the fortifications of the city beginning simultaneous artillery practice. Thunderous detonations and accompanying vibrations tore at Pulitzer's already screaming nerves. In time, he would become so excruciatingly sensitive to sound that the clumsy turning of a book page caused him pain, but even now the guns sounded to him as if the world were ending. Happily, in those days American newspaper publishers were important people, especially if also millionaires. So were the sons of prominent English lords. A desperate Claude Ponsonby rushed to city authorities. The gunnery was ordered stopped for the length of Pulitzer's stay.

At last Pulitzer was forced to accept what doctors had been telling him for years. Facing the fact of his invalidism, he began to adapt his existence to it. He started building around himself a small world, populated by Kate, his children (whose noisy childish enthusiasms his

nervous system could not for a long time bear), Dr. McLane and assorted secretaries who would not only read to him but would be so
impressively educated that he could pick their minds and engage them
in stimulating conversation. While these people shielded him from
the world, the rooms he lived in would be soundproofed or isolated
for silence, and by the use of his great wealth he would always travel
in luxury.

Yet with all this, Pulitzer remained an odd invalid. For one
thing, his decision to cease battling the inevitable brought a kind of
serenity to his once-hectic personality. All the ravages of his sicknesses
(according to McDougall, he also had diabetes) appeared to be inner. The outer man still stood six foot two, and now that the demoniacal haste was gone he stood commandingly straight. Pulitzer's new
personality was further improved when an experienced valet was
added to the entourage. This worthy immediately trimmed Pulitzer's
reddish, tufty beard into a sleek Van Dyck which gave the tall publisher the look of a Spanish grandee—or a Mephistopheles. In addition, the valet usually dressed him in expensive black. The result was
an invalid who paradoxically appeared healthy and majestic.

The impressive new Pulitzer now began a roaming, restless existence. He seemed happiest when traveling and because of this made
long and seemingly purposeless journeys. Life seemed to turn dreary
the moment he tried to settle down. Contrariwise, the thought of
moving cheered him up. While actually in motion he became se-
renely amiable. Pulitzer's first such journey was a return to the United
States in October, 1890. In a moving statement published in the
World of October sixteenth, he abdicated as editor. Almost immediately he sailed back to England, where he purchased an estate in
Surrey. While he tried to rest there, his agents were industriously
buying or leasing alternate estates in Lakewood, N.J.; Bar Harbor,
Maine; Jekyl Island, Georgia; and Cap Martin, France.

All of which made a pattern of the invalid life—but brought
only confusion to Park Row. For Pulitzer, while abdicating as editor,
did not step out as publisher or owner. He first put the editorial department in the hands of a triumvirate composed of Colonel Cockerill; Colonel William Davis, Pulitzer's brother-in-law; and George
Turner, the paper's business manager. In this, there may be visible

the pattern of a man who creates chaos so that of necessity his hand must remain the ultimate guiding one. Pulitzer further increased the ineffectiveness of his triumvirate by discovering that, even as a blind man in exile from Park Row, his sharp journalistic sense remained. There was something uncanny in the certainty with which this man, sitting in near-total darkness, was able to grasp events and discern motives. After only a few weeks of feeling that control of the World lay in their hands, the triumvirate discovered that Pulitzer's constant cables carried as much authority as had his presence. They began again to defer to the master's hand, so that Pulitzer became like the captain of a great ocean liner—a remote but powerful figure on the bridge, seldom seen but whose personality is always felt.

Pulitzer's hidden desire—if such it was—to keep the World in turmoil was further assisted by flaws in his own character. The look of serenity into which his features had fallen was misleading. As his life of blindness continued, he became more impatient and, as he was obliged to depend more on others, more suspicious. This in turn rendered him irascible and peremptory. Like many self-made men, he never seemed able to value those already in his employ. A man attaining a good position on a Pulitzer paper usually remained in it. If the job ahead fell open, Pulitzer brought in someone from the outside. Now he did this on a vast scale. Instead of increasing the responsibility given his staff, the absentee owner began importing outsiders to save what, in moments of depression, he considered a sinking ship.

Colonel Cockerill was among the first on whom such tactics grated. Without Pulitzer's electric presence to divert his mind, the Colonel had time for thought—and the results were not happy. Cockerill believed, not without justice, that his contribution to the Post-Dispatch and the World had been almost as great as Pulitzer's. Yet, it has been said, a colossal success is never big enough to be shared. Had the Pulitzer papers remained moderate earners, Cockerill and his chief might have continued in perfect harmony, reasonably sharing the profits. But the papers had made millions, at which Pulitzer had presented Cockerill a few shares of stock, then taken the millions unto himself. As the invalid publisher began traveling from estate to estate, living in grandiose style, Cockerill examined his sparse quarters in Room One of the Astor House, across City Hall Park from the World Building. He did not like the contrast and began grumbling in his bourbon about his treatment at Pulitzer's hands. Inevitably he sent what Pulitzer considered an insolent message. Stung to the quick, Pulitzer ordered Cockerill to exchange jobs with John A. Dillon, editor of the Post-Dispatch. The redoubtable Cockerill perused the message and exploded into tremendous rage. Grabbing his hat, he left the World forever, and after a brief period of trying to bring his special brand of life to the Commercial Advertiser, became a foreign correspondent for the Herald. As such, he died of apoplexy at Shepheard's Hotel, in Cairo, in 1895.

Cockerill left the World in 1891 and by then Pulitzer was shifting his New York staff as if indulging in a stimulating game of checkers. Dillon was brought East from St. Louis, but before he arrived George Turner, the business manager, had been dismissed for demanding a share of the advertising-department duties of Colonel Davis. Dillon was presented with the responsibilities of both Cockerill and Turner, which did not please Colonel Davis. However, Dillon was so obviously unsuited to business-department duties that shortly he was transferred to the editorial page. One Frederick Driscoll took his place in the business department. But, in Pulitzer's phrase, Driscoll did not wear, and a John Norris was put in his place. In the meantime, S. S. Carvalho was appointed assistant vice-president with absolute power over finances. Again, the urbane Davis was miffed. At the same time, William H. Merrill, who had been put in Cockerill's place as editor, stepped out of that position to become chief editorial writer. From the Brooklyn plant of the World, Pulitzer plucked Don Carlos Seitz, who later became his official biographer.

Into this bubbling stew, Pulitzer—with his penchant for hiring outsiders—kept depositing new ingredients. In his blindness he became partial to confident, flowery conversationalists. He enjoyed the assertive talk of such men, and under its spell would decide that here at last was exactly the man to save the New York World. In time, Pulitzer's Park Row staff came to dread the appearance of prosperous-looking men—usually colonels—clutching letters written on Pulitzer's pale blue stationery. Each would be allowed to function as editor-in-chief until such time as Pulitzer himself caught up with his lack of ability. One was Colonel George B. M. Harvey, who later nominated Woodrow Wilson for the Presidency. In daily and editorial conferences, Harvey would sit in impressive silence until every possible suggestion had been made. Then, selecting the best ideas, he would calmly and solemnly present them as his own. Pulitzer himself had often done this, but it required a master of audacity to get away with it. Pulitzer could do it—Harvey could not.

Slowly becoming conscious of the hostility of the staff, Harvey began editing the paper from the lounge of his uptown club. This did not seem to bother Pulitzer. But when Harvey composed and insisted on printing an article criticizing Mrs. Richard Croker's table manners, Pulitzer at last fired him, explaining, "I knew Harvey wouldn't do from the moment I heard he wouldn't let the elevator stop to pick up anyone else while he was on it."

Still less successful was Colonel Charles H. Jones, whose appearance with a blue letter caused one reporter to state, "The astonishment of the shop was not so much at the Colonel, as at the wide scope seemingly given a man with no knowledge of the field, and Mr. Pulitzer's complete disregard of those who had done so much to hold the paper together so well." Colonel Jones, an out-of-towner, had spent ten days at Chatwold, Pulitzer's Bar Harbor estate, and there made such a deep impression that he was all but given the World. Or perhaps he was merely Pulitzer's most inspired effort to make sure the office could not run without him. Though married to a formidable lady, Colonel Jones appeared somewhat effeminate to the World staff. He aroused further dislike by wearing flowing whiskers while the staff prided itself on being universally clean-shaven.

"His beginnings were full of mistakes," one pundit writes moderately. Indeed, Jones became so despised that Walt McDougall daily caricatured him and his wife in World cartoons, though Jones never seemed to catch on to this fact. Another thing he never mastered was the city's Elevated Railroad. Once he plunged into the city room in a state of high excitement. "I'm going to compel the El to run all night," he shouted triumphantly. Not a voice was raised to tell him the Elevated already ran all night. When an important crisis arose in Washington, Jones set off for that city and, peremptorily brushing aside the World's regular correspondent, began filing dispatches directly contrary to World policy. Carvalho and other executives in New York merely killed these, so they were not known to Pulitzer. But on returning to New York Jones wrote an editorial again at odds with World policy. This was permitted to appear and Pulitzer reacted explosively. Colonel Jones remained adamant. Undaunted, he insisted that he was right and the paper wrong. Shortly, Colonel Jones was seen no more around Park Row.

All this—as the cryptic William Randolph Hearst well knew— produced an inner chaos which an occupant of the World city room later called "a witch's brew of suspicion, jealousy, and hatred—a maelstrom of office politics that drove at least two editors to drink, one to suicide, a fourth to insanity, and another to banking."

Yet even with this internal chaos, the paper offered a prosperous and thoroughly professional front to the reading public. In 1893 a dinner was given as a celebration of the triumphant tenth anniversary of the paper under Pulitzer, and a hundred-page edition was printed in honor of the event. With characteristic extravagance Pulitzer arrived from Europe on the Wednesday afternoon of the dinner and boarded a liner for the return trip on Saturday. He did not go near the World Building, much less enter its city room, but he proved—to his own satisfaction, at least—that he had not lost the common, or city-room, touch.

For it was on this occasion that he summoned Carvalho to the Fifty-fifth Street mansion, there to berate him because of the increasing dullness of the World. Carvalho suggested a shake-up of jobs. Pulitzer would have none of it. "I don't think it is because the staff is stale," he opined. "I think it's because nobody in the place gets drunk. Brad [Bradford Merrill, then editorial manager] never gets drunk; Burton [city editor] lives in Flatbush—he never gets drunk; Lyman [night managing editor], he's always sober. You live in Brooklyn and never get drunk. When I was there someone always got drunk, and we made a great paper. Now, find a man who gets drunk and hire him!"

With these surprising instructions ringing in his ears, Carvalho returned to Park Row. There was no chance that Pulitzer was fooling, for J.P. was not a humorous man. Crossing City Hall Park, Carvalho encountered a notorious rumpot who had been fired from every city room on Park Row. Carvalho hired him at once, by one account "dragging him to the office and nailing him to the payroll." The man was indeed the perfect newspaper drunk, who several times had d.t.'s on the premises and once nearly severed a hand pursuing a purple dog through a glass door. But no matter how outrageous his behavior, the World drunk remained on the payroll until his inevitable death in a barroom brawl. For it was a satisfied Pulitzer's oft-stated conviction that, because of the man's drunken presence, the World had become lively again.

CHAPTER FOUR

"GONE TO GUSH?"

Such was the powerful—if stricken—man whom William Randolph Hearst, in 1895, arrived in New York to combat. "He intended to outdo the World," says one source, "to capture its mass circulation, to defeat it, and if possible wreck it." Hearst's San Francisco Examiner had cost him four hundred and fifty thousand dollars before making money. Success in New York would cost vastly more, but Hearst was quite prepared to risk it—the entire seven million if necessary. On the West Coast the annoying Ambrose Bierce cast a look across the continent at Hearst's embryo activities on Park Row. Bierce understood his employer thoroughly, and as always came up with the perfect phrase for what Hearst intended to do. He called it "the brutal use of money."

Hearst's first step in the newspaper war he alone desired was to re-create the Journal plainly in the image of the World. Page size, column size, number of pages, type, all these were the same. But still there remained a major difference between the existing paper and the projected one. Where the World sold for two cents, Hearst planned to sell his Journal for a penny. "Everybody loves a bargain," he informed his new staff in the fragrance-of-violets falsetto. "I will supply them with a better paper at a penny than Mr. Pulitzer gives them for twice as much."

He planned other innovations, many of them now rendered possible by the fact that, in 1894, a press had been installed in the World Building which registered four colors without results like a

Spanish omelette. On November 18, 1894, the World had used this new press to bring out the first Sunday comic, largely a strip featuring the antics of a wolfhound and a clown created by Richard F. Outcault, a young draughtsman on a trade paper. Hearst had ordered a similar press—it was delivery of this which, among other things, held up the first issue of his Journal—and he also had his eye on Outcault, who, by 1895, had created a new strip called Hogan's Alley. Hearst planned to feature comics daily as well as Sunday, printing them all in the primary colors which were what the new press could at the moment provide. He also planned black-and-white illustrations, which would require a large staff of newspaper artists. The "instantaneous camera," as the photographic camera was called then, was far from instantaneous, while the halftone process for newspaper printing had remained in the development stage. But sketch artists would be no problem: there were almost as many of them in New York as there were reporters. Men like Frederic Remington, William J. Glackens, John Sloan, and George Luks, could be dispatched to the scene of a disaster or crime to return with a drawing almost as good, and perhaps better, than any photograph. Indeed, Hearst at this point may have considered artists more important than reporters. The Journal, as he visualized it, would be so lavish in its use of illustrations and drawn features that it would be possible to enjoy it without reading a word of text.

Slowly the staff he gathered around him began to note quirks on the part of the bland, awkward Western millionaire. His tolerance of the drinking habits of newspapermen appeared to be quite true, for one afternoon Hearst called a meeting of his newly hired reporters only to be told that one man might be found quaffing in Andy Horn's saloon, another in the back room of Perry's Drug Store in the Pulitzer Building, with the others in remaining Park Row watering spots. One staff member had just been taken to a special alcoholics' ward in St. Vincent's Hospital which was fondly dubbed Newspaper Row. Hearst took this in stride. "Dear me," he breathed mildly, "for a man who is practically an abstainer, I probably suffer more from alcoholism than any other human being in the Western Hemisphere." When in due time his convivial staff reassembled—except, of course, for the man in the bed in "Newspaper Row"—Hearst uttered not a word of complaint. "He permits nothing to stir the depths of his strange, agate nature," one of his men noted.

Hearst soon had his men totally enmeshed in getting out the new Journal, and in this his own sleeves were rolled higher than anyone's. In these first days of the Journal, he indulged to the full any desires he may have harbored to be a working newspaperman. In fact, a stranger entering the city room of the newly galvanized paper would have experienced difficulty in selecting the millionaire editor-publisher. Hearst had made for himself a large office in the front of the building, overlooking Printing House Square and City Hall, and had already begun filling it with the heavy antiques and suits of armor that were to surround him all through life. But, for the moment at least, he preferred to spend most of the time in the city room, working like an ordinary member of the staff.

It was he who followed the copy to the composing room and there made up the first edition. Thus Hearst got to know the compositors and pressmen, whom he treated with rare deference and respect. They in turn affectionately called him "Chief" or "W.R." When finally an edition was put to bed, everyone—Hearst, reporters, pressmen—hustled to the plant restaurant on the Frankfort Street side of the building. In these humble surroundings, Hearst demonstrated a great liking for hot dogs liberally coated with mustard. It was while contentedly munching these, he later declared, that many of the important decisions concerning the Journal were made.

What Hearst really wanted was a wholly sensational paper, a mixture of lurid stories, juicy scandals, provocative, strident heads, and new shockers every day: splash-sensations that would paralyze the public. He planned to take the hard-hitting, emotional, factual World technique and carry it to extremes that the more sensitive Pulitzer had never considered. "Get the news and get there first," Hearst lectured his assembling staff. "But be sure and make a great and continuous noise to attract readers."

Hearst had also learned from Pulitzer that intervention in public affairs brings circulation. "Denounce crooked wealth and promise better conditions for the poor," he would continue. "It gets readers." Hearst was fortunate in stepping into the New York spotlight at a time when corporate industrialism was at its height. Rockefeller, Morgan, Huntington, Harriman and other titans were welding great aggregations of capital into monopolistic control of oil, railroads, shipping. Greed on such a huge scale inspired imitation on all levels. Public utilities were trying to control legislatures, courts and administrative offices. Pulitzer had been denouncing this for years but, to Hearst's uncluttered mind, had been doing it in an unnecessarily roundabout fashion. Hearst was always able to reduce complicated issues to beautiful simplifications. This enabled him to crusade largely by leveling thundering attacks at such general targets as "Pirate privilege," "Amalgamated greed," and "Highwaymen of high-finance." At the same time he could view his mission in exalted terms. "I was determined to restore democracy to the United States," he said later. "I had carefully examined the history of the country until I believed I knew what it meant . . ." There were many, however, who felt that Hearst did not know what it meant, and that in crusading in such general terms he was relieving the public of a responsibility for judging issues on real merits. E. L. Godkin, of the Evening Post, especially, viewed this with alarm and for Hearst coined the much-quoted phrase, "The blackguard boy." Yet it was the muckraker Lincoln Steffens who best summed up the dangers in Hearst's glib editorializing. "To give us a better government, he would make us a worse people," he decided.

Hearst worked tirelessly to achieve the right formula. One of those who shortly joined him was a noted foreign correspondent named James Creelman. A dignified man with a small goatee that made him resemble a European scholar, Creelman was nevertheless one of the most adventurous reporters of the time. He had exclusively interviewed such diverse characters as the Indian Chief, Sitting Bull, and the Russian novelist, Leo Tolstoi. In quest of unusual news, he had traveled to Corea, as it was then spelled. Now associated with Hearst, he saluted his new employer's industry by writing, "He realized that he was facing enormous competition and that if the methods developed in San Francisco were to succeed in New York, he had to give them unceasing attention."

When the operation of the new paper began to shake down, Hearst started passing more time in his private office. As he summoned men to the office with its period furniture and curious collectors' items, those surrounding him began discovering new things about the outer and inner Hearst. About the inner, it was found that his seeming shyness and reticence covered an acutely self-centered drive to power. A peculiar facet of the outer man was that Hearst possessed an almost simian skill of movement with his feet, often using them in a manner resembling another pair of hands. His favorite manner of examining an edition of the World, for instance, was to throw it on the floor, then stand above it, examining the front page. After this, using one foot, he turned pages until the end. At home, sitting at his ease in the Hoffman House suite, he would take off shoes and socks to turn the pages of a paper with his toes. Usually, however, he preferred to stand up, and when examining proofs of his own papers, added to the oddness of all this by manifesting curious emotional reactions. One of his early aides was James Coleman, who died as recently as 1956. In language contemporary with his later years, Coleman thus recalls Hearst examining proofs:

> My eyes strained wide and I tried vainly to keep from swallowing my bubble gum when Hearst suddenly spread the proofs [I had brought] on the floor, and began a sort of tap dance around and between them. It was a mild, uncostumed combination of Carmen Miranda, a rhumba, a Russian dagger dance, and Notre Dame shift, with lively castanet accompaniment produced by snapping fingers. After I had observed W.R.'s strange dance, I learned it was his customary method of absorbing pictures and captions on picture pages. The cadence of it speeded up with his reactions of disturbance and slowed down to a strolling rhythm when he approved. Between dances, he scribbled illegible corrections on the margins and finally gave the proofs back to me.

In 1895, Hearst stood on the verge of becoming what Lloyd Morris has called half playboy, half rabble-rouser, all embryonic tycoon. Despite his unwavering efforts with the Journal, he was sometimes seen at Delmonico's, accompanied, as had also been his custom in San Francisco, by two pretty girls. Occasionally he astounded Park Row by appearing in the Journal office for a midnight visit, attired in full evening clothes and still with a pretty girl on either arm. In time the pretty girls became the dancing Willson sisters, one of whom Hearst married when he reached the age of forty. But in the first days of the Journal, such moments of elegance were few. Most of the time Hearst worked with unswerving enthusiasm and ruthless, low-keyed drive. So, according to his lights, did Sam Chamberlain, who had quickly been hailed by Park Row as "Sam the elegant! Sam the drunken!" With the instincts of a fine, if sodden, newspaperman, Chamberlain was quickly getting the feel of New York. How well he did was demonstrated shortly after the Journal commenced publication. Then a young reporter rushed into the city room to announce that there had been a murder on a streetcar. Chamberlain listened, then calmly asked, "What streetcar line?" Told it was the Bleecker Street crosstown, he shook his head sadly. "What happens on a crosstown car never attracts any attention," he said indifferently. "Now, if it had only been a Broadway car. . . ."

Hearst's first great score in a major department of his plans—that of luring the best men from rival papers—came when he persuaded Morrill Goddard and the entire staff of the Sunday World to join him on the Journal.

Goddard, a slight, pale young man who would in time be called a morbid genius, was one of the most unusual newspapermen of his (or any) time. Born in Maine, he had at Dartmouth manifested skill at digging up bizarre and striking bits of historical and scientific information. Small, pale, sickly-looking, he next headed for New York, determined to get a job on a major newspaper. Since he had no experience and appeared so unprepossessing, the ambitious, crafty youth could only become a free-lance reporter working out of various city rooms at space rates. While engaged in this, he discovered that the City Morgue, located on an inaccessible East Side street, got no steady coverage from Park Row newspapers. Goddard established himself there, to become a companion much appreciated by Peg Leg Fogarty, the lonely Morgue attendant. Simply by being on the premises when the bodies came in, Goddard got hold of exclusive stories, which he peddled to Park Row papers, among them the World. Shortly he was on the World staff, where he accomplished one of the record scoops of all time on the day of President Grant's funeral procession through New York. Attired in a black suit, Goddard boldly clambered into the first carriage of the procession and calmly sat himself down beside the bereaved Mrs. Grant. In dark clothes, the pale young man looked every inch the undertaker's assistant, and both the police and the widow accepted him as such. Thus he was able to cover the entire procession from a vantage point beside the widow, which he did not hesitate to stress in the story he wrote for the World. Goddard utilized the same gall when Grover Cleveland married. Where other reporters respectfully withdrew as soon as the knot was tied, Goddard pursued the newlyweds to the door of the nuptial chamber. There he spent the night, all but putting his eye to the keyhole.

With all this journalistic boldness, Goddard never lost his college-boy interest in running down odd facts. Soon his many skills had won him the post of editor of the lurid Sunday World, where his talents at last flowered. From Jules Verne, Edgar Allan Poe, Conan Doyle, the gory Gaboriau, and the obscure scientific treatises, he created weekly features that were a frenzied amalgam of surgery, nudity, monster ape men, criminals of exotic types, and society scandals.

His policy was to use huge drawn illustrations with the smallest possible text, and in his quest for such material was ever vigilant. Once he noted a crowd around a drugstore window and found the people absorbed in a cross section of a ship with the inner sections drawn in bright colors and a shark swimming hungrily below. Goddard needed no more than this to start a journalistic trend. On the following Sunday the World featured a cross section of the human body, and in succeeding weeks cross sections of gorillas, murderesses, buxom chorus girls, prehistoric monsters, and diseased and misshapen bodies lying open on a surgeon's table. Of his success with cross sections, Goddard recalled later, "Some of the staff objected, but circulation jumped four or five thousand a week. On the day I printed a full-page cross section of a gorilla, it jumped ten thousand. All I had to do was cite those figures and all objections disappeared."

Goddard printed almost nothing that was not shocking. Some of his more notable early features were: The Suicide of a Horse; Cutting a Hole in a Man's Chest to Look at His Intestines and Leaving a Flap That Works as if on a Hinge; Experimenting with an Electric Needle and an Ape's Brain; and Science Can Wash Your Heart. Ever a

shrewd newspaperman, Goddard kept his contacts perpetually simmering. To any chorus girl or artist's model who tipped him off to a
story of social high jinks, he made a standing offer of a stylish and expensive cartwheel hat. One day this paid off in a manner that shaped
Goddard's future career as well, perhaps, as the lives of Hearst and
Pulitzer.

It started with the appearance of a young artist's model in Goddard's office in the World's golden dome. Having extracted the
promise of a new hat if her tip paid off, she urged Goddard to find out
what another model named Sally Johnson had done the night before.
Sally was a sixteen-year-old beauty who, according to one of the many
versions of the story, in time killed herself as a result of being sensationally featured in the Sunday World. Goddard wasted no time.
He rushed uptown to find Sally still tousled from a late sleep. From
her own lips—at the price of another hat—he learned the details
of what has come down in history as the Girl in the Pie Dinner.
With no visible reluctance, Sally told of a party, perhaps the ultimate
in Gay Nineties high-jinks, given the night before by the wealthy
bachelor-artist, James L. Breese. It was a stag dinner in his studio
on Sixteenth Street at which a huge Jack Horner pie had served as
centerpiece on the table. As the climax of the evening, the pie burst
open and out jumped Sally, to perform a sprightly dance up and
down the table. She was of course nude—or, as the World story put
it, "covered only by the ceiling."

On Sunday, a seven-column drawing of Sally capering on the
table—most of her nudity hidden by a convenient protoplasmic blur
—filled the first page of the Sunday World Supplement. Beneath it,
creating absolutely no distraction to the eye, a small amount of text
described the dinner. Among the hundreds of thousands who were
brought up sharp by the Girl in the Pie story was William Randolph
Hearst, as he ate his Hoffman House Sunday breakfast. His sluggish
blood quickened and so great was his approval that he did not merely
mutter to himself, "I must have the editor who did that." Instead he
thought, "I must have the staff that did it." Accordingly, on Monday
morning, he summoned Goddard to the Examiner office, which he
still retained in the World Building, to offer him editorship of the
Sunday Journal, with jobs for the entire Sunday World staff. By one

account Hearst, as he made this offer, seemed "so demure, so bashful, so flaccid in manner," that Goddard was totally unimpressed. "I don't want to change certainty for uncertainty, Mr. Hearst," he replied. Then he added, "Frankly, I don't think you are going to last more than three months in this town."

Hearst countered by smiling faintly. Without a word he reached into the pocket of his sporty vest. From it he pulled a crumpled piece of paper which he tossed at Goddard. It was a Wells Fargo draft for thirty-six thousand dollars. "Will that do as a guarantee to you and the rest of your staff?" he inquired.

The ice-blooded Goddard was immediately won over and by displaying the draft easily convinced his staff as well. Taking all the Sunday files and paraphernalia, the group of World men rode down in the elevator, left the Pulitzer Building, turned sharp left, crossed Frankfort Street, and walked up two floors in the Tribune Building to the Journal office. Behind them in the World Tower remained only a single girl secretary, who lost no time in carrying word of the mass desertion to S. S. Carvalho. For that cautious gentleman, it was a crisis far too hot to handle personally. He decided it was imperative to inform Pulitzer who, to complicate matters, was in residence at Cap Martin, France. Carvalho frantically cabled and received back an incredulous reply which asked: GONE TO GUSH?—for Pulitzer killed long hours by lovingly devising an elaborate cable code for communicating with Park Row. He was aware of Hearst's arrival in New York and had assigned him the cable name Gush, perhaps because of some episode when a younger Hearst had worked on the World.

Assured by a cable that his Sunday World men had indubitably Gone to Gush, Pulitzer was both surprised and enraged. HIRE BACK AT ANY COST, he cabled, and Carvalho sent emissaries next door to tempt Goddard and his group back with an offer even better than Hearst's. Goddard listened, then put the Wells Fargo draft back on Hearst's desk, and with his men following, again crossed Frankfort Street and rode up the elevator to the office in the World Tower. They remained there only one day. The contents of Hearst's second offer to Goddard have not been revealed, but twenty-four hours later the Sunday World staff returned to the Journal, where Goddard in time pushed the circulation of Hearst Sunday supplements to thirty million, thus becoming a person of such towering stature that even his employer hesitated to bother him. But in 1895, the second walkout to Hearst persuaded the absentee Pulitzer that in the Goddard matter he must admit defeat. All he could do to bolster his feelings was to order that Hearst immediately be denied entry to the Examiner office in the World Building. This was promptly done. The redwood fixtures in the Examiner office were torn out and delivered to the Journal with Mr. Pulitzer's compliments. The office itself was redecorated in more prosaic fashion and rented to the Boston Globe.

At Cap Martin, the ailing Pulitzer now decided that a return to Park Row was necessary. Sightless, irritable, hideously sensitive to sound, he embarked for New York, there to make one of his few appearances in the building that bore his name. Albert Payson Terhune remembers him being hustled through the Evening World city room "by a cloud of wriggling managing editors and other office chiefs." Having made a suitable tour of the building, Pulitzer returned to his office in the dome, where Walt McDougall pictures his reaction to the Hearst threat as "having received such a jolt that there was no evidence of querulousness nor asperity on his face or in his voice . . . he seemed like a chess player studying a vital move."

It was a necessary attitude, for after the initial success with Goddard, Hearst and his golden checkbook were luring World men in alarming numbers. Indeed, so many of the paper's trusted editors and reporters had already left that it was decided, with Pulitzer back in town, to have a World staff dinner as a boost to editorial morale. Richard Farrelly had just been promoted to managing editor of the World—to take the place of a man who had Gone to Gush—and it was decided to make this event a testimonial dinner to the new managing editor.

Farrelly had begun his newspaper career by a legendary reporting feat during the Blizzard of '88. As the snows of the great blizzard began packing down, he had appeared in Colonel Cockerill's coop in the World city room. A pair of snowshoes hung on his back and he claimed a combination of newspaper skill and long experience in the frozen North. These he offered to utilize by covering the big snow in intrepid fashion for the World. Cockerill, delighted at his good fortune in having such a man miraculously appear, gave the vigorous new reporter carte blanche. Whereupon Farrelly strapped on the snowshoes and clumped off across City Hall Park to the Astor House where, after renting a warm room, he installed himself with a suitable supply of whiskey. From time to time, as the blizzard increased, he emerged to stamp across the Park to the World, making sure that he arrived brushing quantities of snow from his clothes and beard. The liquor he had been consuming gave his eyes the look of a hardy adventurer, and each time, he sat down to write grippingly realistic survivor and adventure stories which gave the World a spectacular beat on the storm.

Worldly-wise in so many respects, Colonel Cockerill never caught on to this monster deception. After the snows melted, he rewarded Farrelly by giving him a full-time reporting job, from which he had slowly risen to become city editor of the Evening World. As the new managing editor of the morning edition, it was fitting that such a man be honored by a testimonial dinner, graced by the unprecedented presence of the great Pulitzer himself. But Farrelly never achieved his rare honor. On the afternoon of the dinner, it was hastily canceled. Farrelly, the guest of honor, had just Gone to Gush.

"William Randolph Hearst broke into New York with all the discreet secrecy of a wooden-legged burglar having a fit on a tin roof," says James Melvin Lee, in his history of American journalism.

It is hardly an extravagant image. Hearst's first issue of the Journal appeared on November 7, 1895, and brought a brief moment of uncertainty to the staff of the World. Along Park Row it was well known that Hearst intended to wreck the World, yet three quarters of the front page of his first edition was filled by a drawing of the wedding of Consuelo Vanderbilt and the Duke of Marlborough. What remained of the page was occupied by a description of the event by Julian Ralph, one of the great reporters of the time who had just been brought over—or bought over—from the hallowed Sun. It was said that Ralph could write five thousand fascinating words about a cobblestone and his description of General Grant's funeral had run to fourteen thousand words. In his initial story for Hearst, the wordy genius outdid himself. His page-one column ran over to fill no less than three tight-packed inside pages. The story, admiring rivals noted, was so intimate it might have been the bride's diary.

But what momentarily surprised the editors in the Pulitzer Building was that by giving such eminence to a social event, Hearst appeared to be drawing his bead on the New York Herald, which had carved out a stately coverage of Society as its special province. On the next day bewilderment in the World Building disappeared. From the second edition of the Journal it was apparent that Pulitzer was Hearst's model—and his target. The most extraordinary dollar-matching battle in American journalism had begun. . . .

Hearst started his efforts to outdo the World not only by sensationalizing World-type news coverage. He also commenced using circulation-promotion as it had never been used in America. The Journal sent bandwagons covered with posters through the streets of New York. Billboards erected in vacant lots shouted the new paper's virtues. Sandwich men paraded the streets, and huge ads promoted the Journal in rival papers and trade organs. Pennies were sent through the mail to registered voters, thus assuring them of the purchase price of the new paper. An early feature on faithless husbands was advertised by postcards sent city-wide to wives and signed cryptically "A Friend." These suggested that the recipients buy the Journal and learn the actual truth about their husbands. "So Hearst," writes Ferdinand Lundberg, who has covered this period of Hearst's life most searchingly, "in his quest for circulation introduced into many households a helpful note of discord."

Hearst even used light verse to blazon his paper. On Journal delivery wagons and billboards he printed such merry lines as these:

Oh, be sure and call me early, mother dear—
I would buy a Morning Journal ere the last one disappear.
I didn't order one last night and I must early rise
To get one from the dealer ere the last one from him flies.

The Hearst credo was: Increase Circulation. In fact, some biographers boil Hearst in essence down to no more than a masterful paper salesman. He believed that only a Journal which alarmed and excited could win readers. By big names and big sensations, shouted from his signboards and delivery wagons, Hearst planned to draw new readers to his Journal. He paid Richard Harding Davis, the famed war correspondent and most glamorous male of his time, an unheard-of fifty cents a word to cover the Yale-Harvard football game. ("How odd," mused the strong-jawed Davis, who had set his price exorbitantly high in an effort to evade the assignment, "to be paid a dollar for writing *For instance*.") He hired Stephen Crane, author of the neglected *Maggie: A Girl of the Streets* and of the just-published best-seller *The Red Badge of Courage*, to write about vice on New York streets. Crane, who had become fascinated by the plight of streetwalkers after seeing a young and attractive girl being mauled by a brutal cop, had ample material for his series, since by 1895 New York achieved a new high of twenty-five thousand Maggies. Crane's articles were highly sensational for the time, but Hearst's advertisements and headlines made them far more so. ("A man must be a drunk, a lunatic, or Sam Chamberlain to work for Hearst," Crane muttered.)

Hearst next decided to utilize the military side of the ambivalent Crane, and sent the frail young man to cover war scares in the Balkans, Venezuela and Alaska. Crane's foreign articles did not match his coverage of New York vice. (Crane knew this and wrote from Alaska, "Little Willie is getting a bad bargain!") Hearst also sent Richard Harding Davis to the coronation of the Czar of Russia and Mark Twain to Queen Victoria's Diamond Jubilee. He hired Julian Hawthorne and Edgar Saltus, and persuaded the expatriate novelist Henry James to sell him serial rights to his new novel, *The Other House*. The prim and proper James nearly suffered an apoplectic stroke on learning that Hearst was advertising the serialization as "Henry James' New Novel of Immorality and Crime! The Surprising Plunge of the Great Novelist into the Field of Sensational Fiction!"

From other papers he hired such top-flight talents as Creelman, Murat Halstead, Robert H. Davis, Alan Dale, James L. Ford, Henry W. Fisher, A. C. Wheeler ("Nym Crinkle"), Julius Chambers and scores of others. To such men the first intimation that Hearst was interested in their talents would be a discreet message, "Mr. Hearst would be pleased to have you call." In the office above Printing

House Square the ink in Hearst's golden pen never seemed to run dry. He also skillfully used the promise of by-lines, then all but unknown in journalism. His purpose in this promiscuous hiring was twofold. Not only did he want the talents of the men he bought—he also sought to injure rival papers, for Hearst was far ahead of his time in recognizing that every man with a distinctive and popular talent is an asset to a paper and that in losing such a man a newspaper loses prestige. Hearst would hire a head of a department and, as with Goddard, insist that the entire staff be brought, too. He bought men, says one source, like bunches of carrots. One day the business manager of the Journal, Charles Palmer, was asked if Hearst's wild extravagance bothered him. "Oh, we don't bother about money here," Palmer answered. "Open any closet door and you'll find money burning."

All this caused romantics among newsmen to believe that permanent prosperity had arrived at last. It had not. Many of the men Hearst hired were fired immediately. After this had happened a few times, those Hearst tried to lure demanded ironclad contracts, which he unhesitatingly gave. When such men failed to work out, the Journal had to humiliate them into resigning. Thus, men making five hundred dollars a week were turned into copy boys or custodians of out-of-town papers. Some were even made men's-room attendants. One such caused the drains to clog every few hours by stuffing them with copies of the Journal, at which the business office gave in and paid his contract in full. Another man loudly informed imbibers in Andy Horn's saloon that he felt his brain cracking under his humiliation at the Journal and that a desire was mounting in him to set the city room afire. He too was paid off.

More fortunate men found themselves capitalizing remarkably. The cartoonist, T. E. Powers, was hired away from the World by one of Hearst's ironclad contracts. Nonetheless, Pulitzer offered him another contract, which Powers signed. Hearst promptly brought suit, at which the court enjoined Powers from working for either party, but ordered that both employers pay him as the contracts dictated. In the course of the long case, lawyers delved into ancient suits involving slaves and indentured servants for precedent. Powers himself paid scant attention. As the happy recipient of two sizable weekly pay checks, he established himself contentedly in Andy Horn's, where he purchased drinks for all and sundry.

Finally, however, the case was settled in Hearst's favor. Powers and his cohorts then reeled across the Park to the steps of City Hall, where a touching scene was enacted. Powers dropped to his knees, while a friend belabored his back with a roll of drawing paper. "You can beat me all you wish," cried Powers, as he endured this punishment, "but my soul belongs to William Randolph Hearst." The tableau attracted such crowds at City Hall that it was repeated at intervals all the way uptown to Fifty-ninth Street. Suitable stops for alcoholic solace were made en route.

In the summer of 1896, Hearst himself sailed lazily in a balloon over New York and Staten Island, to prove to his reporters he would not ask them to do anything he would not do himself. Constantly, he prodded them for sensational stories—or if this were not possible, for unusual ones. Thus a Journal reporter interviewing Sarah Bernhardt asked no questions about her art, but only about the tiny dogs she possessed and the lions and tigers she was supposed to possess. A Hearst interviewer boldly asked Lillian Russell why she had never appeared in tights on the stage. To this impertinence the statuesque beauty made the classic, unruffled reply, "Nature has been too kind." One of Hearst's most successful circulation-getters in San Francisco had been to pose as a benefactor of the poor. Now on hot summer days he transported boatloads of tenement children to Coney Island, and in the cold of winter gave poor children sweaters or distributed coffee and sandwiches around the city.

Always on hand to report these benefactions in highly emotional prose were the sob sisters Hearst had developed—Winifred Black, Dorothy Dix, Ella Wheeler Wilcox and Beatrice Fairfax. But when examined closely Hearst's largesse had a way of turning sour. The man who was willing to pay such vast amounts for journalistic talent was far from generous where his picnics for waifs were concerned. One of his sob sisters later recalled how she was given a single can of ice cream to be doled out on a slum-kid jaunt to Coney Island:

> All the way down I was trembling to think what would happen when I dealt out that one miserable can of cream.

When at last I placed a dab on each saucer, a little fellow in ragged knickerbockers got up and declared that the Journal was a fake and I thought there was going to be a riot. I took away the ice-cream from a deaf and dumb kid who couldn't holler and gave it to the malcontent. Then I had to write my story beginning: *Thousands of children, pale-faced but happy, danced merrily down Coney Island's beaches yesterday and were soon sporting in the sun-lit waves shouting, "God bless Mr. Hearst."*

Hearst also performed his good deeds at disaster scenes, and again the reading public was never allowed to forget it. From one tragic scene a Hearst sob sister wrote:

I was the first to reach the injured and dying."God bless Mr. Hearst," a little child cried as I stooped to lave her brow. Then she smiled and died. I spread one of our comic supplements over the pale, still face and went on to distribute Mr. Hearst's generous bounty.

All Hearst writers had strict orders to insert mentions of comic supplements in their stories. For the cryptic publisher's intuition told him the newly developed comics could be of vast help in securing the circulation that had become his mania. Following this hunch, he wrapped the Sunday Journal in the gaudily colored comics by Outcault, T. A. Dorgan, Rudolph Dirks, and others. Indeed, it was the comics, together with Hearst's determination to feature them, which proceeded to give the entire era in journalism its name. In Outcault's pioneering Hogan's Alley comic strip there appeared a gap-toothed kid with big ears and funny toes. One day a printer at the World complained that its colors were not emphatic enough for the new primary-color printing press. "All right," said Charles Saalberg, whose job it was to color the Outcault drawings, "I'll make the kid's clothes bright yellow."

He did, and the gap-toothed infant stood out from a gang of fellow ruffians like a sunrise. Immediately, New York went wild over the Yellow Kid, though a few intellectuals failed to join the rejoicing. A contemporary deep thinker named Max Nordau wrote: "The Yellow

Kid is the exact and ultimate expression of degeneracy. . . . Notice the bald head (on a boy), the two teeth, the abnormal head and abnormal feet, the formless shirt of yellow—color of decay—covering a multitude of other abnormalities." Others closer at hand failed to appreciate the Yellow Kid's popularity. In the city room of the Evening World young Albert Payson Terhune saw the comic strip's success "spreading like some vari-hued malady." A more important objector was Morrill Goddard, whose passion for sensationalism and drawn art possibly made him blind to—or jealous of—the potential in comic strips. "I'm going to toss out Hogan's Alley on grounds of lack of humor," he sourly informed Walt McDougall. "Whose lack of humor?" McDougall asked. "Yours or Outcault's?"

Hogan's Alley remained, and when Goddard switched over to Hearst, the artist Outcault was one of those who accompanied him. Behind him Outcault of necessity left the title and characters of Hogan's Alley, since they were legal property of the World. The World immediately called in George Luks, later an outstanding American artist, who became the first in a succession of cartoonists to carry on the Outcault characters. On the Journal, Outcault began using the same characters, merely renaming his new strip The Yellow Kid. Like everyone else on Park Row, Ervin Wardman, editor of the New York Press, watched with fascination as the rival Yellow Kids slugged it out. Wardman one day went a step further by characterizing the contest between the World and the Journal as Yellow Journalism, a description so completely apt that it has remained to this day. When the sensitive Pulitzer heard this designation, he cringed. Hearst was delighted. Underlings now began to call him the Yellow Kid and he bowed to the honor with every sign of pleasure.

All this, however, was feature coverage. In the front-page news department, Hearst planned to beat the World with bigger pictures, bigger stories and more sensational coverage of any given event. Where Pulitzer might try to cover news thoroughly, Hearst's would ever be the lurid treatment. "You always had to read the Journal to know whether a woman was shot in the left breast or the right," a Park Row veteran recalls. And in his plans for startling news coverage, Hearst was hugely aided by a new development along Park Row. For big, banner headlines had at last come into being.

One story has it that the morbid genius Morrill Goddard first evolved the idea of across-eight-columns headlines: that on one of his walks around New York he noticed how department stores had begun calling attention to specialties by streamers in large type across display windows. According to this version, Goddard instantly conceived the idea of banner headlines for newspapers.

This may be so, yet most of the facts are against it. The catalyst for the first screaming headline in New York City apparently was Dr. Charles H. Parkhurst, who crusaded so strenuously against prostitution that—where those who crusaded against financial corruption were called muckrakers—he might well be called a sinraker. The formidable doctor's sensational sermons led to the Lexow investigations of 1894, and for one he took as text Proverbs 28:1—"The wicked flee when no man pursueth." A few days after this Boss Croker, the towering head of Tammany Hall, suddenly found it expedient to leave town. It was such a stunning departure that on Park Row the staff of the almost moribund Commercial Advertiser was galvanized into making history. Clearing the space across the top of the paper under the masthead, they set in the largest type available:

THE WICKED FLEES WHEN NO MAN PURSUETH!
BUT RUNS FASTER IF SOMEONE IS AFTER HIM!

It is to be presumed that the editors of the World, on seeing the Advertiser headline, smote their brows in vexation and envy. For the headline was something the World staff had been groping to find since Pulitzer and Cockerill came to town in 1883. The World wasted no time in appropriating headlines, and with the advent of Hearst's typographical sensationalism the headline truly came into its own. Screaming headlines, four or five inches high, became a daily feature of both papers, and Hearst himself finally intervened after Chamberlain and others in the Journal city room devised a wooden font of letters a full seven inches tall. "We've gone far enough in that direction," he said softly.

This, of course, was the era in which strident-voiced newsboys shouted "Uxtry!" all over town, and the World and Journal not only tried to outdo each other in banner headlines but in Extra editions as well. Other papers, alarmed by the way the two titans blanketed the city, desperately tried bringing out Extras themselves, and again the Commercial Advertiser came to life. After its triumph with the first headline, the Advertiser had lapsed back into a sedateness which allowed it to get out two leisurely editions a day—the second, it was said, to enable the editors to correct the grammar in the first. After much deliberation the Advertiser decided it would have to get out an Extra, and picked for its first the day when Henry Ward Beecher died and a wreck occurred on the Second Avenue El. The old Advertiser presses clanged feverishly and newsboys raucously hawked the Advertiser's pioneer Extra around the sidewalks of New York. But only seven copies were sold. The Advertiser sank back to its moribund ways.

CHAPTER FIVE

Yellow Journalism

BEHIND the screaming headlines of Hearst's Journal there was always to be found a certain journalistic emptiness. When proofs from his own presses were rushed to him, Hearst placed them on the floor and performed his little dance around them. With rival papers he stood immersed, turning pages with his foot. Reader interest in his own and rival stories was minutely analyzed in his brain and "what seemed unlikely to divert the lowest common denominator was pronounced unworthy of being included in the Journal." Yet Hearst's love always was more for presentation than for the news carried in the Journal. One necessary reason for this preoccupation was that he held no Associated Press franchise, and as a consequence the Journal's coverage of out-of-town news was weak. For a time the ambitious publisher tried to circumvent this by hiring famous correspondents, but a certain meanness hidden in his opulent character seemed to prevent him from getting along with highly successful men. When Richard Harding Davis became the only reporter triumphantly to crash the coronation ceremonies of Czar Nicholas II, the picture of Davis used with his dispatch on the front page of the Journal was so large that the dashing correspondent might have been the person crowned. Yet by the time Davis had reached Italy on the way home, he and Hearst were engaged in acrimonious cable dispute over expense money.

As a consequence of its lack of an AP franchise and its weak coverage of world news, the Journal depended heavily—and un-

ashamedly—on the columns of its bitter rival, the World. Sometimes
Journal rewrite men bothered to change the first paragraphs of stories
lifted bodily from the World. Just as often they did not. It was no
secret that Hearst took news bodily from Pulitzer (and in 1918 he was
enjoined by Supreme Court order from lifting news stories from other
papers). But in the Yellow Journalism period it was widely believed
that rewrite men and copy editors sat idly waiting in the Journal office
until the first copy of an edition of the World shot off the press.
Then a spy would rush it from one building to the next, at which—
according to legend—the Journal city room set up a chant:

> Sound the cymbals, beat the drum!
> The World is here, the news has come!

A certain validity is bestowed on this story by the frequency
with which Sam Chamberlain, drunk or sober, used to lean from his
managing editor's coop and shout, "Get excited, everybody. God
damn it, get excited." In the early days when the Journal city room
possessed only a single hand-crank telephone, it was difficult to respond to Chamberlain's disconcerting order. But as more phones
were installed a neat solution was found. A reporter merely called the
switchboard and told the operator to ring all city room phones. At
the same time the staff would rush about, creating as much confusion
as possible. This caused Chamberlain to return to his desk, confident
that he had brought industry to the office.

In city coverage, where he was restrained neither by lack of interest nor lack of franchise, the Yellow Kid who was Hearst could be
seen at what he thought his best. With all his love of the promotion
of news—or, if you will, selling papers—he could not hope to publish
a paper as good as the World. He himself was apparently among the
first to recognize this, and to fall back on the commodity that had always sustained him so well: Money. In the Yellow Journalism war
with Pulitzer, Hearst spent—and, in a sense, lost—nearly all the seven
or eight million dollars presented by his mother. It is not difficult to
see how he did this, for in the absence of anything like Pulitzer's inspiration, Hearst developed what might be called Saturation Journalism. Already the employer of enough high-salaried newspapermen to

staff a dozen newspapers, he proceeded to put them to work in a manner which utilized the full quantity of their talents, rather than the quality. A Journal-type story could be assured the most complete coverage in the history of journalism. Where Pulitzer directed his men, "Terseness, Accuracy, Terseness," Hearst made no secret of the fact that quantity and speed were all he desired. "We must beat every paper in town," he would mutter as he walked through the city room. To this end, when a good story broke, the entire Hearst staff ran to cover it. Park Row began calling the mass exodus from the Hearst office the departure of the Hearst Wrecking Crew, but it resembled more an officer leading a battalion into battle. Sam Chamberlain, after hurried consultation with Cosey Noble, would shout excited commands. Members of the staff would leap into coats and follow the running Noble out to the street. Then would come a frantic rush to capture hansom cabs and bicycles (Hearst rewarded his best men with bicycles as gifts).

At first the exodus of the Wrecking Crew was a helter-skelter operation, but in time the Hearst reporters expertly formed into a Wrecking Crew which, it was said, left the citizens gasping. Ahead sped outriders on bicycles, shouting to make way for the carriages whose plunging horses set up sparks from pounding hoofs. When the Hearst affluence became known, the city's wildest cabmen made Park Row their headquarters. To supplement their own talents, some bought fire and cavalry horses to pull carriages. After this wildly careening cavalcade always followed a tail of messenger boys, delivery-wagon drivers, and a legion of stray, yelping dogs. When the story was big enough, Hearst himself went along, leaping wild-eyed and long-legged into a carriage, "to be whisked like a field marshal to the scene of battle."

For a time, the World attempted a Wrecking Crew, but found it lacked the demoniacal drive and the numbers of the Hearst phalanx. For if Pulitzer sent five men out on a story, Hearst sent twenty. If Pulitzer sent twenty, Hearst sent forty. When the story involved crime, Hearst would add to his forces some publicized detective or a "reformed" murderer to write an expert's-eye account. Sometimes it happened that, while the entire Hearst Wrecking Crew was giving saturation coverage to one story, another story broke back on Park Row. Then the one man left to guard the dead city room had a heavy responsibility. He had to recruit a second Wrecking Crew from the free-lance reporters in the Park Row bars or on the City Hall Park benches. It was typical of Hearst, as well as of employment practices of the day, that if such free lances returned with front-page stories they were richly rewarded. If the story failed to turn out well, they were hardly recognized in the Journal office. Hearst men were also instructed by their relentless chief to pose whenever necessary as city detectives or Federal agents. Many a culprit, expecting to land in the back room of a police precinct station, found himself in the Journal office, comfortably drinking coffee while giving the rich details of his crime to a reporter. Many an unhappy girl, believing she was being led to her lover, found herself on Park Row where her story was raw material for Hearst's rolling presses and colored inks. The Hearst Yellow Journalism technique perhaps came to its fullest flowering in the Guldensuppe Murder, which has been called a Gay Nineties version of the Snyder-Gray case. In the summer of 1897, sections of a male torso were discovered floating in the East River, while other sections of the body were found in the Bronx. The discovery was first reported at length in the Telegram, with the World giving it a small paragraph headed GHASTLY FIND! The Journal missed the GHASTLY FIND! completely and as the story grew in prominence the Hearst paper flew into a tantrum over being scooped. It began a series of vitriolic articles accusing the police of suppressing news of this and other murders in an effort to make life easier for themselves. The Journal's implication was that most New York homicides had been shrugged off in this fashion and only the enterprise of newspaper reporters—the Journal's, of course—had forced the police to reveal most crimes.

But while editorially flaying the police, the Journal simultaneously demanded full assistance for the Wrecking Crew in its saturation coverage of the torso case. Both the World and Journal printed on their front pages "exact-size" chalk-plate reproductions of the dead man's hand, claiming each to be exclusive. The stubby thumb in the World's photograph was superimposed on a map showing "Route headless shoulders would take in floating from spot where other part of the body was found." In part because of the efforts of Ned Brown, a young medical student and part-time World reporter, the bits of body were shortly identified as Willie Guldensuppe, who had been employed as a rubber at a midtown Turkish bath.

As this book is written, Ned Brown remains alive and cheerfully reminiscent. He has often told the ingenious steps by which he discovered that the late Willie Guldensuppe had been living with a midwife named Mrs. Augusta Nack. After which, partly because of lack of city-room authority and also because of the Park Row network of newspaper spying, young Ned Brown lost control of the case to a Journal reporter named George Waugh Arnold. The Journal now moved in on Mrs. Nack with an eight-column streamer headline shouting:

MURDER MYSTERY SOLVED BY THE JOURNAL!

Under this, drop-away headlines told the rest of the story:

Mrs. Nack Identified;
Her Husband Held
by the Police

MRS. MAX RIGER RECOGNIZES THE
MIDWIFE AS THE WOMAN WHO
BOUGHT THE OILCLOTH IN ASTORIA

Storekeeper Found by Evening
Journal Reporters and
Taken to Police
Headquarters
Where She
Tells Her
Story

MRS. NACK IS AT ONCE ORDERED
UNDER ARREST BY THE AUTHOR-
ITIES WHEN MRS. RIGER'S
STATEMENT IS
COMPLETED

Herman Nack Is Run Down and
Handed Over to the Police
by Two Journal Report-
ers Who Find Him
on His Bakery
Wagon Near
His Wife's
Home

Behind this lay the fact that a leading clue in the Guldensuppe case was the type of oilcloth in which the various parts of the body were wrapped. Under the supervision of the clever George Arnold, the design of the cloth had been reproduced by Journal artists, while pieces were given to roving staff men assigned to discover its purchaser. Just as Ned Brown finished his deductions, one of these found a Queens dealer who recalled Mrs. Nack as the purchaser of identical cloth. On learning this, Hearst himself, followed by the entire Journal staff in hacks or on bicycles, raced to the building where Mrs. Nack lived. Hearst rented the entire premises and his men moved into all the vacant flats and took possession of the tenement hallways. Guards were posted at all doors to keep out rival newsmen, especially Ned Brown and others from the World. Scouting parties were sent through the neighborhood to locate the few public telephones. These were to be taken over or, if that proved impossible, the wires snipped.

With rival newspapers and police hopelessly out of the case, the Journal prodded Mrs. Nack toward police headquarters and supervised the apprehension of her husband. That night armed sluggers escorted Journal delivery wagons throughout the city to prevent opposition papers from stealing copies of its triumphant Extra. Fed by Yellow Journalism techniques, interest in the Guldensuppe case had risen to the point of mob hysteria and riots occurred at busy corners as people tore copies of the Journal out of the hands of drivers. The Hearst sluggers were in turn slugged by the police. People were knocked down and trodden.

Then it transpired that Herman Nack was innocent. After discarding Willie Guldensuppe as a lover, Mrs. Nack had taken up with one George Thorn, who now forcibly joined her in jail. As the two went on trial in Long Island City, newspapers girded for high-voltage treatment of the event. For a time Mrs. Nack and Thorn seemed headed for acquittal, under the astute guidance of the flamboyant William F. Howe, of the firm of Howe & Hummel. But suddenly Mrs. Nack confessed—exclusively to the Journal!

Other papers promptly charged that a Presbyterian clergyman named Miles, who had been visiting Mrs. Nack's cell daily, was in the pay of Hearst. This was never denied and the extreme rapidity with which the evangelical Miles contributed the personal account of his visits to the Journal lends weight to the claim. If Miles was in the Hearst employ, the psychologists in the Journal city room missed no bets. Accompanying him on his trips to Mrs. Nack had been his four-year-old son, a curly-headed child who climbed into Augusta's lap and asked her, in the name of both heavenly and earthly father, to confess the murder if she had really done it. Pleas from the mouth of a babe had done the trick. "When that adorable child begged me for the truth," confided Mrs. Nack to a Hearst reporter, "I could do no other than tell it to him."

And how did Joseph Pulitzer react to all this?

Since the days of Yellow Journalism, several generations of historians and newspaper analysts have been privileged to rise and, with the crystal clarity offered by hindsight, declare that Pulitzer failed to react correctly. This is perhaps true. With the perspective brought by time, it is possible to say that if the owner of the World had held to his normal course, he might have been better off—or at least spared his reputation considerable tarnishing.

But Pulitzer was ever Pulitzer. He had won eminence in newspaper publishing in New York and was understandably determined to keep it. Yet possibly there was more than a determination to retain eminence involved. In part of his being, Pulitzer may well have welcomed the Hearst challenge, not so much because he wanted a fight as because competition with a ruthless opponent would cause the World staff to make greater demands on him. As for over five years he had traveled from Cap Martin to Maine, to Jekyl Island, to the English countryside, his paper showed signs of being able to get along without him. His only weapon against this had been to keep the staff in a constant state of flux. "No Pulitzer official," recalls Terhune, "knew from day to day when to expect a shift from job to job on the paper, or out into the snow. As a child might shove chessmen from place to place on the board, idly seeking new combinations, so did the blind overlord change his department chiefs."

Yet even the capricious shifting of human beings can pall, and it is possible that Pulitzer subconsciously welcomed the Hearst threat, since it would cause problems to arise which only he could be expected to handle. Without admitting it, he may again have acted in a way to make the World's position worse. Hindsight may show that he would have been better off paying no attention to Hearst, letting the newcomer beat himself out against the impregnable World. But Pulitzer proceeded to do the opposite. He descended to the Hearst level and—in the vernacular of our day—joined in a slug fest with the young millionaire from the West.

He began this unlikely operation with what he later admitted was a serious mistake. For no sooner had Pulitzer returned to New York in January, 1896, than he was informed by a frightened business department that the circulation of the penny-priced Journal had risen to within thirty-five thousand of the World. It was immediately urged by Carvalho, John Norris and others of the business department that the World should meet this by cutting its two-cent price to a penny. This, it was argued, would drive the World circulation up, perhaps to the million mark, at the same time permitting an advertising-rate rise which would more than make up for the loss in circulation revenue.

Thirteen years before, in 1883, the Herald and other major papers had cut prices to meet the threat of the Pulitzer World. Pulitzer always looked back on this price-cut as the turning point in his New York fortunes. He had said at the time, "They have given me the town," and had never ceased to state that the price-cut by established papers brought the World enormous prestige.

In 1896, by reducing the price of the World to that of the Journal, Pulitzer would be doing the identical favor for Hearst. Yet apparently this did not occur to him—or he did not allow it to occur to him. For he began lending his supersensitive ear to the arguments of Carvalho and Norris. These arguments were purely commercial, making no mention of dignity or prestige. If the importance of the last two occurred to Pulitzer, he did not bring the matter up.

In late January, the ever-restless man departed for Jekyl Island. With him went Carvalho and Norris, a sign to Don Carlos Seitz and others who opposed the price-cut that they had lost their fight. The traveling party got no farther than Philadelphia. Returning to New York, they announced that on February 10, 1896, the price of the World would be cut to a penny.

It was the last time Pulitzer ever considered ten his lucky number. From this February tenth on he avoided it. For the slash in price did indeed lead to a circulation rise, but not to the million mark that had been promised. Over several days the World circulation jumped some eighty-eight thousand daily, until it reached the saturation point at six hundred thousand. But more important than any rise in circulation was that Pulitzer had been persuaded his cut in price would harm the Journal. It did not. Instead, the blow fell heavily on the small Park Row papers that were struggling for existence. The Advertiser, Mercury, and Recorder reeled and began moving toward oblivion. It made no perceptible difference to the Herald, the Tribune, the Sun and other well-established papers. But it lifted Hearst, as it had Pulitzer thirteen years before, prominently into the public eye.

In an editorial announcing the price-cut, Pulitzer declared that he preferred Power to Profits. He soon found his power doubtful and his profits reduced about two thirds. Contrary to the persuasive arguments of Carvalho and Norris, new advertisers did not flock to the World, for the merchandise marts did not consider penny-newspaper readers potential buyers. In alarm, the World made another misstep by raising advertising rates, thus actually losing advertisers. This loss in revenue caused features like book reviews and Wall Street closings to be reduced, and readers began falling away. Sitting in the darkened, soundproofed library in his New York mansion, Pulitzer listened to these doleful reports and was heard to mutter, "When I came to New York, Mr. Bennett reduced the price of his paper and raised his advertising rates—all to my advantage. When Mr. Hearst came to New York, I did the same. I wonder why, in view of my experience?"

Further mistakes in judgment showed Pulitzer not as sure-footed as in the past. In the Presidential election of 1896, the Democrats nominated William Jennings Bryan, a man for whom Pulitzer (like many Democrats) had little use. Still, the World was a Democratic paper, and his editors argued that he should support Bryan. He insisted on McKinley. Pulitzer, whose World had always been anathema to Republicans, gained no readers by his stunning move, but Hearst's Journal did. Largely because Pulitzer supported McKinley, Hearst placed the Journal firmly behind Bryan. It was possibly the smartest move he ever made, for the Great Commoner had almost no newspaper backing across the country. To the hinterlands now came word that a great New York newspaper was supporting Bryan and from rural districts Democrats sent in money for subscriptions. Nearly every Hearst biographer has speculated on the surprise these humble folk must have felt on receiving the Journal, since Hearst's support of Bryan, while vociferous, was strangely perfunctory. Daily the Journal seemed content to point out—truthfully—that McKinley was the candidate of monopoly, trust and big-money interests. Then it turned with obvious relief to such Yellow Journalism features as exposure of the fact that a pretty young burlesque queen of the day possessed a husband in the insanity ward of Bellevue Hospital. The Journal took the position that his wife's heartless conduct had driven the man there and with a great show of moral indignation printed a picture of the girl in what can only be called bloomers. Under this it ran a headline story demanding:

HAS PUBLIC TASTE SUNK TO THIS DEGRADING LEVEL?
IF THE NEW YORK THEATER-GOERS UNBLUSHINGLY FLOCK TO SEE A
VULGAR YOUNG WOMAN UNDRESS HERSELF ON THE STAGE, WHAT MAY
WE EXPECT NEXT?

SHOULD BE SUPPRESSED, SAYS DR. PARKHURST

LEWD AND INDECENT, SAYS CHARLOTTE SMITH

ALAN DALE SAYS, THEY ARE THE LIMIT

The Shocking Performance
of Miss Leona Barrison at
a New York Theater

It was to such depths of Yellow Journalism that Pulitzer now took an ignoble downward step. He did this without considering Hearst a journalist. He respected his Park Row rival, but merely as "a master of the great art of attracting attention." Himself he considered pure journalist. Yet despite this, he willingly entered into an attention-attracting war with Hearst. His staff, noting that Pulitzer thought it necessary to battle Hearst, lowered the paper's sights accordingly. Even so, there were moments when Pulitzer suffered qualms over his drop to Yellow Journalism. These usually came with arrival at one of his several estates, after a soothing train or boat ride. Once he telegraphed back to the World for the personal history of all his editors, hoping to find one of poor family background on whom he could place the blame for the editorial excesses he was now condoning. The case histories showed all important World men to be of good family. Most were college graduates and a surprising number the sons of ministers. Unable to find a whipping boy, Pulitzer sulked.

Next he belatedly became alarmed over the lurid sensationalism of the Sunday World, which since the departure of Morrill Goddard had been edited by the brilliant young Arthur Brisbane. Of all members of the World staff, Brisbane had the greatest feeling for Yellow Journalism and once a week exercised his genius to the utmost. But from the throes of a fit of respectability Pulitzer now wired him: "Please have on the front page of the magazine in next Sunday's World, the fine portrait of General O. O. Howard, head of the Army."

Such instructions did not please Brisbane, whose god was rapidly becoming that of yellow-type circulation. He disregarded Pulitzer's orders, then on Monday morning wired: "Sorry we did not have that O. O. Howard picture. Instead, on the front page, I had a wonderful picture of Kate Swan in the electric chair and circulation is up 15,000."

Pulitzer's inner conflicts are all too apparent in the reply he sent back: "You know perfectly well I am blind, and must rely on you. Congratulations."

It was with Brisbane and Carvalho that Pulitzer proved his errors in judgment were not limited to prices and politics. At a time when Hearst was industriously stealing his best men, Pulitzer chose to

antagonize these two important cogs. First came Carvalho, whom Pulitzer immediately blamed for the disastrous drop to one cent. By personal remarks and a gradual withdrawal of authority, Pulitzer let his
general manager know he had fallen in favor. It took a little more
than a month for Carvalho to become fed up. On March 31, 1896, he
wired Pulitzer that unless the majority of his powers were returned he
would resign. No answer came and Carvalho departed, to join Hearst
a few days later. As with many others, this process seemed to turn a
bearable man into an unbearable one. Old-timers recall Hearst's
Solomon Solis Carvalho as

> . . . the watch-dog of the Journal exchequer. While Hearst
> was out scattering money, Carvalho went about the office
> turning off lights and picking up stray bits of paper. Once
> he even invaded the ladies' lavatory to snap off the lights. A
> young lady screamed, and Carvalho darted out just in time
> to be observed.

The case of Brisbane was more complex, since this son of a
notable American social reformer and idealist had become a great favorite of Pulitzer. In New York, Brisbane often rode in Central Park
with Pulitzer, and frequently was called for lengthy stays in Bar Harbor and Jekyl Island.

Even as a young man, Brisbane was monumentally self-assured.
One day he rocked Park Row by stating that it was unfortunate that
American Presidents had to be middle-aged men. He would have to
wait about twenty years before the American public could have the
pleasure of sending him to the White House. "At that time I was full
of ambitions," he later recalled, "and deeply resented that the Constitution of the United States fixed the minimum age of the President
at thirty-five. I felt I had too long to wait." In 1890, when he joined
the World, Brisbane was still under thirty, with a brow already
marked by deep washboard furrows. Once he opined that, since the
ebullient Walt McDougall's brow was unlined, the cartoonist must
be a man who never thought. "I don't think with my skin," Mc-
Dougall snapped back.

But with all his conceits and posturings, Brisbane could be a highly competent writer. For the World, he described Theodore Roosevelt, who, as a member of New York City's three-man Police Commission, went about wearing a pink shirt and a cummerbund sash, the tassels of which hung to his knees:

> His teeth are big and white, his eyes are small and piercing, his voice is rasping. He makes our policemen feel as the little froggies did when the stork came to rule them. His heart is full of reform, and a policeman in full uniform, with helmet, revolver and night club, is no more to him than a plain, everyday human being. . . . The new Commissioner cannot be described as an intellectual type . . . but he does look like a determined man.

Despite this ability, however, Brisbane nursed curious ambitions as a writer. He wanted to write editorials so simple that they could appeal only to the masses. His plan was a style so elementary that the ideal sentence would consist of three words. Further, in order that his columns bear no stigma of the high-domed editorial page, he visualized them on page one, column one. Several times, in his closer moments with Pulitzer, he broached this idea, only to have the publisher irritably refuse. "Nobody expresses editorial opinions in my papers but me," he stated flatly.

With the constant reshufflings on the two Worlds, Brisbane, in late 1896, found himself editor of the Evening World. He was quite aware that, in the Tribune Building next door, Hearst was laying plans for an Evening Journal. Indeed, Brisbane had already received a Mr. Hearst-would-be-pleased-to-see-you message. He had done nothing about it, for Pulitzer was about to leave for Europe, and it was Brisbane's plan to start running his own editorials on the day Pulitzer left. Thus more than ten of them would be published before the publisher could do anything. Brisbane was convinced that, after reading these, Pulitzer would be splendidly won over. He wrote and published a dozen, without hearing a word, and became convinced that he got away with his bold stratagem. But he had not. Suddenly he received a cable: "Stop editorials at once. If you want good ones, rewrite those in Morning World."

Several hours later Brisbane engineered his famous meeting with

Hearst, at which he stunned the Croesus-like publisher by announcing: "I don't want Mr. Pulitzer to think I'm leaving him because of money. I want just what I'm making now, two hundred dollars a week, plus a dollar a week extra for each thousand in circulation I bring to the Evening Journal."

Hearst was quick to grant this innocent-seeming request, but in time Brisbane's paltry two hundred dollars a week became thirty thousand a year and eventually two hundred and fifty thousand. For, as editor of the new paper, Brisbane's will to succeed was such that he ordered the staff to report for work at four thirty A.M. Heretofore Park Row's afternoon newspapermen had come to work at eight A.M., with the first edition appearing at noon. Brisbane was determined to have his edition on the streets first, and added to such heroic industry was the indisputable pulling power of his editorials, which began appearing on page one, column one, of the Evening Journal. With complete freedom to perfect his stylistic eccentricities, Brisbane shortly became master of a style which read as simply as this editorial in favor of labor unions:

> You see a horse after a hard day's work grazing in a swampy meadow.
> He has done his duty and is getting what he can in return.
> On the Horse's flank you see a leech sucking blood.
> The leech is the trust. The horse is the labor union.

Next came such a fury of sensations that the words Yellow Journalism began to seem mild.

Among the active participants in the Battle of Park Row was the Socialist-to-be, Charles Edward Russell, who had been Pulitzer's morning city editor until, shortly before Brisbane, he deserted to Hearst. Thus he saw the fight from the inside and declares, "A better name would be the Bedlam Period of Journalism. Human ingenuity was all but exhausted as we now began devising typographical and other eccentricities with which to diversify pages and torment readers. We got out editions with exclamation-point heads. For a murder the heading would be BLOOD! For a fire FLAMES! For a collision

SMASH, CRASH! It was all a great hit, but it was bedlam too. How else can I better indicate the depths to which we had fallen?"

No idea seemed too mad. One day a Journal editor, passing a group of newsboys, heard one say to the other, "You bet your life, we're the stuff"—thus neatly combining two catch phrases of the era. Back in the office, he issued orders that the phrase *You bet your life, we're the stuff* be inserted between all Journal stories, in place of the usual black rule indicating the end of one story and the beginning of the next.

One of the managing editors of the World saw the Journal innovation and vastly admired it. It was the day of an Irish sports victory and the World editor decided to borrow the Journal idea and insert A *Great Day for the Irish!* at the end of each World story.

But aside from the sports victory, it was no great day for sons of Old Erin. It was one of those awful ones when every local news story seemed unhappily to involve an Irishman. In Brooklyn, one Patrick Hennessey, janitor, playing on the roof with children, fell off and was killed. Grim Recorder Smyth had before him a notorious burglar named Shaughnessy, whom he sentenced to sixty-five years in Sing Sing. The body of a floater in the East River was identified as Patrick Doolan. James Kelly and Michael O'Brien were arrested for fighting on a barge, with O'Brien so badly mauled he had to be taken to Bellevue. William Mulrooney, a well-known philanthropist, choked to death on a chicken bone. And at the end of each story ran the World's sprightly declaration—A *Great Day for the Irish!*

CHAPTER SIX

Park Row Makes History

With the lurid sensationalism of Yellow Journalism turning into the unbridled moon-madness of Bedlam Journalism, there seemed few other stages through which the two newspapers, locked in such a furious circulation struggle, could pass. A few of the saner heads around Park Row—still led by E. L. Godkin—must have sighed sorrowfully as they watched the colossal waste of editorial energy by the two fiercely battling titans. Thus it is altogether possible that someone involved with matters on Park Row may have ruefully thought, "There is nothing further for the World and Journal to do but start a war."

For this, in effect, is precisely what they now did. There were, of course, long-standing political factors concerned in the Spanish-American War. The American people, according to Walter Millis, were acquiring a taste for the grand manner. Less elegantly phrased, this means that ours had become an ambitious, robust country, enormously self-satisfied and quite eager to throw weight around, even if it meant a fight.

The idea of a European country like Spain controlling the Caribbean Islands a few miles off our southeastern coast rankled with most Americans, whose country was based firmly on the idea of independence. Further, Cuban patriots fleeing the Spanish rule had inevitably come here. Largely they had settled in New York, from whence spread a tireless propaganda campaign detailing atrocities by the cruel Spaniards on patriots, women and children. The Cuban patriots' flag, today the symbol of a free country, was first given to the breeze on the flagpole atop the Sun Building in 1850.

In politics, the Democratic platform had come to contain a plank favoring the annexation of Cuba, but Grover Cleveland, a Democratic President, had turned out to be the possessor of what has been called an obstinate conscience. Dispassionately examining the Cuban situation, he could see no real justification for annexation. It was true that some Cubans were fiery revolutionaries, but the majority seemed to be living in passive contentment under the ruling Spaniards. Also, the atrocity stories which sounded so bloodcurdling in the United States had a way of turning out to be minor infringements of liberty, or of disappearing completely, when studied closely. Cleveland's levelheadedness, however, was highly unpopular. Theodore Roosevelt, while still in the police period of pink shirts and tasseled scarf, declared that the President's foreign policy was "brutal stupidity and cowardice." A far more measured opinion came from the well-connected Chauncey M. Depew. "The United States is too conservative as far as the annexation of property is concerned," he pontificated.

With the election of the Republican McKinley in 1896, it was expected that the national policy toward Cuba and the smaller islands would change drastically. But though the possessor of no obstinate conscience, McKinley could not bring himself closer to involving the country in war than his predecessor. Among the men around him was Theodore Roosevelt, now elevated to the post of Assistant Secretary of the Navy. In case of actual conflict Roosevelt had made plans to resign so that he could take part in what he was convinced would be a "bully war." But though the war-group pressures were constant, McKinley would not budge. Ordinarily, in such a situation, the next step would be to inflame the public, but already the American people were inflamed. "The combustibles were all there," says one account. "All that was needed was a man who would set fire to the combustibles." And to the delight of those favoring war, such a man now appeared, as neatly as if summoned by the supernatural: "He was an enterprising newspaper publisher anxious to gain the widest possible circulation for his paper. A man who, at the same time, had a typical schoolboy conception of war as a romantic enterprise."

It was, of course, William Randolph Hearst, whose fling with

Yellow Journalism had by the end of 1896 brought Journal circulation
to four hundred and thirty thousand daily, where it now matched
the World. Hearst began, as soon as McKinley's passiveness toward
war became apparent, to play up Spanish atrocity stories, supplement-
ing them by gruesome drawings, usually faked. From the war-monger-
ing Journal, the public learned that it was the daily practice of Spanish guards to take Cuban prisoners from jail and cold-bloodedly shoot
them; that Spanish troops had a habit of beating to death anyone
who stood in their way; and that unarmed peasants, women and children were ruthlessly attacked. "The columns of the Journal," says
Millis, "built an increasing resentment against Spain on the part of
hundreds of thousands of Americans."

The exact moment at which Hearst decided that a war with
Spain would benefit this country, no less than the circulation of the
Journal, has never been determined. But surprisingly, it was a decision in which he was joined by Pulitzer. For seemingly the publisher
of the World had sunk so far into the mire of Yellow Journalism that,
like Hearst, he could think only in terms of wildly extravagant sensations. But where no Hearst aide apparently ever faced his chief with
a warning of the tragedy he might be fomenting, one Pulitzer associate did. On the record is Pulitzer's frank admission that war might result from excesses of Yellow Journalism. Having admitted this much,
he paused slightly before uttering one of the most extraordinary sentences of all time: "I rather like the idea of war—not a big one—but
one that will arouse interest and give me a chance to gauge the reflex
in circulation figures."

Others besides Pulitzer thought a small, neat, beneficial war
could be arranged. Naturally one was the effervescent Roosevelt, now
writing his family that he had plans for a "jim-dandy regiment" in
case of war and "it would be awful to miss the fun." To an associate
in Government, he wrote in more reasoned words: "I do not think war
with Spain would be serious enough to cause much strain on the
country or much interruption to the revival of prosperity. I certainly
wish the matter could be settled this winter." In such an atmosphere,
it was not hard for the New York World and the New York Journal
to begin a newspaper propaganda campaign of unparalleled distor-
tion. The commander of the Spanish forces in the Caribbean Islands

was General Valeriano Weyler, yet no Yellow paper honored the general by calling him that. He was "Butcher" Weyler and the bloodiest of crimes against humanity were placed on his conscience. By magnifying the cruelties of General Weyler and his men, Cuba was made to seem a country united in bitter hatred of the Spaniards. Subtly assisting all this was a fatal Spanish instinct for doing the wrong thing at the wrong time. Rendered panicky by the American newspaper attacks forwarded from Washington by the Spanish Ambassador, Weyler created off-limits areas in towns and branded an outlaw anyone traveling without a Spanish passport. Roused slightly from a customary inertia by these measures, the Cubans retaliated by burning and pillaging. Hearst reporters, sent on forays into the Cuban countryside, returned to write stories declaring that this pillaging was done by Butcher Weyler's Spanish troops.

So, long before diplomatic relations between the United States and Spain became acutely strained, the two great Park Row papers, engaged in a circulation war of enormous proportions, began using the sufferings of Cuba and its unhappy people as a convenient kind of private ammunition. When one side sprang a war-scare surprise the reflex action of the other was to spring a better one.

Usually Hearst led the way. A full year before war was declared, the Journal ran a headline quoting John Sherman, Secretary of State:

SHERMAN FOR WAR WITH SPAIN
FOR MURDERING AMERICANS

Behind this jingoistic headline—which, incidentally, was totally untrue—lay the exploit of a Hearst writer named Francis Lawrence, who, having touched foot on Cuban soil, sent back a dispatch describing the death of a group of American freebooters in a fight with the beastly Spaniards. Lawrence was soon forced to admit his story was a fake. Only then did Secretary of State Sherman dare state that he had never come out in favor of war with Spain. Already, it was noted, both President McKinley and Sherman abjectly feared the Journal.

Delighted by the sensation caused by the Lawrence dispatch, Hearst sent the artist, Frederic Remington, to Cuba. Remington was

a notable delineator of cowboys and Indians. He had orders to sketch
the atrocities which Hearst apparently believed took place daily on
every street corner. But in Remington, the Journal had a man of integrity, who not only landed on Cuban soil but traveled extensively
inland. He found no atrocities, merely a people too sunk in lassitude
to care whether they lived under Spanish rule or not. A few firebrands
worked hard to stir them up, with small visible success. Arriving in
Havana with pencil and sketch pad unsullied, Remington cabled
home:

W. R. Hearst
Journal, New York.

Everything quiet. No trouble here. There will be no war. I
wish to return.

Remington

To which Hearst sent his memorable reply:

Remington
Havana

Please remain. You furnish the pictures and I will furnish
the war.

Hearst

In efforts to fulfill this modest promise, the Journal publisher
was greatly assisted by two factors. One was the talents of Arthur
Brisbane, whose inspiring effect on the Evening Journal quickly became such that Hearst made him editor-in-chief of both Journals,
thus placing him over the elegant, hard-drinking Sam Chamberlain.
Almost from their first working moment together, Hearst and Brisbane functioned like journalistic twins. Hearst instantly admired
Brisbane's simple, declarative-sentence editorials, and from that point
on it became impossible to figure where Hearst ended editorially and
Brisbane began. Future Hearst writing would be of the simple style
pioneered by Brisbane—or was it Hearst who somehow crystallized
Brisbane? No one will ever know.

Like Hearst, Brisbane seemed able to make himself believe in the total rightness of any crusade he undertook, at least during the time the crusade was in progress. If any vestiges remained of his reformer father's idealistic influence, these evaporated rapidly under Hearst. So did his dreams of the White House. Brisbane now began to see the Presidency as suitable only for Hearst. In addition—to make himself more than ever the perfect assistant—he turned an early love of athletics into driving office energy. His biographer, Oliver Carlson, has pictured him in early days as a Journal editor-in-chief, dashing madly from desk to desk issuing orders, inventing startling new methods of treating news and writing his flamboyant editorials. "It was a happy time in Brisbane's life," Carlson concludes.

The second factor aiding Hearst in his warlike dreams was destined to become an even more durable feature of American journalism than Arthur Brisbane. This was the use of pretty girls. In performing his prodigies of jingoistic politics, Hearst was in fact assisted not only by one pretty girl, but by two. Likewise involved was Richard Harding Davis, who, despite his acid feelings over the expense account in Czarist Russia, had allowed himself to be sent to Cuba by Hearst for an awe-inspiring three thousand dollars a month and expenses. There Davis satisfied his war-hungry employer a bit more than Remington, who by now had returned to Park Row. Davis filed some mildly bellicose dispatches, in the course of one reporting that the American steamship *Olivette* had been held in Havana harbor while three young Cuban girls were searched for papers of a traitorous nature.

When dispatches concerning the Cuban situation arrived in the Journal office, they were rushed directly to Hearst, who read them with every instinct alert for potential scoops. Reading the long Davis dispatch, he stopped short at the *Olivette* incident. Summoning Remington, he informed him (the artist always insisted) that a Cuban girl had been stripped naked on the deck of the *Olivette* and roughly searched by bearded Spaniards. "Draw a picture of it," Hearst ordered. Remington did, creating a girl standing slim, proud and startlingly nude, while being searched in the dark of night by three sinister-looking men. It was a picture to stir anger in the hardest breast, and to arouse reader-emotions further Hearst placed above it this howling query—

DOES OUR FLAG PROTECT WOMEN?—INDIGNITIES PRACTICED
BY SPANISH OFFICIALS ON BOARD AMERICAN VESSELS—
RICHARD HARDING DAVIS DESCRIBES SOME STARTLING PHASES
OF CUBAN SITUATION—REFINED YOUNG WOMEN STRIPPED AND
SEARCHED BY BRUTAL SPANIARDS UNDER FLAG OF THE OLIVETTE

In the gold-domed building next door, the World was caught completely off balance by the shocking account of the nude girl on the *Olivette,* which now became the first story in any American newspaper to approach a sale of one million copies. But the wary World, which had two star correspondents, Sylvester Scovel and William Shaw Bowen, in Cuba, smelled a fake. Surely one of its men would have learned of such an insult to young womanhood. Reaching back for the epithet the Sun had applied to the Journal under his brother Albert, Pulitzer dictated an editorial saying that the Journal was still "edited by fools for fools." Coldly, he branded the *Olivette* story a fake and announced that the World had chartered a tug to meet the boat at sea where it would interview the young lady herself. This was accordingly done and the girl admitted that she had indeed been searched but—fortunately for the World—by a police matron. At no time had she been stripped nude, much less been forced to stand naked, surrounded by men.

Pulitzer made much of this, declaring it proof-positive that the Journal was indeed edited by fools. Then he received support from a most surprising source. In Havana, the great Richard Harding Davis had learned the fate of his story and reacted with fine fury. Well aware of the conflict between the World and the Journal, he performed an act unprecedented in journalism. To the World he sent a long cable disowning the Journal's story. Any suggestion of girls standing disrobed before male examiners was wholly a product of the Journal's imagination, he stated, and the World splashed the Davis denial luridly over its front page:

MR. DAVIS EXPLAINS—THE OLIVETTE OUTRAGE IS NOW MADE CLEAR—
A LETTER FROM THE WRITER—THE PAPERS HE REPRESENTED, NOT
RICHARD HARDING DAVIS, GUILTY OF DELIBERATE FALSEHOOD

No denial, even a headline, ever quite catches up with a story. The Journal had enjoyed its scoop, one of the mightiest of all time.

With no visible regret, it now scratched Richard Harding Davis and his three thousand dollars a month off the books. But Hearst, his appetite whetted by the circulation jump produced by the *Olivette* story, increased the intensity with which he perused the Cuban cables. For a time they reported only routine atrocities. Then on a torpid afternoon in August, 1897, he was—according to James Creelman, who should know—lolling in his office chair, mentally bewailing the fact that in such heat even tremendous headlines failed to stir the crowd.

As he sat, continues Creelman, a copy boy entered bearing a cable from Cuba:

EVANGELINA CISNEROS, PRETTY GIRL OF 17, RELATED TO PRESIDENT OF CUBA, TO BE IMPRISONED TWENTY YEARS ON AFRICAN COAST FOR TAKING PART UPRISING CUBAN PRISONERS ON ISLE OF PINES.

Hearst stared long at the little slip, continues Creelman, then slapped his knee and laughed his high laugh. Walking to the door, he called Brisbane and Chamberlain. "We've got Spain now," he told them. "Wake up our correspondents all over to start getting names of prominent women on a petition for this girl to be sent to the Queen of Spain. Enlist the women of America. Notify our Minister in Madrid. . . ."

Once again the entire Hearst organization roared into action over the plight of a young girl—this time on a scale that made the *Olivette* story seem like a minor incident. Shouting headlines and stories on *Journal* front pages told the world that Evangelina was sitting wretchedly in a cell in Havana Prison, awaiting sentence to an even worse jail. No member of the Hearst press had ever seen her, but she was pictured as "ignorant of the world, cloistered as a nun—delicate, refined, sensitive and unused to hardship."

In vain did the *World*—whose function at extreme moments of Yellow Journalism seemed to be pointing out facts closer to the truth —report that Evangelina had been on the Isle of Pines because the Spaniards had gallantly permitted her to accompany her radical father into exile. On the island, she had engaged in partisan activity. This was never mentioned by Hearst, who maintained from the start that the fiery young female had got in trouble for defending her charms from the overtures of a bestial Spanish jailor. Still, no matter how Evangelina had got herself put into the Havana jail, she was definitely there. She was also pretty, and in real danger of being sent to an African penal colony. Soon Hearst was cabling the names of two hundred thousand protesting American women, in gross lots of fifteen thousand, to the palace of the Spanish Queen Regent in San Sebastian. Julia Ward Howe saved him one cable toll by sending her cable to Pope Leo XIII. Mrs. Jefferson Davis, Frances Hodgson Burnett and the mother of President McKinley willingly put their names to Hearst's petitions, urging, in a phrase baldly borrowed from melodrama, that Evangelina be saved "from a fate worse than death."

The possibilities in the Evangelina Cisneros story seemed limitless, and now Hearst dispatched Karl Decker, one of his more adventurous reporters, to Havana, with orders to rescue the girl. After reconnoitering, Decker—according to stories in the Journal—found that, far from being chained to a dark wall, Evangelina had the freedom of the prison and prison yard. The prison itself was rotting away, bars in cell windows being so rusted as to be little more than powder. On the night of October 10, 1897, Decker climbed to the roof of the house adjoining the prison and Evangelina's cell. He attracted her attention, then leaned down and with his bare hands wrenched out the rotting window bars. Then he took Evangelina by the arms and pulled her through the window to the roof. Together the two dashed to a hideaway in Havana, where Evangelina remained for two days. Then she was smuggled aboard ship for New York.

This clean-cut version of the rescue, however, is the Journal account of Decker's exploit. Some researchers—notable among them John Tebbel, in his biography of Hearst—picture the adventure in comic-opera terms. According to Tebbel, the dashing Decker used co-conspirators and the rescue of Evangelina was far from clean-cut:

> . . . Decker and his little helpers demonstrated that they were really only amateurs at international jailbreaking. They bungled the whole business. They got their ladder across the space between the roof of the house and the prison roof; one man climbed across to hold it, and in the process knocked off a chunk of cornice which resounded

cheerfully below in the still Cuban night. Decker pulled
back the ladder, leaving his man stranded, while the warden
stepped outside, made a sleepy, perfunctory examination,
and went back in. Decker threw out his ladder again and
made the passage himself this time, armed with a saw. . . .
He found the prisoner waiting at the bars, where she had
been for the last two and a half hours while her rescuers
fumbled about in the darkness.

Decker began hacking away at the bars with his saw,
but they rattled enough to wake the dead. . . . Evangelina
must have uttered a few pungent observations in Spanish,
but the semi-official biographer swears that all she said in
English was a frightened "Go! Come back tomorrow night!"

Nothing if not resourceful, Decker was on hand the following midnight, equipped this time with a couple of Still-
son wrenches and a handy carriage poised in the side streets.
As an added precaution, he sent an aide with a bottle to get
the warden drunk, a mission easily accomplished. Again the
ladder, again the agile Decker, and this time, taking advantage of the dent he had made in the main bar the night
before, he wrenched it apart with his wrenches. Evangelina slipped out . . . and tripped across the ladder to safety.

However it was done, the rescue actually was accomplished, and
Hearst in New York rose to signalize the event by indulging in a
paroxysm of typographical pride. Huge type was hauled forth to make
a gloating headline over Decker's cabled account of the rescue:

AN AMERICAN NEWSPAPER ACCOMPLISHES AT A
SINGLE STROKE WHAT THE BEST EFFORTS OF
DIPLOMACY FAILED UTTERLY TO BRING ABOUT

Beneath this were two large drawings of Evangelina—Before and
After Fifteen Months of Incarceration. One showed a beautiful
young girl, the other a broken old crone.

Even as this triumphant Journal was being hawked through the
streets, Hearst applied what Walter Millis calls his extraordinary and
fertile mind to the problem of exploiting Evangelina when she arrived in New York. The results were apparent when the Journal an-

nounced a huge rally at Madison Square, where New York multitudes could welcome the heroic girl. Following this public event, Mr. Hearst would give a private reception at Delmonico's. To this he invited, a later account states, "all the political hacks, retired military leaders, and dusty wives of dead and forgotten heroes." On the day of her arrival Evangelina was rushed post-haste to the Madison Square rally, where observers noted that despite fifteen months of brutal imprisonment she looked the picture of radiant health. At the Delmonico reception, others observed that Hearst, having conceived this splendid demonstration, played a curious part in it. He hastily shook Evangelina's hand, then retired behind a row of potted palms, from which vantage point he watched proceedings in a manner which, James Creelman states, clearly indicated he now thought them sordid and distasteful.

Such ambivalence in the Hearst nature was often noted by his men, and in a sense took the spirit out of many of them. While in the throes of conceiving one of his sensations, Hearst seemed to believe in it with every fibre of his being. Once the story was successfully ended, he just as plainly believed in it no more, and made little effort to hide his cynicism from the reporters around him. This was, in part, what Ambrose Bierce meant when he compared working for Hearst to masturbation. The result was a growing bitterness in many of the excellent talents on the Journal.

Evangelina provided a month of hysterical, chauvinistic excitement. But still the country refused to go to war, even though in Cuba the Spanish instinct for doing the wrong thing continued to give Hearst and Pulitzer new atrocities to keep the public aroused. The Journal began to agitate for American warships to be sent to Cuba to defend American interests. Both papers accused the unhappy McKinley of betraying Cuba, and relentlessly the circulation of the two sensation-laden Yellows approached the million mark, with only Editor Godkin raising his voice to state:

> Nothing so disgraceful as the behaviour of these two newspapers has ever been known in the history of journalism. Gross misrepresentation of facts, deliberate invention of tales calculated to excite the public, and wanton recklessness in the construction of headlines which outdid even

these inventions have combined to make the issues of the most widely circulated newspapers firebrands scattered broadcast throughout the community.

But though the methods of the Park Row rivals appeared identical, there had in fact been one slight change. With the arrival of the ever-shrewd Brisbane in the Hearst camp, a noticeable tightening in the Journal followed. Where the World had been the paper to pull tricks showing up Hearst exceeses, the Journal began displaying a sharpness of its own. Each paper tried daily to outdo the other in printing Extras, and it was not unusual for Eighth or Ninth Editions to appear on the sidewalks of New York before bedtime. One day the World came out with a screaming Tenth Edition. Brisbane, smiling a cold smile, printed an offer of fifty dollars to any citizen who would bring to his office a copy of the Eighth or Ninth Edition of that day's World. His money was safe: there had been none. Where formerly the Journal borrowed news shamelessly from the World, the World now began plucking juicy items turned up by Hearst's Wrecking Crew coverage of the Spanish situation. Brisbane immediately noted this. Soon the Journal ran a story saying that Colonel Replive W. Thenuz, an Austrian observer sent to Cuba to report the true state of affairs to his government, had been killed by a sniper's bullet. The World solemnly reprinted this, causing Brisbane to erupt into howls of mixed jubilation and rage. Replive W. Thenuz, he explained in large type on the first page of the Journal, was a phonetic anagram for We Pilfer the News. Faces at the World attained a remarkable shade of red.

Then came the event which propelled America into war. On the night of February 15, 1898, the battleship *Maine*, ordered to Cuba in answer to the Journal's demands for protection to American citizens, was blown up in Havana harbor. Of its crew, 259 officers and men were killed, to give this country one of the most terrible jolts in its history. "With the destruction of the *Maine*," says Walter Millis, "the match had at last been applied." On Park Row, the two mighty papers took steps to see that prompt declaration of a shooting war did not evade them this time. The World immediately sent a tugboat to Havana, complete with divers, to discover the truth about the *Maine*.

Next door, at the Journal, a strange atmosphere seemed to pervade the office. Around Hearst there was

> . . . pandemonium. Artists were illustrating just how a torpedo was placed under the vessel and detonated by means of an electric wire from the shore. Hearst and Chamberlain were like madmen. The morning headlines were black and red, ominously demanding "Who Destroyed the Maine?" and offering $50,000 reward for "information" revealing the culprit.
>
> An extra edition of the Journal on the morning of February 17th flatly declared: "The War Ship Maine Was Split in Two by An Enemy's Secret Infernal Machine!" The first eight pages were devoted to imaginary portrayals of how it had been done. . . .

The sinking of the *Maine* has remained one of the great mysteries in our nation's history. No one, despite the Journal's fifty-thousand-dollar reward, has ever stepped forward to provide even the slightest clue to the explosion. Yet in the minds of some, a shadowy possibility has always persisted. Captain Sigsbee of the *Maine* was himself the first to voice it when he stated that he considered the detailed Hearst drawings and diagrams to be proof that there had been a plot to blow up the *Maine* and that *the Journal knew of it!* Yet Sigsbee never went so far as to put in words what others have thought: that Hearst may actually have co-operated in the plot, or even conceived it. No one can imagine that he intended an explosion that would kill 259 men, but Hearst may have thought a harmless explosion—similar to Pulitzer's "small war"—would be justified as a move to involve the country in a war which to Hearst had by now become both a matter of personal pride and a burning obsession. After which, the Cuban patriots detailed to execute the plot may have panicked, got out of hand, or made a terrible mistake. Among those who support this theory is Ferdinand Lundberg, who writes:

> The man in the United States most interested in plunging the country into war was William Randolph Hearst. The Journal had led the campaign to have a warship sent to

Havana, although none was needed. An "incident" was, there is no doubt, hoped for by Hearst. The Journal made the first accusation against Spain, whom history has since exculpated, shielding the Cuban Junta with which the Journal had very close connections. All the Hearst men in Cuba carried letters from Cuban conspirators in New York. Richard Harding Davis, in one of his published letters, states: "We have the strongest possible letters from the Junta...." This point is at least certain: If the Junta directed the explosion, then it was caused by a group with which the Journal had intimate connections.

In this connection Hearst's slogan flashes upon the mind: "While others talk the Journal acts."

Yet in the spring of 1898, no sane man would accuse Hearst of abetting the blowing up of the *Maine*. His Journal was the super-jingo paper, the most violently patriotic in the entire country. As the excitement following the *Maine* began to subside, Hearst clamored louder than ever for war, and on Park Row the strain of almost-wartime Yellow Journalism was taking a toll of newspapermen.

One was Ernest O. Chamberlain, who had been made city editor of the Evening World when Brisbane deserted to Hearst. Chamberlain was a thin little man with a big head, waxlike complexion and huge black mustache. In speech and manner, he appeared to be nervelessly quiet. He was also a glutton for work, in the best tradition of city editors of the time. Usually he worked twenty hours a day, seven days a week, and the only meal his staff ever saw him consume was a bowl of crackers and milk. Yet now this man was pitted against the brilliant Brisbane, who knew that every thousand he added to the Evening Journal in circulation brought a dollar more in his pay check that week. Chamberlain, though a fine newspaperman, was hopelessly outclassed. As his desperation mounted, it seemed to him that the only method of saving himself was to scoop Brisbane on the declaration of war. Abandoning his four hours of daily rest, he began spending entire days and nights at his desk, so that when the war declaration came in, he would be there to handle it personally.

Suddenly, the flash he dreamed of came—but to him alone. In the middle of the night of April tenth, Chamberlain's reporters (among them Terhune) were roused from sleep by frantic wires ordering them to report to the city room at once. There they found a triumphant Chamberlain waving an edition headed WAR! Then, as his astonished staff watched, Chamberlain sank to his desk and began to weep.

Simultaneously, the foreman of the composing room appeared with a World executive. Park Row was, after all, a small locality and news of tremendous stories ran rapidly from one composing room to the other. While setting up the War Extra, the World composing room had listened for sounds of activity in other shops. None was heard. Nor was there the exciting sound of horses' hoofs striking sparks from cobblestones, as the wagons waited restlessly for papers to deliver. It all made the foreman suspicious and he made a visit to the city room where, from Chamberlain's glittering eyes and feverish enthusiasm, he rightly deduced that the editor had gone mad.

He did not remain to investigate further. By now some copies of the War Extra would be shooting off the presses, to be stacked and lifted into delivery wagons, then, behind whipped-up horses, rushed into the night. Inevitably, a few wagonloads would already have departed, and the important thing was to get those papers back. Typesetters of the World, plus a few hastily requisitioned reporters, fanned out over the City Hall area, pulling back all copies of the War Edition. By morning all had been found. This was Chamberlain's swan song as a newspaperman. Four days later he was dead, the first Park Row casualty of the Spanish-American War.

On April 25, 1898, no one rushed to haul back the Extras howling WAR! which flooded from the presses of Park Row. This was the real thing—the war of which Walter Millis says: "Seldom can history have recorded a plainer case of military aggression; yet seldom has a war been started in so profound a conviction of righteousness." At the Journal, Hearst took considerable personal credit for the war against Spain, belated though it might be, and was noted to be in a state of proud ecstasy. His paper broke into a new madness of big-type-and-red-ink appeals to public passion, and circulation of both World and Journal shot upward to record-breaking heights, with the World boasting a sale of five million copies in a single week. Even this mark would soon topple, however. Before the unhappy conflict ended, the two Park Row titans would be selling one million three hundred thousand papers a day!

Having blanketed the town with his own War Extra, Hearst consulted the Journal exchequer and decided that he could afford to spend five hundred thousand dollars on Wrecking Crew coverage of the war. He also telegraphed Washington offering his yacht *Bucentaur* to the Navy, with himself as captain. His services were politely refused, though the yacht was accepted. Later, Hearst was given the simulated rank of ensign, but for the moment, having presented his own yacht to the Navy, he bought another, named *Sylvia*, and led a fleet of twenty cutters to Cuba. In this fleet reposed an entire Wrecking Crew of "writers, artists, war authorities, biographers, medical men, and astrologers." With Hearst himself leading, the brave flotilla proceeded at full steam to Tampa, where the United States Army, the Militia and thousands of enthusiastic Volunteers were scheduled to be molded into a fighting force by Regular Army officers. Behind him in New York, where crowds packed Park Row to read the bulletins pasted on ground-floor windows by the newspapers upstairs, Hearst left Arthur Brisbane. The new editor-in-chief immediately proceeded to develop a new type of come-on headline, which all but contradicted itself once the purchaser had bought his paper. Often, through the Spanish-American War, the Journal trapped readers by headlining:

BIG BATTLE
Is Expected

CHAPTER SEVEN

The Correspondents' War

O N Park Row special copy desks were installed to cover the influx of news. Feature stories were run about the Knickerbocker Theatre, where audiences went patriotically mad as the song *Unchain the Dogs of War* was introduced into the musical comedy *The Bride Elect*. One Extra after another spilled from the presses, making newsboys hoarse as well as weary from the weight of the coins jangling in their pockets.

But with all this the real story of the war was far to the south. In fact, the Spanish-American War has often been called the Correspondents' War. "Never was nor will be again," writes Fairfax Downey in his biography of Richard Harding Davis, "such a field day and mob scene of war correspondents as the Spanish War inaugurated in Tampa." Hearst was one of the first to arrive and soon his forces were augmented by the arrival of the peripatetic James Creelman. The World dispatched its own Wrecking Crew, featuring Sylvester Scovel, who would distinguish himself strangely in the course of conflict. Outstanding, of course, was Richard Harding Davis, fully prepared to cover the war for the New York Herald, the London Times, and *Scribner's* magazine. Abroad, the frail Stephen Crane, who had settled in England after ceasing to be a roaming correspondent for Hearst, was agreeing by cable to join the World as special correspondent in Cuba. Stephen Bonsal, Ralph Paine, Caspar Whitney and other topflight newspaper correspondents of the day quickly arrived on the scene, and for every newspaperman there seemed to be an artist. Already among them were Frederic Remington, Howard Chandler Christy and Rufus Zogbaum. The young art of news photography was less well represented, but a bright part of the Tampa scene was that irrepressible pioneer, Jimmy Hare.

Still, these were the stars of the American newspaper firmament. For each star reporter arriving in Tampa, there appeared to be fifty average city-room types. Continues Fairfax Downey:

> Scores flocked in every day until hundreds were present. Almost every newspaper in the land had seethed with intrigue for the prized post of "Our special at the front. . . ." Rank amateurs and outsiders offered their services, and sob sisters sobbed to go. . . . The very copy boys mentioned that they were especially qualified for carrying messages. An agricultural paper dispatched a representative toward the field of combat, and not a few religious weeklies sent observers.

All in all, it made a colorful, carefree sight, if not a particularly warlike one. Among those present was Acton Davies, a pudgy dramatic critic whose appearance in military garb would be compared by Stephen Crane to that of a crushed peony. Davies was accustomed to detecting sham in the theatre and noted that the hundreds of correspondents in shiny new campaign outfits looked a trifle ridiculous. "You never saw such a collection of shiny boots and pith helmets and field glasses in your life," he wrote home. "It looks like a rehearsal for a military melodrama."

To the surprise of none, Richard Harding Davis was the first to score with his dispatches. Assistant Navy Secretary Roosevelt, as hungry now for Navy publicity as he would shortly be for his jim-dandy Rough Riders, permitted Davis to board Admiral Sampson's flagship, the *New York*, as it blockaded Havana. The noble Davis was chewing fire like everyone else, and his dispatches stated the belief that Sampson bombarded Cuba's shore batteries with a distressing lack of frequency. When he did bombard, however, it made a stirring sight: "like watching the burning of the Waldorf-Astoria from Brooklyn Bridge." Davis's meticulous dispatches included one especially strange note. During the heavy cannonadings, he reported, the ship's band on the *New York* provided loud accompaniment by booming out themes from Richard Wagner.

In letters home Davis opined that this would be a merry war. At the same time he demonstrated why he was the top correspondent of his time. Like other successful newsmen of the period, he was in many ways an uncritical enthusiast. Yet with this went great powers of description and an absolute lack of fear in writing what he observed and thought. "However confused his appreciation of other values, he was never at a loss to recognize news value," a later critic has written of Davis. This was equally true of other correspondents in the Correspondents' War. Charles Rosebault, who as a cub reporter scored the scoop on General Grant's illness, put it this way, "That rare bird, the real reporter, has sources of penetration which seem like magic to the average newspaperman." Correspondents like Davis preferred covering wars, since battle brought the greatest tests of their talent. "The good reporter, like the good soldier, must look upon war as the supreme adventure in the short drama called Life," wrote the humorist, Finley Peter Dunne, in a moment of dead seriousness.

So between rapturous dispatches evoking the Waldorf-Astoria, Richard Harding Davis did not hesitate to mention his uneasiness over fire discipline in the Navy. In a dispatch which caused outrage in New York, and made the firebrand *Journal* accuse him of treason, Davis described the informal manner in which the *New York* fired its guns:

> . . . The ship seemed to work and to fight by herself; you heard no human voice of command, only the grieved tones of Lieutenant Mulligan, rising from his smoke-choked deck below, where he could not see to aim his six-inch gun, and from where he begged Lieutenant Marble again and again to "Take your damned smoke out of my way." Lieutenant Marble was vaulting in and out of his forward turret like a squirrel in a cage. One instant you would see him far out on the deck . . . and the next pushing the turret with his shoulder as though he meant to shove it overboard; and then he would wave his hand to his crew inside and there would be a racking roar.

In time, Navy ineptitude and cannonading to the strains of Wagner palled on Davis. He disembarked to return to Tampa. There he confounded the hundreds of correspondents who were attempting to ape his smart field attire by appearing in white ducks, double-breasted blue coat and natty straw boater. On a tour of Army camps, Davis concluded that if the press corps stood ready for war, the Army did not. Far more time would be needed before the scattered representatives of the Regular Army could beat fighting discipline into the ranks of the vociferous Volunteers, among whom were two gangling Midwestern youths named Sherwood Anderson and Carl Sandburg. Davis announced that this was the Rocking-Chair period of the war and sat down with the others to rock. While he did, Theodore Roosevelt resigned from the Navy and, wearing a Brooks Brothers uniform and carrying a dozen extra pairs of what he called specs, rushed to join the First Volunteer Cavalry as it trained in the dry heat of San Antonio, Texas.

The First Volunteers—soon to be famous as the Rough Riders or Teddy's Terrors—were an undisciplined, colorful mixture of clubmen and cowboys, most of them close friends of Roosevelt's. "It was the society page, financial column, and Wild West Show all rolled up in one," a correspondent wrote. Almost all the New York clubmen had insisted on joining up as rough-and-ready sergeants, and soon Lieutenant Colonel Roosevelt was in trouble for drinking beer with his enlisted men. "Sir, I consider myself the damndest ass within ten miles of this camp," he told General Leonard Wood, who was forced to reprimand him. Nevertheless, Teddy continued to mingle. When the Rough Riders moved on to Tampa, Davis observed Roosevelt dining in the company of enlisted men. This violated the strict Davis code and he wrote: "Last night Roosevelt dined with two sergeants as his guests. That stopped me from giving him a clean bill of health. He gave the regiment a bad name."

These two strong-willed, self-righteous men had clashed before, when Roosevelt was a tassel-wearing member of the New York City Police Board. In a glaring, finger-shaking exchange, the harsh word *Liar* had passed between them. However, old antipathy did not prevent the ambitious Roosevelt from feeding Davis exclusive stories which glorified the Rough Riders, thus allowing them to attain a strategic position on the front page from which they were never dislodged. Nor did Davis, on his part, hesitate for an instant in making his decision that the Rough Riders were the news feature of the war. His presence in their midst at all important moments has been cited as an example of the famous Davis luck, but it was more like a gift for swift evaluation of any given situation. Once he had discovered the Rough Riders, Davis also became impatient for the war to begin. He informed General Miles it was high time Cuba was invaded and, perhaps because of this impatience from such a celebrated person, steps toward an actual invasion were at last begun.

Before Cuba was attacked, however, Park Row passed through an episode which has come down in the annals of newspaper reminiscence as the Sad Scoop. In the Far East, Admiral Dewey—unhampered by the splendid confusions of Tampa, though possessing a few of his own—demolished what has since been called a feeble collection of Spanish gunboats in Manila Bay. Still, the gunboats did not seem feeble then, for Yellow Journalism had built up the wooden-decked, fire-prone Spanish fleet as a marvel of modern power. As Dewey performed his epochal feat, three correspondents were aboard his flagship: Edwin Harden of the World, J. L. Stickney of the Herald, and John T. McCutcheon of the Chicago Tribune. This was before the days of wireless and all three, of necessity, had to wait until they reached the cable office in Hong Kong before filing dispatches. Finally, at one A.M. on a Monday morning, they arrived. Stickney and McCutcheon immediately cabled stories at press rates. The astute Harden used the expensive full rates, which gained him three or four hours in transmission time.

But Monday morning in Hong Kong is Sunday morning in New York. Harden's cable, containing perhaps the biggest scoop of the war, arrived just as City Editor Van Benthuysen was putting on his hat to go home. The final edition of the Sunday World was on the streets, being hawked loudly by newsboys. The staff that had created it—from editors and reporters to pressmen—had for the most part left for home. Delivery wagons were beyond recall. Van Benthuysen immediately recognized the mighty importance of the cable and somehow pulled together a skeleton staff which produced an Extra blazing MANILA OURS! Beneath this, he simply printed Harden's first dispatch:

> I have just arrived here on the United States revenue cutter Hugh McCulloch, with my report of the great American triumph at Manila.
> The entire Spanish fleet of eleven vessels was destroyed.
> Three hundred Spaniards were killed and four hundred wounded.
> Our loss was none killed and six slightly wounded.
> Not one American ship was injured.
>   E. W. Harden
>   (World's Staff Correspondent)

With this Extra in print, Van Benthuysen found a few newsboys to shout it through the streets. But of the five hundred thousand copies of the World sold that day only twenty thousand were the MANILA OURS! edition, which thus earned its name of Sad Scoop. Sale of twenty thousand copies of the Sunday World profited the paper only $120. Harden's next cable, describing the battle of Manila in full detail, cost five thousand dollars. (Stickney's longer one to the Herald cost eight thousand). When the originator of the Sad Scoop returned to Park Row, these blunt facts were for some reason pointed out to him. Perhaps because of this, he shortly entered the business of stocks and bonds.

On a morning in mid-June, 1898, an American convoy of thirty-two tightly packed, stuffy and decrepit coastal vessels left Tampa Harbor, guided in the general direction of Santiago, Cuba, by armed United States Navy vessels. In the ships was the Fifth U.S. Army Corps of 815 officers and 16,072 enlisted men, together with 89 correspondents. The sea was brilliant and burning, and the quarters acutely uncomfortable, but few of the men complained. During the past week the same ships had sat hot and motionless in Tampa Harbor, some—like the *Yucatan*, which the privileged Rough Riders had vigorously commandeered—in the center of a stream of sewage from the city. This had been a sorry and unnecessary delay, caused by a combination of impatient orders from Washington and clumsy preparations in Tampa. Correspondents capable of deep thought now felt confirmed in their suspicions that during the Rocking-Chair period of the war, as Thomas Beer later wrote, "Windy patriotism and romance had been supplanted by hot veracity. The men of the press saw a willing army, ill fed, badly dressed for a climate grown tormenting, and made ready for transport in ships hardly fitted to carry uncritical cattle. . . . Many eyes saw the beginning of a crime on men rendered defenseless by discipline."

One who was critical, though perhaps not on so high a plane, was the stalwart Richard Harding Davis, who as the armada moved toward Cuba paced the deck of General W. R. Shafter's headquarters ship, the *Segurance*. As the convoy moved toward combat, Davis found matters to criticize, reporting:

> We travelled at the rate of seven miles an hour, with long pauses for thought and consultation. Sometimes we moved at the rate of four miles an hour, and frequently we did not move at all. . . . We could not keep in line and we lost ourselves and each other, and the gunboats and torpedo boats were kept busy giving us sharp, precise orders in passing through a megaphone to which either nobody on board made any reply or everyone did.

Yet when the armada anchored off a small and familiar (to him) hamlet called Daiquiri, Davis could not but allow his spirits to rise. Here was war at last. Though a future historian would picture the landing as "like everything else in this most amateurish of wars, a mad scramble," Davis saw it through romantic eyes. Of the boats now being lowered from the sides of the unhappy-looking transports, he wrote:

> Soon the sea was dotted with rows of white boats filled with men bound about with white blanket rolls and with muskets at all angles, and as they rose and fell on the water and the newspaper yachts and transports crept in closer and closer, the scene was strangely suggestive of a boat race, and one almost waited for the starting gun.

By approaching Cuba aboard General W. R. Shafter's headquarters ship, Davis had temporarily abandoned his favored Rough Riders, who steamed behind in the *Yucatan*. The reason for this was contained in the remarkable person of General Shafter himself. The general was sixty years old, a gout-ridden mammoth of three hundred pounds who had won a Medal of Honor in the Civil War. Davis, compact, vigorous and gallant, regarded Shafter with ill-concealed aversion and considered his presence as commander typical of the stumbling way in which the war had so far been carried on. In Davis's opinion, a commanding general should be prepared at any moment to grab a sabre and lead a charge. This Shafter, who seldom moved from a sitting position, would obviously never do. Indeed, as the convoy anchored off Daiquiri, he was further from such a possibility than Davis or anyone imagined. In later testimony before the Dodge Committee, Shafter recalled the invasion days in these words: "I was nearly prostrated . . . when I would sit up it would make me dizzy. I had a beastly attack of gout so that I could not wear a boot. I had to wear a gunny sack on my foot. I could not mount my horse."

It was Davis's fear that, when battle came, the gout-tortured General might feel resentful toward the dashing Rough Riders and keep them in the rear. But Davis should have known his Rough Riders— nothing could hold them back! Instead, it was Davis himself who for a time seemed destined to be thwarted by the suffering Shafter. As the landing boats were lowered from the *Segurance*, Davis discovered that by order of the general no correspondents would be allowed in what today would be called the first wave of landing craft. Such a thing was unheard of in the experience of the most famous reporter alive. Angrily he strode across the deck to the mountainous general, and launched into a vigorous protest. In the words of Shafter's harried aide:

> He was told that the order did not indicate any unfriendliness to reporters. . . . Davis persisted in his argument and . . . said he was not an ordinary reporter but a descriptive writer. At this the General's patience, never very long, gave way and he replied in a sharp tone: "I do not care a damn what you are. I'll treat all of you alike." Mr. Davis was offended at the abruptness of the reply. . . .

But this was war, and all the indignant Davis could do was descend to his cabin, there to salve feelings by attiring himself more correctly in the correspondent's outfit that had become his trademark: wide-brimmed campaign hat, high white composition collar, blue coat and trousers stuffed into high-laced field boots, with field glasses conspicuously slung. Thus adorned he rose to the deck, only to find that his argument with General Shafter had been totally unnecessary. In his absence below decks, the nine other correspondents aboard had merely climbed into a boat, lowered it, and shoved off. An astounded Davis spotted the journalistic boat from the deck and shouted for it to return. One of the important minor decisions of the Spanish-American War now faced the correspondents in the boat. Should they return for their highly publicized colleague, or leave him ignominiously behind in his best war-covering regalia? In another war, Davis might have been hooted at and abandoned, but in the Spanish War correspondents were gentlemen. "We've got to go back for Dick Davis," Stephen Bonsal shouted. The others set up a happy, unanimous cheer of accord. The boat returned.

As the invading army landed through high surf, it was found that the Spaniards had withdrawn inland. Nevertheless, there were casualties. Two soldiers were drowned disembarking and a reporter named Archibald of the San Francisco Post was grazed on the arm by a bullet—whose, the record does not say. Davis immediately rejoined the Rough Riders, who were ashore early as a result of their policy of commandeering boats assigned to others. Lieutenant Colonel Roosevelt and Davis had buried all past differences and the Rough Rider now greeted the handsome correspondent with the grin of comradeship. It was Roosevelt's conviction that General Shafter's bulk was too unwieldy to allow him to proceed far inland, and in this he was joined by nearly all his brother officers. Shafter's orders had been to remain on the sandy beach until he at length arrived, but the Rough Riders and others felt—possibly rightly—that immediate pursuit of the Spaniards was imperative. Brigadier General B. S. M. Young, in charge of the brigade, and Major General Joe Wheeler, an old Confederate who persisted in calling the Spaniards "Damn Yankees," decided that they felt justified in misunderstanding Shafter's order. With Regular Army men led by Young and Wheeler, and the Rough Rider Volunteers behind Wood and Roosevelt, the brigade headed into the jungle.

As the Rough Riders advanced, General Wood, in the lead, could hear Davis explaining the flora and fauna of Cuba to Roosevelt, who had never been on the island. In this informal fashion, the Rough Riders—even though the experienced Wood deployed his men and sent scouts ahead—may have committed the militarily unpardonable by walking into ambush. The Rough Riders themselves, of course, always denied this, but Edward Marshall of the Journal immediately cabled home that the men had been ambushed. Davis, the man of vaunted integrity, wrote the same, though in 1910 he somewhat reversed himself, perhaps because Roosevelt had been in the White House.

But whether taken by surprise or not, on the morning of June 24, 1898, the Rough Riders found themselves undergoing the baptism of fire they so ardently desired. Mauser bullets from unseen rifles suddenly ripped into their ranks and Davis, who knew exactly how to behave in battle, promptly whipped binoculars to his eyes. On a hill ahead, a group of Spaniards, unmistakable in cockaded sombreros, leaped into his vision. He indicated them to Roosevelt, who also peered at them through field glasses, seemingly fascinated by such a bully sight as the enemy. Roosevelt continued to examine the men on the hill lingeringly—for so long, in fact, that it was Davis who directed the fire of Rough Rider sharpshooters at the Spaniards. A bigger enemy volley answered and the men on either side of Davis fell wounded.

Davis, too, fell to the ground, but only for safety. Starting to rise, he found that from the sudden fall (or, modern psychology might say, for psychosomatic reasons) an agonizing sciatica had begun to rack one leg. Nonetheless, he assisted one wounded man back to the dressing station. Returning for the other, Davis was greeted by words that only could have been spoken in battle by a Rough Rider. Davis had gone to Johns Hopkins and Lehigh, but in his bestselling books the stern-faced heroes had always attended Harvard, Yale or Princeton. In addition, Davis himself had been a familiar figure on Ivy League campuses. Now the wounded Rough Rider whispered, "I met you at Harvard on the racquet court."

Davis helped him back to the doctors, then returned to find that young Captain Capron, one of Roosevelt's favorite officers, had been killed. "Death had given him a great dignity and nobleness," the Davis dispatch that night would say. Near Capron sprawled the body of a young sergeant. This was Hamilton Fish, Jr., "his very attitude one of attack, his fists clenched, his jaw set, and his eyes, which were still human, fixed with resolve." Davis, searching the body for a keepsake to send his parents, discovered a watch engraved with the words, *God Gives.* To Davis, writing of this skirmish at Las Guásimas, it seemed that God had given the young man a noble end: "To die in the forefront of the first fight of the war, quickly, painlessly, with a bullet through the heart, with his regiment behind him, and facing the enemies of his country."

While leaning over the body of young Fish, Davis heard Roosevelt calling for a bully charge. He straightened, the exaltation of battle filling him. Still suffering the pains of sciatica, Davis hobbled forward under a shower of bullets to pick up a carbine dropped by a dead man. Again looking through the field glasses, he noted that the Spaniards had taken refuge in a tin shack. To his own amazement, Davis found himself ordering Captain Capron's uncommanded men to charge the shack. The Rough Riders dutifully plunged onward, Davis with them, firing, loading and emptying his carbine again and again.

By now the Regulars under Young and Wheeler had heard the shots and were pushing through the jungle to the assistance of the Rough Riders. Seeing this, the embattled Spaniards retreated from the shack. Trailed by Fighting Joe Wheeler's yell, "We've got the Damn Yankees on the run," they vanished into the jungle. Only then did Davis remember that as a noncombatant, by the rules of war, he was forbidden to fire a gun. In dispatches to the Herald, he abjectly confessed this breach of international law. But the country, as always, found it easy to forgive Dick Davis. After all, "he was an American and he had to do his part . . ."

As landing boats had moved toward the Daiquiri beach, a cutter manned by William Randolph Hearst and selected members of his

Cuban War Wrecking Crew used a megaphone to hail the first boat-load of landing troops. The nervous soldiers, about to set foot on a beach that might be infested with Spanish sharpshooters, pulled back, believing the shout through the megaphone was a military order. All Hearst wished was to learn the name of the soldier in the prow of the boat, for presumably this man would be the first to land. Now another boat shot ahead. As an unhappy reward for its Yellow Journalism enterprise, the New York Journal never was able to give the world the name of the first soldier who set foot on Cuban soil in the Spanish-American War.

Other curious events befell Hearst and his writers as the American troops completed the landing and, with the hulking General Shafter aboard what he properly called a stout-hearted mule, advanced in the direction of Santiago. Edward Marshall, the Journal correspondent with the Rough Riders, was shot in the spine and carried from the field in a litter, still writing the dispatch which maintained that Teddy's Terrors had been ambushed. "He was suffering the tortures of the damned," states a fellow correspondent, "but after he finished the dispatch he began singing, with astonishing pluck, a song that was popular then called On the Banks of the Wabash Far Away." Perhaps because of the pluck, Marshall survived his serious injury to live well into the 1930's.

James Creelman, Hearst's most notable man in the field, performed deeds which bore comparison with those of Richard Harding Davis. As the troops came to the blockhouses of El Caney, a stiff battle began and Creelman found himself in its bullet-whistling midst. Like Davis, he observed that under fire some American troops behaved like sleepwalkers. The military books Creelman had read all stressed the importance of the bayonet charge and, striding importantly up to an officer, the goateed correspondent in natty uniform suggested one. Probably the officer thought a charge was being ordered by a superior officer. At any rate, he signaled one, and it was gloriously successful. But the Journal's military tactician was unable to savor his triumph. He was shot in the shoulder just as the charge began. Creelman was not left untended, however. As he recalled later in his book On the Great Highway:

Someone knelt in the grass beside me and put his hand
on my fevered brow. Opening my eyes, I saw Mr. Hearst,
the proprietor of the New York Journal, a straw hat with a
bright ribbon on his head, a revolver at his belt, and a pencil and a notebook in his hand. The man who provoked the
war had come to see the result with his own eyes and, finding one of his correspondents prostrate, was doing the work
himself.

Slowly he took down my story of the fight. Again and
again the tinging of Mauser bullets interrupted. But he
seemed unmoved. That battle had to be reported somehow.

"I'm sorry you're hurt, but"—and his face was radiant
with enthusiasm—"wasn't it a splendid fight? We must beat
every paper in the world."

After doing what he could to make me comfortable,
Mr. Hearst mounted his horse and dashed away for the sea-
coast, where a fast steamer was waiting to carry him across
the sea to a cable station.

Not every Park Row correspondent covered himself with such
glory. Wandering vaguely around American encampments on Cuba
was the World's special correspondent, the reserved, slow-spoken,
twenty-seven-year-old Stephen Crane. Before leaving England Crane
had been ill from a difficult-to-diagnose intestinal consumption. Accompanying this depleting sickness was the conviction that, either
in this war or shortly afterward, he would die. Nor did Crane seem to
be of the rugged stuff from which front-line correspondents are
made. He had made his reputation from *The Red Badge of Courage*,
which he wrote from experience gained in studying a series of magazine articles on Civil War battles. He was in Cuba because now he
wanted to see American warfare at first hand. He should never have
been there. "Sense and the warnings of friends should have kept
him away from Cuba," says his biographer Thomas Beer, "but his
curiosity took him there quite inevitably."

Ironically, Crane, for all his sickness and retiring nature, was perhaps the first correspondent to reach Cuban soil. On June tenth,
fourteen days before Daiquiri, he landed with six hundred advance-
guard Marines on the eastern bank of Guantanamo Bay. For a time,
Crane seemed beside himself with excitement at actually taking

part in a war. He had befriended an Army surgeon named Gibbs and the two held happy discussions around late-night campfires. Then *The Red Badge of Courage* type of war suddenly hit Crane. Dr. Gibbs was horribly wounded, and the correspondent sat beside him through a night-long vigil:

> Every wave, vibration, of his anguish beat upon my senses. He was long past groaning. There was only the bitter strife for air which pulsed out into the night in a clear, penetrating whistle with intervals of horrible silence in which I held my own breath in the common unconscious aspiration for help. I thought this man would never die. Ultimately he died.

After that, war was hell for Stephen Crane. He went through the outer duties of correspondent, riding on horseback forty miles around Santiago, guided by half-clad Cuban scouts. Fatigue from this danger-filled journey, physical sickness, despair, the brandy he drank, the quinine he took—all combined to drain Crane completely. "I did not discover my condition until we were well through the Spanish lines," he wrote later, "and then I discovered I was a dead man. The nervous force having evaporated, I was a mere corpse. My limbs were dough and my spinal cord burned in me as if it were a red hot wire."

In this condition, all Crane seemed able to think about was death. Yet he kept on. He and his Marines were near the Daiquiri beach when General Shafter and the Rough Riders landed. Lacking Richard Harding Davis's miraculous intuition, Crane elected to follow General Young's Regular troops. Thus he missed the major part of the skirmish at Las Guásimas, but as the hospital tents of wounded multiplied, he horrified other correspondents by remarking that it must be interesting to be shot. He stored up such gory details as the fact that men struck in the chest ran forward before falling, while those wounded in abdominal regions crumpled in their tracks. Crane was no longer drinking, but he was dosing himself heavily with quinine when a message from Park Row arrived demanding to know why he did not file more dispatches. Momentarily, he pulled himself together to examine the activities of the 71st New York Regiment under fire near Santiago. He thought the men cowardly and his dispatch said so. On Park Row, the World printed the dispatch, giving Brisbane another chance to hurl accusations of treason at a rival newspaper. New York, the home of the 71st, rose in an uproar. Then a reluctant War Department report confirmed Crane's story.

Wearing a conspicuous gray English topcoat which he was afraid to take off for fear it would be stolen, Crane followed the Army to the foot of San Juan Hill. There his behavior under fire became incredible—an almost-insane combination of death wish and determination to see war at closest possible range. Crane stood upright atop trenches, drawing fire until infuriated soldiers hauled him down. He walked from trench to trench, battalion to battalion, constantly fired at but never hit. At San Juan, he wandered close to a depression sheltering General Leonard Wood and Richard Harding Davis. Soldiers shouted at him to lie down, but he did not seem to hear. Davis finally became annoyed and called him loudly. "Crane jumped," reported Davis, "as if waking from a nap, and looked at me, astonished by my voice, perhaps."

For a moment, Crane flattened out like the others, crawling behind a small hillock. Soon he was upright again, drawing fire as he dazedly walked about. Davis, knowing there was nothing exhibitionistic in Crane's behavior, tried sarcasm. "You're not impressing anyone by doing that, Crane," he shouted. Crane crouched down again and Davis crawled toward him to say, "I knew that would fetch you." Again Crane seemed to wake up. "Oh, so that was it?" he answered.

Before long he was up again, fascinated by the smoke and flame coming from the line of Spanish entrenchments. Davis heaved a long sigh of resignation and himself got up. Stepping over soldiers, he seized Crane by the shoulders and, using old football muscles, forced him to the ground. As he did this, a bullet sent his famous campaign hat spinning and the leather of his binoculars was clipped by another. Crane saw this and for a time kept flat again. But soon, says Beer, "he wandered away to play his game elsewhere."

As the Rough Riders started up San Juan Hill—or was it Kettle Hill?—Crane appeared again. While the American flag was jubilantly planted atop the hill, he was seen trying to hammer back a loose heel on his shoe. Thus it is fitting that Richard Harding Davis was the one most memorably to report San Juan Hill for Park Row newspapers:

> They drove the yellow silk flag of the cavalry and the Stars and Stripes of their country into the soft earth of the trenches, and then sank down and looked back at the road they had climbed and swung their hats in the air.
> And from far overhead, from those few figures perched on the Spanish rifle pits, with their flags planted among the empty cartridges of the enemy, and overlooking the walls of Santiago, came, faintly, the sound of a tired, broken cheer.

With this, the Spanish-American war all but ended, though the outsize General Shafter did not seem to realize it. Nor did Theodore Roosevelt, living out his great day in military history. Indeed, had the battered Spanish troops ventured an attack on the night after San Juan Hill the results might have been both ironic and interesting. For on this night, Shafter was beset by nagging fears and actually was on the point of ordering a retreat when word came that the forlorn Spanish fleet had made an attempt to break out of Santiago Harbor.

Here none other than William Randolph Hearst had all the journalistic luck. The Journal cutter with Hearst and his Wrecking Crew aboard was circling the American fleet at the moment of breakthrough. For a while the overanxiousness of the Hearst craft brought it within range of American guns, causing the entire fleet to remain mute. But eventually Hearst pulled out of range, and American guns mercilessly bombarded the Spanish ships racing along the coast with decks afire, boilers bursting and guns helpless. The American fleet pursued and behind it came the Newspaper Fleet, indomitably led by Hearst. As sailors from the burning Spanish battleships leaped overboard and swam for shore, the Hearst cutter veered to follow. Hearst himself heroically rolled trousers above knees, and before his cutter reached the shore, clambered out to pursue the fleeing Spaniards. Brandishing a revolver, he shouted to the unhappy men to halt. This they did, to be hauled aboard the Hearst cutter and then transferred to the Hearst yacht, where they were in-

terviewed and photographs taken. The results were rushed to Park
Row, where the Journal announced a historic battle, led by the
Hearst yacht!

So ended the glamour period of the war, leaving intermittent
skirmishing, details of the Spanish surrender, and the malaria and
yellow fever which now attacked American encampments with a
fury the enemy had never shown. At home came a sudden awareness that, though this had been one of the shortest wars on
record, it had brought a heavy toll in casualties, as well as revela-
tions of Government and military stupidity. The theme song of
the war, *There'll Be a Hot Time in the Old Town Tonight*, took
on an exceedingly hollow ring and seldom was heard. That other
song favorite, *Good-Bye, Dolly Gray*, now seemed in its sadness to
pertain to sick and wounded rather than to chaste farewell kisses
in the swings of vine-covered porches.

No less than the unfortunate Government did the Park Row
newspapers have difficulties during the declining period of the war.
Joseph Pulitzer, already rendered unhappy by results of the small
war he had desired, was made acutely uncomfortable by an incredible
event involving his top Cuban correspondent, Sylvester Scovel. As
the American flag was about to be raised over Santiago, the enterprising Scovel, dreaming of carrying Yellow Journalism to measureless heights, decided it would increase the World's prestige if he were
visible in the official photographs.

Accordingly he clambered atop a roof which would bring him directly in the line of cameras. He was ordered down by Army officers,
but steadfastly refused to budge. For this occasion, the mountainous General Shafter had been lifted off his mule and stood in sweaty,
saluting dignity waiting for the flag to rise. Shafter had come to
nurse a bitter hatred for all newspapermen. "Throw him off," he
thundered when he saw Scovel's position on the roof. Several soldiers advanced to do so, at which Scovel jumped down. But instead
of disappearing unobtrusively, he proceeded straight toward General
Shafter and began to give him an angry tongue-lashing. "One word,"
says Shafter's later report to Washington, "led to another." Then suddenly Scovel astoundingly threw a punch at the jaw of the Commanding General of the Fifth Corps. So great was his rage that the

blow missed, but he was instantly placed under military arrest and ignominiously ordered to stand on a pedestal from which a statue had been toppled, guarded by two armed men. After the ceremonies he was taken to a moss-covered calaboose, while on Park Row the World was duly informed that its number-one correspondent languished in jail. Fortunately, Scovel was a close friend of President McKinley. This and Pulitzer's influence eventually got him free. But, far from reflecting credit to the World, his action was a considerable blot on the paper's prestige.

The Journal fared even worse in the final weeks of the war. With the surrender of Santiago, Hearst correspondents—possibly on orders from Park Row—posted inflammatory signs in an attempt to arouse the Cuban population against the unarmed Spanish prisoners. At this, the long-suffering Shafter finally had his fill. He declared that such action deserved the penalty of death and informed Washington that he intended to place Journal correspondents before a firing squad. Horrified cables shot back to warn him this could never be done. So Shafter decreed a fate perhaps worse than death for the Journal. He banned all Hearst correspondents from Cuba, thus making it possible for every paper in the country to scoop the mighty Journal. Hearst was outraged and bombarded Washington with threats and appeals. Washington, in turn, bombarded Shafter with messages which read, "The Journal is in deep distress—the Journal has been doing good work." But for once the gout-ridden man remained adamant. The Journal's disgrace at the end of the war was greater than the World's. It was not getting the news.

By this time Hearst had reappeared on Park Row, there apparently to indulge in realistic thinking. For nearly three years he had been trying to ruin the World. Into the Yellow Journalism battle he had dumped most of his mother's seven million dollars. True, this had not been a total loss, for the Journal was now established and, with the horde of immigrants increasing the population of New York, finding an increasing readership. But Hearst was shrewd enough to realize that he had failed in his most cherished dream. The World, which had even descended to meet him on his own terms, still stood firm. He had not wrecked the man he had picked as his rival: he

could never be the controlling force in New York that Pulitzer once
had been. It meant an admission of defeat for the ruthless Westerner,
a switch in plans for the future. Now, seemingly, had come the time
to try politics or newspaper publishing on a national, rather than
local, scale.

The blind, incessantly questing Pulitzer was also thinking. He
had sickened of the Spanish-American War, which had run up expenses in World tugboats and correspondents cabling dispatches at
$2.12 a word. Though both the World and Journal had upped
price to two cents, domestic losses had also run high, for dealers had
been so swamped with Extras that thousands of unsold papers had
been returned, at enormous cost. Now, with the war's decline, came
reports of unspeakable conditions in Volunteer camps and on transports. Back came the crusading Pulitzer of the past. "The instant, ur-
gent necessity is to break up the pest camps and disband the Volunteers," he wrote as the opening of the type of editorial campaign
that had made the World famous. "There is not the slightest reason,
nor the slightest need, for this enormous Army. The Navy has force
enough to take care of remote contingencies."

With such thoughts occupying the minds of both men, it is small
wonder that concrete steps toward peace were taken on Park Row.
Perhaps Hearst, the junior in years, at some point approached Pulitzer. Whether he did so personally is not known, but Pulitzer soon
informed associates that overtures had been made. To William H.
Merrill he wrote from Bar Harbor: "There is a proposition before me
to stop all unfriendly utterances between the World and the Journal.
I don't know whether the proposition will be carried through or not,
but in the meantime you might suspend such utterances until there
is provocation. You might tell the others also, but very discreetly, as
I doubt whether the thing will finally go through. This until further notice."

Further notice never came, but a lessening in competition between the two papers was soon visible. With its crusading for better
conditions for troops, the World began a move back to its former
posture of integrity, while the Journal continued to hack out its own
peculiar province in New York. The day came when Pulitzer even
issued instructions to his editors to scrap the huge headline type

which had played such a part in the conflict of Extras with the Journal. He had never seen this horrendous type, but his sensitive, experienced mind told him what typographical atrocities it could produce. World editors obediently collected the large letters and had the foreman melt them down, but shortly orders were quietly issued to have them made again.

Yellow Journalism was not—and never would be—that dead!

CHAPTER EIGHT

The Satrap—I

S TRANGELY enough, two other Park Row newspapers—almost in spite of themselves—profited greatly from the Spanish-American War.

One was the New York Times, purchased on August 13, 1896, for the relatively small sum of seventy-five thousand dollars, by a young man from Chattanooga, Tennessee, named Adolph Ochs. Ochs hesitated a long time before buying the sickly Times but finally, with a show of considerable courage, paid over the money for the newspaper with offices at 41 Park Row. Having gained possession of the Times, the canny Ochs decided to offer New York a paper which presented the news in straightforward, unembellished fashion, at the same time providing the greatest possible physical contrast to the Yellow titans locked in struggle at the north end of Park Row. Ochs set out to make a clean paper typographically, with readable print and a dignified appearance. For this enterprise he was rewarded by a slow, steady rise in circulation and the plaudits of churchmen and leading citizens who saluted the new Times as a decent, readable paper, fit for any home.

Having achieved this important step, Ochs next found himself facing the Spanish-American War, to which his towering rivals were prepared to give expensive and unprecedentedly large coverage. Where Hearst could afford yachts and Wrecking Crews, and Pultizer cutters and Stephen Crane, Ochs had only the comparatively tepid and impersonal reports of the Associated Press. It appeared a moment

of acute crisis, and gloom temporarily filled the office of the Times.
But Ochs neatly solved the problem by deciding to sharpen and increase his coverage of New York news, while at the same time giving
more space to thought-provoking features like book reviews.

It was an eminently sensible decision, for a public quickly tired
of the Spanish-American War turned with relief to the more relaxing
local news stories in the Times. Yet it was not enough to spell financial success and Ochs resorted to the old trick of reducing price. He
dropped the Times from three cents to one cent (the World and
Journal had just jumped to two cents). At first this was viewed with
alarm by those who had so far approved the new Times. It was
thought that the paper had changed policy and planned to outdo the
Yellow Journals. Indeed, for a few unthinkable days some Times
staff members seemed to labor under this delusion, turning in stories
written in riotous, exclamation-point Yellow fashion. But soon both
public and staff were reassured. Where the World had undergone a
visible cheapening by reducing price to compete with the Journal,
the Times did not. It still stood forth proudly among its Park Row
rivals.

The success of the Times, though it increased in circulation from
25,726 to 76,260 in the years 1898-99, was in those days a minor
matter compared to the new vigor infused into the New York Herald,
second of the papers suddenly to find itself benefited by the Spanish-
American War. By seeming to rise above the Cuban conflict, the
Herald may be said successfully to have cashed in on it. In fact, it has
often been stated that the Herald now behaved in the manner Pulitzer should have adopted when Hearst first challenged him on Park
Row. The Herald did little to inflame the jingoism of its readers before the conflict, and when war did come it aloofly hired the best
available correspondent, Richard Harding Davis, with great dignity
featuring his honest, graphic dispatches. Even the Yellows, licking
wounds after the Spanish surrender, had to admit that the Herald had
unexpectedly come out on top where Park Row was concerned.

Such success on the part of the Herald becomes the more remarkable when placed beside the fact that James Gordon Bennett,
Jr., the tall, aquiline-nosed, drooping-mustached proprietor of the
paper, almost never entered the office. Even so, the first-off-the-press

copy of every edition was rushed to a place atop Bennett's unused, uncluttered desk. So great was the Herald's fear of the swaggering, arrogant Bennett that his staff remained absolutely convinced that the publisher, no matter where he might be on earth, would *know* if this first copy of an edition were not put on his desk. Terror of the saturnine Bennett extended even to the Herald's star reporters. In the city room many old-timers followed the tradition of working with hats on. It is said that whenever Bennett's name was mentioned, these men could not help respectfully touching a finger to hat brim.

There was reason for this. Bold, strapping, aggressive, Bennett had been born with a silver spoon in his mouth, and the spoon rapidly turned to gold. In a long lifetime, he was privileged to spend no less than thirty million dollars, largely on personal pleasures. To view Bennett charitably, he was one of the rudest and most erratic men who ever lived. To be more realistic, his behavior bordered on madness and frequently crossed the line. Most of his life—for a very definite reason—was spent in Paris, where he started the still-existing Paris Herald as an outlet for his considerable journalistic talents. The fact that it lost him an annual hundred thousand dollars bothered him not at all and may even have spurred him into establishing an ill-fated London Herald. When not resident in Paris or London, Bennett cruised the world aboard what was probably the most luxurious yacht of his time. From it he communicated endlessly with the New York Herald, putting his slightest wish into irritable, individualistic cables. When Venezuela popped up in the world news, the impatient man could not bother to learn the proper spelling of the country's name. He merely cabled instructions about "Venezoo." Bennett, in fact, made such heroic use of transatlantic cables that one year the Western Union Cable Company hailed him as its best single customer. This proved to be a mistake. The millionaire John W. Mackay had in mind a rival and more direct cable company. Now, reading about Bennett, he asked him to invest as a partner. Bennett instantly agreed. To be co-owner of a transatlantic cable company was life on precisely the scale he liked.

Bennett had many personality problems, chief among them the fact that he was a drunkard. Drink ignited his latent madness, setting it aflame with a bonfire roar. "Sober, he was the coldest and most calculating of men, drunk he was a madman," a contemporary has stated. Still, there was great irony in Bennett's drinking. It took no more than a sip or two of the champagne he adored to create in him a raucous, belligerent mood which the average hard drinker works hours to attain. "By some wise provision of nature," the contemporary goes on, "it took but little liquor to upset Bennett. Two glasses of champagne would completely destroy his equilibrium." If this was a wise provision of nature, it was also a baffling one. Bennett's antics as a drinker were well known, and medical men aware of his reputation as a drunkard were always astounded at his robust physical health. The truth seems to be that he actually drank so little that the alcohol made no inroads on his magnificent constitution or, as one doctor said, "His potations did little interior damage, though they often imperiled his person."

Drunkenness, rudeness and one of the largest fixed incomes of his time made Bennett an outstandingly domineering and unpleasant person—but a good newspaper publisher when he wished to be. This was the result of inheritance and training. He was the son of the James Gordon Bennett who, from 1835 on, was as much of a catalytic agent to New York journalism as Pulitzer became in 1883. The elder Bennett, says Elmer Davis, in his history of the New York Times:

> . . . was the inventor of almost everything, good and bad, in modern journalism. He was the first editor who gave his chief attention to the collection of news, and before long his competition had compelled all newspapers which made any pretension to influence to undertake unheard-of expenditures and to compete with him in the utilization of the railroad, the steamship, the telegraph and other new inventions just coming into use . . . he discovered and encouraged the popular taste for vicarious vice and crime. . . .

Being a bold journalistic pioneer got Bennett no thanks from the people of New York. He became perhaps the most hated man in the city. Several times he was horsewhipped and spat upon in public. Polite people shuddered at his name and the wealthy would not permit him past the door. Bennett loudly maintained that he thrived on such hatred and financially he did, accumulating millions over

the years. But as if stung by the hatred of his fellow men, he made
the columns of his paper increasingly shrill and abusive. Seldom, if
ever, has a paper contained such vitriolic writing as the New York
Herald, which in its time called Abraham Lincoln "an imbecile rail
splitter," "a smutty joker," and finally "a traitor." People loudly despised the Herald's publisher, yet they were forced to buy his paper
for lively, realistic news. Bennett's Herald never launched flaming
crusades or provided mature editorial stimulus—this was Pulitzer's
later contribution—but while he lived, the elder Bennett drastically
changed the country's concept of news.

For all his provocative behavior before an ungrateful public,
the senior Bennett was a good husband and father—in the case of his
son, too good. Bennett was Scotch, his wife Irish. This allowed Dr.
George Hosmer—a physician whose curious preoccupation with newspapers caused him to pass his adult life in the entourage of both
Bennetts and Joseph Pulitzer—to state that Bennett, Jr., had inherited the worst features of both nationalities. "When sober he displays the worst qualities of the one, and when drunk the worst qualities of the other," Hosmer stated from the safety of the Pulitzer payroll. The younger Bennett was born on May 10, 1841. When he
reached the age of five, his mother decided that a city that reviled his
father was hardly a place to bring up the boy. She took the children
—Bennett had a sister—to Paris, where, under the exclusive guidance
of tutors, James Gordon, Jr., began the process of becoming half
European and total monster. One problem he faced was that from
New York his father showered him with money. Even as a child, his
personal income—if it can be called that—exceeded the wealth of
many rich men in America. Bennett was big for his age and this, with
the money, caused him to investigate the fleshpots of Europe while
still practically in short trousers. It did not help his personality adjustment. "Isolation abroad, combined with plenty of money, made
him dissolute when very young," a biographer sadly writes.

From time to time Mrs. Bennett and her children returned to
the United States. Then the elder Bennett took over, concentrating
on his son's newspaper training. On either side of his own large desk
in the building at Broadway and Ann Street, Bennett, Sr., placed
two smaller desks. In one he sat his son and in the other an attrac-

tive redheaded contemporary of his son's named Edward Townsend
Flynn. The senior Bennett, in what turned out to be a sagacious
move, plucked young Flynn from among his son's acquaintances to be
trained with him. Thus, in later years, while Bennett roamed, Flynn
remained in New York to run the paper. Bennett, Sr., a man of no
mean intuition, seemed to know this was precisely what would happen.

Long before he reached the age of twenty young Bennett's character began displaying glittering facets. Perhaps the most colorful was
his love of gentlemanly sport. This remained his passion through life.
He took part in, or offered Bennett cups in, yachting, polo, coach-
driving, auto-racing, ballooning and aviation. In what remains of
American society Bennett is still recalled primarily as the man who
introduced polo to Newport—Newport, of course, being the entire
United States. Yet in the world of sport Bennett's first love was
yachting. In 1857—at the incredible age of sixteen and a half—he was
elected a member of the New York Yacht Club, the youngest skipper
ever to be accorded this honor. Older members grumbled, but it
was impossible to keep the brash youngster out. Though just out of
knee pants, he had recently built the seventy-seven-ton yacht *Rebecca* and under his own command was skillfully racing it against top
sloops of the day. Bennett's interest in yachting never waned and
his later transatlantic races have become exciting chapters in the annals of sport. His yachts brought world-wide publicity to both himself and the Herald, but at the same time contributed many a throbbing headache to the offices on Park Row. Bennett's interest in general news was always perfunctory, but he read every word of every
Herald on the chance that it might contain something pertaining to
the sea or navigation. All copies of the paper were sent him with the
name of the writer over the story in crayon. If the writer attributed a
crow's nest to a ship that did not have one, described a shipwreck in
landlubber terms, or made a mistake in reporting the tides, Bennett's blast would rock the city room.

Posted in the city room was also a list of Bennett's high-society
friends whose names must be spelled correctly and mentioned as frequently as possible. This was a fairly simple task, since Bennett employed as society reporter Nicholas Biddle, the Beau Brummel of

Park Row and a man more blue-blooded than any of the New York aristocracy he wrote about. But the elegant Biddle could not be present on all occasions and sometimes copy readers, rendered nervous by Bennett's multitudinous strictures, made distressing mistakes. Once the names of guests at a costume ball given by Mrs. Stuyvesant Fish were transposed with those attending a lowly prize fight. Mrs. Fish, reading that she had entertained Tammany politicians and gangsters, shattered the peace of upper Fifth Avenue with her wrath. Nicholas Biddle was hastily dispatched to soothe her, using his most polished manners to present Bennett's apologies. Mrs. Fish flatly refused to accept them. When this was relayed to the egotistical Bennett, he reacted furiously. New York society was all very fine, but James Gordon Bennett, Jr., apologized to almost no one, and when he did the apology *had* to be accepted. "All right," he shouted. "Never mention her name in the paper again."

Hand in hand with the sporting Bennett went a rambunctious playboy, for with his ability to get roaring drunk on a few sips of wine, Bennett was a social-behavior problem from the beginning. Frank Squier, a New York City Park Commissioner, paid a call at the Bennett home when young James was sixteen. He found a children's party in progress and reported to friends that young Jimmy was disgustingly drunk. Bennett's subsequent career as the town's most notable hell-raiser also had aspects of irony. A New York society that would not speak to his father was unable to disregard the young millionaire sportsman. The reactions of James Gordon Bennett, Sr., as his headstrong offspring sailed into the upper circles of New York society, are not known. But however successfully New York had ostracized the father, it could do nothing to stop his brash son. By the time he was twenty, Bennett, Jr., was not only a member of the New York Yacht Club, but of the Union Club and the Jockey Club as well. All three, as a contemporary social record puts it, "were domains limited to the elect."

Of them, the Union Club was by far the liveliest. Located on the corner of Fifth Avenue and Twentieth Street, it was the happy haunt of the gayest of New York blades, featuring such names as Leonard Jerome, Herman Oelrichs, Pierre Lorillard and Freddie Gebhardt. Some of these notable sporting men were approaching middle age, but younger members of Bennett's generation made up for any sedateness contributed by older members. "One of the privileges of belonging to the Union Club," writes a member, "was that of being wild and respectable at the same time." In other words, any escapade on the part of a Union Club member was quickly forgiven. The portals of this cheery establishment were never closed and seldom was a sober breath drawn by the younger members who lounged within its four walls. Fittingly, it was at the high club windows overlooking Fifth Avenue that young Jimmy Bennett conceived the first of the escapades that were to make him famous as a playboy. Idly peering out a club window one afternoon he noticed that the girls' finishing schools in the vicinity marched their young charges—and some not so young—through the streets to and from recreation periods in nearby parks. The sight of pretty girls marching demurely two by two inflamed the destructive urges ever-latent in Bennett. He charged out of the Club and raced his heavy bulk straight into one line of girls. Plunging between the first couple, he enfiladed the line and threw it into screaming confusion. At the rear, he quickly darted away to escape the wrath of the teacher in charge. Other young bloods of his age—then about twenty—delightedly joined him in this game. In the quiet New York of the time, the pastime achieved wide emulation and was solemnly dubbed "Bennetting."

After this strong start, Bennett began emerging as the town's playboy *par excellence*. His summertime love of sailing turned in winter to coaching, and from this expensive activity came stories of wild night rides and startling adventures that lent support to the belief held by many of Bennett's friends: that at times he was actually insane. With coaching companions like Gunning S. Bedford, he would race along the roads of upper Manhattan, whipping his horses until they foamed at the mouth or fell. Often, instead of stopping at the finish line of a race, Bennett would charge off on rampaging coaching trips of several weeks' duration. Buying new coach-and-fours along the way, he would plunge through New England, shouting wildly as the coach attained what for the time was a dizzying speed. There are even weirder stories of Bennett's coaching. Sometimes in night rides he tore off his clothes, so that he could sit in the box stark

naked as the coach hurtled along country roads. In Paris he topped
all his mad exploits by wagering friends that he could drive a coach-
and-four under a narrow archway. It could not be done. Bennett was
scraped off the box and tumbled to the street nearly dead from shock
and concussion. He lay in the hospital for two weeks, to emerge absolutely unrepentant. Immediately, he fearlessly resumed his wild
coaching.

If his outdoor exploits were maniacal, Bennett's indoor behavior was boorish. It was his pleasure—in Paris, perhaps, more than
in New York—to walk through restaurants yanking the tablecloths off
tables as he went. The reaction of diners to this caprice is not
known, but restaurant proprietors seldom minded. A well-padded
bill sent the next day to Mr. Bennett would be paid without question by one of his secretaries. In the various exclusive clubs to which
he belonged Bennett's actions were equally impetuous, but because
of his money, sporting superiority, and an overwhelming arrogance he
was tolerated and even fawned upon. "The candle flame never lacked
its attendant array of admiring moths," a diarist of the time glumly
set down.

Even so, Bennett's trigger temper kept him constantly embroiled, and on occasion rendered him downright ridiculous. Once he
entered Delmonico's alone, took possession of a table, and loudly ordered a bottle of champagne. When it did not appear instantly, he
flew into a rage. Leaping to his feet, he shoved bull-like through the
double line of men around the bar. "I ordered a bottle of champagne fifteen minutes ago, where is it?" he thundered. A small man
near him said calmly, "You'd think he ordered a case." Bennett heard
this impertinence and, wheeling, drove a ferocious punch into the
face of the smaller man. It struck only air and a return clip to the jaw
dropped Bennett insensible to the floor. As usual on such occasions,
Edward Townsend Flynn materialized to take care of his problem
friend. The groggy Bennett allowed himself to be led peacefully
home, but in the morning noisily demanded the identity of the brute
who had attacked him. Flynn informed him the man was Billy Edwards, a lightweight boxer. Bennett immediately swelled up with
perverse pride. In his odd lexicon it was an honor to be knocked out

by a professional. "Invite him to lunch," he ordered. Soon Bennett and Billy Edwards were boon companions.

Bennett was equally unpredictable on a night he dined in the company of Jim Fisk and the great actor Edwin Booth. For such occasions the swarthy man attired himself in full evening dress, with shiny boiled shirt, jeweled studs and dazzling watch chain. This night, as the three men toasted one another, he was filled with a mighty expansiveness. Suddenly, a fire engine raced by the club. Some erratic impulse, or perhaps a sip of wine, caused him to inform his companions that he was a masterful fire fighter. Another engine clanged by and, convinced by his own words, Bennett leaped up to chase it. Around the corner he found the city fire department battling a dangerous blaze. Elbowing his way through the crowd, the resplendently attired man started to assume direction of the fire fighting. Shortly he had made himself such a nuisance that a fire chief ordered his men to turn the hose on him. The jet of water struck Bennett full in the chest, causing him to fall back ignominiously to a sitting position on the watery ground. From there he was pulled to his feet by Fisk and Booth, who had followed their impetuous friend to the fire. Next morning Bennett again summoned the omniscient Flynn. "What did I do last night?" he inquired foggily. "All I remember is being damned soaking wet."

"You made a fool of yourself," Flynn told him bluntly. "You interfered with firemen, trying to tell them how to fight a fire, which they understand a good deal better than you."

Bennett looked quite pleased with himself. "Send a new rubber raincoat to every man in the department," he directed. "I'll pay the bill." Then he thought a moment. "You know," he said, "I never felt so wet in my life."

When Bennett's father died in 1872, the son was thirty-one, in full career as a hell-for-leather sportsman and playboy. Despite this, his father's will gave him complete ownership of the Herald, and the staff of the paper waited in trepidation to see whether he would bring his robust antics to the operation of the paper. Bennett did. Albert Stevens Crockett, a long-time Bennett aide, has written, "If impulse

called, he obeyed, and no rule existed except to be broken." This
was especially true of Bennett the publisher. He sometimes appeared
in the Herald office on Broadway and Ann Street and from his desk
there more or less ran his tangled affairs. Occasionally, but not often,
his attention strayed to the newspaper. One of his favorite sayings was
"Nothing can hurt the Herald," and this allowed him to take a
debonair attitude toward his duties as editor and publisher. At the
same time, his oft-stated belief seemed to be more right than wrong.
Even after Pulitzer's inroads on the prosperity of the city's newspapers, the Herald flourished. Nothing seemed able to keep it from
being one of the most profitable and potentially most powerful papers in the world. Under the elder Bennett the paper had made millions. Under his madcap son, it made more.

In his rare moments devoted to the Herald, Bennett had some
good ideas. Nor were these always editorial. It was Bennett who conceived the idea of the first real-estate advertising department in a
New York newspaper. There was method in his sanity, for Bennett
himself had large real-estate interests on Washington Heights and
wished to develop them. At the same time, real-estate advertising
brought the paper a lead in the field which it never lost. Almost
simultaneously Bennett saw the need for want ads in the growing
city, and another large source of revenue was added. To the news department, he pointed out that nearly every newspaper on Park Row
was devoting itself to a sensational Sunday supplement. He recommended a dignified one, "full of reachings-out beyond the routine,"
was the clear way in which he outlined it. Coupled with this was his
interest in Society, which he insisted be covered in meticulous detail,
and an excellent coverage of foreign news, the result of Bennett's
years abroad, as well as his ownership of the Paris Herald. Thus with
real-estate and want ads, society coverage and foreign news, Bennett
was making a bid for all types of readership. The financial success of
his paper showed how well he got it.

Even more important was Bennett's rare genius for exclusive
news. "He knew how to make news, not by the simple and unsatisfy-
ing process of creating it out of whole cloth, but by starting something that would find an echo in the popular imagination and
stimulate a demand for more," says Crockett. In part, the secret of

this lay in Bennett's wild extravagance. Reporters with a thirst for
travel always tried to get jobs on the Herald, for at any moment Bennett might dispatch them to some faraway corner of the globe on an
adventurous stint that could be featured excitingly in the Herald.
Keep the People Guessing was one of Bennett the publisher's
maxims. This may have been an offshoot of his lifelong delight in
tormenting and teasing those around him, but in newspaper terms it
meant stories that could be tantalizingly drawn out while public interest mounted. One young reporter, dispatched to far-off Abyssinia
on the strength of a letter of recommendation to Bennett, was
Henry M. Stanley. At their first interview, Stanley found the publisher "a tall, fierce-eyed, imperious young man." Their second meeting came several years later, after the famed Scotch-Presbyterian mis-
sionary, Dr. David Livingstone, had disappeared into the vastness of
Africa. Stanley was peremptorily summoned to Bennett's presence,
for a session which started badly when Bennett, reclining indolently
in bed at three P.M., failed to recognize the man he had sent for.
"Who are you?" he demanded. Stanley identified himself and the
two talked of Africa. Then Bennett sat up, adjusted the pillows, and
from a more comfortable position uttered the famous command,
"FIND LIVINGSTONE!" The interview continued on a jagged course,
since Stanley was aware of Bennett's drinking habits and considered
that a man lolling in bed in midafternoon would issue such a
grandiose instruction only if drunk. Eventually he became convinced
that Bennett meant his words and began preparations for what remains probably the greatest newspaper story of all time. For a full
year Stanley's dispatches from Africa to the Herald held the world's
unflagging interest. On November 10, 1871, as other Park Row papers were beginning to scoff and call the story a hoax—the Herald's
past contained some notable ones—Stanley found Livingstone, an
event he described in a crowning dispatch:

> After a few minutes we came to a halt. The guides in
> the van had reached the market-place, which was the central
> point of interest. For there the great Arabs chiefs, and re-
> spectabilities of Ujiji, had gathered in a group to await
> events; thither also they had brought with them the vener-
> able European traveler who was at that time resting among

them. The caravan pressed up to them, divided itself into two lines on either side of the road, and, as it did so, disclosed to me the prominent figure of an elderly white man clad in a red flannel blouse, gray trousers, and a blue cloth, gold banded cap. . . .

Under all these circumstances I could do no more than exercise some restraint and reserve, so I walked up to him and, doffing my helmet, bowed and said in an inquiring tone,—

"Dr. Livingstone, I presume?"

Smiling cordially, he lifted his cap, and answered briefly, "Yes."

This ending all skepticism on my part, my face betrayed the earnestness of my satisfaction as I extended my hand and added,—

"I thank God, Doctor, that I have been permitted to see you."

"I feel most thankful that I am here to welcome you."

Having scored so heavily with Stanley and Livingstone, Bennett pursued the hunt for adventure stories that would keep people guessing. His enthusiasm was somewhat dampened by the ill-fated, Herald-sponsored Jeanette expedition to the North Pole, but after the turn of the century he could not be restrained from paying twenty-five thousand dollars to the dubious Dr. Cook for the exclusive story of his alleged discovery of the Pole. A part of the impetus for Bennett's transatlantic sloop races, as well as his Bennett cups for racing, ballooning and aviation, always lay in his Keep-the-People-Guessing policy, for the Herald coverage of such events was always the exciting best. At least one unexpected reward came to Bennett for his enthusiastic sponsoring of adventure. There is a Bennett Island in the Arctic, and in Africa a Bennett Mountain and a Bennett River, both named by the intrepid Henry M. Stanley. As the result of a Herald-sponsored expedition into Alaska, led by Frederick Schwatka, there is also a beautiful Lake Bennett in the upper regions of this continent. Flowing into it is a Flynn River, gallantly named in honor of the long-suffering Edward Townsend Flynn.

The amazing thing is not that Bennett should do these things well, but that he should do them at all. For his behavior around the Herald office is the stuff that Park Row legends are made of.

When Bennett took over the paper, the city room was populated with men who had labored hard for his father. The young man could have showed at least token respect to them. He did not. With the possible exception of his contemporary, Edward Townsend Flynn, he never seemed to value anyone on the paper. "I want you fellows to remember," he once lectured a staff, "that I am the only reader of this paper. I am the only one to be pleased. If I want the Herald to be turned upside down, it must be turned upside down." Contempt for editorial underlings was not one of his numerous passing moods. He meant every word. When anyone in the Union Club congratulated him on having a fine Herald staff, he exploded into raucous profanity. "All the brains I want can be picked up any day at twenty-five dollars a week," he would shout.

One of his first acts on taking over the Herald was to order everyone in his employ to write a report on the fitness of fellow workers. Thus he quickly found those on the staff willing to spy on others and carry tales to the Commodore, as he was always called in the office. These spies were rapidly dubbed White Mice by the rest of the Herald staff, and the result of their existence was that Bennett, even when in Paris, knew every bit of gossip about New York. Usually the tales passed along by White Mice, and greedily devoured by Bennett, were cruel and unpleasant. Occasionally, though, the results were humorous. From Paris, Bennett once sent for Edward D. DeWitt, a young Princeton athlete who had been appointed Herald advertising manager. The bewildered man boarded ship and in ten days found himself in Bennett's presence. His employer looked him up and down searchingly. "I've been getting reports about you," he snapped. "They say you're getting fat. Napoleon and his generals won their battles when they were lean. I don't want any fat men around me, but I can see you aren't getting fat. So, all right, get back to New York."

Gross inaccuracy on the part of his White Mice never dampened Bennett's enthusiasm for their undercover reports. He always listened avidly to what they had to say, and acted on their advice. Important men like City Editor George J. Taylor suddenly found themselves in Brooklyn supervising the efforts of a few district reporters as a result of the whispering White Mice. Unlike Pulitzer and Hearst, who often transferred men on whims, Bennett contributed a final twist of the knife by reducing pay as well as rank. Pulitzer and Hearst at least continued to pay the man his old salary.

On at least one occasion Bennett apparently felt twinges of conscience about his raw treatment of subordinates. But in no time he came up with a characteristic rationalization. By abusing his men, he was testing them. As summed up by Thomas G. Alvord, one of his associates:

> The seemingly erratic, unjust, contemptible conduct now and then shown the most deserving members of the staff was designed to put to the severest test the loyalty of the individual. . . . Came he through demotion, reduction of pay, undeserved suspension, designed humiliation, and still remained, steadfast in his devotion to the Herald and its master, taking his dose without complaint or the seeking of a place on some other paper, then Mr. Bennett believed he might be trusted in great temptation and relied on in all emergencies.

The Commodore's fiercest hatred was ever reserved for those who tried to curb him when drunk. Frequently he would race from a fashionable dinner table to the Herald office with an editorial idea to be featured in the paper. His editorials were clumsily written and trite in content, but he printed them in large black type across two columns, so that none could possibly miss his pearls of thought. In the highly alcoholic state in which he usually wrote, Bennett made silly mistakes. One midnight he appeared downtown in full evening attire to insert in an editorial: "This is the last dying kick of the Tammany anaconda." His night city editor, J. I. C. Clarke, tried to explain to his glittering-eyed boss that an anaconda does not kick. It was precisely the wrong thing to say, for Bennett exploded, "That's what m'friends uptown say, that an anaconda can't kick. Got no legs. But that's the fun of it. I want it in, and I'll have it in." Clarke made another try. "Suppose you say squirm," he suggested. Bennett ap-

peared ready to strike him. "Stick to kick," he shouted. Then, liking
the sound of this, he repeated over and over, "Stick-to-kick, Stick-to-
kick, Stick-to-kick." Clarke stuck.

In spite of such lunatic behavior, good men stayed faithfully
with Bennett and even seemed proud to work for him. According to
Don Carlos Seitz, these men developed a hair-shirt attitude toward
working for the Herald. "Some who left or were demoted never felt
themselves again," he states. "They missed the plentiful excitements
of the Herald office." Seitz also finds "something compelling about
the tigerish proprietor with his fickleness and brutality." It was Bennett's loud boast that he never fired a reporter, yet the distinction is
exceedingly fine, since he was a past master at humiliating a man until, spirit broken, the man quit. However, few actually got pink slips
at the Herald, but by the same token the autocratic Commodore was
fanatically determined that no one was ever to resign from his employ. When Managing Editor Ballard Smith went over to Pulitzer,
Bennett's fury of humiliation shook the building. Rampaging
through the office, he shook fists at the ceiling and vowed brutal
vengeance on Smith's person. Smith, however, had wisely departed the office, so the threats were empty. Bennett then decided to
humiliate him in absentia. "Any man can fill that job," he roared.
"Why, I'll make my stenographer managing editor. I'll make the
baseball reporter managing editor. It's no trick to be managing editor." This did not completely satisfy him and, in a burst of inspiration, he turned his spleen on the job itself. "I'll have no managing
editor," he shouted in triumph. "I'll abolish the job." This he instantly did, creating the position of News Editor to handle cable and
telegraph news. Ever as good as his angry word, he first gave this job
to his stenographer (male) and later to the paper's baseball reporter.
Both did well and progressed to greater things.

There was never another managing editor on the Herald.

CHAPTER NINE

The Satrap — II

A<small>T</small> one point, the city of New York, where he could so easily find hard-drinking, hard-driving companions of his own age and background—not to mention a metropolitan newspaper on which to impose his vagrant whims—seemed well on the way to becoming the idiosyncratic Bennett's favorite world city. But after the playboy-publisher had passed the ripe age of thirty-five, he precipitated an event which soured him forever on New York. Or perhaps it is better to say that the city soured on him.

By this time Bennett was the most celebrated member of the Union Club, from which he led gay-blade companions in such drink-induced escapades as riding horses up the steps of Fifth Avenue mansions and into the Newport Casino. It is said that when the notable English playboy Lord Rosebery visited these shores, he found no more compatible spirit than Commodore Bennett. "The two made New York glow together," one chronicle recalls. Rosebery was accounted the most brilliant young man in England, and one memorable night at the Union Club he confided that he had three aims in life: to marry a great heiress, win the Derby, and become Prime Minister. All these he eventually achieved (he married a Rothschild) and each step of accomplishment was wildly applauded in print by his rowdy drinking companion, James Gordon Bennett.

Bennett's escapades were usually of the type that only men could enjoy, but occasionally he permitted himself the company of women. Not unexpectedly, he was partial to flashy girls from the

152

new, daring musical shows in which females wore tights. For a time he showered attention on a reigning Broadway beauty named Pauline Markham, from whose slipper he ostentatiously drank champagne. Yet his interest in a girl was always short-lived. When Pauline fell on evil days Bennett did absolutely nothing to help her, though her sad plight was featured in a story in his own newspaper.

Then it became apparent that Bennett's heart, though seldom visible in the give-and-take of ordinary existence, had been touched by feminine loveliness. Near the Union Club lived the family of Dr. William May. One day the bloodshot eye of James Gordon Bennett fell upon young Caroline May, and soon word circulated through the Four Hundred that the rip-roaring playboy had fallen for her spirited charms. It was then, far more than now, the New Year's Day custom to move merrily from home to home for Egg-Nog parties. On the New Year's of Bennett's devotion to Caroline May, he arrived in due course at the home of the girl he loved, where had also gathered the cream of New York Society. Bennett, of course, was gloriously lit, pounding men on the back and regaling the ladies with crude stories. High Society was quite accustomed to overlooking such antics on the part of the multimillionaire Jimmy Bennett, but it could never overlook what he did next—"a breach of the most primitive good manners." For suddenly Bennett felt a strong urge to relieve himself. In his sodden, happy state, he realized dimly that the nearest bathroom was some distance away. Drunk or sober, Bennett was always a supremely practical person, hewing through obstructions until only the stark reality of his personal desire remained. Now he acted completely in character. In a room crowded with members of New York Society, James Gordon Bennett calmly unbuttoned his trousers and urinated into the roaring fireplace. . . .

As he sobered up the next day, Bennett realized that he had forever lost lovely Caroline May and that from now on, like his father, he would be barred from the better New York homes. His ruthless character probably did not mind either of these losses, but he could also see an end of jolly days at the Union Club. For a fellow member was Frederick May, brother of Caroline, and Bennett well knew that he could expect a considerable reaction from Fred May. In the shortest possible time he discovered what this would be. A day later, as Bennett stepped into his sleigh after a Union Club lunch, Fred May approached with a cowhide whip and began to thrash him, while members of the Club lined the windows to watch.

Bennett stoically endured the first few slashes of the whip, shouting as he did, "Why don't you kill me and get it over with?" Then he made a dive for May, and the two fell fighting in the snow. Club members rushed out to separate them, but now it was Bennett who felt that his honor had been outraged. He challenged Fred May to a duel which, unlike most affairs of honor at this late date, actually was fought. The two men with their seconds journeyed to the aptly named Slaughter's Gap, in Delaware. There Fred May, who appears to have had a redeeming sense of humor, shot into the air. According to his second, Bennett was too nervous to fire accurately and his shot went wild. The two men then considered honor vindicated and departed. Back in New York, Bennett promptly boarded a steamer for Paris, declaring that his native city had dreadfully let him down.

Over the years following, Bennett rampaged Europe like an angry bull, yet he never relaxed his hold on the New York Herald. In a manner that seems fantastic today, he maintained from Paris absolute control of his New York newspaper. At the Park Row office a fresh copy of each edition was tenderly placed on his desk and in the city room the old-timers respectfully touched hats when his name was mentioned. The terrible man was still present.

Partly this was achieved by Bennett's voracious reading of the reports of his faithful White Mice. A more tangible method of keeping well informed was to summon members of the New York staff to Paris. At the slightest whim, the impatient satrap would order a New York Herald reporter to make the long, expensive ocean voyage to Europe. When Bennett decreed, it was useless to refuse or evade. One New York editor was bold enough to rebel when a valuable Herald reporter was senselessly ordered to Paris. "Impossible send So-and-So," he cabled. "Man indispensable." From Paris came the immediate answer, "Send list indispensable men." The names of some ten or twelve important cogs were cabled to Paris. Bennett, who proudly boasted that he never fired anyone, ordered all these men fired. "I will have no indispensable men in my employ," he informed his secretary.

The Commodore summoned men to Paris with such frequency that he often forgot they were coming. At one time he imported a brace of important executives who waited for Bennett in the Paris Herald office. "What in hell are you doing here?" he shouted, on seeing them. "You sent for us," one stammered weakly. "Well, get the hell back to New York," the Commodore commanded.

Worry over the reception to be expected from the irascible Commodore caused some Herald men to lean heavily on liquor before turning up in his presence. Usually the Paris office staff hustled any drunks away before the publisher saw them, but once he called an artist named Dan McCarthy from Park Row for the sole purpose of sketching Bennett and some of his aristocratic friends seated in his plush coach-and-four. McCarthy arrived in Paris and was instructed to continue to an inn in Trouville, near the Bennett stables. Wholly in the dark as to the purpose of his trip, McCarthy got drunk in Paris and in Trouville set about improving his knowledge of the local cognac. Days passed before the coach-and-four driven by the Commodore rolled up to the inn, filled with male and female specimens of European nobility. By this time the cognac in the rugged McCarthy had turned sour. He staggered over to the handsome equipage and inquired, "Say, Bennett! How much do you pay these kings and queens for riding around with you?"

Where some fell back on drink, others tried strategy. Bennett's fondness for tiny dogs was one of the better-known facts about him. Though a big man himself, and ever partial to the larger aspects in life, he was pathologically devoted to small dogs such as Pomeranians and Pekingese. In a period of Chihuahuas, Bennett would have remained in a state of permanent rapture, but as it was he had to get along with such small breeds as his era offered. He constantly issued orders to his editors to print stories praising the intelligence of midget dogs. One of his firm beliefs was that small animals were excellent judges of human character, and he gauged the qualities of callers by the manner in which they were received by his hordes of little animals. Usually Bennett's cables summoning men to him were empty of clues as to the purpose of the summons, but once an indubitably angry blast brought an English correspondent hastening to Paris. Aware that he was in extreme disfavor, the Englishman decided to operate through the dogs. Dressing in top hat and Prince Albert coat, he placed a slice of liver in the hat, while sticking an anise-scented handkerchief in the tail of his coat. Bennett was icy when he appeared, but not so the dogs. They swarmed upon the visitor, sniffing happily, fawning and frolicking about him. Bennett was delighted. Setting aside whatever unpleasant matters had been on his mind, he treated the visitor with the utmost cordiality. He was especially impressed when, at the interview's end, the dogs had to be restrained from following the visitor out the door.

Bennett's interest in tiny animals is one of the more bewildering aspects of a character that has been called fitful and tantalizing. He was, of course, a forceful and aggressive talker, bluntly imposing his own opinions on any conversation. Yet he would always listen quietly to talk of small animals. Once Edward Townsend Flynn and others on the editorial board of the Herald sent him an important cable requesting a change in newspaper policy. For a week the men awaited word from Paris. Finally a cable arrived, to be torn open eagerly. "Send two mockingbirds by special messenger," it read.

The Dog and Bird editor of the Herald was ordered to find a dealer who sold mockingbirds. Two splendid specimens were purchased and dispatched to Paris by trusted messenger. Then the council of editors began again to await an answer to the policy matter. Days passed before the cable spoke. Then it said, "Send mockingbird food." Once more a messenger was dispatched with the proper food. In time he returned to report that Bennett's interest in mockingbirds had been aroused when he regaled a dinner table with praise of the melodious merits of the American mockingbird. A British lady guest had dared to contradict him, insisting that the English mockingbird sang a sweeter song. To prove the correctness of his statements, Bennett had cabled for the birds. Then it was found that no mockingbird food was available in France. No reply, incidentally, ever came in answer to the council's query on policy.

Another matter capable of arousing the Commodore was human hair. Though possessed of a luxuriant, drooping mustache himself, he

liked those around him to be clean-shaven. He also objected violently to unusual haircuts. Through the tireless reports of his White
Mice he at one point learned that Charles Henry Meltzer, a music
critic newly hired by the New York Herald, affected what in those
times was called a Buster Brown haircut. The Commodore imperi-
ously cabled: "Tell Meltzer cut his hair."

Meltzer, made of stern stuff, refused. This was duly relayed to
Paris by anonymous letter. Bennett decided to give the culprit one
more chance and cabled: "Has Meltzer cut his hair?" "No," the
New York office replied, at which Bennett cabled: "Send him St.
Petersburg." Meltzer had no sooner completed the arduous journey
to Russia when the Herald correspondent there received the query:
"Has Meltzer cut his hair?" Informed that Meltzer still resembled
a superannuated Buster Brown, Bennett wired: "Send him Berlin."
After being shunted to other European capitals—but not, it must be
noted, to Paris—Meltzer was ordered home. On landing, he was fired
by the man who never fired anyone. Meltzer sued and, it is gratifying to report, collected damages from Bennett and the Herald.

With his crudeness and arrogance, Bennett was not without a
certain mordant humor. One issue of the Paris Herald carried a letter
signed "Old Philadelphia Lady," requesting information about how
Centigrade thermometer readings could be rendered into Fahrenheit.
Bennett was delighted by this naïve epistle and when, by a printer's
error, it was repeated a second day, ordered that it be run daily. For
years the old lady's request solemnly appeared in the Paris Herald.
But this was not the only use to which the letter was put. When
replying nastily to letters which had annoyed him, Bennett often
signed himself "Old Philadelphia Lady."

If Bennett, the satrap, functioned as a hair shirt to those around
him, he could also do the same for himself. This was made quite apparent by his choice of a permanent Paris mistress. In middle life,
he fell under the spell of the wife of a Russian general resident in
Paris. Long before he met her, this large, commanding female had
the reputation of being the most unpleasant woman in Paris. By
some alchemy, Bennett—who may well have been the most unpleasant man—felt drawn to her, and the two begun a liaison that lasted
for years. However, they seldom appeared together in public, and

because of this few members of Bennett's staff had an idea what the Commodore's mistress looked like. Albert Stevens Crockett, dining one night in a quiet Paris restaurant, found his meal ruined by a woman talking loudly in a rasping, disagreeable voice. Never had Crockett seen a female order men about with such viciousness, relish, or bad humor. "Who is that?" he finally inquired. The headwaiter bent low to whisper, "That, sir, is the *chère amie* of your chief."

The headaches of the New York and Paris staffs—already weighty—increased hugely when Bennett used six hundred and twenty-five thousand of the thirty million dollars he spent in his life-time to build one of the most elegant steam yachts of his yacht-conscious time. This he named the *Lysistrata* after, he would say, a Greek lady reputed to be very beautiful and very fast. Contemporary accounts state that *palatial* was the only word to describe the *Lysistrata*: no royal yacht was so splendidly equipped. Bennett's peculiarities immediately became manifest when he ordered a suite of rooms built for himself on each of the *Lysistrata*'s three decks so that he could always make use of the one nearest him.

One hundred men—all clean-shaven—were required to operate the *Lysistrata*, which also boasted a complete Turkish bath for Bennett's use. But perhaps the most unusual feature of the sleek and gorgeous craft was that it provided quarters for an Alderney cow, since Bennett insisted on fresh milk with certain meals. A young Paris Herald reporter felt deeply honored when Bennett invited him to weekend on the luxurious yacht. But instead of taking him out to sea, Bennett piled him in a gig and the two began scouring the countryside for another Alderney cow to take the place of a current one, which showed an unfortunate tendency toward seasickness. About twenty miles inland Bennett found a satisfactory cow. He immediately bought it and handed the rope to the young reporter. "Here," he said, "lead the cow back to the yacht." He himself raced off in the gig.

No one who boarded the *Lysistrata* ever quite knew what to expect. For no fathomable reason, the Commodore objected to card-playing aboard. On arrival the baggage of all guests was searched for decks of cards. If found, these were carried to the Commodore, who personally rendered them useless by tearing up the aces. It was often Bennett's expensive pleasure to anchor in a harbor and bring a local theatrical troupe aboard to entertain his guests. At Amsterdam, he enjoyed such a performance so much that he put out to sea, taking the protesting actors with him. By far the most trying of the Commodore's nautical peculiarities was his firm refusal ever to change the *Lysistrata's* course. Battleships, transatlantic liners, the most formidable craft afloat, had to make way for the James Gordon Bennett yacht. The Commodore's iron-willed steering cowed all vessels in his course.

Soon after the Spanish-American War, the goateed James Creelman wearied of Hearst's employ. Bennett learned this and immediately hired him for the Herald. Creelman was ordered to report to Bennett aboard the *Lysistrata,* but at the gangplank found his way barred because no bearded men were allowed aboard. "But Mr. Bennett expects me," Creelman protested. The quartermaster was adamant. "You can't set foot aboard until you've shaved your beard off," he stated. "The Commodore permits no one aboard who isn't clean-shaven."

Creelman, like the heroic Meltzer, refused to be shorn. He obtained the itinerary of the *Lysistrata* and followed the yacht from port to port, attempting to board at each. He abandoned this in Fiume and returned to Paris to await a dry-land meeting with his new employer. Had he continued to follow the *Lysistrata,* he might have witnessed what remains perhaps the most Bennett-like incident of all. On the Greek coast the publisher debarked with his guests to inspect a monastery which boasted a lamp that had been burning for over a thousand years. This impressed Bennett greatly. "You say this lamp has never been out in all that time?" he barked at one of the guiding monks. The monk assured him the lamp had indeed been lighted for more than ten centuries. At which Bennett leaned over and blew out the tiny, flickering flame. "Well, it's out now," he announced.

Like Creelman, another Hearst stalwart now surprisingly entered the Bennett service. This was Sam Chamberlain, who, perhaps because of jealousy over the eminence of Arthur Brisbane, quit the Journal in 1899. Bennett immediately imported him to Paris, to act as a right-hand man. Oddly enough, working for a man made mad by drink seemed to have a soothing effect on the elegant drunkard of Park Row. In all stories concerning the two, Chamberlain soberly protects Bennett from the results of his wild excesses. Perhaps the most notable of these occasions came when, in the course of some sustained tippling, Bennett suddenly decided that the New York Herald had been accused of pro-Catholic bias. "I'll show them," he bellowed. To Chamberlain, he dictated an editorial containing such pyrotechnic phrases as *To Hell with the Pope. . . . Tear down the monasteries. . . . Drive out the monks. . . . No more political interference from Rome.* Then he cocked a crafty eye at Chamberlain. "You've fooled me before by not sending cables you thought would get us in trouble," he said. "This one I'm going to send myself."

So saying, he lurched to the office of his own cable company where he carefully filed the editorial. Not for ten days did he sober up sufficiently to remember the indiscretion. Then, summoning Chamberlain to his bedside, he nervously asked if something had not been sent to the Herald abusing the Catholic Church. Chamberlain was equal to the occasion. Straight-faced, he replied, "Commodore, I thought the editorial might not be strong enough. I called it back from the operator with a view to letting you read it over again." Whereupon he produced the editorial. Bennett read it, then put his throbbing head back on the pillow. "Thank God," he breathed fervently. That afternoon, as he and Chamberlain went for a carriage ride, Bennett unexpectedly ordered a stop at a jeweler's, where he purchased an expensive cat's-eye ring. Wordlessly he handed it to Chamberlain.

Such episodes the experienced Chamberlain could take in stride. But nearly a year later, in Marseille harbor, he stood beside the Commodore in the steering cabin of the *Lysistrata* while Bennett headed straight toward an American man-of-war which he cursed roundly for being off course. Chamberlain urged Bennett to give way to the larger ship. Bennett profanely refused, continuing a course which would strike the battlewagon directly amidships. Suddenly Sam Chamberlain could take no more. Grabbing the wheel in Bennett's hands, he gave a violent wrench, swinging the *Lysistrata* away from the battleship. Never in his lifetime had James Gordon Bennett been so violently thwarted, and he stood speechless and apoplectic while the enormity of it sank in. Chamberlain, after one look at the Commodore's vengeful face, departed the cabin. As fast as a boat could be lowered, he left the ship, never to set eyes on Bennett again. For a time the elegant Sam worked in Paris on Le Matin. Then, having had his fill of independence, he returned happily to Hearst.

One day in Paris, Bennett sat down in a comfortable armchair in his apartment, only to find something digging unpleasantly into him. It turned out to be a large roll of bills in his trouser pocket. In a shouting fury he extracted the roll, cursed it and hurled it into the fireplace. A newspaperman to whom he was talking watched with fascination as the flames drew closer, noting that the roll seemed to be American fifties and twenties. When Bennett turned aside for a moment, the newspaperman grabbed the bills from the fire and gave them back, with the remark that he had just saved the bills from burning.

"Perhaps that's how I wanted them," Bennett roared. With that he threw the bills into the fire again. This time they landed irredeemably in the middle of the fire. . . .

Back on Park Row, William Randolph Hearst heard such stories, as well as accounts of the adventures of Creelman and Chamberlain. They caused him to ponder the curious expatriate existence of James Gordon Bennett. Could the man's frenzied existence in Paris indicate a lack of interest in the New York Herald?

Since 1898 Hearst's career had undergone some involutions. He had branched out to buy a newspaper in Chicago and was wet-nursing publishing properties in other American cities. Still, his reputation as a publisher had suffered a severe blow. With the end of the Spanish-American War, Hearst's hatred of President McKinley had not abated. It even seemed to grow, with Journal editorials becoming so vitriolic as almost to advocate the assassination of the beleaguered President. In an editorial deploring McKinley's election to a second term, the Journal actually said, "If bad men cannot be got rid of except by killing, then the killing must be done."

Then, in 1901, McKinley was assassinated. In the eyes of many,

Hearst was to blame for planting the idea in the madman's mind. Among many other things, the jingoist publisher was now accused of being un-American. To thwart these charges, he deftly renamed his New York newspaper the American-Journal. He also began to think seriously of a political career and formed a close alliance with Tammany Hall. On November 4, 1902, he was elected to the House of Representatives from the Tammany-controlled Eleventh District in New York. So came a proud and happy moment for Hearst who, despite the calumny still being heaped on his head, began looking down the golden road to the Presidency.

But as so often happens omissions in his character thwarted him. Hearst's election from the Tammany district had been a foregone conclusion, and to celebrate, the American-Journal sponsored a monster election-night fireworks display at Madison Square. A large crowd gathered to enjoy the excitement. The actual display was to begin only after the results came in, but before this an explosion shook the pile of fireworks. Others followed, and in minutes the ground reverberated from one ominous explosion after another. Heavy smoke drifted over the area and the frantic crowd panicked, running in all directions at once. Seventeen people were killed and an equal number crippled for life.

This was bad. But worse was Hearst's apparent cowardice in accepting responsibility for the explosion. Every New York newspaper except the American-Journal carried a front-page story of the tragedy. The American-Journal buried it on page five, with no mention that the explosions had occurred at a Hearst-sponsored rally. Nor would Hearst ever admit personal connection with the tragedy, though suits against him (charging carelessness) mounted to three million dollars and took twenty years to settle.

Coming so soon after the McKinley assassination, the fireworks explosion finished Hearst with thinking people. But the new member of the House of Representatives did not appear aware of it. Indeed, he took two steps calculated to win great favor with the voting public. He married and changed his manner of dress. No longer did he wear the clothes of a sportsman or gambler. Instead, he began affecting a black frock coat and black slouch hat. According to Frederick Palmer in Collier's: "The outsiders who saw him did not meet a man in a check suit, accompanied by two or three beautiful girls, but a silent, listening man in that inevitable frock coat."

It was this new, serious Hearst who, after considering the seemingly irresponsible antics of James Gordon Bennett in Paris, decided that the New York Herald might be available for purchase. Accordingly, he one day cabled James Gordon Bennett: "Is the Herald for sale?" As Hearst knew, Bennett's contempt for him was of the monumental variety. Where Pulitzer would give his Yellow Journalism rival credit for being a genius at exploitation, Bennett would credit him with nothing except overweening gall. Whenever Hearst's name was mentioned in his presence Bennett would snort, chew his mustache and mutter profanely. To receive such a cable from this ludicrous upstart was a downright insult to Bennett, yet with great difficulty he controlled himself and answered: "Price of Herald three cents daily. Five cents Sunday. Bennett."

So began a feud of considerable magnitude and in time Hearst, pride stung by Bennett's cable, had another reason for resenting the arrogant absentee publisher. When Hearst papers proudly announced that their publisher planned to run for the office of Mayor of New York, the Herald responded by promising to oppose Hearst if he ran for so much as catcher of dogs. This was, perhaps, a mistake. For the Herald, vaunted family newspaper though it might be, possessed a vulnerable spot. From his father's regime, Bennett had inherited a Personals column. With his pioneering interest in want ads and real-estate columns, Bennett had been highly partial to the Personals.

In the elder Bennett's day, the Herald Personals had unashamedly become a place where whores advertised their wares and announced changes of address. Shortly before his death, the elder Bennett had been forced to clear this up and the Personal column had remained pure until 1894. Then Dr. Parkhurst's moral crusade temporarily drove prostitution underground, and the Herald Personals again began to display a wide-open aspect. Eccentrics and the romantically inclined continued to advertise, yet covertly but unmistakably prostitutes and houses of prostitution began taking over. Some such ads seemed innocuous, for instance: "YOUNG LADY, Good Figure, wants to pose for artist; references exchanged; positively no triflers." But in others advertising Swedish massage parlors with "young lady masseurs," Turkish baths, and dubious rooming houses with "female clientele," triflers were plainly encouraged. In addition, some of the more enterprising Personals users employed anagrams which spelled out obscenities. Several times Edward Townsend Flynn and other Bennett aides had called the Commodore's attention to the abuses of the Personals column, adding for emphasis that along Park Row the Herald Personals were called The Whore's Daily Guide and Handy Compendium. Bennett impatiently swept these words aside. Personals rates were high, alone bringing the Herald some two hundred thousand dollars in annual revenue. But a more compelling reason for Bennett's attitude may have been that the earthy man believed his Personals provided a necessary public service.

Every New York newspaper was aware of the excesses of the Herald Personals, but from a sense of journalistic fair play kept silent. Still, anyone anxious to injure Bennett had an easy course laid out before him. Hearst was eager to harm Bennett, and to the task of exposing the Herald Personal ads he assigned Victor Watson, a reporter so ruthless that Hearst himself once declared that there was room for only one such man in any organization. For a full year Watson tracked down the Herald ads, discovering manicure shops where manicures were unheard-of, massage parlors where massages were rare, and Turkish baths better left undescribed. His findings broke in a lurid series of articles in the Hearst papers—by that time the Morning Journal was called New York American—while simultaneously Solomon Solis Carvalho, acting for Hearst, gravely presented Watson's fascinating material to the United States Grand Jury. This august body read it avidly and was so shocked that it indicted Bennett for using the mails for obscene purposes. At a trial, he was found guilty in absentia and fined twenty-five thousand dollars.

This was a harsh blow to the Herald, which began drastically to lose its family circulation. The Sunday Herald declined particularly, allowing Hearst to lure away some of its more potent comics. In Paris, Bennett fulminated and vowed he would never pay the fine which, since it had been levied on him personally, could be evaded as long as he remained abroad or on the *Lysistrata*. Yet he obviously felt the

stigma of the fine, for one day in the summer of 1907 the lovely
Lysistrata suddenly appeared in New York Harbor, where it sailed ma-
jestically up the Hudson to dock at Seventy-ninth Street. Bennett remained aboard until late afternoon, then was whisked by a devilish
motorcar to Federal Court, where he contemptuously paid the fine
in cash. Returning to the *Lysistrata,* he immediately set sail for Europe: it was a day when millionaires' yachts crossed the Atlantic as
easily as ocean liners.

For the second time in his life, in Bennett's candid opinion, his
native city had let him down.

One final distinction remains to James Gordon Bennett. He was
the first newspaper publisher to leave Park Row.

From distant Paris, as early as 1894, the real-estate-conscious Bennett became aware that the heart of New York was slowly moving
uptown. But there was another motivation behind Bennett's
thoughts of moving. The irascible man could not tolerate tenants in
any building he owned. In the Herald Building on Park Row were
several, impossible to dislodge because the leases had been given in
perpetuity by Bennett Senior.

Smoldering over this, Bennett began thinking of an exclusive,
small building which would be his alone. After consultation with
Stanford White, the big gun of the architectural firm McKim, Mead
and White, he decided to build a duplicate of one of the most
beautiful buildings the world has ever known: the Palazzo del Con-
siglio, in Verona. With White as architect, the building was erected
on Broadway between Thirty-fifth and Thirty-sixth Streets. This site
was then so far uptown that the beautiful Herald Building brought
great prominence to the district. A guidebook puts it this way: "The
Herald's uptown move boomed uptown. Great stores and hotels
sprang up around it and in due time the huge terminal of the
Pennsylvania and Long Island Railroads added importance to the
center then named and still called Herald Square."

Throughout the construction of his delicate new building, Bennett remained in Paris, but he also remained Bennett. He bombarded Stanford White with conflicting orders and feuded with his
business manager because, on White's recommendation, that func-

tionary bought from Tiffany a fourteen-thousand-dollar silver desk set of the Palazzo period for Bennett's personal use. "Pay for it out of your own salary," the cable thundered. The general manager, visioning such a large sum being extracted from his weekly stipend, quickly faded from the scene, but as always Bennett had the last word: he left the man the embattled desk set in his will.

Then, having maintained he would endure no tenants, Bennett was persuaded to offer space to a branch post office because this would greatly benefit his beloved advertising columns. Having reluctantly acquiesced in this, he immediately presented a snag by refusing to accept rent from the Government. The Government, in turn, declared that it could not use the premises free. Finally a nominal rental of fifty dollars a month was agreed upon, and the Herald Square Post Office began functioning.

Yet the crowning irony was the building itself. Undeniably beautiful, it was only another monument to the Commodore's temperament and idiosyncrasies. The idea of crowding a lusty American newspaper office into an Italian palazzo may have appeared sensible to his boiling mind, but those who began working in the building quickly found otherwise. In the words of the sapient Don Carlos Seitz:

> The building was a model of good taste, but not convenient. Situated on an island, so to speak, it had no room for expansion such as was soon needed. The composing-room, up under a hip roof, was hot and low. The typesetting machine operators had to sit under the eaves. Besides, the building was on leased land with but twenty-five years to run. Pulitzer once told Bennett in Paris, when he heard this, that he [Pulitzer] could not sleep nights with his building on another man's land. Bennett dryly replied that he would not be on hand to worry about it, which became true, though he worried a good deal just the same.

CHAPTER TEN

The Favored Ones: DAVID GRAHAM PHILLIPS

O NE evening several months after the turn of the century, a tall, wide-shouldered, beautifully attired editorial writer on the World, named David Graham Phillips, stood at the top of the steps to the Hotel Brevoort on lower Fifth Avenue. He was conversing with the French author-explorer Paul Du Chaillu, whose first books about the wilds of Africa had been greeted in the United States as exaggerated, but now were recognized as truthful accounts of such areas as the Gorilla Country, which in fact was the name of Du Chaillu's most celebrated book. The Frenchman was a voluble talker, with an explorer's freedom of speech. Standing with Phillips on this particular night, he had over his arm several skins of rare African monkeys, and as he gesticulated a pungent odor from them is remembered as wafted into the warm spring night.

As the two men talked, a Victoria drew to the curb below and through the light of the lamps on the sidewalk, Richard Harding Davis could be seen handing out a beautiful young girl. As the handsome pair of young celebrities mounted the steps—the girl's glove white on Davis's black sleeve—Du Chaillu stopped talking. As they moved by, he craned his neck to watch the slim girl pass into the doorway. Only after the ethereal couple had disappeared did Du Chaillu realize that Davis, whom he knew well, had not spoken. Nor had he given David Graham Phillips more than a quick nod. Du Chaillu's volubility turned to anger. What was the matter, he demanded furiously. Why had his friend Davis not spoken and why—

far more important to the Frenchman—had he not been introduced to the lovely young girl?

It may have been an embarrassing moment for David Graham Phillips. More likely it was not. For Du Chaillu's indignant questions were of a kind he was well equipped to answer. Every bit as confidently as Richard Harding Davis himself, he was in a position to inform Du Chaillu that his robust conversation, flowing rapidly between two languages and tinged with an adventurer's roughness, might in some way have given offense to a delicately reared young lady. Du Chaillu looked astounded, but Phillips went on. It was the duty of a gentleman, he said, to protect any lady companion from embarrassment, from the slightest contact with the sordid side of life, or even reality. Such was the first tenet of a strict gentleman's code, and it was incumbent on correspondents and Park Row newspapermen to enforce it more vigorously than other males. For were they not the outstanding men of their time . . . ?

As the 1950's approach the 1960's, newspapermen are universally taken for granted. Their photographs, when printed, show them to be only too average in appearance and their work, though somewhat different, operates on the same principles as other business. A newspaperman today is just another workingman. Hence it is almost impossible to conceive of an era when the newspaperman, as represented by Richard Harding Davis, held one of the most important of contemporary jobs.

Davis was the handsomest man of his time, the most envied male alive, the Clark Gable-and-infinitely-more of the period. Anyone backward enough to remain unaware of his front-page dispatches from far-off regions where wars were fought knew instead that Davis's square-jawed handsomeness, with his clean-cut profile, high gentlemanly collar, and hair parted in the middle, had been taken by the artist Charles Dana Gibson as the model for the fortunate companion of the most famous girl of the era. Richard Harding Davis was the model for the Gibson Man, whose amorous involvements with the gorgeous Gibson Girl set the pattern of romantic love for the time. True, Gibson had done his close friend a slight favor in making him into the Gibson Man, for Davis—if the truth be known —was a trifle compact and solid to be the masculine beau ideal. Gibson had given him an additional inch in height, and an attractive angularity as well, to create the most celebrated male figure alive. Thus, while young men gazed at the willowy, high-pompadoured Gibson Girls, young girls in greater quantity sighed over the resolute, immaculate Gibson Man, knowing full well he was really the great newspaper correspondent, Richard Harding Davis.

However, the Davis eminence was largely the result of his own accomplishments. He not only covered wars and the coronations of kings and queens, but was the author of short stories glorifying the excitements of newspaper life. He also wrote best-selling novels and hit plays, and had created a character named Cortlandt Van Bibber who, though a trifle languid and disdainful, dressed perfectly and in moments of crisis forgot his aristocratic hauteur to behave according to the high gentleman's code Davis personally advocated.

Van Bibber's speech, attire and manners had much affected the behavior of his time, but in 1900 Davis had ceased writing of him. Instead, by his own eminence as the most successful writer of the time and as the Gibson Man, Davis was personally influencing his time as much as Van Bibber had done. Young boys no longer dreamed of becoming President: they dreamed of becoming Richard Harding Davis. In the words of Thomas Beer, "He mounted into celebrity as gracefully as he might have swung his fine body in its handsome clothes to the cushions of a waiting hansom cab. He rode, a figure of pleasant sophistication and fresh good humor, among passengers who lacked those qualities . . . and boys laboring with manuscripts looked up and saw a star."

On Park Row, where he began his New York newspaper career on the Sun in 1889, Davis had become something of a remote star as a result of his world fame. Where once he had covered the city like any other reporter, his superior dispatches now came from places like the Balkans, Mongolia, South Africa, or Honduras. Davis loved New York and returned there as often as possible, but even so he was seldom seen around Park Row. He did his gentlemanly drinking at the Waldorf Bar, an uptown shrine of Bacchus far beyond the pocketbook of the average newspaperman, where the popping of champagne corks was never stilled during the cocktail hour. When Davis dined, it would be at Delmonico's, which he would enter strikingly with a society or theatrical beauty resembling the Gibson Girl on his arm. After the theatre he might appear at Rector's, escorting Ethel Barrymore or Cissie Loftus, the two most spectacular ingénues of the day. The paragon couple would be the center of discreet attention, their table visited only by such comparable celebrities as the rotund Victor Herbert, or Lillian Russell and Diamond Jim Brady.

But if Park Row appeared to have lost the great Richard Harding Davis, it still possessed a star of its own. This was the wonderfully dressed David Graham Phillips who had conversed with Paul Du Chaillu on the Brevoort steps. Only slightly less than Davis, Phillips appeared before the world as the ideal male of his time. His face was as clean-cut and strong-jawed as that of Davis, though perhaps not quite so preternaturally stern. Where Davis fell an inch or so below classic male perfection, Phillips did not. He stood a strapping six foot three and had the spare, casual leisureliness that had been given Davis in the drawings of the Gibson Man. Where Davis's hair was black, his was brown, also parted severely in the middle. His eyes were deep blue, his face serious, his smile sunny, winning and magnetic. On close acquaintance, Phillips offered more. According to one friend, "he had that rarest of gifts, which is charm." His biographer, Isaac F. Marcosson, has expressed it more succinctly. "He was pure personality," he recalls.

Phillips was born in Madison, Indiana, at a time when the Hoosier state was contributing enormously to the literary flavor of the United States. General Lew Wallace, author of the mighty seller *Ben Hur*, had practically made the state a literary shrine. Younger writers like James Whitcomb Riley, George Barr McCutcheon, George Ade, Meredith Nicholson and (shortly) Booth Tarkington, made Indiana and successful popular writing synonymous. Even so, as a growing boy, Phillips manifested no interest in such a career. His father was the local banker, making the family well-to-do if not rich. For reasons never quite explained, young Graham was educated at home by private tutors, which may account for the somewhat remote attitude toward his fellow men that accompanied him through life.

Phillips went to Princeton—then known as the College of New Jersey—where he became friendly with the four sons of the Halstead family of Cincinnati. Murat Halstead was a well-known figure along Park Row, and others of the family owned newspapers in Ohio. Stories of newspaper adventures recounted by the four Halstead boys kindled a fire in Phillips. Graduating from Princeton at the early age of nineteen, he immediately hastened to Cincinnati for a newspaper job. His method of attack is revealing. College graduates were much in demand in city rooms of the era, and Phillips might also have used the influence of the Halstead family. He did neither, since even at an early age the upright code by which he had decided to live precluded the use of friends for personal gain.

Phillips placed still another barrier in his own path. At nineteen he had already begun to affect the sort of extravagant attire which would later cause him to be hailed as the most perfectly dressed man in Manhattan. The strapping youth first appeared on the premises of the Cincinnati Times-Star wearing a high, white starched collar, conspicuously patterned suit, pink shirt, high pearl-button shoes and waistcoat of flowery hue. All this was bad, but far worse, he ostentatiously puffed a cigarette, when he-men of the day would touch only cigars. (Later Richard Harding Davis bravely wore a wrist watch, thus putting this effeminate timepiece on the road to universal use.)

Against the unfortunate impression made by his dandified attire, Phillips's college degree and pure personality were of little use. He was curtly informed that no job was open on the Times-Star. As his later newspaper career would show, Phillips was a man of determination and resource. He requested permission to remain around the office for a few days, familiarizing himself with newspapers that came in from other cities. There was no valid reason for refusing such an innocent request to the overdressed young college man, and he was given a desk. There he calmly established himself and in time the inevitable happened—as he was confident it would. One day when all available reporters had been dispatched to cover one story, a fire broke out elsewhere. In desperation the city editor sent Phillips. He returned with his remarkable attire as unsoiled as ever, and the story he wrote fully matched his appearance. It showed that, instead of studying out-of-town papers, he had been studying the Times-Star. The story was impeccable, even to such stylistic matters as commas and capitals. All the city editor had to do was write a heading and, having done this, he peered up at the elegant young man waiting beside his desk. "You don't need any training, you're a born newspaperman already," he admitted grudgingly. Phillips nodded. He had known this all along.

It was merely a matter of time before the talented Phillips made his appearance on Park Row. It also goes without saying that, once there, he would work on the distinguished Sun. Phillips climbed the spiral stairs to that paper's city room in May, 1890. As he did he may have heard the uncertain clicks of the typewriter just purchased for the office (Dana's male secretary used it), or noticed on the wall the single hand-crank telephone, which was equally new. Dana, who knew of his work in Cincinnati, promptly hired Phillips at fifteen dollars a week. Though he had gained rich experience in Ohio, he was, like all cubs, broken in for New York by an assignment to the most sordid story in the city. This was the Jefferson Market—or Prostitute's—Court.

Some young reporters seemed able to take Jefferson Market in stride, but men like Lincoln Steffens, Charles Edward Russell and Phillips never could. The sight of the hollow justice meted out to women young and old shocked all three into thinking along sociological lines—though Steffens, of course, had started before reaching New York. It was plain to anyone who set foot inside the court that it functioned as an adjunct to the underworld. A prostitute brought there under arrest had usually been turned in by pimp, procurer, or venal cop. Her arrest was merely a warning of what might happen if she did not obey or pay off. Just before sentence was passed, the pimp would step up to pay the girl's fine. Then, with a menacing grip on her arm, he would lead her out.

Pimps and procurers also stood around waiting to pay the fines for new girls brought in by the police. But most distressing to any thinking person was the lack of real justice or attempt at rehabilitation. For most prostitutes, a ten-day sentence on Welfare Island was merely a necessary interruption of activity. Shortly the girl would be standing before the same judge again, receiving precisely the same sentence. It was a pointless judicial treadmill, steeped in all the viciousness which the era was capable of displaying.

Also in the Sun city room in 1890 was Richard Harding Davis. He, too, had been disgusted by Jefferson Market Court and, having been relieved of that assignment, felt obliged to write home that, though his stories of Tenderloin brothels and dance halls where girls gathered were graphic and knowing, he had visited them only in line of duty. He, too, had first appeared in the Sun city room resplendently attired and because of his clothes had almost immediately gained the attention of New York City.

Davis was riding the Jersey City ferry one day when a notorious con man named Sheeny Mike noted his forthright countenance, ruddy complexion and fine clothes and decided that here was a newly arrived young Englishman ripe for swindling. The con man approached and opened negotiations for the sale of a rare painting. Davis listened with every evidence of belief. But when the boat landed, he collared the plausible rascal and shouted loudly for the police. In the Sun office, he wrote a humorous story of his exploit, and New York roared with approving laughter. Because it was such a personal story he was permitted a by-line. Thus for the first time the metropolis heard of Richard Harding Davis.

In looks, talent, sartorial interest and ambition Davis and Phillips seem almost identical. Yet the two never became close friends, or even friends at all. The reason remains hidden deep in the personalities of each. Davis had already decided that he wished to travel the world, covering wars and other tremendous events, then write novels and plays based on them. Phillips's ambition was the same: he also dreamed of writing novels and plays. It was one of the paradoxes of his character that this seemingly relaxed and leisurely man nursed a relentless ambition. "Get a fixed purpose and never deviate from it," he liked to advise his fellow man. Sometimes he amended this dictum in a manner with which many will disagree. "Remember," he once counseled a struggling young author, "that working with a fixed purpose in life can be just as amusing as drinking champagne." From his first days as a reporter, Phillips's own fixed purpose was to work as a newspaperman for ten years, then start writing novels. The novels would be something unusual for those times. They were to be unsparingly realistic, spelling out such sordid scenes as the Jef-

ferson Market Court. "I will have no mission, no cult," Phillips
stated. "I will just be a novelist, telling as accurately as I can, what
I see."

Where Davis seemed to feel it necessary to roam the world to
find material, Phillips seemed to consider New York—or the United
States—made to order for him. This may have been the reason for
the lack of real understanding between the two men. Each possibly
respected the other's aims, as well as the province in which the other
chose to work. But there was no solid ground—interest in fancy
clothes was not a primary preoccupation with either—on which the
two could meet. Park Row may have been another factor which kept
the two apart. For oddly enough Davis, though enthusiastic, frank
and friendly, was not much liked by his working-press colleagues.
According to Chester A. Lord, one of the famed managing editors
of the Sun, "his enthusiasm and naïveté, his rigidity of code and
self-dramatization . . . clashed with the cynicism and surface sophistication of many newspapermen and caused them to dislike him."

Strangely Phillips—so stalwart, rugged and stern—had precisely
the quality which others found lacking in Davis. Though seemingly
so favored by life, Phillips's outlook could be cynical, almost defeat-
ist. A later critic would call this "a confused Nietzscheism," for his
cynicism remained immature and callow all through life. Exactly as
if he had never been able to assimilate the discovery in adolescence
that all females are not pure, he remained forever bitter about
women. "The American woman is hopeless," he wrote in one novel.
"Her vanity is triple-plated, copper-riveted."

He felt the same way about the institution of marriage, apparently for the same reason. "Even if you are by some accident happily
married . . . ," he wrote a friend. Always it seemed that Phillips,
reared in a God-worshipping family, had failed to assimilate the
youthful discovery that this is an impure world and that women
and marriage can be among its impurities. Still, it was this quality
in such a handsome man which largely won Phillips's colleagues to
him, when they could not like the outgoing Davis. It even increased
his charm, for it was a quick cynicism, the sort that in his epic novel,
Susan Lenox: Her Fall and Rise, allowed him to insert a sally which
shocked the nation. Susan, an occasional streetwalker, flounces past a

Salvation Army lassie who calls out, "The wages of sin is death." To which Susan replies, "Yes, but it's often a mansion on Fifth Avenue." Phillips's own cynicism was of the same amusing variety. It was also tempered by tolerance and good feeling. "There was no sting to it," states Isaac F. Marcosson.

After he had been on Park Row for several years, Phillips uttered a much-quoted remark that did almost as much as Richard Harding Davis to encourage contemporary boys in dreams of becoming big-city reporters. "I would rather be a reporter than President," Phillips declared. He meant it. This feeling he carried to every story he ever wrote, and it made him similar to Davis in that, no matter what his personal immaturities, he could put color and distinction into accounts of anything that took place before his eyes. This skill as a newspaperman, together with his great size, also allowed him to get away with his colorful excesses in dress. He was perhaps the gaudiest dresser of his time, a man who stepped into tailor shops and ordered entire suits made of fancy waistcoat material. Proudly he wore the stiffest, most upright starched collars of his period. He alone seemed able to wear these. Once he loaned such a collar to a Park Row colleague, who wore it into the city room of the Journal. There he was instantly spotted by Arthur Brisbane who, in a rare moment of levity, quipped, "Somewhere behind that collar there must be a face."

Phillips not only wore the highest collars of his—and perhaps any—time, but each morning he fixed in his buttonhole the largest white chrysanthemum his florist could provide. Bedecked in his extravagant clothes, wearing the sprawling chrysanthemum and a gaily patterned shirt, as well as puffing one of the cigarettes the world called effeminate, Phillips went out on routine assignments in his early days as a New York reporter. Besides the Jefferson Market Court, he covered fires, domestic squabbles, gang fights, suicides, murders, rapes and collisions. But no tough Boweryite ever picked on him or mocked his flowery dress. He looked so rugged and strong that his picturesque garb was accepted as a personal idiosyncrasy and left at that.

It has been said that fortune favors those who conspicuously bid for it, and a man like Phillips did not remain a routine reporter long. After less than a year on the Sun, he was sent to Hudson,

New York, on a story involving the disappearance of a child. He accompanied search parties through the woods and was present when the child was found. The result was the kind of story that makes editors cheer and the public weep. Today it seems saccharine, but Phillips's lost-child story was then considered a Park Row classic. Almost overnight, the critic Granville Hicks has written:

> Phillips name became almost legendary. Wherever he went journalists gathered about him, though even his friends were amused at the height of his collars and the conspicuousness of his clothes. . . . But they could not deny him the position of leadership he had unconsciously assumed. Tall enough to stand out in any group, he attracted attention by the impressiveness of his name and the severity of his expression.

To Phillips, ever alert to his master plan of ten years of newspaper work before attempting realistic fiction, it soon became apparent that what has been called the seasoned serenity of the Sun was failing to provide a storehouse of material for the future. In 1892, he switched to the World, finding it all he had hoped: "a maelstrom of ideas and action." The maelstrom increased when Joseph Pulitzer learned that such a talented young man had joined the World staff. Pulitzer sent for him immediately. The blind publisher could not see, but easily could sense, Phillips's commanding physical presence. He liked this, and also enjoyed his stimulating talk. "I need you to cheer me up," he frequently wired Phillips from one or the other of his American estates.

Pulitzer traveled to England early in 1893 and took Phillips with him, placing him in London as that city's World correspondent. Unlike Davis, who quickly became an Anglophile and bought Bond Street clothes, Phillips never warmed to the English. Rather, he retained an Indiana-like suspicion of them as foreigners. He soon indicated to Pulitzer that he wished to return home, but the crafty publisher kept him in London by dangling a promise of that nirvana of the newspaperman's dreams—a by-line. This was the period in which the Park Row offices of the World were kept in seething turmoil by the regimes of Colonel Harvey, Colonel Jones and other irritating Pulitzer appointees. Practically the first idea to smite any new Park Row editor was to cable the London correspondent, ordering him to secure an exclusive interview with Queen Victoria. Phillips became increasingly annoyed by the frequency of this cable, with its impossible order. He increased pressure on Pulitzer for a return to the United States.

Of necessity, however, he entertained some warm feelings for London, since it was there that he achieved the all-but-impossible by scooping the world on a major story. On June 23, 1893, during fleet maneuvers off Tripoli, the British warship *Victoria* collided with the *Camperdown*, with the result that the *Victoria* quickly sank with a loss of 386 lives. The British Admiralty released only these stark facts, adding that Queen Victoria had been desolated by the loss of life. After that came official silence, while all Fleet Street, together with foreign correspondents, hammered fiercely on Admiralty doors.

Days passed as the newsmen became frantic, aware that just beyond reach lay one of the great disaster stories of the decade. Still, there seemed nothing possible to do—until Phillips recalled an old American newspaper trick, and in desperation decided to try it. This act—together with an incredible combination of coincidence, newspaper instinct and astounding good luck—resulted in the New York World scooping the universe on the *Victoria-Camperdown* disaster.

How it happened has been told by Phillips himself, though it is well to remember that a salient feature of the rigid Phillips-Davis gentleman's code was a becoming modesty. In his account of the tremendous scoop, Phillips plays his own part far down, referring to himself as "The London Correspondent." In his words, the story is this:

We of the New York *World's* London bureau assumed that the great London journals, certainly the *Times*, would have a full report for the next morning early enough for us to send it on to New York, thanks to the five hours' difference of time in our favor. But we also thought that it would be a good idea to have our own special on a news event of such magnitude, of such world-wide interest. So we looked up Tripoli on the maps.

It proved to be a sea town about forty miles north of

Beirut, and about seventy miles northwest of Damascus—
a sleepy little city that was born of Tyre and Sidon when
they were in their glory, and that had finished its senile activities and entered the state of suspended animation soon
after Godfrey de Bouillon became king of Jerusalem. There
was no British consul, no American consul, nobody to whom
we could telegraph, offering a liberal honorarium for an account of the disaster. We knew that the British journalists
must have friends among the several thousand men of those
eleven great ships of the Eastern Mediterranean squadron,
to whom they would telegraph, and from whom they would
get the story. But we had no such resources.

Now, in America it often happens that a tip comes over
the wire, of some unexpected news event at an obscure vil-
lage where a newspaper is published and no newspaper correspondents live, and to which it is impossible to get a rep-
resentative in time. In these circumstances, the average
American night editor wires the telegraph operator at the
point nearest the scene, asking him to send at once as many
facts as he can gather, and assuring him that he will be paid
well for his trouble. Ninety nine times out of a hundred, the
night editor reaps some return.

Why not try this plan on Tripoli? It is a telegraph station on the Turkish government lines. There must be a
telegraph operator and he must have some intelligence and
the passion for easy money.

The London correspondent was at the general offices
of the Eastern Telegraph Company, in the East End, as
soon as a cab could get him there, and was immediately in
consultation with the general manager. He listened, he
smiled—politely, for he was an extremely courteous man,
was the general manager—but with the tolerant superiority of experience observing the antics of inexperienced folly.

"You would be throwing away your two shillings a
word," he said. "The operator is a Turk. He does not know
one word of English. You ought to see the mess he has made
of every private message that has come through today. And,
furthermore, he never heard of your paper, or of New York,
or even of the United States. Why, he would not even know
a message had been sent him."

This was certainly common sense, and depressing. To persist seemed folly.

The American correspondent hesitated, and then said:—

"Well, it's a small stake for a big return, a sort of ten-thousand-to-one shot, as we say in what you call 'The States.' I'll risk it. You'll do your best to get my message through in a hurry, won't you?"

"Oh, yes," replied the general manager, and he seemed to look a little incredulous. He seemed to be a bit infected with the gambler's spirit.

The correspondent wrote, and scratched out, and wrote again, the general manager assisting with increasing interest. Finally he was speaking of it as "our telegram" and was not trying to conceal what might almost be called excitement. The telegram was sent, and read something like this:—

To the Telegraph Agent, Tripoli, Syria.

The New York *World* will pay you five hundred dollars for a full account of the Victoria disaster. We hope you will send about two thousand words. Please send as soon as possible.

And so it went under the sea, past the confines of civilization, and after a wait of many hours, down that remote, inaccessible coast of Asia Minor, so near to Europe geographically, so near to civilization, yet for the purposes of a newspaper more distant than scores of places of the same size in China and Japan.

There was nothing to do but wait—and, of course, telephone to the friendly general manager at intervals. That twenty-third of June—a Friday—wore on until midnight, and then the four early hours of Saturday, during which any message that might have come could have been sent to New York for publication in the Saturday morning paper. But nothing came from the "unspeakable Turk."

The London Saturday morning papers were about to appear, and they would surely have all the details. The general manager was right. The scheme was preposterous. The correspondent had wasted hope and money on a foolish telegram to "nobody, nowhere."

It was a crestfallen group that attacked the pile of freshly printed London morning newspapers at dawn in the correspondent's chambers. Despondency soon changed to wonder, wonder to amazement. Not a single London journal, not even the all-seeing *Times,* had any account of the disaster. Beyond a few names of the lost, given out at the Admiralty, and long descriptions of the intense anxiety throughout the Empire, there was nothing.

A few hours later the correspondent was again in the offices of the general manager. That official looked keenly disappointed, and at the same time a little ashamed of himself.

"Nothing," he said, gloomily shaking his head. "I"— he certainly meant to say "told you so" but stopped and finished with "fear we shall get nothing."

The correspondent drove back home and ordered the evening papers sent in as fast as their various editions might appear in the streets. He was just looking through the first installments for the story that was not there when the general manager burst in. He had come in a cab from the far East End, but he looked as if he had run every step of the way.

"Here it is—an answer!" he said excitedly, and the correspondent was devouring a few words on a big, square, thin sheet of the Eastern Telegraph Company's paper. It read about like this:—

> Prepay telegraph tolls or telegraph the money to pay. Will send account.
>
> PIERRE

"Let's get the money off at once," said the correspondent, seizing his hat.

"You can't," groaned the general manager. "If you could, I think I'd have sent it myself. But we can only send to the end of our lines, and the Turkish government will not take it on. There's no way in the world of getting a cent of money to Tripoli from here, except by mail."

Here was a story that the whole world was waiting for, and that every great newspaper in England and on the Continent had been moving heaven and earth to get. And it was just within the grasp of the American paper—when the unbusiness-like methods of a barbaric government intervened, and refused to move.

"What can be done?" asked the correspondent.

"Nothing," exclaimed the general manager, looking as if he were planning personally to wipe out the strain of "the Great Assassin" from the map of Europe.

"We'll send another telegram," said the correspondent. "We'll throw ourselves upon the mercy of friend Pierre."

And so the following was sent:

Pierre, the Telegraph Station, Tripoli, Syria.

Impossible telegraph money from here. You will put us under greatest obligation if you get money there. Telegraph us amount paid out. We will mail draft at once. Many thanks for courtesy. Your dispatch sent at once will probably be first account *Victoria* disaster published anywhere.

"That man is no Turk," said the correspondent. "He seems to understand American newspaper methods, for all his French name."

Another day of waiting. It was now late in the afternoon of Saturday. No news in the afternoon papers. No news from Pierre all that night. No news in the Sunday morning papers. No news from Pierre Sunday morning, Sunday afternoon, Sunday evening, Sunday midnight, the early hours of Monday morning.

Again the anxious scanning of the London Monday morning newspapers, and again relief and amazement because there was no news of the disaster, only more and angrier remonstrance that the public had been kept in suspense for four days, when the officers of the fleet had access to a wire and must, as a matter of course, have received messages from, and sent messages to, the Admiralty office in London.

At eleven o'clock on that Monday morning the correspondent was at breakfast over a particularly trying cup of the proverbially vile English coffee. In rushed a messenger from the Eastern Telegraph Company. It was the first sheets of the long-expected "special"—a half dozen sentences describing the appearance of the British fleet as it began to maneuver just off the harbor. The mysterious correspondent at Tripoli was "beginning at the beginning"—an unfailing sign of a good story.

Within ten minutes came another messenger, and so on at intervals of about ten minutes, until the correspondent had before him a pile of loosely-written sheets, containing a complete, logical, and admirably clear account of what had happened. His story went on to tell how Vice-Admiral Sir George Tryon, commanding the eleven warships that were advancing in double file, had given, from the flagship *Victoria*, the signal to turn inward so as to make a sort of "right about face" movement; how Admiral Markham had signaled from the *Camperdown* that the movement was impossible in such close quarters; how Admiral Tryon had merely repeated his order; how the *Victoria* and *Camperdown*, leading the two files, had turned each toward the other.

The bow of the *Camperdown* crashed into the side of the *Victoria*, and the *Camperdown* drew back. The *Victoria*, with a great hole in her side, staggered, then started ahead at full speed through the smooth waters for the shore. Admiral Tryon signaled that he needed no assistance. Presently the *Victoria*, having got quite a distance inshore from the rest of the fleet, plunged forward and went down bow first, like a "sounding" whale. There was a vortex, at the bottom of which whirled the great blades of the screws. Into this maelstrom, down upon those frightful, swift-revolving knives, were drawn several hundred British sailors, marines, and officers. They were torn into pieces, the sea was reddened all around, and strewn with arms, legs, heads, trunks. Then the boilers, far down beneath the surface, burst, and scores of those still alive were scalded to death—and the sea smoothed out again and began to laugh in the superb tropical sunlight of the summer afternoon. A few survivors were picked up. Twenty-two officers and three hundred and thirty-six men had perished.

It was a wonderful story of an insane commander, of valor and coolness and discipline triumphant, of tragic death. And the "unknown" at the Tripoli telegraph station had told it well.

The special was written in admirable English sentences, so far as form went, but the spelling, the distortions, of words and phrases, the breakdown of sense here and there, showed that an operator who knew nothing of English had sent it. We translated it into connected English, and cabled it on to New York, sending with it a technical explanation of the maneuvering by William Laird Clowes, the famous English naval expert.

It reached New York at half-past seven o'clock (New York time) in the evening of Monday, June 26th. Soon came a cablegram from the managing editor:

Eight this evening your special on streets in extra. Great beat. Congratulations. Who's Pierre?

It was not telegraphed back to London by the New York correspondents of the English journals in time for their Tuesday morning editions. So, while England and Europe were still waiting, the United States knew the whole terrible story of Admiral Tryon's insane order and its appalling consequences.

The American paper published the story on the morning of June 27th in its regular editions. Then it was cabled back to London, and on the morning of June 28th—six days after the disaster—the London *Times* and the London *Telegraph* printed the first story of the *Victoria* disaster, with full credit to the American newspaper.

The London afternoon dailies promptly tried to discredit the "American special." It was clearly impossible, they pointed out, that an American newspaper should get a detailed account of the disaster. Was it not a disaster to a British ship? Did it not occur three thousand miles nearer England than America? Therefore, could anything be clearer than that the alleged "special" was a "fake"? A visit to each of these logical editors and an exhibition of the telegram from Tripoli before his amazed and envious eyes produced courteous retractions in later editions, and caused the *Times* and the *Telegraph* to assert the authenticity of the news next morning.

It was not until the morning of July first that any English newspaper had a "special" of its own, giving an account of the disaster. That first English "special" came from Malta the day the Eastern Mediterranean squadron arrived there. It simply repeated the story, with less detail. So the "special" sent by the correspondent at Tripoli remains to this day the most complete and accurate newspaper account of the *Victoria* disaster ever published.

Who was "Pierre"?

That is the most curious part of the story. Let him tell it in his own words, in the following letter received by the correspondent about a week after the "beat":—

Tripoli, Syria, June 26th

DEAR SIR:

I am the only American here now, and the only foreigner who speaks English. I know of only five natives who speak English, and that with difficulty.

I happened to be in the telegraph office when your telegram came. The agent, a Turk, whose name is in French Pierre, and who can't speak a word of English—only French and Arabic—instead of throwing it away, gave it to me to translate for him. When I did so he said:—

"I don't know about this newspaper. Do you?"

I told him I had good reason to know it, for I had been a subscriber for the past four years, "and you are sure of your money." But he would not do anything about it. I saw that if you got anything I must do it.

The operators never work after sunset, and only by the governor's orders did they work until ten at night during the stay of the English fleet. When I showed the article, they said:

"Tomorrow will do."

I replied: "Must, at once."

"But we must go to the city"—two miles inland from the port. So it was after ten at night before I could get a second operator—a new hand, in fact, a learner—to go with me. Then we had to wait thirty-five minutes for a tram car, then another thirty-five minutes to get to the office, then half an hour for the operator to smoke a cigar and get Beirut.

Then I had to spell every word, for the boy who sent my story did not know English. If the copy was mixed, or anything was wrong, you must blame the operator. I tried my very best to get it off in time and in right order.

I had to borrow the cash necessary to pay for so big a telegram from an old merchant I know in the town. And mighty hard work I had getting it, when he found out what I wanted it for. He thought the hot sun had turned my brain.

This is the first time I ever tried my hand at reporting, and may the good Lord deliver me from any such work again—especially in Turkey. I am the American doctor here, and have a large practice.

Several requests came for items from the London papers, but I bought them off. So you had the only full account that left the telegraph office. The official report for the Admiralty was sent by mail Saturday night.

I got the story of the accident from a midshipman who was on the bridge with the Rear Admiral (Markham, of the *Camperdown*) at the time the fatal order to turn was given. This was only an hour after the accident. All he told me has been confirmed by many eye-witnesses. I myself was standing watching the maneuvers, and saw the *Victoria* disappear.

IRA HARRIS, M.D.

Here is a series of coincidences that staggers imagination. A telegram is sent anonymously into Asia Minor. It reaches a Turk who does not understand its language, and would not understand its purport if he could translate it. A man who knows English just happens to drop into the telegraph office. The man happens to be not only English-speaking, but an American. He reads the telegram. He happens to be a subscriber to the very American newspaper that sent it. He is interested, and his American "stick-to-itive-ness" is roused by sundry exasperating and fatiguing and disheartening obstacles. He gets together the very considerable cash needed—borrows it, if you please—and all in order that his newspaper published in his native land may "beat the world" on a great news event. . . .

The *Victoria-Camperdown* scoop was stupendous enough to win Phillips the praise of the entire newspaper world, but it failed to win a by-line from the tantalizing Pulitzer. Nor did the publisher produce another London correspondent for the World, so that in time Phillips became much nettled and tendered his written resignation. Pulitzer, who retained a warm regard for the impressive young employe, flatly refused to accept this. He hastily ordered Phillips back to Park Row, where in 1894 the young, imaginative Charles Edward Russell had become the city editor of the World.

Russell was the perfect editor for Phillips, since he considered it a waste of talent to send a would-be novelist on routine stories. He turned Phillips into a special feature writer, among other assignments sending him to a Thanksgiving dinner at a home for the incurably ill. Phillips produced another Park Row classic and when taxed for the secret of his success with heartthrob stories, answered, "I always write about the human beings involved, no matter what." Even as a feature writer Phillips never lost his uncanny sense of the curious ingredients that make news. At a political banquet, he sat at the press table listening while the oratorical war horse, Joseph H. Choate, sawed his way through a familiar speech. Suddenly, Choate departed from his usual pattern to remark, "It would be a good thing for this country if all the Irishmen, instead of trying to control politics here, would go back to Ireland and try to govern their own sorely misgoverned isle." Only Phillips was astute enough to realize that from such slurs are front-page stories made. His story alone featured Choate's remarks, and again the World scooped the town.

When Charles Edward Russell departed the World for Hearst's Journal in 1896, one of his last acts was to recommend that the resplendent Phillips be broken in as an editorial writer. Pulitzer acquiesced and Phillips moved from a city room desk to the dignity of a cubicle under the dome, just off the publisher's richly paneled, never-used Tower office. Under the absent but powerful guidance of Pulitzer, and the closer supervision of William H. Merrill, Phillips became one of the World's molders of opinion. It paid him eight thousand dollars annually, a princely sum for a single man of the time, but he was not altogether happy in the post, since the constant restrictions set down by Pulitzer and Merrill left little room for the expression of his own definite opinions. Yet from the remoteness of the World editorial rooms Phillips had an Olympian view of the ugly Yellow Journalism war being waged below and perhaps because of this inspiration now began—several years before his projected ten-year period—his first novel, *The Great God Success*.

The Great God Success was about the newspaper world, and to-day it seems mild indeed. But when published in 1899 it was sensational, so much so that Phillips signed it under the nom de plume John Graham. As a story of the newspaper world it showed only too plainly the reason behind Phillips's determination to soak up every observation possible: he seemed unable to write imaginatively about anything unless it had actually passed before his eyes or gone into his ears. In the first chapter a young college boy applies for work—exactly as did Phillips in Cincinnati—in a city room, plainly the World:

> It was a large, bare room, low of ceiling. Across one end were five windows overlooking from a great height the tempest that rages about the City Hall day and night and with few lulls and no pauses. The Managing Editor's roll-top desk was at the first window. Under each of the other windows was a broad, flat desk—for copy readers. At the farthest of these sat the City Editor. . . . Sloping desk tables—those near the windows lighted by daylight, farther away by electricity. Even on that cool, breezy August afternoon the sunlight and fresh air do not penetrate far into the room.

After describing this, Phillips gives rein to his celebrated cynicism. One of the older hands in the city room tells the newly hired boy:

> They say of other professions that there is always room at the top. In journalism the reverse is true. The room is all at the bottom. It is easy to enter . . . impossible to leave. It's all bottom, there is no top.

Also included in *The Great God Success* was a portrait of a newspaper publisher which caused Pulitzer, as the book was read to him, to become greatly incensed. Soon, however, he decided to for-

give his favored Phillips, and even write him a letter of congratula-
tion. In this he became one among many, for the book, hailed as
hard-hitting and meaty, was highly praised by reviewers. Stepping
out from behind the nom de plume, Phillips announced himself as
the author. But far more interesting than the content or success of
The Great God Success—or, indeed, of any Phillips novels, short stories and articles—was the manner in which it was written.

One critic has said of Phillips, "The resoluteness of purpose that
his face suggested was undeniably genuine." But even this is something of an understatement, for Phillips's ambition to be a writer
seemed to have grown into an obsession. On Park Row he would
work in the World Tower until midnight. After that, he did not ad-
journ with other newspapermen to a nearby bar, or to Delmonico's
or the Hoffman House, which his large salary would allow him to
frequent. Instead, he hastened to his rooms at Thirteenth Street and
Third Avenue, where he stood himself behind a high, pulpit-like desk
and commenced to write. Phillips always referred to this curious,
especially constructed desk as the "Old Black Pulpit," and in time it
became quite famous. His public believed he used it because of his
excessive height, but the real reason was that he nursed a morbid fear
of appendicitis, which he believed might result from bending his
huge bulk so many hours over a sitting-down desk.

Phillips's stand-up, night-owl writing habits never changed, nor
did his consuming passion to write novels, articles and short stories.
To Pulitzer's annoyance, he quit the World in 1902, after the success of *The Great God Success* and several Graustark-like romances
had brought him a sufficient income. But instead of taking life easier,
he worked harder. "I write every night from eleven until five or six in
the morning," he once told an aspiring writer. "Sometimes it is seven
or eight. I write every night seven nights a week. Let me urge you
to work the same number of hours every day and never, never, never
to let anything or anyone interfere between you and these working
hours. I don't wait for mood or inspiration and I don't give up because I don't begin right or am writing rubbish. I think it is fatal
to give way to moods."

Employing his strong energies in this manner, Phillips averaged
some six thousand words a night. In his ten years of productivity

after *The Great God Success* he wrote the staggering number of twenty-three complete books and several hundred short stories and fact articles, to make a literary output almost unprecedented for that length of time. Driving work seemed to satisfy him completely, for when asked if he regretted the absence of wife and family, he cited his need to write at least five thousand words every night. "Don't forget," he added, "that if you have a family it holds you down."

Phillips needed surprisingly little sleep and often awoke refreshed and fit at nine in the morning after working until six A.M. Nor did he waste the daylight hours. Part of his day was taken by engagements unavoidable to a man who became one of the most successful writers of the day. More time was devoted to conferences with his publisher, talks with magazine editors and revision of typescript and galleys. In his contacts with editors, he always seemed unhurried, friendly and outgoing: so much so that one editor wrote, "The more you saw of him, the more you wanted to see."

Still, this was business. Phillips never really sat back at his ease, though plainly he desired to do so at times and even seemed to be fighting to let himself do so. His motto was Emerson's "Every man is as lazy as he dares to be," and he wryly admitted that—for no perceptible reason—he dared not be lazy for a moment. Phillips's only seeming relaxation was to turn from writing one book to writing another. For this, he always kept two books going simultaneously. Or was it three? For invariably one night of his seven-night work week was devoted to the novel he considered his epic: the massive *Susan Lenox: Her Fall and Rise*. Phillips visualized this as "a huge gash out of life, a span of society that reaches from the depths to the heights." In this he succeeded—in his own era, at least. *Susan Lenox* is today a forgotten novel, remembered (if at all) because Greta Garbo and Clark Gable appeared in a movie based upon it. But contemporary critics hailed the book, seeing it less as a gash of life than as a heady libation. "Here is life," one reviewer rhapsodized, "life brimming to the cup's edge, quaffed to the cup's dregs."

Far more than a writer, Phillips was a rewriter. If Pulitzer was perpetually dissatisfied with the World, Phillips was equally dissatisfied with every word he put down. It is said that when he wrote editorials for the newspaper, the World charwomen signed a petition complaining about the number of discarded sheets of paper found cluttering the floor of his cubicle. He applied this same method to writing books. He revised endlessly in pencil, using a minute, meticulous script. Having tirelessly worked over a page, he then turned it over to the operator of a newfangled typewriter. When the typescript came back he revised again and again. Finally the book came back to him in galley proof and he rewrote once more on the margins—possibly more than any writer since Balzac. "I write and rewrite, going over my stuff again and again," he once declared. "Sometimes to turn out a book of one hundred thousand words, I write a million words. I am not exaggerating this. I know it's awful, but that's the only way I can do it."

Having resigned from the World to become a novelist, Phillips abandoned his rooms on Third Avenue and moved to a picturesque apartment at 119 East 19th, at the rear of the National Arts Club. Here he was joined by his sister, Mrs. Carolyn Frevert. In the days when Phillips was a beginning reporter in Cincinnati, Mrs. Frevert and her husband lived nearby. When Phillips came to New York, Mrs. Frevert followed alone. While in London, Phillips wrote her daily, and never allowed a day to pass without a letter to her whenever he was otherwise out of New York.

Mrs. Frevert appears to have been his favorite feminine companion. In the many mentions of Phillips by contemporaries, she is the only member of the opposite sex with whom his name was coupled. He did not, like Davis, become famous as an escort of willowy, pompadoured young ladies. This is particularly strange for a handsome man in the turn-of-the-century metropolis which, one writer recalls, was "In many ways the most picturesque city in the world. There was sin there, but it had a romance about it, a lavishness, a glitter that was almost gold."

Surrounded by every temptation the provocative city offered, Phillips remained tight in the grip of his obsessive writing. With all the lavishness around him, he appeared to see nothing but material for his novels. While the city sinned, he wrote, piling up so much work ahead that his publisher accepted the finished novels, then stored them away for future publication. "If I should die tonight,"

Phillips would impress friends by saying, "I would be six years ahead of the game." This statement was destined by events to turn out both eerie and utterly correct.

Phillips's better novels vacillate between exposure of the emptiness of financial success on the robber-baron level and straightforward treatment of sex. For, strangely enough, the man whose name was never romantically linked with a woman's was a pioneer in an open-eyed approach to the sex urge. Though his opinions on many matters were muddled and adolescent, Phillips, the fiction writer, seemed able to view the world around him with the unerring vision he could bring to a newspaper account. In doing this, he noted both the self-centered ruthlessness required for Wall Street financial success and the hypocrisy with which sex was currently treated. While the times were adjusted to disillusionment with financiers—Theodore Roosevelt used the phrase "raking the muck" for the first time in an attack on Phillips's sensational fact book, *The Treason of the Senate*—few were prepared to accept realism when applied to sex. Yet Phillips clearly perceived the sexual motivation in human relationships, and uncompromisingly transferred his observations to books. "Treat the sex question as you would any other," he recommended. "Don't treat it reverently and don't treat it rakishly—treat it naturally."

Sex in the Phillips novels seems tepid today but at the time he was hailed as a magnificent realist. A young H. L. Mencken praised him as "the greatest living novelist." The prurient Frank Harris unhesitatingly lifted him to a top position among literary immortals. Later critics have compared him to Dreiser and F. Scott Fitzgerald, though he did not possess the fumbling comprehension of the former or the skill of the latter. What Phillips lacked was the true novelist's imagination. For all his desire and industry, he could only report. His novels remain rooted in the first decade of the century when they seemed readable and important because they dealt with the current scene. Now they are at best documentary fiction. Anyone wishing a meticulous prose photograph of the era can find it in Phillips's books, most successfully in *Susan Lenox*. But his characters never come alive. For pleasurable reading, Phillips's books are dull and dated.

Yet Phillips's output is inevitably obscured by the human image
of a tall, handsome, virile man standing erect in the highest of stiff
collars and the most flowery of dressing gowns, writing through the
night before a pulpit-type desk. At such times he was utterly alone, a
state he thought inevitable for *homo sapiens,* since he once wrote:

> Every man goes through the world absolutely alone.
> He may be married, but he is alone nevertheless. Friendship
> makes no difference. . . . He is alone in the midst of a
> crowded street as much as in the middle of the desert, al-
> ways alone to the end. Only the few men who can stand
> being alone ever get anywhere. Everything worthwhile is
> done alone. . . .

How to explain Phillips? Behind his noble façade, what forces
made him so limited and negative in thought? What caused such a
fortunate man to be imprisoned in such a narrow, almost bitter
sphere? What kept him from marrying, tied him to a merciless drive
for success as a writer, then refused to let him go when success was
achieved?

Two explanations seem possible. One, of course, is psychologi-
cal. For all his seemingly superb equipment to conquer life, Phillips as
a child may have received too much adoration from parents (who
provided him with a tutor), and from the sister who became Mrs.
Frevert. This may have caused him to remain emotionally unde-
veloped, despite his physical impressiveness. The childish narcissism
of his clothes gives some support to this. Phillips's emotional imma-
turity may have led to fear of women, making him sexually impotent.
Or his problem may have been the cliché of our Freudian era:
latent homosexuality. In his time, it was possible for a man with
mild homosexual urges to go through life without the slightest comprehension of what was wrong with him.

The other explanation is more practical—and at the same time
less so. Phillips may have been one of those rare human beings who
lived under a premonition of violent death. The man who so often
said, "If I should die tonight . . . ," may have labored desperately
for fear death would reach him before he fully realized himself as a

writer. A psychic—or, if you will, metaphysical—premonition may have driven him to shut out the world so that at least he could finish *Susan Lenox: Her Fall and Rise* before the day a murderer's bullets tore through a manuscript carefully folded in his inner breast pocket. . . .

CHAPTER ELEVEN

The Favored Ones:
STEPHEN CRANE, RICHARD HARDING DAVIS

I N 1900 anyone anxious to find a writer whose existence was be-
clouded by a premonition of death need not look as far as David
Graham Phillips. It was only necessary to locate Stephen Crane,
who in the Spanish-American War had appeared to seek death, but
had got no more than a peculiar fever which gave him on arrival in
Tampa a wild craving for pickles and orange ice cream. Shortly the
twenty-seven-year-old Crane was back in New York, where he shocked
people by saying, "I'm not much account any more, I don't think I'll
live long." More specifically he announced that he did not expect to
live beyond the age of thirty-one.

These morbid statements were given corroboration by Crane's
sorry appearance. Actually he was wiry, broad-shouldered, slim-
waisted, a young man whose seat on a horse was exceptional. As an
undergraduate at Syracuse he played baseball with such fierce intensity that, had a literary life not seemed more attractive, he probably could have played shortstop in the contemporary big leagues.

But little of this athletic potential was ever visible to those who
observed Crane. The broad shoulders and narrow waist made
clothes hang on him lumpily, bringing his spare frame what has
been called an air of starved neglect. Though his mind worked with
the speed of light, he spoke slowly and moved deliberately, as if
depleted by the physical effort. His face was lean, hollow-eyed and

194

sallow, with a lock of fair, limp hair usually hanging over his forehead. When tired or in need of sleep, heavy black circles appeared under his eyes. An air of abstraction made him always seem in a moody trance.

For a man apparently able to soak up experience through his pores, Crane had a strange puritanical streak. He was morally opposed to women smoking cigarettes, which at the century's turn a few ladies of fashion were tentatively beginning to do. On another level, he solemnly warned a girl that she was injuring her reputation by rooming in a house that had been built by a wealthy man for his mistress. At the same time—in part, perhaps, because of an unhappy awareness of the decadence of his looks—Crane liked to shock friends by hinting of orgies and debaucheries. Even in his Park Row days there were whispers that he took drugs, and it is likely that Crane started most of them himself. His sallow, trancelike appearance only made the job easier and the fair-minded Richard Harding Davis had to admit, when later defending his friend, "Appearances are against him. He smokes constantly and is very sallow and very thin. To see him through the smoke of a restaurant and to be told that he ate morphine would not have surprised me. But I know a great deal about the signs of the drug habit and Mr. Crane has none of them."

Bad as Crane customarily appeared, he looked far worse on his return from Cuba. He seemed ill and restless, and any vitality of manner was gone. He wanted to sleep all the time and when awake would say, "I'm too tired to breathe." This obvious languor, combined with tales of his curious behavior in the Spanish campaign, brought fresh rumors of drug-taking and general depravity. Soon these had forced Richard Harding Davis into violent action. At Delmonico's one night he heard a hulking photographer named Thomas McCumber

> . . . gabbling that Crane was dying from disgraceful diseases. Davis rose and ordered the fellow to keep still. The photographer, towering above him, glared and mouthed more filth. Then Davis, blushing furiously, towed the big gossip out of the place and came back with his customary dignity and a cut lip to ask such men as he knew to forget the affair.

Crane was vulnerable to charges of dissolute living for reasons other than his jaded appearance. Infinitely more difficult to explain away was his fascination with the seamy side of New York and, particularly, with the streetwalkers whom as a writer he called women of the city's painted legions. Indeed, it is still a moot question among his biographers as to whether, after the Spanish-American War, he married a woman who had, to use another celebrated Crane-ism, been on the turf or, at least, managed a bawdy house.

Crane, the fourteenth child of a Newark clergyman, arrived in New York in 1890, aged nineteen. Pale, unpromising in appearance, he tramped Park Row day after day, climbing grimy stairs, timidly approaching city editors with requests for work. He received scant encouragement, but at first this did not seem to matter. He had fallen in love with New York, especially with its sinful life after dark. All night he walked the teeming, dangerous Bowery, no doubt saved from real injury by his seedy appearance. One day he appeared in a newspaper office with an eye terribly bruised and discolored. Happily he recounted that he had been sitting in a Bowery saloon when a thrown bottle struck him.

No record tells what young Crane first thought of the thousands of girls and women who paraded their flesh around the Bowery and the uptown Tenderloin on Sixth Avenue from Twenty-third to Forty-second Street. New York then had nearly twenty-five thousand prostitutes, a surprising number still new to the game, young and attractive. In the early days of his wanderings Crane may only have seen them against the drama that was nighttime New York. But at some point he watched a spirited young streetwalker being beaten to her knees by the hammy fist of a brutal cop. This incident probably took place on the Bowery, but a more romantic telling places it in the Broadway Gardens, a Tenderloin hangout. One version neatly identifies the brutal policeman as Lieutenant Charles Becker, who in time went to the electric chair for the murder of the gambler Herman Rosenthal. It further states that Crane was locked up for a night in jail as a result of insults to Becker and pictures him boyishly proud of the incident. Whatever actually happened, Crane began to observe the city's multitudinous professional girls with considerable sympathy.

As a writer Crane was sharply different from David Graham Phillips in that he never appeared to labor over what he wrote. Instead, he gestated material until the precise moment came. Then he quietly began to write. "I have seen him sit down before a blank sheet of paper, dip his pen, and go on without haste or pause for hours," his friend Joseph Conrad eventually wrote. Once Crane had done this, the work was finished—he seldom bothered to rewrite. And now, in 1891, he began to gestate a novel about a young slum girl driven into prostitution, and the environmental and emotional factors that put her on the turf. Later, when attacked for choosing such a sordid topic, he stated, "I had no other purpose . . . than to show people to people as they seemed to me, and if that be evil make the most of it." Yet even in selecting a subject no other contemporary dared touch, Crane did not see his novel solely in terms of realism. He was a novelist instinctively prepared to break through the rigid confines of existing American literature. "He swayed clean from the national orbit," writes Thomas Beer, who goes on to describe the twenty-year-old Crane pondering a book on a young streetwalker:

> Here came a boy whose visual sense was unique in American writing and whose mind by some inner process had stripped itself of all respect for those prevalent theories which had cursed the national fiction. . . . Upon what segment of the visible scene would he commence his sardonic operations? Perhaps it was simple recoil from the lukewarm current of letters, or perhaps it was deeper curiosity that took Stephen Crane headlong and resolute into the slums.

Crane possessed a great independence. Even at twenty, he resented accepting money from older, married brothers. Thus while prowling New York at night, storing up material for novels, he continued to haunt Park Row by day in the hope of making enough money to support himself. For a time, he was permitted to sit in the city room of James Gordon Bennett's Herald on a free-lance basis. Crane had a simmering curiosity about life and should, by all surface indications, have made an excellent reporter. But this rare curiosity was never directed at the matters editors wanted. House numbers, names and ages of injured persons, the figures of a crowd: such practi-

PARK ROW

198 PARK ROW

cal items seemed unimportant to him. Says Thomas Beer, "Crane's shadowy term with the Herald exactly prophesied his whole career as a journalist. He could not report. Apparently he did not try to report."

Sent out by the Herald city editor to cover a fire in an office building, he returned to write a description of the scene, but not of the fire. In it, the impatient fire horses "kicked grey ice of the gutter into silvery angles that hurtled and clicked on frozen stone." Next he interviewed a fat city alderman "who sat like a rural soup tureen in his chair and said *Aw!* sadly whenever ash from his cigar bounced on his vest of blood and black." Of a street cleaner knocked down by a runaway horse, Crane wrote, "he flattened his face toward heaven and set up a jet of violet, fastidious curses." In another story, an ancient egg had "a snarling smell." The feather in the hat of a pretty girl was "a quivering invitation." (Later, his short story "The Open Boat" would have one of the most famous opening sentences of literature: "None of them knew the color of the sky.")

When such flashes of phrase were angrily blue-penciled from his copy little remained of any Crane story. Finally he was informed by the Herald that he could not expect any more assignments. But in Park Row of the period it was usually possible to find a few crumbs. Someone on the Tribune had heard of his vivid phrasing and encouraged him to do interviews and descriptive stories on his own initiative, then bring them to the Tribune city room where there was a good chance they would be bought at space rates.

Crane was by now living in the high-ceilinged, barracks-like Art Students League on East Twenty-third Street. This was a building old even for the time, and, Crane wrote, it

> . . . squatted, slumbering and old, between two exalted commercial structures which would have to bend far down to perceive it. . . . The northward march of the city's progress had happened not to overturn this aged structure, as it huddled there, lost and forgotten while the cloud-veering towers strode on.

The chambermaid who took care of Crane's room in this ancient edifice was a pretty girl named Jennie Creegan. She had been born on the Bowery, never attended school, and by some happy miracle escaped life on the turf. Crane and the other young artists, actors and writers in the building nicknamed her Bunny, and she often perched on a trunk in Crane's room, chewing gum "like a slim, reminiscing cow." Under Crane's verbal prodding she reminisced of her Bowery childhood and possibly Bunny's tough, lively chatter provided the impetus that started him writing. For in January 1892 a boyhood friend named Wallis McHarg sought out Crane in the Art Students League room. Crane immediately took him on a tour of the Bowery, showing him the saloon where the flying bottle had given him a black eye, and pointed out the spot where a few nights before he had seen a young streetwalker throw her body over the face of her drunken procurer when a gang of vengeful Bowery Bhoys tried to stamp him to death. Then the two young men—both only twenty—returned to the League. There Crane suddenly reached for a package of manuscript. "I want you to read my book," he said. "I wrote it in two days before Christmas."

So begins the saga of *Maggie: A Girl of the Streets.* As a novel, it is less a description of a prostitute's life than of the pressures that made her one—"the sordid squabbles of a besotted tenement family become titanic struggles and mud puddles are magnified into measureless oceans." Richard Watson Gilder, whose vastly respected *Century Magazine* had just stirred up a storm by printing the word *rape*, gingerly handed Maggie back to Crane on March 23, 1892, with the excuse that it was "too honest." Other book and magazine editors hardly said that much, so eager were they to rid the premises of the shameless manuscript. In despair, Crane borrowed one thousand dollars from a New Jersey brother and had eleven hundred copies of a paper-bound *Maggie* printed at his own expense.

For obscure reasons, he decided not to put his own name on the book. Instead, the mustard-colored cover bears the hastily improvised name of Johnston Smith. Even so, bookstores were as reluctant as editors to have anything to do with it. Brentano's accepted a dozen copies, then all but buried them from sight. Gradually all the copies Crane had been able to put out for sale came back to him at the Art Students League, to make several ceiling-high piles in his room. One copy he sent to a friend with the inscription: "This work is a mud puddle, I am told by the best authority. Wade in and have a swim." Came an icy night in the winter of 1893-4 and Jennie Creegan, eager for Crane's room to be warm when he returned to write a story for the Tribune, grabbed up an armful of the yellow-covered Johnston Smith editions and used them to start a fire in the fireplace. Crane, when he found what she had done, shrugged sardonically: at least the room was warm. Today, the price of each copy of Jennie's armful of *Maggies* would be about $250.

Crane now owed his family the sum of one thousand dollars which he could see small likelihood of paying back. Though he was ever welcome in New Jersey, a great pride held him in New York. So he began what has been called "that period of starvation so much admired in the history of artists by comfortable critics, sure of next week's bread." At this point Crane was bothered by more than lack of money. The familiar block that strikes sensitive writers whose works do not sell hit him hard. He could not bring himself to write even newspaper features, and there are stories of his appearing frantic and disheveled in Park Row city rooms to borrow a nickel to buy a glass of beer and gorge himself on the sumptuous free lunch at Andy Horn's. At other times, he was seen lurching through City Hall Park in a condition that looked like drunkenness, but probably was the dizziness of hunger. Once in a while a working friend bought him a meal, and as an aftermath of one such welcome repast he found himself in the throes of a brainstorm. If he could not sell his piles of *Maggie*, he could at least give them away. He began sending them to well-known writers of the time. Hamlin Garland, one of the first recipients, answered with words of unexpected praise. Crane promptly walked the four miles to Harlem, where Garland lived, to show a short story called "An Ominous Baby." Garland sent it to a magazine called Arena, which bought it for twenty-five dollars.

But infinitely more important, Garland forwarded a copy of *Maggie* to William Dean Howells, the foremost literary figure of the day. Howells, now also a New Yorker, liked the book. Suddenly a dazzled Crane found himself invited to the luxurious Howells home for dinner. Attired in a suit borrowed from a friend at the Art Students League, he heard himself introduced around the parlor by a phrase which has since become famous—"Here is a writer who has sprung into life fully armed." Bolstered by this and a few encouraging words from other critics—among them a young and temporarily liberal thinker named Rupert Hughes—Crane found himself able to throw off his writing block. Since playing childhood games with tin-soldier toys, he had been fascinated by warfare and now, after searching libraries, he complained to friends that no one had written anything good about the Civil War. He passed the summer in New Jersey and from a neighbor borrowed the copies of the *Century Magazine* containing a series of graphic articles called "Battles and Leaders of the Civil War." When he returned them, it was with a note saying he expected to write a novel on the Civil War.

Crane did not write *The Red Badge of Courage* in one inspired sitting, as he apparently had written *Maggie* and could on occasion write short stories. He seems to have produced it chapter by episodic chapter, pondering each of the twenty-four separately before setting it down in his unhurried fashion. Thus, in October, 1893, he returned to New York with three quarters of the manuscript in his valise. Immediately he needed to spend every cent in his pocket for a pair of shoes. Then it began to rain and in a drenching downpour he walked to the Art Students League to collapse with cold and fever. Through weeks of recuperation, he wrote the remaining chapters of the book and in February, 1894, turned the completed manuscript over to a typist. Her price for typing the short novel was thirty dollars. Crane could muster only fifteen. Taking half the typed script, he trudged to Harlem to show the chapters to Hamlin Garland. After one quick look, Garland advanced the other fifteen. Downtown, Crane retrieved the remainder of the manuscript. He was in such desperate need of cash that he could not wait while a book or magazine editor weighed its merits. Instead, he carried it to a newspaper syndicate, where it was immediately bought for one hundred dollars.

The Red Badge of Courage is probably one of the few works of fiction to be recognized as a masterpiece by the printers who set it up. The book was first serialized in the Philadelphia Press, most of whose linotypers had fought in the Civil War. They called this story of a boy's effort to find courage and manhood on the battlefield the real thing. When Crane visited the Press office, the printers left machines to cluster around offering congratulations. Recognition from more exalted sources came immediately after publication. On the fragile basis of serialization in newspapers throughout the country, Stephen Crane was hailed as a genius, the possessor of a style as clear as polished glass and a gift for lighting up an individual scene—more so perhaps than a character—by the use of an odd and striking phrase.

Success of the serialized *Red Badge* allowed Crane to do what every young man—even a genius—dreamed of doing in the 1890's. He took a trip through the West and Southwest, introducing himself to authentic cowboys as "A tough jay from back East"—jay being Boweryese for guy. The sallow, boyish-looking Crane easily made friends with the rugged cowboys, who were delighted by the ease with which the tough jay sat on a saddle. This trip—he also went to Mexico—was Crane's last and perhaps only period of great happiness in life. Returning to New York, he found that *The Red Badge of Courage* had been published in book form. "The history of a triumph is always dull," states Thomas Beer, and *The Red Badge*, though attacked for many reasons, was a triumph. It outsold Kipling, Zola and Tolstoi, the best-selling authors of the time. Crane, who gulped and stammered whenever he found himself the focus of attention, was now a literary lion. It was not a happy sensation. The young man who had lived on free lunches and five-cent beers, spending nights walking the slums of the city, now found he could never be by himself. In a remark that might have been disputed by David Graham Phillips, he said, "It seems I can do anything, any damn thing I want, but be alone."

Crane's notoriety increased when *Maggie: A Girl of the Streets* was published in hard covers, and it was probably to save himself from controversy and lionizing that he accepted the 1896 Hearst assignment to become a roving correspondent. Crane traveled to Alaska, Paris, Greece and the Balkans, sending colorful cables back to Park Row. Resting in England, he discovered the Surrey countryside, which seemed to bring him singular peace. Among his new English friends was Joseph Conrad, who actually stood in awe of the young man because of *The Red Badge of Courage*. Conrad later said, "I discovered early in our acquaintance that Crane did not have the face of a lucky man."

Conrad also found himself saying to Crane, "Stevie, you brood like a distant thundercloud." For even before the Spanish-American War had apparently sharpened his desire for death, Crane expressed the premonition that he would die young. "Let it be stated that the mistress of the boy's mind was fear," a critic has written. "Here stood the great death and here, mentally or in the flesh, stood he."

Crane's feeling for death had a physical basis. Consumption made him languid and weak. Accompanying this was a dispiriting conviction that *The Red Badge of Courage* was his best work—that he would never write so well again. In New York Crane had also become the victim of another circumstance which took much zest from life. In the days of his Park Row poverty and early success, it had seemed amusing to be considered a drug addict and a riotous liver. But now with literary fame such stories multiplied hideously. Alive in Crane's period was Dr. S. Weir Mitchell, an author of successful historical novels and a pioneer in psychiatry. As a doctor-author, Mitchell was uniquely qualified when he wrote: "The phenomena of envy are very much more marked among artists than in other professions. Invariably or nearly so, these take the form of gossiping stories about the personal character of a successful writer and the stories always show the same trend: the writer is given to heavy indulgence in alcohol or to irregular use of drugs."

Stories of drink, drugs and consorting with fallen women now hung around Crane's head like an evil cloud. It did no good for Richard Harding Davis to thrash one man spreading such tales. A dozen others immediately appeared. Incredibly, they seemed to emanate largely from Park Row, for if nothing else newspapermen of the day could recognize good writing, and knew that as a writer Crane towered above them all. In the eyes of the envious, Crane was unforgivable for still another reason. Despite his careless dress and frequently sour conversation, he was an instinctive gentleman. Richard Harding Davis and David Graham Phillips might firmly set their jaws, dress immaculately, live by a courtly code, and thus inform the world that they were noblemen of the breed. With them both, it always appeared to be something of an act. Crane was neither courtly nor handsome, but he was gentle, compassionate, fair and always completely himself. This, too, made him hard to swallow as a youthful success. As his friend James Huneker later wrote: "There must have been people who hated the boy monumentally. Three or four times when he had been spending the whole evening with Ryder and myself, I would be told in the morning how drunk and disorderly he had been the night before by men who had not seen him. For a mild and melancholy kid he certainly had fallen completely into the garbage can of gossip."

Perhaps to escape the garbage can, Crane in 1899 returned to England, where, in a castle in the quiet Surrey countryside, he found energy to write more short stories. To guests from America, he delighted in making the shocking declaration that he did not expect to live beyond the age of thirty-one. He discussed life and death with Conrad, who after one such bleak conversation thought, "Stevie's life has been anything but a stroll through a rose garden." The turn of the century brought him close to his twenty-ninth year, strengthened by the belief that he could look forward to two more years on earth. He could not. In March, 1900, Crane leaned over from the dinner table to pat a dog. His mouth filled with blood. Three months later he was dead.

Of the three favored men who used Park Row as a stepping-stone to success, the greatest in his time always remained Richard Harding Davis. For whatever his fate as a creative writer, Davis had a special distinction in life. He brought glamour to his world. "Romance was never dead while he lived," a writer has stated, and prose of the period echoes with variations on this theme. Davis's admiring colleagues called him Richard-the-Lion-Harding. It was his custom to walk into a room (or a general's tent on a battlefield) and with sublime assurance announce, "I am Richard Harding Davis." According to his biographer, Fairfax Downey, "that name meant the breath of romance and the spirit of adventure . . . it was a symbol of youth and success, a token of friendship or disinterested kindness, a gauge of chivalry."

The image of Davis's dashing exploits as a war correspondent, his gallantry in the better restaurants of New York and London, brought a taste of bygone chivalry to the lives of workaday men. To women, the Gibson Man became the beau ideal of masculine beauty. But most of all, Davis inspired the young. One young man who looked up to him was Booth Tarkington, who years later wrote:

> All ages read him, but the young men and young women . . . turned to him when his fame made him their idol. They got many things from him, but above all they lived with a happier bravery because of him. Reading the man beneath the print, they found their prophet and gladly perceived that a prophet is not always cowled and bearded, but may be a gallant young gentleman. This one called merrily to them in his manly voice and they followed him. He bade them see that pain is negligible, that fear is a joke, and that the world is poignantly interesting, joyously lovable.

Handsome, healthy, strong-profiled, with a well-trailored outfit for every possible occasion, Davis appeared to have few conflicts in life. He was the son of an editor of the Philadelphia Public Ledger, and of Rebecca Harding Davis, a pioneer American realistic novelist. With such a heritage it was inevitable that he would want to be a writer. At the same time it was characteristic of him that, despite a literary inheritance, he never minimized the problems involved. He was superbly adjusted to life, fully aware that to become an outstanding writer would require hard labor. After somewhat lackadaisically spending his college years at Swarthmore, Johns Hopkins and Lehigh, Davis attained his real desire: a job as a reporter on a Philadelphia paper. But even then he was busy planning ahead. Taking humble pen in hand, he wrote Robert Louis Stevenson, saying that he hoped to become more than a mere city-room reporter and asking advice on how best to rise from that lowly beat. It is interesting to speculate on what might have happened to the Davis adjustment had Stevenson replied that writing is a matter of sudden inspiration. But he did not. RLS replied with exactly the kind of advice Davis expected:

If you are to escape unhurt out of your present business, you must be very careful, and you must find in your
heart much constancy. The swiftly done work of the journalist and the cheap finish and the ready made methods to
which it leads, you must try to counteract in private by
writing with the most considerate slowness and on the most
ambitious models. And when I say *writing*—O, believe me
it is rewriting that I have chiefly in mind. If you will do this
I hope to hear of you some day.

By following Stevenson's adjurations, Davis soon made himself
the most famous writer of his day. But unlike Phillips and Crane—
and contrary to his own youthful ambitions—he remained primarily
a newspaperman. Or, to be more exact, a war correspondent. There
was considerable of the poseur in Davis, and he always kept in mind
the backdrop against which he was currently appearing. He liked to
cover wars, since they provided the most bravura background against
which it was possible to move. So, despite the best-selling books,
the Broadway hit plays, and the inspiring legend of Davis gallantry,
he always remained the world's foremost correspondent, and eventually caused his death by the energy he put into covering the early
months of World War I. Even by the turn of the century, it had become a cliché that no war could be a success until Davis had arrived
to cover it in the style that only he could provide:

A perfect day for Mr. Davis [one author wrote] would
consist of a morning's danger, taken as a matter of course. In
the afternoon a little chivalry, equally a matter of course to
a well-bred man. Then a dash from hardship to some great
city, a bath, a perfect dinner nobly planned. Shrapnel, chivalry, *sauce mousseline*, and so to work the next morning on
a story which pre-supposed in others the virtues his code
compelled him almost to ignore in himself. Richard Coeur
de Lion would not have disliked such a day, once he was
used to shrapnel.

To the period in which he lived, the name Richard Harding
Davis became a synonym for the ultimate in courage. Yet from our
vantage point in time it is possible to surmise that the Davis career

—noble though it was—may conceivably have been motivated by a kind of cowardice instead of intestinal fortitude. David Graham Phillips erected between himself and the world a fence compounded of aloofness and industry. Davis, by gearing his life to the most exalted code of gentlemanly behavior, may also have protected himself from the slings and arrows of ordinary living. A benevolent Providence had given him outstanding handsomeness and enough talent to achieve world fame. Yet with all this, Davis may have feared life. By passionately embracing his elaborate, strong-jawed code of upstanding behavior, he handily isolated himself from the terrors of everyday existence. By his code, certain things in life were white, the remainder black: there was a convenient lack of gray. He married twice, the first time unhappily, but his behavior with the Gibson Girl beauties he escorted before and between marriages only gives credence to inner fears. It was well known in beautiful-girl circles of the day that to be escorted by Richard Harding Davis meant being treated with a respect amounting almost to reverence. "To the ladies, God bless 'em," was a favored toast of the era, and Davis carried through on this in extravagant fashion. Never for him was the possibility of rejection on emotional or sexual basis—it would have injured his protective image of male perfection. How much easier, how much less dangerous to the self-esteem, to escort a young lady directly home after an evening at the theatre or a supper at Rector's. Then assist her to the sidewalk, doff the high silk hat in old-world farewell, and step back into the hansom cab for a quick trip to Delmonico's, there to enjoy a proud, solitary nightcap.

With less glamorous matters in Davis's life, it was the same. By sternness of countenance and correctness of code, he sought to keep himself free of the petty annoyances with which he perhaps felt unable to cope. As a war correspondent, he worked daily with other newsmen, often begging his colleagues to leave to him colorful episodes which might be woven into his short stories and novels. But in the evening Davis retired within himself. He went to his tent—or, if possible, his hotel—to change into full evening dress, as a true gentleman should. Immaculately attired, he ate in solitary splendor, even if the meal were served to him under a Central American banana tree. From a distance the other correspondents in whose per-

sonal affairs he did not care to mingle watched with either admiration
or amusement, and only once by the record was he rudely interrupted. Then an English correspondent named Oliver Madox Hueffer stepped up to greet Davis familiarly as he ate. Davis was not
pleased and promptly delivered his crusher. "I'm afraid, old chap," he
said, "that I've forgotten you." Hueffer cocked a bleary eye. "That's
quite all right, my dear fellow," he replied. "You may have forgotten
me, but I certainly haven't forgotten you. How could anyone ever
forget meeting Jack London?"

Davis seemingly encountered only one obstacle on the road to
newspaper fame. This came when, reporting as a beginner on the
Philadelphia Record, he extended a yellow-gloved hand to the city
editor. He thus made an enemy who turned his first newspaper days
into a sheer hell. Yet his reaction, when inevitably he got fired, was
pure Davis. Extending the same yellow-gloved hand, he said, "Well,
old chap, I guess I'll have to take my medicine." Davis was no fool
and on the Philadelphia Press shed gloves, cane and ulster, to become
a working demon. Even so, he was always too large for a city room.
The immaculate attire, rigid code and straightforward manner made
the other reporters uneasy. So did his effort to assist them in becoming successful writers of short stories. "Don't look at the dirt, admire
the picturesque," he would cheerfully instruct. "That's what I do
and that's why I get five hundred dollars for a short story." Such excellent advice, no matter how well intentioned, never failed to sound
smug and patronizing.

At last the generally unfriendly atmosphere of city rooms pushed
him toward becoming a roving correspondent. He could not function well as a member of a team: alone he operated superbly. Another factor which contrived to remove him from the city room was
that he milked every milieu for short stories and novels. He made
newspaper work glamorous—and himself famous at twenty-five—with
short stories about Gallegher, an inquisitive copy boy. This field exhausted, he turned to Cortlandt Van Bibber and New York society.
With New York duly utilized, he was ready to accept Mr. Hearst's
offer to become a full-time foreign correspondent. When he and
Hearst quarrelled over the *Olivette,* it made no difference to Davis.

His reputation was made. When he landed in New York, newspaper and magazine editors called on *him*.

It is easy to make fun of the upright and—it would seem—humorless Davis. At the same time, it is impossible to dislike him. There is a special reason for this. Davis was in many ways a muddled, routine thinker, but above everything he did towered a remarkable sense of fair play. In the city room, he was invariably the first to congratulate a reporter who had written a good story. As a young man just turning nationally famous author and Gibson Man, he traveled every Sunday to Philadelphia to pass the day with his mother and father. There he learned of a young lady who for some minor misdeed was being ostracized in her neighborhood. Next Sunday the Gibson Man bounded up her porch steps to ask if she would do him the honor of accompanying him to church.

The Davis gallantry was not always of such an obvious variety. He was noted along Park Row for returning to the city room penniless, having given all his money to unfortunates encountered in slum sections. Davis's ever-present sense of justice became moral courage in his defense of Stephen Crane. It was absolute heroism in his 1906 defense of Stanford White, the redheaded, ebullient architect who was shot to death by Harry K. Thaw. In life, it was said that the extroverted White had never lost a friend. As he lay dead, he seemed to have none. Not one of his fine-living, girl-chasing companions appeared for his funeral. Davis had never been a close friend of White, but apparently he alone could see the injustice of the public's revulsion. While the papers blasted White as a Nero, Davis boldly wrote in an article for *Collier's*:

> He was big in mind and big in body, he was incapable of little meannesses as of great crimes. He loved life and got more out of it in more intelligent and in more different ways than any other man of his day in New York. He admired beautiful women as he admired every other beautiful thing that God has given us. . . . In New York it is impossible for the poor man, the rich man, the man of taste and the man with none, to walk abroad without being indebted to Stanford White for something that is good and

uplifting. Is it then intelligent to believe that one whose work was fine, big, and far-reaching could have himself been degraded and contemptible?

For this ringing defense of a dead man, Davis, universally considered a knight of decency, had the unusual experience of being denounced from pulpits. A library in New Jersey dumped his books in the nearest gutter, while the headmaster of a prominent school for boys warned his pupils not to read Davis's *Soldiers of Fortune* and *Princess Aline* "as foul emanations of a depraved romancer." In the teeth of this tempest Davis kept his resolute poise. "I have never known an attack to be made on anyone as undeserved, as unfair, as false, as the attacks upon White," he reiterated.

Only once in his life, it would seem, did Davis lose his celebrated instinct for doing the right thing at the right time, and it is characteristic that he publicized the uncomfortable incident himself. It happened when he was sent to cover the Russo-Japanese War, perhaps the only war assignment Davis failed to enjoy. The Japanese considered journalists the equivalent of spies and Davis, as the foremost correspondent of all, was considered the most suspicious spy. He was kept in Tokyo as long as possible, then for four months sent on a wild-goose chase around Manchuria in search of a major battle. It was Davis's own hunch that a big battle would be fought over the city of Liao-Yang, but a helpful Japanese officer assured him the city had already fallen to the Nipponese armies. The experienced Davis should have trusted his own intuition but, says Fairfax Downey, "In that dark, frustrate hour, the intrepid spirit of risk and resource, the once unerring instinct for action, were gone from him." Davis threw up his hands and headed for the coast. Arriving at Chefoo, he found the cable office, where the Chinese operator surprisingly said, "I congratulate you." As Davis tells it, in *The Notes of a War Correspondent*:

> For a moment I did not lift my eyes. I felt a chill creeping down my spine. I knew what sort of blow was coming and I was afraid of it.
> "Why?" I asked.
> The Chinaman bowed and smiled.

"Because you are the first," he said. "You are the only correspondent to arrive who has seen the Battle of Liao-Yang."

The chill turned then to a sort of nausea. I knew then what disaster had fallen, but I cheated myself by pretending the rumor was unfounded.

"There was no battle," I protested. "The Japanese told me themselves they had entered Liao-Yang without firing a shot."

The cable operator was a gentleman. He saw [my] distress, saw what it meant to deliver the blow with the distaste of a physician who must tell a patient he cannot recover. Gently, reluctantly, with real sympathy, he said: "They have been fighting for six days."

I went to a bench and sank down. . . . by the space of three days, I had missed the greatest battle since Sedan. . . .

But if Davis let his public down in this one instance, he more than lived up to the romantic conception of the Gibson Man in his second courtship and marriage.

Davis was a top Broadway playwright, as well as a fabled man about town, on the night he attended a performance of the musical comedy *Three Twins*. In the course of this otherwise undistinguished production a girl named Bessie McCoy appeared onstage to sing and dance a number called *The Yama Yama Man*. "No one who saw Bessie McCoy," says a contemporary, "can ever forget the picture of grace and sparkling vitality she made, the charm she wafted over the footlights." Strong men fell madly in love with Bessie before she finished singing, and the redoubtable Davis was no exception. He could have secured a formal introduction to the Yama Yama Girl as easily as he picked up the evening cane he carried with his top hat, gleaming shirt front and Inverness cape. Or (even in the early 1900's) he could have knocked on her dressing-room door and, as a distinguished personage, introduced himself.

None of these, however, fitted the Davis code, a salient feature of which was that the ideal woman is worshipped from afar. For eighteen successive nights Davis expressed his love by occupying a seat in the front row of the theatre, where chin on hands, hands in white gloves folded on cane, he watched only the Yama Yama number, then ostentatiously departed. After three weeks of devoted theatregoing, Davis stopped at Churchill's restaurant to dream of his love over a quiet drink. He had several, and suddenly Miss McCoy appeared in the doorway, squired by Frank Ward O'Malley of the Sun and other newspapermen. O'Malley saw Davis and called for him to join the party. It is possible that Davis hesitated a moment before subjecting his dream to reality, but there was nothing he could do without being rude. And for once, reality matched the dream. He found Bessie McCoy enchanting offstage as well as on, even though the young lady admitted that she had heard of Richard Harding Davis for so long that she classed him with Dickens and Thackeray.

Next evening Davis appeared in Miss McCoy's dressing room and ceremoniously asked her hand in marriage. Such haste may have fitted the Davis code, but it was psychologically unsound. Both Miss McCoy and her mother became alarmed at the speedy proposal and sternly requested him to leave. Davis was undeterred. The Gibson Man showered the Yama Yama Girl with flowers and continued his nightly visits to the front row of the theatre. This disconcerted Miss McCoy further. Before stepping on the stage, she would peer through the curtains to see if Davis occupied his usual prominent seat. "Make him go away," she would direct the stage manager. "He makes me so nervous I can't work." When an usher relayed this message, Davis would rise and make a dignified but flourishing departure, only to return the next night.

When *Three Twins* closed, the determined lover transferred his presence to the Florenz Ziegfeld production in which Miss McCoy next appeared. "The glamour of Richard Harding Davis' good looks, reputation, and personality has turned the head of many a girl," said a contemporary publication, "but Bessie McCoy is famous in her own right." Slowly, however, the young lady relented, allowing Davis to visit her backstage or take her to Rector's. Then it was noted that the Yama Yama Girl was wearing a celebrated cameo brooch that had belonged to Rebecca Harding Davis. "Stout heart has won fair lady," the romantic publications of the day opined. This indeed was the case, and on the day of the wedding the ever-generous Davis sent five hundred children from the slums on a steamer outing

to Coney Island. He also carried through nobly on his stern gentleman's code. For he and Bessie McCoy Davis lived happily ever after.

Davis's novels, plays, short stories, articles and news dispatches
brought him over a million dollars, an incredible amount in literary
reward at the time. Yet today, with Crane established as a genius and
Phillips occasionally mentioned as a milestone in literature, Davis's
literary output is all but forgotten. The sad truth is that his stories,
so closely resembling news accounts, are as dated as the newspaper stories of the time. Yet according to his biographer Davis
would not have minded literary oblivion: "For him it was enough
that men and women, boys and girls, eagerly awaited the appearance of his novels. That they who were too poor to buy magazines
haunted public libraries for issues with stories of his. That people
laughed at his farces or were thrilled by his plays. That so many
youngsters found inspiration for their writing careers in his success."
Davis's own existence was more romantic than anything he ever
managed to write. His rewards came to him in life, and who can say
that this is not the best way to have it happen?

CHAPTER TWELVE

Reporters

For every reporter who used Park Row as a road to fame, there were hundreds who, in varying degrees of contentment, remained working newspapermen. Yet even those among them who chafed at the insecurities and other unhappy aspects of the contemporary journalism retained a great intrinsic pride in the profession. In this era, the newspaperman was a very definite type. His work broadened his horizons far beyond those of the average man, who did not have such things as films, radio, or television to make him knowledgeable. Further, the reporter's contact with flamboyant figures in and out of Park Row usually added a flavor to his personality that was lacking in most other men of the day.

This was, in fact, the reporter's high point in history—a period when he was given a respect and importance he had never enjoyed before and would never enjoy again. According to Irvin S. Cobb, who arrived on Park Row from Paducah, Kentucky, in 1903, "The time of the Great Editor had waned and faded, the time of the Great Reporter succeeded it." Even if a Park Row newspaperman did not become a truly great reporter like Davis, Phillips, Julian Ralph, or James Creelman, he could at least bask in their reflected glory, and in his way live a life adventurous for the time. As a result, most Park Row newspapermen considered themselves a group set apart. They stuck together and drank together. At Andy Horn's, Perry's Hole in the Wall, Lipton's and other downtown watering places, they might grumble into drinks about the cruel peculiarities of James Gordon

Bennett, the eccentricities of Joseph Pulitzer, and the less remote offenses of managing and city editors. But through it all ran the unstated belief that the newspaperman's life was withal a beautiful one.

"The editorial life has been my destiny and delight," declared John Swinton, who, as reporter and city editor, worked on nearly every Park Row newspaper of his long day. Others were not quite so rhapsodic, seeing pitfalls as well as pleasures. Don Carlos Seitz, in an effort to capture the essence of newsmen, wrote: "Of course, no one with real sense or any hope of the hereafter would work for a metropolitan daily, even of the best sort. Journalists are, however, seldom sensible persons. They prefer irregularity to routine and excitement to ease. Money is secondary in their eyes. . . ."

Though the hours were long, the abrupt dismissals frequent, and the high points of real excitement few, the reporter of the day never seemed to lose the feeling that his was the most truly romantic of professions. He might take violently to drink, become cynical and embittered, or prematurely old and dropsical in the service of the ruthless city desk. But he never appeared able to dislodge somewhere in himself the feeling that newspaper work was indeed his destiny and delight.

Just as much, if not actually more than ever, Park Row after 1900 represented the real newspaper world to ambitious reporters across the country. Most of them dreamed of local scoops that would attract the attention of New York editors, or that friends who had moved on to Park Row would recommend them for jobs. Many receiving no call to New York took independent action. At this time a cartoonist also had to be a writer, since he was required to write any story accompanying his drawings unless the story were a major one. In San Francisco, a young cartoonist named Rube Goldberg decided to take the Park Row plunge on his own. Goldberg's parents lived in San Francisco and he loved the city, but the pull of the hub of the newspaper universe was too strong. He arrived in New York and immediately hastened to the office of the Journal, which was the inevitable first stop of any young job-hunting San Franciscan. Unable to get a job from Arthur Brisbane, Goldberg ultimately reached the New York Mail where he was put on salary. In doing this, he covered a familiar path. Other young men, unable to get jobs on the World, the Times, the Herald, the Sun, the Tribune, or the Journal, dropped their aspirations a peg and went to work for the Mail, the Globe, the Telegraph, the Press, or other papers of lesser stature. For Park Row in those days was bristling with newspapers. For once in history, the New York newspaper world seemed able to take care of its own. . . .

A young man employed on a Park Row paper after the century's turn would find his starting salary higher than it would have been in the 1890's. Instead of beginning at fifteen to twenty-five dollars, he would get twenty-five to thirty-five. This was not altogether a boon, however, for the cost of living had risen. Gone—or in the process of going—was the noble institution of space rates, by which a reporter could be rewarded by payment of eight to ten dollars a column above his regular salary for an extra-good, or extra-long, story. Nor were space rates the only colorful institution disappearing from Park Row. The free-lance reporter, once encouraged to hang around the outskirts of the city room, was becoming a man of the past. Increased use of telephones, the work speed-up of typewriters, the growth of wire services, all made it possible to estimate the number of men needed for any possible news-covering emergency. An organization-minded managing editor could now tell exactly how many men he needed in his city room.

But if Park Row had already lost some of its picturesque informality, with city rooms taking on faint outlines of business efficiency, the young reporter newly arrived there could hardly be expected to notice the fact. Park Row was still a romantic spot where, as another arrived-from-San-Francisco cartoonist named Harry Hershfield recalls, a young man could encounter in City Hall Park a distinguished, white-haired, white-suited man with a small cigar butt nearly burning his generous mustache. The white-suited man would be Mark Twain, who frequently contributed special articles to Park Row newspapers, especially to the Herald. Again, a pudgy, careless-looking man, whose breath usually smelled of liquor, appeared every week at the Sunday World to collect $50 for a short story about New York. The stories always had surprise endings, and the pudgy man signed them O. Henry, though those he encountered on his brief weekly visits usually referred to him as Sidney—or Sid—Porter.

But Park Row was not the only section of New York City in which such magical things happened. Beyond it stretched the entire growing metropolis, which at this point has been called "An adolescent city which, like all adolescents, was in love with itself." New York was the vibrant, poignant city of O. Henry's Four Million, of Floradora, hansom cabs, Diamond Jim Brady and Fritzi Scheff. To an impressionable young man from out of town, it could be an intoxicating place, for in the words of Thomas Beer:

> . . . the show was good. Victor Herbert's increased orchestras made silky melody in theatres where shoulders were naked at last, after a long discussion of a gentlewoman's right to dress as she pleased. Each autumn the groomed horses trotted in the new Madison Square Garden. . . . Each winter the opera dazzled. . . .

Probably the young newspaperman would first venture into the Bowery, since fifty years of strenuous propaganda had made this a place of national fame. But after the turn of the century the Bowery had begun losing its flavor. The city's march uptown took the headquarters of sin along with it, and now the Tenderloin, along Broadway, Sixth and Seventh avenues, was lined with dance halls, bars, theatres and night clubs. Most of all, the Tenderloin offered girls, many young and highly attractive. "Girls grabbed my arm and pulled at me the first night I took a walk up Sixth Avenue in the Tenderloin," an old-line newspaperman recalls. "They were young and heavily made-up, but still some looked a lot like my sister back home. They wore big hats and swung large bags, just the way they were supposed to. They were insistent, hanging on my arm and saying, *Come on, dearie. It's only a dollar and I got the room.* Some had pat stories about starving mothers or putting kid brothers through college. It was all sad and exciting, fascinating and frightening, to a youth just in from the sticks."

New York's prostitute population was still, despite several highly publicized vice investigations, at the twenty-five thousand mark, for the eight-dollar-a-week salaries, endless work hours, and colorless occupations conspired to drive girls onto the streets. It was a period when fourteen-year-old girls were allowed to work in department stores. Faced by days of almost sweatshop-level labor and nights of hopeless monotony, girls still fought a losing battle against a profession that was also hopeless, but at least seemed to offer temporary excitement. O. Henry gives a picture of a girl teetering on the verge of prostitution, leaving little doubt as to which way she will fall:

> Nancy you would call a shop-girl—because you have the habit. There is no type; but a perverse generation is always seeking a type; so this is what the type should be. She has the high-ratted pompadour and the exaggerated straight-front. Her skirt is shoddy, but has the correct flare. No furs protect her against the bitter spring air, but she wears her short broadcloth jacket as jauntily as though it were Persian lamb! On her face and in her eyes, remorseless type-seeker, is the typical shop-girl expression. It is a look of silent but contemptuous revolt against cheated womanhood; of sad prophecy of the vengeance to come. When she laughs her loudest the look is still there. The same look can be seen in the eyes of Russian peasants; and those of us left will see it some day on Gabriel's face when he comes to blow us up. It is a look that should wither and abash man; but he has been known to smirk at it and offer flowers—with a string tied to them.
>
> Now lift your hat and come away, while you receive the sardonic, sweet smile of Nancy that seems, somehow, to miss you and go fluttering like a white moth up over the housetops to the stars.

By far the most notorious spot on the Old Tenderloin was a dance hall called the Haymarket, immortalized by the artist John Sloan and numerous other painters and writers. Actually the Haymarket, for all its riotous color, was a blatant house of assignation where on the most realistic basis men could meet the liveliest and most temptingly sinful girls the city offered. One reason why the Haymarket girls were prettier, and the place itself more obvious than its many rival establishments, was that the Haymarket habitually paid five hundred dollars a month to the police commissioner and other high police officials. The Haymarket itself was on Sixth Avenue in the Twenties, while these police officials lived miles away from such a bawdy locality. Yet they calmly complained to the management that the music and noise from the Haymarket interfered with their peaceful slumbers. In return for this breach of the peace, the Haymarket forked over the monthly payments. Another curious—and perverse—feature of the place was that, as the night hours grew small, drunken girls were encouraged to mount the bottle-strewn tables and sing hymns, in which the entire crowd would lachrymosely join.

The colorful aspects of the Haymarket drew artists and writers, but reporters knew it for a vicious spot where girls were unceasingly brutalized by procurers and police. In order to maintain its reputation for offering the newest, freshest girls, the Haymarket needed a steady stream of new talent fed into the place. Even from the Park Row days of Richard Harding Davis, reporters used the thought of this heartless place to cushion the shock when sent to cover the story of young girls who had committed suicide, been murdered, or killed in accidents. "At least she'll never get to the Haymarket," Davis and an entire generation of reporters muttered, looking down at the young bodies. Somehow it always made them feel a little better.

Up and down Broadway, Sixth and Seventh avenues, the girls—most of them young, many middle-aged, and others downright old—promenaded, leading any men successfully solicited to rooms rented in houses along the gloomy side streets. Also on the side streets—now, in the 1950's, New York's teeming garment district—were the more sedate houses of pleasure, some richly subsidized by the Pittsburgh millionaires who were at the time as prominent a feature of the American scene as Texas millionaires are today.

Most of the Pittsburgh millionaires had traveled to Paris and returned with varying ideas of what a brothel should be. To handsome young Harry K. Thaw, it would be a place where young girls could be tied to four bedposts and sadistically whipped. Others displayed more refined tastes. One brothel, stemming from the largesse of a Pittsburgher, actually had become a salon where newspaper and literary men gathered to talk. This was a tribute to the refinement and personality of the presiding madam, a woman of such copious charm and wit that Irvin Cobb, one of those who came to talk, could only refer to her as a "courtesan." Cobb, at the time of his visits to this select establishment, was quite proud of himself, since as a young reporter on the Evening World he had just coined the term *innocent bystander* to describe a man unwittingly present at the scene of a crime. Now, as he joined in the conversation in the salon, he watched the courtesan wave elegant hands in the air while seeking words to describe a pompous client of her establishment. Suddenly she found the perfect ones—*a stuffed shirt* she called him. Cobb had never heard the expression before and neither, apparently, had anyone else. Cobb appropriated it, and by his newspaper writing placed it beside *innocent bystander* in the language.

The young man arriving in New York would seldom penetrate into such a plush establishment—nor, for reasons of caution and timidity, was he likely to go into the bawdy Haymarket. It was much easier to discover places like Maria's, the Black Cat and Duquesne's. In Maria's the dinner cost fifty cents and it was, says one reminiscence, of a lofty and generous quality. Cocktails were fifteen cents, or two for a quarter, in most New York City restaurants, but at some bars they cost a mere dime. Beer cost a nickel, and with a five-cent schooner went the privilege of eating one's fill at a free-lunch counter which today would not be matched for variety or excellence in the most elegant restaurants. Coffee, too, cost a nickel, and a sumptuous breakfast could be had for fifteen cents, where lunch might be twenty-five. The best theatre tickets cost a dollar and a half, and for only three dollars a night it was possible to hire a hansom cab which would drive a romantic couple to the theatre, wait throughout the performance, take them to a supper place, wait again, then drive home by the circuitous route of Central Park.

In particularly festive moments a young reporter could—and after a few months in New York invariably would—go to Jack Dunstan's, known proudly and plainly as Jack's. There fifty cents would buy a porterhouse steak weighing a pound. With it went all the rolls possible to eat, together with a piled side dish of French- or German-fried potatoes, and piccalilli sauce. In addition to steaks and chops, Jack's was noted for steamed clams, broiled lobsters, oysters, lobster fat on toast, scrambled eggs and Irish bacon, Welsh rarebits, and broiled pigs' feet with deviled sauce. Yet with all this, the most satisfying dish was Jack's famous canvasback duck. This cost three dollars and, says a contemporary account, "no reporter ever paid more for a single dish."

The food may have been magnificent, but this was the last reason one went to Jack's. Where the Waldorf, Rector's and Delmonico's possessed a steady, high-toned clientele, Jack's by some necromancy became the place to which the colorful remainder of the world thronged. Recalls Donald Henderson Clarke, who over the years was a steadfast Jack's regular:

> Jack's was the most renowned of all oases in New York, where upper and underworlds met; where stars of the stage met with noted sportsmen; international crooks sat down with newspaper reporters, artists, and editors; where ladies of the evening rubbed elbows with sightseeing matrons from the hinterland; where I have sat at table, unidentified and unnoticed in those early days, with Rex Beach, Jack London, and Samuel Gompers. . . .

White-haired and contrastingly red-faced, Jack Dunstan threw away the key to his restaurant on the day it opened. This was no empty, publicity-seeking gesture. Jack's was never closed for a moment thereafter until the unhappy advent of Prohibition in 1919. Then Jack had to summon a locksmith to fashion him a new key. On an ordinary night Jack's would be filled to capacity, from its comfortable Center Room out, with crowds patiently waiting to get in. Because some of his more motley guests on occasion became obstreperous, Jack organized a Flying Wedge of waiters which in time became as famous as the restaurant itself. In the hope of seeing the burly Flying Wedge in action, visitors to New York made a special point of visiting Jack's, much as out-of-towners now attend the Radio City Music Hall primarily to see the Rockettes.

But Jack's was uptown—at Sixth Avenue in the Forties—and the young reporter who had just found a job on Park Row would first of necessity become familiar with the restaurants and convivial spots in his downtown neighborhood. One was Meehan's where the proprietor himself stood in the window during meal hours, invitingly carving huge slices of corned beef. Another—still in existence—was

Hitchcock's in the Tribune Building, famous for beef 'n beans: large portion ten cents and a larger one fifteen, with a two-pound slab of creamy butter automatically gracing every table, and limitless bread without asking. The young reporter would also learn that on the fourteenth floor of the World Building was a restaurant called Hesse & Loeb's (later Wharton & Winne), which would extend credit on a week-to-week basis to men working on New York newspapers. The result of this happy arrangement was that on paydays many a total check went straight to Hesse & Loeb, while its owner was required to eat and drink there for still another week.

For this reason—and the fact that the Hesse & Loeb premises were usually tainted by the presence of World executives—many Park Row newspapermen developed a violent dislike for the place. Standing at the Hesse & Loeb bar, one celebrated city-room drunk began declaring in October that he would not eat Christmas dinner at Hesse & Loeb's, as he had been forced to do over many previous years. He evolved a plan whereby he mailed his pre-Christmas check to a trusted friend who lived respectably with his family in Brooklyn. But he neglected to warn the friend of his plan and, on arriving in Brooklyn on Christmas morning, he found that the friend and his family had gone elsewhere for the holiday. In the mailbox he could see the envelope containing his check, but he could not reach it. A forlorn and broken figure returned to Hesse & Loeb's for Christmas dinner as usual.

Far more elegant than Hesse & Loeb's, and used by World men for special lunches and dinners, was Mouquin's on Fulton Street. Food there was straight French, and for a dollar it was possible to dine with wine and a ten-cent cigar thrown in. Lunch was fifty cents. A bottle of Swiss or French wine cost twenty cents, and the thirty-cent bottle was among the best in New York. A small sirloin steak at Mouquin's came to thirty cents, while poultry and game cost fifty—always with vegetables and French bread and butter free.

One of the major surprises of Park Row was that Perry's Drug Store—better known as Perry's Hole in the Wall—served spiritous drinks. Indeed Perry's, on the ground floor of the World Building, was perhaps the most celebrated of all Newspaper Row drinking places. It was small, dingy and deceptive (since it posed outwardly as a drugstore), and newspapermen have immemorially preferred to drink in such surroundings. Perry's was a crutch on which World men leaned heavily in any crisis. One morning George Cary Eggleston, a massively rotund editorial writer, arrived for work to find the building's only elevator undergoing mechanical repairs. As an editorial writer Eggleston had an office on the fifteenth floor, in the gilded dome, whereas most other World men worked in the city rooms on the eleventh floor. His immense girth made the task of climbing fifteen flights seem almost superhuman, but Eggleston managed with much grunting, groaning and heavy perspiring. He reached the top, only to be greeted by the sight of the elevator simultaneously arriving at the same floor. Eggleston immediately decided that his noble exertions had earned him a drink at Perry's, and he stepped aboard to ride to the ground floor. There he was informed that this had been a trial trip, to find out whether the machinery had been successfully repaired. It had not: there would be no more elevator trips that day. Says one observer of this shattering scene, "Eggleston's language, on finding he must re-climb all those steep flights to the fifteenth floor, was a liberal education."

Having familiarized himself with both the city and the territory in which he would work, a young reporter next found it necessary to fit himself into one of several Park Row groups. Inspired by the example of Richard Harding Davis and David Graham Phillips, he might choose to devote his spare time to writing short stories, articles, novels, or plays. No other Park Row figures ever reached the heights achieved by Davis and Phillips, but Albert Payson Terhune, Maximilian Foster, Jesse Lynch Williams, Guy Wetmore Carryl (who uttered the classic line, "It takes two to make a seduction"), and others rose from newspaper work to become successful writers of the time. Largely this was done by means of the *Saturday Evening Post*, for George Horace Lorimer, the new editor of that publication, believed that ambitious newspaper reporters were potentially good fiction writers. Albert Payson Terhune not unexpectedly wrote for Lorimer rugged he-man fiction, but others discovered a neat formula. In those prim and proper days it was possible to say many things lightly that could not be said seriously, as David Graham Phillips was struggling to say them. Park Row writers with the proper deftness and facility began writing the light-touch, romantic short stories for which the *Saturday Evening Post* under Lorimer became famous.

If a young man nursed no aspirations beyond the newspaper world, he could make friends with older reporters and city editors. In due course he might be invited to visit their homes, there to meet a sister-in-law or daughter, marry, and settle down to proper suburban domesticity. A large number of newspapermen asked no more of life than this, and it was to quicken the blood of such types that Joseph Pulitzer ordered that the drunk be placed in the World city room. At the same time, the era worked against a young newsman finding easy wedded bliss. Reporters were suspect in respectable homes, for their work brought them in contact with murderers, light ladies and all the sordidness and excitement from which well-brought-up ladies were protected. Says Ned Brown, who, after his youthful triumph on the Guldensuppe case, abandoned medical studies to become a top sports writer on the World: "Being a newspaper writer gave you stature then, everywhere except in society. But elsewhere, a first-string reporter on any recognized paper—especially one of the World's—had a lot of prestige. *Civis Romanus erat*. He was a citizen of no mean state." Such citizens found themselves most welcome in the homes of other newspapermen, and much professional inbreeding resulted.

A third alternative lay open before a Park Row reporter. If he were lighthearted, liked to drink, and enjoyed the companionship of his fellow man—women play an exceedingly small part in sagas of Park Row—he could become one of the irresponsible and high-spirited reporters typified by Donald Henderson Clarke, who got a job on the World before he went to college. Even as a young man of twenty, Clarke—later to become the author of much popular fiction and many movies—was one of those free souls who could stay up all night drinking, yet perform capably in the city room all through the next day. In his nostalgia-laden words:

> Those of us newspaper reporters in New York of the early 1900's who were unwitting Bohemians lived in a sort of ecstasy of unreality, a sort of blissful dream. Like birds

intoxicated with the sun we fluttered aimlessly in response to any breeze, any attractive sight, scent or sound.

Yesterday was a golden haze, tomorrow a golden fog; today might produce a bruise or two, quickly forgotten in the sensuous enjoyment of a new thrill.

Newspaper business, although it required long hours and hard work on occasion, was also for us an escape from reality. It was the Land of Dreams, a fairy land of romance and high promise.

As a typical episode of his youthful newspaper days, Clarke recalls a night when he spent all his money at Jack's, then summoned E. Lloyd Sheldon from the city room of the World to rescue him from his predicament. Continues Clarke:

Sheldon paid the check. He bought some drinks. We ate. We had some more drinks. We were riding in a hansom cab—Lloyd and I. The driver drank with us. He went to sleep. I carried him into bars and poured drinks down his collar. I drove the cab. I rode the cab horse.

Clarke's frequent companion on bibulous forays was a fellow reporter named Arthur Somers Roche, who in years to come became a writer of successful serials for *Collier's* and the *Saturday Evening Post*. At the time of his World apprenticeship, however, Roche was a debonair young man who stuffed newspapers in the holes in his shoes and used his money for drinks and hansom rides with pretty girls. Roche has summed up the life of the happy-go-lucky reporter even better than Clarke. "We were in Bohemia then," he once stated, "but we didn't know it. If we had known it, it wouldn't have been Bohemia."

Still around to inspire young reporters who lived the rowdy life were a few representatives of a fast-disappearing breed—the picturesque newspaper drunk of the Eighties and Nineties, the man with a gargantuan appetite for liquor. One such who had lingered into the new century was named Frank Butler and in the early 1900's his favorite drinking companion was a stunningly handsome young Journal cartoonist named John Barrymore. By later standards, Jack Barrymore—as Park Row called him—would no doubt be considered the best-looking young man ever to step into a New York newspaper office. But these were days when the image of strong-jawed Richard Harding Davis's good looks still filled the public mind. Barrymore was considered fragile and effete in appearance. Even so, for a time in 1902 he performed the difficult feat of capturing the precocious interest of a sloe-eyed, full-lipped girl named Evelyn Nesbit, considered the most sensationally beautiful girl on Broadway. She was also the youngest. "Madame, I am running a theatre, not a baby farm," said the first Broadway impresario to whom Evelyn's steely-eyed mother took her. Other producers were not so particular, and soon Evelyn was cavorting behind the footlights in a show called *Wild Rose.*

Most of the men who instantly began bidding for her still-childish favors were middle-aged connoisseurs of beauty, among them Stanford White. All considered her the most surpassingly beautiful young thing they had ever seen. Evelyn's beauty was not the pure, spiritual type, however. Rather it filled men's minds with thoughts of the bedchamber. For a time, Evelyn and dazzling, hard-drinking Jack Barrymore were so much together that Park Row and Broadway considered them secretly married. But at this point, the ambitious Mrs. Nesbit conveniently decided to adopt the popular prejudice against newspapermen. No newspaperman, she loudly declared, was a fit person to associate with her daughter, even if he was a Barrymore and not really a newspaperman, but a cartoonist. She then proceeded to steer Evelyn—with a financial assist from Stanford White—in the direction of Harry K. Thaw, the wild-eyed Pittsburgh playboy whose bizarre pleasures were causing whispers about town.

Such treatment by a greedy-eyed stage mother drove Barrymore back to steadfast masculine drinking companions like Frank Butler, who was over six feet in height and carried some 240 pounds of flabby weight. Butler seemingly never washed and his clothes, a contemporary has said, were monogrammed with the remnants of the meals of numerous past years. He possessed a voice of stentorian resonance—at least an octave lower, legend assures us, than anyone else ever possessed. As if in deference to this astoundingly vocal instrument, Butler affected a frock coat of ancient vintage and a

picturesque, wide-brimmed black hat. It all blended into a porten-
tous appearance worthy of a United States Senator. "He reminded
me," Albert Payson Terhune has said, "of a dropsical eagle that had
spent the night in a coal bin."

Butler labored for the Daily News, a minor Park Row paper for
which he occasionally performed a major news beat. Invariably, he
achieved these because of his towering impressiveness of manner.
When a prominent New York financial magnate fell ill, doctors and
family barricaded the millionaire invalid in his Fifth Avenue mansion and refused to issue bulletins. While the city speculated as to
whether the important man could be living or dying, reporters tried
every known trick to persuade doctors or bribe servants to give information.

All this was to no avail until, through a murky fog of alcohol,
Frank Butler learned what was going on and hauled himself into
action. Leaving his comfortable station at a downtown bar, he
visited the premises of a friendly pawnbroker, where he exchanged
his artistic black hat for a tall silk one. From a police autopsy surgeon, he borrowed a black medical bag. Almost as an afterthought,
he sponged the more conspicuous food spots off his frock coat. So ar-
rayed, he presented himself at the portals of the Fifth Avenue mansion. His majestic figure and Jove-like vocal tones gained him immediate admittance and he was taken up the stairs to the sickroom.
There a twittering nurse informed him the patient was not expected
to live more than twenty-four hours. This was all Butler cared to
learn. Turning abruptly on his heel, he departed, only to be inter-
cepted on the stairway by a surprised male secretary who demanded,
"Pardon me, are you from Johns Hopkins?" "No," Butler thundered, "I am Old Doctor Grindle"—that being the name of the spon-
sor of a much-publicized quack remedy of the day.

Butler, who usually reserved his talents for such scoops as this,
continued alive largely because he was the possessor of a shiny gold
front tooth. This could be extracted at will and pawned for the sum
of seventy-five cents, which in a day of ten-cent cocktails and fifteen-
cent breakfasts was a not inconsiderable sum. Says a contemporary,
"Frank's financial condition could always be learned by the tooth's
gleaming presence or its gaping absence in his mouth."

Next to Barrymore, who soon quit cartooning to go on the stage, the disreputable Butler favored as a drinking companion a young man named Robert Owens, a nephew of the eminently respectable William H. Laffan, publisher of the Sun. Where Butler's mighty frame allowed him to drink vast quantities of alcohol while preserving an unfailing dignity, Owens rapidly became a barbrawler and frequent occupant of a bed in the Newspaper Row ward at St. Vincent's. At one discharge from these premises, he hastened to Perry's Drug Store, there to inform the assembled imbibers that in the hospital a railway train had crashed through one wall of his room, then ripped its way out the wall opposite. "The God damn craftiness," he shouted. "It never made a mark on either of the walls, coming in or going out. That was to get me in bad with the doctors. They thought I was lying when I told them about it."

Eventually a crisis came in the firm drinking relations between Butler and Owens. After his many bar fights, the younger man's front teeth were in worse state than Butler's. His prosperous family outfitted him with three gold front teeth. To Butler, this represented wealth. Between them, the convivial pair now commanded three dollars in ever-pawnable gold teeth. But for obscure reasons Owens stubbornly refused to part with his, no matter how sorry the financial condition of the duo. Butler, it is said, would sit staring ruefully at his friend's effulgent teeth—"as a child would peer into a Christmas toy shop window." At first he exhorted Owens in the name of comradeship to part with his teeth. After that, he took to denouncing him as a self-centered scoundrel. Neither worked. Owens stubbornly refused to give over so much as a single gold tooth. Soon the two were no longer friends.

CHAPTER THIRTEEN

Stories

W HILE such activities, reminiscent of the old Park Row, were going on, indications of a new one were in the air. As early as 1902, Adolph Ochs, after only six years as publisher of the New York Times, had become so prosperous that he was considering plans for the finest newspaper plant in the world—even including a Times Tower to match that of the New York World. Ochs's policy of quiet, complete, impartial news coverage, together with scrupulously honest advertising, had paid off handsomely. To the surprise of everyone, including himself, the self-effacing publisher had become a phenomenon of Park Row. When praised for this he would modestly state, "I do not understand the tributes that come my way. I merely proved that, if given the chance, the reading public would choose a paper that served up news without coloring it."

Ochs first considered purchasing the land across City Hall Park where the Woolworth Building would eventually stand. When this deal fell through, he was not disappointed. For having thought seriously about the future of New York, Ochs joined his eccentric colleague James Gordon Bennett—with whom he agreed in no other way than this—in realizing that the trend in New York was strongly northward. He also came to the conclusion, says a biographer, "that Park Row was dying, just as old persons must die."

Like Bennett, Ochs now decided to remove himself a long distance from the old neighborhood. In 1903, he bought the triangular plot at Broadway and Forty-Second Street, facing what was called

Longacre Square but would soon be rechristened Times Square. Other newspaper proprietors shook their heads over Ochs's bold move, since a location so far uptown presented hazards in newspaper distribution. The Times would, for instance, lose valuable time in getting the important Brooklyn papers back to Park Row, where thundering wagons hauled them across the Brooklyn Bridge. But Ochs had cannily taken into consideration the fact that New York's first subway was about to open. Indeed, this had been behind his selection of Times Square as the site of his new building. The station there would be the hub of the new underground system.

Through 1903 and 1904, hordes of workmen labored on the new Times Tower. A block north, the Hotel Astor neared completion and two blocks east the cornerstone of the New York Public Library had been laid. It is curious to note that even in 1903 New York was full of so-called sidewalk superintendents. Under the headline DEEP- EST HOLE IN NEW YORK A BROADWAY SPECTACLE, the rival Herald wrote (without mentioning the Times by name), "Never before has a similar undertaking been watched by so great an audience. The excavation is highly interesting by night, the jagged rocks standing out in striking relief against the shadows. The great throngs which surge along the brightly illuminated sidewalks of Broadway look down at an abrupt angle into what appears to be a bottomless abyss."

The great Stanford White did not design the Times Building, but it was patterned—in the manner of White—after Giotto's Florentine Tower. Aided and abetted by the lively interest of the citizenry, the new edifice stood all but completed in December, 1904. Then on New Year's Eve, 1904, the Times Building was used for one of the great newspaper-promotion displays of all time. Writes Meyer Berger:

> Times Square was crowded with hundreds of thousands of horn-blasting, bell-ringing celebrants, come to witness a brilliant fireworks display touched off in the Tower. Midtown skies reverberated with the thunderous bursting of flights of bombs. Skyrockets and flares streamed against the midnight sky in the first Times Square New Year's Eve show, centered around the Tower. These assemblages be-

came traditional with Times electricians controlling incandescent figures that spelled out the dying year, and spelled in the new. The signal for the old year's passing was a massive illuminated globe that slid down the Tower pole while the crowds far below on the sidewalk cut loose with ear-splitting din. A final burst of fireworks "1905" in flame against the heavens, and the throngs screamed and shouted themselves hoarse.

As the last, lingering members of the New Year's Eve crowd drifted home, the Times began moving its plant uptown. January 1, 1905, was a Sunday and, as the presses at 41 Park Row stopped rolling off the big Sunday edition, an army of men from the Mergenthaler Linotype and Hoe Printing companies took over, together with the entire Times staff and hundreds of special workers hired for the event. Everything usable from the old office was piled into horse-drawn drays and hauled the three and one-half miles uptown to the new building. There eleven Mergenthaler machines, with four to five thousand parts apiece, replaced twenty-seven old-type Park Row machines.

Other machinery was similarly up to date, with the actual presses on the bedrock-basement of the building, adjacent to the subway station, so that handlers could throw the first bundles from them onto "new shiny subway trains bound downtown. They dropped papers off for dealers who waited at stations along the route. At Park Row they unloaded the rest. There bundles were hustled to waiting wagons, drivers laid on the whip and the first Tower issue went skidding across Brooklyn Bridge in the crisp winter starlight. . . ."

But if Park Row was doomed, the short stretch of street gave no inkling of awareness of the fact. It was still the destination-in-dreams of nearly every newspaperman in America: still the place where the biggest news stories could happen—and did.

Park Row was, of course, suitably hysterical in its coverage of one of the first sensational murder cases of the century. The so-called Hansom Cab Murder took place on June 4, 1904, when a radiantly beautiful girl named Nan Patterson shot her lover—a man picturesquely named Caesar Young—as he bade farewell to her in a hansom just before he was due to set sail for Europe with his wife. By this time the Gibson Girl had been supplanted by the Floradora Girl as the national symbol of feminine beauty. To make the rich Nan Patterson case incredibly richer, Nan was a Floradora Girl: not one of the original Sextet, to be sure, but she had indubitably been hired when an original girl left the cast. Nan was young, breathlessly lovely and—her lawyer later claimed—madly infatuated with worldly Caesar Young. She sat demurely through two trials with her distinguished-looking father solicitously at her side. Her spirited defense was conducted by Abe Levy, trickiest criminal lawyer of the day. At both trials, Nan declared—through Levy—that in the hansom cab Caesar Young had tried to kill himself over sorrow at leaving her, that she had tried desperately to prevent him, and that as the pair wrestled, the gun went off.

All this occured in a day before tabloids, gossip columns, or scandal magazines. Thus still another advantage to being a reporter on Park Row becomes visible. For only newspapermen seemed to have the inside story of the Nan Patterson case: that, curiously, a Tammany lawyer-private eye named Dan O'Reilly had been allowed to see the sobbing girl alone immediately after she was brought to the station house. O'Reilly, known as the Irish Cupid of Park Row, did not need his masculine wiles to obtain Nan's co-operation for what he immediately suggested. From her slender arms he stripped the elbow-length white gloves, the right one bearing a telltale spit of burned powder grain in its crotch. O'Reilly wadded up the gloves and stowed them in his pocket. No one ever saw them again, but O'Reilly, who owed much to the newspapers, was not one to keep such a secret from the gentlemen of the press. In both Nan's trials, two infatuated juries—to use Alexander Woollcott's phrase—found it impossible to believe that such a pure-looking girl could kill a man in anger. Nan went free, with the world largely believing her story. But Park Row knew Nan had shot her Caesar dead.

Eleven days after the Hansom Cab Murder—on June fifteenth—Park Row was jolted by a story of an altogether different sort. Robert H. "Bob" Davis has written that it shook New York to its very vitals, but this is the mildest of understatements. The tragedy, which took place only ten miles from Park Row itself, still remains among the most terrible marine disasters of all time.

News of it arrived first in the city room of the Evening World by one of the odd miracles that make newspaper legends. In 1904, there were few telephones in New York, and it would be many years before the city's population began the quaint custom of promiscuously phoning city rooms for information, argument and demands for simple justice. The World and Evening World had three or four wall phones apiece, each so conspicuous by its presence as to be designated by the numbers, 1-2-3-4. When a call came in on any of these phones, a rewrite man immediately answered with pencil and paper in hand, ready to take down the facts of a story. So when, at approximately eleven A.M. on June 15, 1904, phone number 2 in the city room of the Evening World rang, the call was answered by Martin Green, one of the top rewrite men of the day. As Green clapped the clumsy receiver to his ear, he heard a far-off voice say, "There is a boat burning up here in the East River." Green jotted *Boat burning* on his writing pad, then asked, "Where are you?" "In an office overlooking the river at One Hundred and Thirty-seventh," replied the man, who after the event never stepped forward to be identified, though the World searched long and hard for him. "The boat is downstream from me at about One Hundred and Twenty-fifth Street, coming north," he added.

Green cupped his hand over the phone's mouthpiece to call to the city editor, "There's a boat burning in the East River, at about One Hundred and Twenty-fifth Street."

The city editor immediately ordered another reporter to call Eugene F. Moran, of the Moran tugboat company. Moran had just been alerted by one of his tugboat captains who had phoned in, "There's a ship blazing like hell up here in the river!" "Can you get us up there in a tug?" the reporter asked, when Moran confirmed the story. "Take the El, it's faster," the practical Moran replied.

At phone number 2, Green was slowly getting his story. "What's her name?" had been his next question. "I can't make it out," the man at the other end answered, continuing:

"The breeze from the south is driving smoke forward from the stacks and from the cabin windows. She's a side-wheeler. I can see women and children running madly about the upper and lower decks. Some are attempting to leap overboard while others pull them back. Women holding children up are clustered in front of the pilot house. Smoke is rolling up from the main deck. . . ."

"Try to make out her name," Green urged, "it should be forward or on the pilot house. Watch for it."

"I will, but the smoke is getting thicker. Wait a minute; the breeze is shifting. I got it: The first word is G-E-N- . . . Can't get it; too much smoke. When she comes opposite me, perhaps. . . . Good God! Flames are bursting from the upper cabins. Women and children are climbing on deck chairs and beckoning to the shore. Boats are putting out from the docks. . . . Children are being herded astern, but cannot be controlled. Panic is on. A woman with a child in her arms has just jumped overboard. . . . Another. . . . A girl in a blue dress struck the hood of the paddle wheel, slipped off and has gone under the blade. I can hear screams. The crew is serving out life preservers. Slocum, Slo-cum. . . . General Slocum. S-L-O-C-U-M. That's her name. She is now opposite me. God, what an awful sight! Everybody on board has gone mad. Women on fire and holding children in their arms running about the deck. In another five minutes the boat will be a furnace. . . ."

With the name General Slocum, Green had again shouted to the city editor, and now for the first time the awful enormity of the story's possibilities struck Park Row. A quick check showed the *General Slocum* to be an excursion boat hired to take seventeen hundred parishioners—nearly all women and children—of St. Mark's Lutheran Church on the lower East Side on an annual picnic to Locust Grove, on Long Island Sound. With these facts established, a dozen or so reporters were ordered to race to One Hundred and Thirty-seventh Street and the East River, while two were delegated to go to St. Mark's Lutheran in the hope that someone remaining there would be able to provide a list with the names and addresses of all ticket-buyers for the excursion. Meantime, on the phone, Green was asking the question that millions would ask through several official investigations—for the captain of the blazing ship, who survived to be sent to jail for criminal negligence, stubbornly passed Randall's Island, where he could have beached. He kept going, with the breeze from the motion of the ship further fanning the flames, until the boat grounded herself on North Brother Island.

"Why doesn't the captain put her ashore?" Green yelled. "God knows," the man's frantic voice answered:

> "He is still holding to mid-stream. The deck is filled with burning torches. . . . Women and children are now going over the rail by the dozens. . . . The ship is veering toward the Bronx shore in 130's. She is going in. . . . She's struck on North Brother Island and is listing. Smoke and flames envelop her. God, man, I can't stand any more. I'm sick at the stomach. You'll have to get along now without me. I'm all in. Goodby."

Because of its anonymous informant, the Evening World scored one of the most famous of all Park Row news beats. Within an hour, its Extras exclusively told the city of the fearsome burning of the *General Slocum*—not only by Martin Green's story which, when written, became still another Park Row classic, but with its list of those aboard the ill-fated side-wheeler. Even so, the tragic *General Slocum* story was just beginning. Reporters arriving on North Brother Island beheld one of the ghastliest sights the earth has ever known. The final death toll mounted to 1,021, almost all women and children. Charred and mangled bodies lay in high piles on the North Brother beach or floated hideously in the bloody, blackened water. For perhaps the only time in newspaper history, experienced reporters found a story too gruesome to cover. Some turned their backs on the scene and went home, to sit speechless, unwilling or unable to tell wives and children of the horrors they had seen. In the city rooms of Park Row papers, toughened reporters taking the details over the telephones were seen to break down and weep, while the rewrite men whose job it was to write the succeeding stories jumped from typewriters to rush to the men's room to vomit.

And still the awful story continued. . . . In the section of the East Side known as Little Germany, from whence most of the excursionists had come, two hundred hearses, both black and white, took three endless days to return those bodies that could be found and identified. Hardly a family in the district escaped at least one death, and in many families only the working father was left alive. Suicides and mental breakdowns followed the *General Slocum* disaster and soon, as if by tacit understanding, the Lutheran families began leaving lower Manhattan. Today, on Tompkins Square, just off East Tenth Street, a small stone memorial stands to the children who perished in the inferno of the *General Slocum*. *"They were the earth's purest children, young and fair,"* it reads.

All the sensational scoops of the day were not those attained by the World and Evening World—though from the number of Pulitzer men who later wrote books about their exploits, this would seem to be the case. Even after the death of Dana in 1897, the New York Sun remained the newspaper favored by superior writers. Its staff now included Frank Ward O'Malley, a pixieish man known as the reporter's reporter; Edwin C. Hill, a splendid sartorial figure and a splendid writer, who died as this book was being written; George Van Slyke and others. Of these, the most notable in his time was O'Malley, whose curious sense of humor was left totally unbridled by the Sun. Every year O'Malley covered a Tammany function and annually, to make a feature that grew increasingly famous, his story began in the same way:

> All roads led to the Terrace Garden last night, where the Larry Mulligan Association held its annual high carnival. Champagne flowed like water. Amid garlands of flowers and the sweet strains of the light fantastic, leading Tammany statesmen, the city's more prominent wine agents and song pluggers, and the elite of the Bowery danced the hours away with their lovely ladies.

Like all Sun reporters, O'Malley was strikingly versatile and could move from humor to pathos with the switch of an assignment. His most famous story, perhaps the newspaper story most often re-

printed in anthologies, was written when a young policeman named
Gene Sheehan was killed by an East Side bully boy. In true Sun
fashion, O'Malley did not go to the station house for the bare facts
of the case. Instead, he went to see the patrolman's mother and in
part wrote:

> Mrs. Catherine Sheehan stood in the darkened parlor
> of her home at 361 West Fifteenth Street late yesterday
> afternoon and told her version of the murder of her son
> Gene, the youthful policeman whom a thug named Billy
> Morley shot in the forehead down under the Chatham
> Square elevated station early yesterday morning. Gene's
> mother was thankful that her boy hadn't killed Billy Morley
> before he died, "Because," she said, "I can say honestly,
> even now, that I'd rather have Gene's dead body brought
> home to me, as it will be to-night, than to have him come
> to me and say, 'Mother, I had to kill a man this morning.'
> "God comfort the poor wretch that killed the boy,"
> the mother went on. . . . "he is more unhappy tonight
> than we are. Maybe he was weak-minded through drink.
> He couldn't have known Gene, or he wouldn't have killed
> him. Did they tell you at the Oak Street Station that the
> other policemen called Gene 'Happy Sheehan'? Anything
> they told you about him is true, because no one would lie
> about him. He was always happy, and he was a fine-looking
> young man. He always had to duck his helmet when he
> walked under the gas-fixture in the hall as he went out the
> door.
> "After he went down the street yesterday, I found a lit-
> tle book on a chair—a little list of the streets or something
> that Gene had forgot. I knew how particular they are about
> such things, and I didn't want the boy to get in trouble,
> so I threw on a shawl and walked over through Chambers
> Street toward the river to find him. He was standing on a
> corner some place down there near the bridge, clapping time
> with his hands for a little newsy that was dancing; but he
> stopped clapping—struck, Gene was, when he saw me. He
> laughed when I handed him a little book and told him that
> was why I searched for him, patting me on the shoulder
> when he laughed—patting me on the shoulder.

" 'It's a bad place for you here, Gene,' I said. 'Then it must be bad for you, too, mammy,' said he; and as he walked to the end of his beat with me—it was dark then—he said, 'There are lots of crooks here, mother, and they know and hate me, and they're afraid of me'—proud, he said it—'but maybe they'll get me some night.'

"He patted me on the back and turned and walked east toward his death. Wasn't it strange that Gene said that?"

In 1902, a young San Francisco reporter named Will Irwin followed the well-beaten path across the continent and, by dint of a friendly personality and reportorial experience on West Coast papers, extracted a job from Chester S. "Boss" Lord, then the awesome managing editor of the Sun. Irwin, it soon transpired, was a pithy writer and a careful craftsman, factors which quickly made him conspicuous if not prominent along Park Row. For two years he worked happily on the Sun. Then his contentment was rudely shattered by the offer of a roving-reporter staff position on *McClure's* magazine. Irwin was in a quandary. He thought of himself primarily as a working newspaperman and he loved the Sun. But *McClure's* offer represented advancement and perhaps fame, for this was the magazine of the muckrakers, led by Ida M. Tarbell, Ray Stannard Baker and Lincoln Steffens. Steffens, a fellow Westerner, had, by his attacks on big business for *McClure's*, made himself world famous. Reluctantly, Irwin made up his mind to leave the Sun.

He had been in the McClure office only two days when, on April 18, 1906, word reached New York of the San Francisco earthquake. Irwin instantly ceased being a magazine writer, to resume his old role of reporter. He walked out of the magazine office and headed straight for Park Row, where he reappeared in the city room of the Sun as if he had never left. "Send me to San Francisco," he begged Boss Lord.

Irwin's arrival was something of an answer to Lord's muttered prayers. Ten years before, the irascible Dana had quarreled bitterly with the Associated Press and had thrown back the Sun's AP franchise, valued at a mere five hundred thousand dollars. To show that he could not be bullied, Dana had then established the Sun's own nationwide news service, which he called the Laffan Bureau. For the most part this sent out the feature stories used in the Sun, but it also received news from special correspondents around the country. However, the Laffan Bureau had one particular weak spot. This was on the West Coast, where a single man covered the area between Seattle and Los Angeles. Now, with only one intact telegraph wire leading into the turmoil of San Francisco, the Laffan correspondent—provided he was in San Francisco at all—would have to compete with such powerful adversaries as the AP, the Hearst Examiner reporters whose stories would automatically be wired to the New York Journal, and special writers for the World, the Herald and the Times. Lord was an eminently realistic man, who cherished no illusions. The Sun was in a tough spot and he knew it.

When Will Irwin suddenly appeared in the city room, the desperate Lord conceived an idea. He would not, as Irwin requested, send the prodigal reporter to San Francisco. That would take five days, with no assurance that he would be able to enter the city. But Irwin loved his San Francisco and, even as a Park Row reporter, had reminisced about it constantly. Lord decided to feed Irwin every possible bit of news about San Francisco and let him try writing about the scene as if there. News was almost nonexistent at first and to get material Lord and Irwin telegraphed California editors outside San Francisco and alerted the Sun Bureau in Washington to forward any information from Government sources. With only the sparsest of information to begin on, Irwin took pencil in hand—through a long journalistic life he remained a pencil-wielder—and started to write. In the first afternoon, he wrote enough to fill eight columns of tight-packed, atmospheric story, and from this point it became apparent to all Park Row that the Sun—by a method which would only later be divulged—was furnishing the best descriptive accounts of the San Francisco earthquake.

Yet even this feat appears minor when placed against the fact that Irwin, with time out for hasty naps, bolted food and quick trips to a Turkish bath, wrote steadily on the earthquake story for eight days. Following the first afternoon, he averaged fourteen columns a day. To do this, he not only had to write, but also assimilate news from outside the office and the verbal briefings given him by

Lord. Where another paper might have been content to await the early editions of other papers, then rewrite the rival stories, the Sun with its proud heritage could not do this. Irwin's accounts, in order to sustain the Sun's hallowed tradition, had to seem more up to the moment and better written than those taken from eyewitness accounts relayed by the telegraph wire from San Francisco. (Later it was learned that the Laffan Bureau correspondent in San Francisco was furiously filing stories. But the military commander of the disaster area had issued orders that only accredited news services could use the precious wire facilities. The telegraph operator had never heard of the Laffan Bureau and, after accepting copy for the Sun, calmly filed it on the floor.)

As Irwin wrote his memorable account, the first four days were a period of intense strain. At the end of them he was, in his own words, "quaking and drooling like a nonagenarian." Then, by way of another Park Row city room, he learned that a San Francisco reporter had inserted in a telegram the news that Irwin's family was safe. This appeared to bring him a new lease on life and, after a quick trip to a Turkish bath, he returned to the Sun to labor four more days in a state he later recalled as "a calm, high, god-like state of consciousness." From that moment on, throughout his life, Irwin remained fascinated by the psychic aspects of his heroic endurance. He began to think with William James that "ordinary work brings fatigue; extraordinary hard work under great strain sometimes puts us into a state of being where the mind seems to burn with its own light and fatigue seems impossible."

In this state, Irwin actually seemed able to *see* the city of San Francisco in all its desolation. Several times, when stories of the disaster were put before him, he brushed them aside with the words, "That's not true." Later reports certified the accuracy of his hunches. Also, in the course of his second four days Irwin took a period when he might have been napping to write a background piece called "The City That Was," which began:

> The old San Francisco is dead. The gayest, lightest-hearted, most pleasure-loving city of this continent, and in many ways the most interesting and romantic, is a horde

of huddled refugees living among ruins. It may rebuild; it probably will; but those who have known that peculiar city by the Golden Gate, and have caught its flavor of the Arabian Nights feel that it can never be the same.

It is as though a pretty, frivolous woman had passed through a great tragedy. She survives, but she is sobered and different. If it rises out of the ashes it must be a modern city, much like other cities and without its old flavor.

Irwin's total eight-day writing exploit has come to be referred to under the title "The City That Was." Actually, this was only a small part of his entire stint. Yet "The City That Was" story possessed such high literary merit that it was published in book form and remained in print for over twenty-five years as an example of remarkable newspaper writing.

After eight days, the Laffan Bureau correspondent in San Francisco made his presence felt. His stories began getting through. This left Irwin free to abandon his prodigious feat and obtain some sleep. But in his still-exalted state, he did not. Instead he attended a testimonial dinner to a newspaper colleague and had an excellent time. Irwin was in no way opposed to alcohol, but during his eight strenuous days had not touched it for fear his senses would be dulled. Now he lifted highballs along with the rest, and went home to bed as if his day had been a thoroughly ordinary one. But the impression of his experience never left him. Thirty-five years later he wrote:

> Somewhere in the mysterious background of human consciousness there exists an area of higher space. Let a man once enter it, and he rises above himself; all his powers, and especially that endurance-at-speed which is the mark of intellectual superiority, seem to multiply themselves by ten.

On the night of June 25, 1906, a new musical comedy called *Mamzelle Champagne* opened on the roof of the Madison Square Garden, America's largest entertainment building. Built in 1890 at a cost of four and a half million, and designed by the ubiquitous Stanford White, the New Garden, as it was still called, occupied an en-

tire block bounded by Madison and Fourth Avenues at the northeast end of Madison Square. Its main feature was a huge arena, three
hundred feet long and two hundred feet wide, covered by a high
arched ceiling supported by curved steel beams under a sliding sky-
light. Around this cavernous space ran tiers of elegant boxes, mez-
zanine floors and balconies, accommodating seven thousand in all.
Traditionally the Madison Square Garden arena was the home of
circuses, horse shows and similar spectacles. For prize fights, wrestling
matches, political rallies and conventions, spectators could be seated
in the arena itself, thus making it possible to accommodate almost
fourteen thousand.

In addition to this celebrated arena, the Madison Square Garden boasted a sumptuous theatre and concert hall, a restaurant and
lodge rooms. Two years after it opened, the Roof Garden was added
with elegant though informal atmosphere, supper tables and a stage
suited to frothy entertainments like *Mamzelle Champagne*. With all
this, however, the most unique feature of the Garden remained the
Tower, which rose a majestic 341 feet above the sidewalk. As was
his custom, Stanford White had gone abroad for inspiration, pattern-
ing his Tower after the Giralda Tower in Seville. Atop the Tower
stood the beautifully poised, fourteen-foot gilded-copper statue of
Diana, created by St. Gaudens. This lithe figure of the Goddess of
the Chase was bare to the waist, and held a bow and arrow which
always pointed into the wind, since the statue was based with extreme delicacy on forty steel balls. Even so, when the city fathers
pointed with pride to the many marvels of Madison Square Garden,
the lissom Diana was usually slighted. For the idea of a bare-
bosomed female, even one revolving gently over three hundred feet
in the air, was a shocking one for the time. Clergymen on occasion
attacked the statue from pulpits, and mothers wrote indignant letters
to newspapers stating that, while minding children in Madison
Square Park, they had observed men with spyglasses turned upward
to view the nearly nude Diana. "Is our city safe, when such things
are permitted?" they demanded.

Over the years the daring statue of Diana had merged in the
public mind with whispers of scandalous activities in the luxurious
bachelor apartment Stanford White had created for himself high in

the Tower. These were later found to be largely untrue, but it was exciting to hear and pass on stories of bedrooms with ceiling mirrors, divans covered with leopard skins, nude paintings and sculptures and erotic tapestries, as well as sliding panels and secret doors through which young ladies could scamper when outraged husbands or lovers pounded on the door.

These were all intangible whispers, but one thing was tangible. Any girl Stanford White entertained anywhere, anytime, would be young, for his love of beauties in the late teens or early twenties—never more—was as well known as his genius as an architect. Tall, redheaded, barrel-chested, energetic, beginning at fifty-three to run over into fat, White strode through New York as if it were a feudal domain over which he held sway—as, in a sense, it was. White was married, with a son at Harvard. Yet his flaunting of beautiful young girls was something the puritanical city had perforce to accept as a price for the superb buildings he designed for it. As Richard Harding Davis would shortly be the only person to point out, beautiful girls aided White's genius no less than the ancient palaces of Verona or the towers of Seville.

No one really expected any artistic merit in the frothy shows produced on the Madison Square Garden Roof, but perhaps because of the elegant and relaxing atmosphere New York drama critics never failed to attend Roof openings. On June 25, 1906, though, there was one drama critic absent. Charles Darnton, of the World, was in Europe on his honeymoon. In his place, the city room had sent the experienced and hard-working Albert Payson Terhune, whose assignments were usually of a far more robust sort. Terhune had looked forward to this as a pleasant change of pace, and had brought his wife along to enjoy the evening. But *Mamzelle Champagne*, of which little had been expected, offered even less. Once the viewer had become accustomed to the sight of chorus girls in tights, there was little else. Terhune watched with some interest until the beginning of a number in which the girls began fencing with one another on the stage. This was plainly another excuse by the director to get the girls in tights and Terhune let his eyes wander, noting the presence of Stanford White in the space close to the stage where celebrities were permitted to dine.

The red-haired, fatty architect was attired in immaculate evening dress. Strangely enough, on this night the connoisseur of young beauty was alone, supping without the usual female companion. Terhune was trying to assimilate this unusual fact when he saw a young man suddenly appear, to begin pacing up and down before White's table. White quickly became aware of him, but pretended not to be. Writes Terhune: "Every time the tall youth passed the table he would pause to glower furiously down on the ostentatiously oblivious older man." Terhune, like most members of the audience, well knew the reason for the glower, and slowly the drama before White's table drew the attention of the entire audience. On stage the girls broke into the chorus of their song, *I challenge you to a du-u-el, I challenge you to a du-u-el,* then joined ranks to march to the footlights with weapons drawn. As they did, the young man finished pacing. He was now, by one account,

> . . . a scant two feet from the man at the table. Unhurriedly and without visible emotion, he drew from the shadows of his coat a shining revolver and, still unhurried, lifted the weapon to the level of the seated man's eyes. With three well-aimed bullets, he shot him dead.

Terhune saw him fire three times "in slow and rhythmic succession." But, however the shots were fired, they were unmistakably effective. White toppled over and fell to the floor, while the young man lifted up his arms in a gesture that seemed to mean victory. Then he dropped his arms, broke the revolver, unloaded it and handed the remaining bullets to a Garden policeman who, with unusual presence of mind, had rushed forward to seize him. To the policeman the young man remarked casually, "He deserved it, he ruined my wife." He accompanied these words with an indifferent nod at the corpse.

Most of those watching first considered this murderous byplay a practical joke or a part of the show, perhaps a tie-in with the girls-in-tights duelling number. But now a radiantly beautiful, dark-haired young girl in obvious distress ran between the tables and threw herself on the neck of the young man. It was Evelyn Nesbit Thaw, who cried out, "Oh, Harry, I never thought you'd do it *that* way!"

Terhune waited no longer. Instinct told him there was still time to catch the first edition of the World. Rushing through the stunned audience, he began—to make a scene that might have been used to advantage in the numerous literary and motion-picture re-creations of the crime—plunging down the elegant red-carpeted stairs of the Madison Square Garden Roof. Public telephones were rarities in June, 1906, but Terhune recalled a wall phone on the first floor of the building. This he found infuriatingly in use by a man holding a smirking conversation with a girl named Tessie. Terhune signalled that he needed the phone for an important purpose. The amorous man shook his head in foolish negative. The bruiser-like Terhune glared for a moment, then used his amateur-boxer muscles to yank him bodily from the phone. Then Terhune impatiently began jiggling for the operator.

There were many hazards to telephoning in 1906. It was necessary, in placing a call, to reach the central operator, or Hello-girl, then give her the desired number. If the operators on a given night were busy or indifferent, this could take time. Terhune was calling on one of those nights. As he stood jiggling the receiver of the wall phone, another hazard appeared. The man he had pulled from the phone returned with several friends, all armed with chairs and eager to do bodily harm to the burly reporter. While Terhune jiggled with one hand, he desperately fended off his attackers with an arm and a leg. While thus occupied, he got his call through to the city room of the World. "Harry Thaw just killed Stanford White," he shouted.

With this spirited scene, Terhune fades from the scene of the Thaw case and Irvin S. Cobb takes over. As a beginning reporter— it seems impossible ever to refer to Cobb as a cub—on the Louisville Press, Cobb had once left the scene of a Kentucky murder trial for a weekend trip with his new bride. It had been a terrible blunder. Though assured by the presiding judge that there would be no sessions over the weekend, Cobb awoke the next morning to discover that court had unexpectedly convened in dramatic night session. Hastening back to the trial, he found that a friendly telegraph operator, aware of his absence, had secured a transcript of the night's proceedings in court and wired it to Louisville under Cobb's by-line. With the addition of only a lead paragraph by the city desk, this had made such an exciting story that Cobb was congratulated by his city editor.

It also brought Cobb a new slant on trial reporting. Stick to the proceedings, he told himself—don't try to embellish. With the coming of the trial-of-the-century Thaw case, Cobb astounded the city editor of the New York Evening World by asking permission to cover it alone. Other newspapers were assigning from two to four star men to the trial, among them Samuel Hopkins Adams (World), Roy Howard (Scripps-McRae), Alfred Henry Lewis (Journal), and Roland B. Molineux, himself recently acquitted of murder (Herald). In addition, most papers were sending sketch artists like Alonzo Kimball, C. Allen Gilbert, Homer Davenport, Richard Boehm, Wallace Morgan and the two World stalwarts, Perley and Stein.

Yet in the face of all this opposition, Cobb insisted on working for the Evening World alone. He worked out a system by which a single copy boy (other papers had dozens dashing in and out) took his copy, sheet by scrawled sheet, to a basement corridor of the Criminal Courts Building, where the script was read over a private telephone wire to a stenographer in a booth in the World city room a few blocks away. By doing this, Cobb averaged some twelve thousand words a day: more than the teams of reporters representing other papers. Further, the quality of his writing was such that the London Daily Dispatch commented editorially on its excellence.

But perhaps the most potent factor in Cobb's favor was his state of mind concerning the case. Drawling, homely, the perennial country boy turned big-city reporter, Cobb was frankly dazzled by the Thaw case. Like other American males, he was especially intrigued by the figure of Evelyn Nesbit Thaw, who in the courtroom tried to wipe out recollection of a freewheeling past by appearing decked out in a reefer jacket, demure flat collar and big bow tie. All this made her look like a virginal schoolgirl innocently trapped in a hideous web of circumstance. Cobb, like all young men who saw her, never forgot her luscious beauty. The man who covered the first World War, numerous succeeding trials-of-the-century, and became one of the top fiction writers of his time, could still look back on the 1906-7 courtroom and write in his autobiography, *Exit Laughing,* published in 1941:

> In her latter teens and her early twenties she was, I think, the most exquisitely lovely human being I ever looked at—the slim, quick grace of a fawn, a head that sat on her flawless throat as a lily on its stem, eyes that were the color of blue-brown pansies and the size of half dollars; a mouth made of rumpled rose petals.

CHAPTER FOURTEEN

The Incredible Chapin

THE reporters assigned to cover the two shocking Thaw trials—the first resulted in a hung jury, at the second Thaw was declared insane and committed to an asylum—were widely considered the most fortunate of men. Yet there were a few alive who would never consider any reporter lucky. These comprised the select group of newspapermen who had once been, or were still, city editors. Charles Edward Russell was typical. After serving as city editor of the World and the Journal, he never ceased to look back on the post as the most enviable journalism had to offer. Of the city editor, Russell wrote:

> He is an artist. As a painter before his easel, so sits the city editor every day before the paper he is to make. He can lay on the crime and give his paper a red hue; he can develop the humorous side of a day's life in the city; he can seize on a story in low tones from the hearts of the lost-and-found advertisements; he can work out every contrast of scarlet and purple, for every tint is supplied by the events before him. He has but to choose, combine, and study the results. And all the time he can derive from his weavings the satisfaction that pertains only to the exercise of art, which is now and always a means to transfer a feeling.

In the early years of the century—and indeed until a certain dark day in 1918—the words *City Editor* immediately conjured up in Park Row minds a single terrifying figure. Even among a good many newspaper readers the man was well known. As recently as 1934 Stanley

Walker, in his book *City Editor*, would call him, "Quite possibly
. . . the ablest city editor who ever lived."

This was Charles E. Chapin, the city editor of the Evening
World to whom Martin Green shouted the first news of the *General
Slocum* when it came in over the telephone. Chapin was ever a curious figure in the city room of a newspaper. He invariably dressed like a
bird of rich plumage in the contemporary high style of wasp-waisted
double-breasted suit, spats, pearl tie pin, watch fob and bunched
ascot tie, the gaudy colors of which bespoke a partiality for such hues
as baby blue, pink, orange, purple and red. He was granite-faced,
and under a close-clipped military-type mustache, his mouth seemed
a tight, straight slash. On the bridge of his thin nose perched a
tortoise-shell pince-nez, anchored to his buttonhole by a dignified
black ribbon. Sparse gray hair covered his head and of his eyes Irvin
Cobb, the Evening World's most prized reporter, once wrote:
"Ophidians have such eyes, but they are rare in human heads." His
voice was called a blend of snarl, whine and nasal modulation. In all
a contemporary pictured him this way: "His face was a gray paving
block, with jaw as square as a lynx's jaws and as tight. His snake eyes
were dull and empty. The shallow light from these eyes never seemed
to come from within but from without. His voice seemed to match
the rest of him. Big game hunters say that a hostile leopard has a
voice like that."

Chapin's high point in outrageous newspaper behavior no doubt
came as the shocked and queasy rewrite men beat out the Evening
World's coverage of the *Slocum* disaster. Then his trim, erect, fop-
pish figure capered about the city room with every trace of enjoyment, to make him seem a figure of jerking, hysterical life in a ballet
with a background of morbid death. He would run up and down,
peering over shoulders to read the nauseating details of the tragedy as
they were typed out. Then, standing erect, he would shout, "Women
and children jumping overboard with clothing afire! Water full of
charred bodies!" And between these jackal outcries he would strut
exultantly up and down, humming a simmering, happy, tuneless
tune.

Many are the stories told about Charles Chapin, or Hardboiled
Charlie, as his staff called him. Most deal with his sadistic, bullying

cruelty, for as lord of the city room of the Evening World he was an iron-handed dictator, a relentless despot, a whip-cracking slave driver. Chapin would fire a man for being two minutes late, for staying home to minister to a sick family, or for getting knocked unconscious in pursuit of a story. Cobb, his star reporter, spoke for all Chapin staffs on one of the rare days when Hardboiled Charlie phoned in to report sick. "Let us hope it's nothing trivial," Cobb muttered. Yet the hatred of the men who worked under him failed to deter Chapin. He even seemed to glory in it. "In twenty years, I never saw or spoke to a member of the staff outside the office or talked to them in the office about anything except the business of the moment," he boasted once. "I gave no confidences, I invited none. I was myself a machine, and the men I worked with were cogs. The human element never entered into the scheme of getting out the paper. It was my way of doing things."

In the city room of the Evening World Chapin considerably increased his awesomeness by sitting in splendor behind a large flat desk on a raised dais in the center of the room. From there the snarling whine of a voice whiplashed orders. After years of dealing with flaring headlines, Hardboiled Charlie spoke almost exclusively in newspaper terms. His vocabulary consisted mainly of the short, quick words favored by headline writers: *Probe, rift, fray, slay.* Not only did Chapin prefer such terse words, but headlines dotted his conversation. As he snapped out orders in the city room, he could not say, "Hurry up with the story of the child who was killed." Instead it would be, "Hurry up with TINY TOT WITH PENNY CLUTCHED IN CHUBBY HAND DIES UNDER TRAIN BEFORE MOTHER'S EYES."

Most of the reporters clustered around Chapin's raised dais tried at one time or another to picture the demon city editor in words. One pictured him as "Something of Caligula, with a touch of Barnum, a dash of Narcissus, a spicing of Machiavelli." Another was struck by "the unblinking stare of those opaque eyes." Still another saw him as "all pouter-breasted and springy, like an old gray cock pigeon, strutting to his place on the city-room platform."

Chapin himself was a firm believer in brevity in writing and posted signs around the city room which spelled out TERSENESS in block letters. Thus it is perhaps fitting that the aptest phrase ever ap-

plied to him is also the tersest. This was "gnarled genius." Chapin
was a gnarled genius indeed, and never seemed more so than when
he sat behind his throne-like desk stuffing his mouth with sweets—for
a reason. As a young man Chapin had been a problem drinker. He
had taken the pledge and the contemporary Keeley Cure, but continued to maintain that the desire for drink flamed high within him.
In the belief that sweets fermented in his stomach and to some ex-
tent soothed his still raging thirst, he lived on a diet almost totally
sugar. One member of his staff remembers: "Every few minutes
Chapin sent a copy boy out for food. He ate ice cream cones, canned
peaches, jam, candy, sticky nut bars, and coffee that was half
sugar." And when not stuffing this endless assortment of sweetments
into himself, the stone-faced man assauged his nervousness by puffing at a cigar or clamping the cold butt in his mouth, holding it tight
in his iron jaw.

One day, as Chapin sat munching a mouthful of candy, he discovered something he did not like in a piece of copy. He called its
author to him and there followed a short, taut verbal exchange. The
reporter departed in the general direction of his hat and coat and
Chapin turned to address the entire city room. "That is the one hundred and eighth man I've fired," he announced with vast satisfaction.
(Legend today has it that Chapin fired 108 men in his entire career,
but this number actually was reached when he had many years to
go.)

On another morning, the dapper, pouter-pigeon figure strutted
into the city room to pause before the rewrite desk behind which sat
his rewrite staff of Irvin Cobb, Martin Green and Lindsay Denison,
three of the finest newspapermen in New York of the day. "I was telling Mrs. Chapin this morning that everyone thinks I am a mean son
of a bitch," Chapin stated. "Do you think I am a mean son of a
bitch, Cobb?" Cobb quickly declared he did not, as did Green and
Denison in turn. Chapin then proceeded to his desk, apparently reassured, and set about being a mean son of a bitch for the rest of the
day. On still another occasion, he summoned to the dais a reporter
who was about to leave on a well-earned vacation. Chapin fixed him
with a baleful eye and whined, "I just want to tell you that if, on
your return, your work does not materially improve, the Evening

World will no longer require your services." To a newly hired reporter named Richard Schayer, he was similarly comforting. When
his first week's pay check got to him, Schayer found that he had not
been paid for one day's work. "Don't let it worry you, Mr. Schayer,"
Chapin said, in the snarl and whine. "When it comes time to fire
you, I'll make sure to do it a day ahead of time, so you won't lose
anything."

Chapin's cruelties never ceased. He lived in an era when Broadway producers traditionally sent large blocks of free opening-night
seats to newspaper city rooms. At other Park Row papers, the city editor would see that the drama critic got his pair, then reward other reporters with the rest. Not so Chapin. He presented the drama critic
his two and usually kept another pair for himself. Then he awaited a
moment when he knew the eyes of the entire city room were upon
him and ostentatiously tore the remainder up. It was a sad sight to
underpaid reporters anxious to entertain wives or sweethearts, but it
also affected the copy boys who might have liked a night at the theatre. One former copy boy who well remembers this is Walter Marshall, son of Hamilton Laidlaw Marshall, a World editor. On school
vacations Marshall, who grew up to become a reporter on the Daily
Mirror, filled in as a copy boy on the Evening World. "I used to keep
one eye on that batch of theatre tickets all afternoon," he recalls. "My
heart would begin to sink when Chapin grabbed them in his bony
hands and began to arrange them in tearing position. He never tore
them neatly in two, so that any could be retrieved and pasted together. He tore them into tiny bits, then let them fall like snow—
not into a wastebasket, but into the spittoon he used all day. There
was never any hope of getting a free theatre ticket after that. The
whole staff knew it."

Yet men worked heroically for Chapin, and at times appeared
even happy to do so. At other times, they were torn between admiration for his newspaper craftsmanship and hatred for his city-room
meanness. One reason men could stand Chapin was his wholehearted
respect for straight news. The seemingly souless man actually appeared to worship what Cobb called "that inky-nosed, nine-eyed,
clay-footed god called News." Chapin approved the photographs just

coming into newspaper prominence, but he despised serials, comic strips, contests, puzzles, and other features which were supposed circulation-getters. By his estimate, these only stole space which rightly belonged to straight reporting of events. His city-room staff, news reporters all, approved heartily of his attitude.

Men also found it possible to labor under the city-room tyrant because a curious quirk in newspapermen—and, perhaps, in everyone—makes them inclined to admire the man who works hard. And no matter how hard Chapin drove his reporters, he drove himself harder. He rose at five A.M. daily, took a brisk canter in Central Park atop a fifteen-hundred-dollar horse given him by a grateful Joseph Pulitzer. He was at the Evening World office by seven A.M. and at eight was crouched ready to fire any of his staff who arrived a minute late. From that instant he labored like a maniac. Unlike many executives who overload themselves with work, everything Chapin did made sense. His work counted: there was no waste motion, no show, no show-off. His men respected him for this, as well.

Chapin possessed enormous competence. "This malign, vulpine, competent creature," he was once called. Similar descriptions begin with abuse and end in grudging tribute to his all-around newspaper genius. He could, it was often stated, smell disaster and sniff scandal a mile away. Chapin's true uniqueness as an editor lay in an uncanny ability to subordinate his human feelings to greed for news. Thus with the East River glutted with the charred bodies of women and children, Chapin had no thought for the dead and bereaved. To him this was New York's most dreadful disaster and he, Charles Chapin, was fortunate enough to be sitting in an editor's chair with the responsibility for covering it. It filled him with a wild, gloating glee—which made him, in turn, a great newspaperman.

Though Chapin contained no visible milk of human kindness, he did show odd respect for the men working under him. He reviled them, fired them, permitted no personal contact. At the same time he rendered a special tribute. Having hired a man, he gave him more responsibility than was customary among city editors of the time. In the rather high-flown prose he developed after leaving Chapin's influence, Irvin Cobb summed it up this way:

Chapin, having set this man or that on a stint, thereafter left them to their several devices. For him there was no harassing of legmen over the telephone, no shouted demands that all concerned make sure every possible pump was being siphoned, every possible rat hole being watched—and no nervous hovering over some hard-pressed rewrite man. Chapin plainly figured that it would be a reflection on his own judgment were he to display uneasiness, either with the chore or with the outcome.

Ensconced behind his throne-like desk, munching candy or clamping the remains of a dead cigar in his tight mouth, Chapin never manifested the slightest sense of humor. Infrequently he showed signs of being human. As an editor he had a great partiality for what he fondly called daffy stories. These were the kind—written best by Frank Ward O'Malley of the Sun—in which a minor incident (or no incident at all) was built by hyperbole, satire, or whimsey into an amusing feature. The men Chapin never fired were the rare reporters who could, to his satisfaction, write the daffy stories. His tolerance of such men once caused him to undergo considerable personal humiliation. A reporter with a gift for daffy stories customarily added to his Evening World income by writing extravagant serials for rival newspapers. In the course of one, he invented a murderous explosive which threatened the existence of all mankind. The author then produced the perfect name for this horrendous substance. He called it Chapinite. This resulted in such a happy reaction along Park Row that soon the entire serial revolved around Chapinite. At his desk on the dais, Chapin would growl, snarl and hurl black looks at the offending genius. But he never fired him. His daffy stories were too good.

Chapin printed news in blaring, exaggerated fashion which a large segment of the New York population liked. When taken to task for this sensationalism, he would virtuously declare, "I never printed anything worse than some human being did. If God permits such things to happen, how can they be too terrible to print?" By this rule, the Evening World never ceased to make money, a fact which gave Chapin the convenient delusion that his paper was keeping the

Pulitzer enterprises afloat. He saw the World as the respectable but money-losing member of the family, while his Evening World was the unruly provider of necessary finances. "The Morning," he later declared, "was J. P's pet, but the Evening paid the bills. When I was city editor my rag made a clean profit of half a million every year. That gave the old man plenty of money to sink in sweetness and light for the Morning. Sweetness and light are pleasant, but seldom profitable."

Pulitzer himself did much to encourage Chapin's feelings of high self-satisfaction. The absentee publisher left his demon city editor almost completely alone, something he rarely did with other editors in his organization. He even permitted Chapin to fire Joseph Pulitzer, Jr., for when that young man was deemed ready to begin a newspaper career his father had immediately assigned him to Chapin for training. Chapin, in turn, gave him over to the guidance of a veteran court reporter. One afternoon he felt an urge to commune in person with the new cub and phoned the pressroom of the court, only to be informed that young Pulitzer was not there. "Where is he?" Chapin demanded. "He had an appointment with his tailor, Boss," he was told. Chapin's straight mouth tightened. "Have him report back here and get his pay," he snapped. "He's fired." Chapin was every bit as good as his threat. Young Pulitzer was fired from the Evening World. The elder Pulitzer said not a word.

So while other city editors fell decapitated along the byways, the ghoulish Chapin walked proudly with head erect, to attain remarkable longevity on Park Row. He even became, if anything, more the complete newspaperman. It was the fanatical Chapin who created the rewrite man as he is known in city rooms today. When telephones began coming into common use, Chapin immediately recognized the great part the new instrument could play in newsgathering. While other city rooms still dispatched men to cover stories, Chapin, ever greedy for news to fill the Extras he loved, made a checkerboard chart of the entire city and placed a reporter in each of the squares. The reporter was responsible for news in his square. Then, instead of rushing back to the office to write it, he phoned in the story to a rewrite man.

In getting scoops for his beloved paper, Chapin appeared to op-

erate with an uncanny sixth sense for news. "He was an inspired
tyrant," one of his men recalls, "with a kind of occult instinct for detecting an unsuspected or craftily hidden sensation." When Chapin
himself was asked how he always seemed to know where news clouds
were gathering, the terrifying man would turn winsome. "A little
birdie tells me," he would say in what he considered a cute voice.
Having seen Chapin's unerring intuition at work many times, Cobb
and others came to believe that this was possibly the case—or,
more concretely, that Chapin actually did possess psychic powers. Yet
in retrospect Chapin's hidden powers would seem to be a mixture
of ceaseless drive to cover every news event possible and a major
general's power over the men under him. "Journalism is the art of
knowing where hell is going to break loose next and having a man
there to cover it," one of Chapin's fellow editors once defined.
Chapin seemed to live in terror that hell might break loose without
the Evening World having a man on the scene. As a result, he assigned men to nearly any activity he heard about. Thus when he
learned that Mayor Gaynor of New York was leaving on what seemed
to be a routine trip to Europe, Chapin ordered a reporter to accompany him from his Brooklyn home to the pier. He also told a
photographer to be at the pier to take the Mayor's photo. As the
Evening World photographer lifted his camera an assassin stepped
forward and shot Gaynor, to make what still remains one of the
greatest of all news photographs. It also produced a classic Chapin
story. For when the developed photograph was handed to the man
who could inhumanly subordinate human emotions, he chortled with
pleasure. "What a wonderful thing," he cried. "Look, blood all over
him—and exclusive, too."

Chapin's other sensational scoops came from the same determined drive to know everything possible himself and to have his men
cover every possible news source. Once he boarded the French
steamer *La Burgoyne* to bid farewell to sailing friends. Passenger lists
were being handed about and Chapin instinctively grabbed one.
Two days later the city room of the Evening World was electrified
by the flash that *La Burgoyne* had been sunk off Halifax. In those
days shipping companies kept careless records, and all printed passenger lists had gone down with the ship. No one alive was sure who

had been aboard—except Chapin who had held tight to his list. That night, and for days thereafter, the Evening World alone had thorough coverage of the *La Burgoyne* story.

In the last analysis, however, it is not for hard work and uncanny news intuition that Charles Chapin has become a legend. It is for sadistic cruelty. During the years he was behind the city desk, nearly a hundred men on his staff went to their graves, most of them under forty. As a result, the few hardy souls who found it possible to continue working under Chapin were gruesomely dubbed the Happy Pallbearers. These were days before the Newspaper Guild and, like any employer in any contemporary business, Chapin could fire men without warning or explanation. It was a weapon he used ruthlessly. Indeed, in his more than 108 opportunities he became something of a connoisseur of firings. Some he planned in advance, savoring his secret knowledge of the blow to fall. "He would carry a grievance for days," recalls one colleague, "hugging it to him like a possession dear and fragile, before he loosed the vials of wrath on the condemned man."

Most of the men Chapin fired nursed an undying hatred of the freakish city editor. One was a reporter named Kenneth Coolbaugh, who wrote: "Red letter days in Chapin's calendar were those on which he deprived a fellow worker of a chance to earn a living. There was always an extra measure of enjoyment if the victim was well along in years and fighting to keep pace with the younger men around him; a kid who was filling the role of head of the house for a widowed mother; or happened to have a wife in the hospital. . . ." When firing a failing old-timer, Chapin sometimes delightedly twisted the knife by coupling him in his last assignments with a young reporter. In this way he gave a final blow to the man's spirit by making it apparent that he had become old and spavined at the game. When this had penetrated sufficiently, Chapin unceremoniously gave him the boot.

One morning a reporter hobbled in with his foot bandaged. "I scalded my foot, Boss," he explained. "Had to go to the doctor." Chapin made no comment at the time, but the following Saturday he beckoned the man to his desk. "I didn't fire you the other day," he said, "because I wanted to see how long you would fake that phony limp. Now get out."

Chapin was a demon for punctuality but after a period when his staff had been seriously depleted because of firings for tardiness, he refined his technique. He developed semi-firing: that is, he would fire temporarily. "You," he would snarl at an offender, "you know eight o'clock is the hour to report for work around here. It's two minutes past. Suppose you just turn around and go home for a week, without pay." Chapin fought tenaciously against having female reporters on his staff, but finally on orders from above he hired Zona Gale, who later became a famous short-story writer and novelist. After a fine start, Miss Gale became as unpunctual as the men. She was late one morning, at which Chapin warned her. The next morning she was late again. He fired her, and she began to cry. In Chapin's pious code respect for sweet womanhood carried enormous weight. His staff watched fascinated as emotion battled across his usually bleak countenance. Finally he put a forgiving hand on Miss Gale's shoulder. "Run along, child," he soothed. "They don't pay me enough salary to make girls cry."

No less than unpunctual reporters, Chapin disliked those who were unable to handle assignments. When a young reporter covering a big fire phoned back for instructions, Chapin directed him tersely, "Find the hottest place and jump in." His prime hatreds merged when reporters phoned late to report that they had failed on a story. For such occasions Chapin evolved a splendid technique. "Your name is Smith, isn't it?" he would ask with elaborate politeness. "You work for the Evening World?" When the reporter admitted this, Chapin's voice switched to full snarl: "You're a liar. Smith got fired from the Evening World an hour ago." Once, however, a bibulous reporter beat Chapin to this punch. Disguising his voice, he phoned the frosty-faced Chapin. "Have you a man named Arthur Hogan working for you?" he asked. "Yes," Chapin answered politely, "Hogan works for me." "You're a goddam liar," Hogan then yelled in his normal voice. "I've just resigned."

Perhaps the most famous Chapin story—or at least on a par with Cobb's, "Let's hope it's nothing trivial"—stems from the time the martinet dispatched a reporter to interview an Irish contractor whose wife had run away with a Chinese delivery boy. The burly, infuriated husband threw the reporter down a flight of stairs. "He says he'll kill me if he ever sees me again," the young man reported to Chapin over the phone. Irvin Cobb and others always considered Chapin a notable physical coward, but on the telephone he was ever the mighty man. "Go back and tell that so-and-so he can't intimidate me," he shouted.

Chapin governed himself by such an old-fashioned code that he tried to avoid profanity, and always held himself in high, humorless regard. It would seem that anyone who outwitted him in tricky fashion would earn his vituperative wrath. Yet when Chapin was fooled, he reacted by exhibiting a charity and forgiveness that might well have been applied elsewhere.

Once, for instance, it was announced in the World offices that any reporter who became a father would receive a five-dollar weekly raise. Almost immediately a bright young fellow stepped up to Chapin's throne and said, "Congratulate me, Boss. My wife gave birth to triplets last night."

Chapin, so harsh, so eternally suspicious of humanity, believed him and with a flourish signed the voucher for an added fifteen dollars weekly. Soon he discovered that he had been tricked, but instead of firing the brash young scoundrel he allowed him to keep the raise and thereafter favored him. Chapin also reacted unaccountably on the day an office spy—like James Gordon Bennett, he encouraged his men to tell tales on each other—reported that one of the star reporters had taken a young girl under his protective wing. Though married and a father, the reporter had established a love nest for the sweet young thing. The informant who whispered this titillating bit expected Chapin to soar to moral heights and fire the offending reporter. Instead, Hardboiled Charlie assimilated the spicy item, then licked his lips and admiringly said, "The son of a gun! Double his salary, he'll need it now."

Nowadays Charles Chapin, with his driving lust for news, his unrefined sadism, his rigid moral outlook and other eccentricities, seems like a psychoanalyst's nightmare. Oddly enough, it was Chapin who, in 1898, succeeded Ernest Chamberlain as city editor of the Evening World when Chamberlain went mad on the eve of the Spanish-American War. Later, irreverent sources opined that where it took Chamberlain only twenty-four hours to go mad, it took Chapin considerably longer. But the fact remains that from the moment he mounted the city editor's dais peculiar forces seemed to attack Chapin. Another man might have fought them off, but apparently Chapin was at their mercy while they chipped away at his sanity, bringing him the complexes and delusions of grandeur which resulted in the isolation and awful sadism of the Evening World years of his life.

Chapin was born in Watertown, New York, in 1858, and like most other boys of his generation arrived in a household as poor as any described in the books of Horatio Alger or G. A. Henty. Yet in one feature the Chapin family—poor, obscure, sometimes hungry—was set apart. Chapin's mother's sister had married a tight-fisted Albany gentleman named Russell Sage. Sage had started working at the age of ten in a grocery store, for two dollars a week. Displaying a will to succeed that might have appalled even Horatio Alger, he prospered in Albany. After the Civil War he moved on to New York, where he confidently planned to conquer the giant money marts.

Russell Sage has come down to us as a benevolent philanthropist. Actually he was the most miserly of men, as niggardly with emotions as with actual cash. The Chapin family well knew how Uncle Russell was faring in New York: plunging full-speed-ahead toward a final eighty million dollars. The poverty-ridden family also knew there was no point in asking their whiskered relative for financial help—robber-baron relatives never did such things in those days. When at the age of fourteen, Charles was told he would have to leave school to go to work, no one thought of appealing to Uncle Russell for funds to keep him in school. Uncle Russell himself had begun at ten. "What's the boy been waiting for?" the forbidding man would have grumbled angrily.

At fourteen, Charles was thin and tiny, "an underfed and woeful little fellow." For reasons never quite explained, this woeful youngster journeyed to Ohio to start his working career. There, he got his first opportunity, that of selling papers. For this he was paid the sum of four dollars a week and permitted to sleep on a pile of old newspapers in a corner of the cellar pressroom. Even for a boy bent on living out the Alger legend, this was insufficient income.

Charles needed more money and applied for work at the telegraph office in the local hotel. He was hired to deliver telegrams at thirteen dollars a month and perquisites—this last being the right to demand an extra twenty-five cents for messages delivered a long distance from the office.

It was a drab existence, plodding the city delivering telegrams, distributing newspapers in the cold, pre-dawn hours, sleeping wrapped in a musty quilt on a pile of messy newspapers. From his hard-wood seat in the telegraph office, Charles could easily see into what seemed to him to be the richly furnished lobby of the local hotel. This ornate lobby came to represent to him the utmost in luxury, a type of existence at an extreme pole from his own. It also brought the lifelong conviction that hotels were the ultimate in luxury and privilege. Later, as the best-paid city editor of his time, Chapin would never live anywhere but in hotels. He also became a man who liked to pontificate, "I can do without the necessities in life, but I must have the luxuries." It always brought amused chuckles, but the statement happened to be true.

"I had no boy friends and made no attempt to cultivate them," Chapin would write of this period in his youth. "My associates were men, chiefly men from whom I could learn something useful." It was a stern, colorless life for a growing boy, the only apparent bright spot coming when Chapin began to dream of someday becoming a newspaperman. Yet before this could happen, the friendless youth fell under the spell of an older boy who wanted to be an actor. Surprisingly, he persuaded Chapin to join him in thoughts of an acting career. More surprisingly, the two boys immediately got jobs with a barnstorming theatrical troupe. Reporters who later worked under Chapin in city rooms were never surprised to learn that their sadistic boss's most successful role as a boy thespian had been in *Uncle Tom's Cabin*. He played Simon Legree.

He also played Romeo—and now enters another matter which drastically shaped his life. In 1879, he married Nellie Beebie, who on occasion had played his Juliet. Though she did not appear so at the time, Nellie was several years older than Chapin, who was twenty-one. The wedding was a hasty, between-shows affair and at its end Nellie Chapin suddenly realized she was wearing a black dress. "Black is an evil omen for a bride," she said, in alarm. In many ways, it was a prophetic remark, for life with Chapin was no lark. This immediately became apparent when the status of married man seemed to rekindle all his old desire to be a newspaperman. He rapidly lost interest in acting and, seizing upon some ill fortune that befell the company, gave his notice. He hustled Nellie to Chicago where he settled her in the inevitable hotel—in all their married life, the pair never lived elsewhere—and set out on a tour of newspaper city rooms. When he got home one night he was a reporter on the Chicago Tribune. Chapin's real life had begun.

No editor who hired Chapin as a reporter ever regretted it. While Nellie Chapin amused herself as best she could at the hotel, Charles proceeded to demonstrate his genius for the newspaper game. As a beginning reporter on the Tribune, he was under city editor Fred Hall, who for twenty-seven years had worked sixteen hours a day, seven days a week, without a single vacation during the entire period. On his head in the city room, winter and summer, Hall wore a battered straw hat. There is no doubt that Chapin's idea of what a city editor should be was much shaped by Hall. He immediately began emulating his boss by devoting his spare time to tracking down stories, even solving murders the Chicago police called hopeless.

After four years he went to the Chicago Star as city editor, and one of the first acts of his new, responsible position was to hire a promising young man named Finley Peter Dunne. Chapin was then only twenty-five, and at this time held such warm feelings for the human race that he started a series called City Slave Girls, exposing working conditions in local sweatshops. This and other features, including an equally humane one urging that the well-to-do leave Christmas presents for the poor at police precinct stations, soon won him a better job as city editor of the Chicago Herald.

In those days of intense Park Row newspaper rivalries, New York City papers scouted the hinterlands for talent, much as big-league baseball teams today cover minor leagues, colleges and high schools. In July, 1891, Chapin made his first visit to New York. Characteristically, he repaired immediately to Park Row where, beside a Nellie Chapin who already looked older than her age, he stood lost in awe and wonder as he gazed up at the gilded dome of the World

Building. Suddenly Chapin felt an impulse. "I'm going in there," he informed Nellie. Leaving her to sun herself on a City Hall bench, Chapin entered the building. He took the elevator to the dome and had himself announced to Ballard Smith. Instantly a figurative red carpet appeared. Smith himself rushed out to shake his hand and lead him inside. A dazed Chapin, who had expected to identify himself laboriously as a Chicago newspaperman, found that Smith knew all about him. Chapin could hardly believe his senses when he heard Smith asking if he would like to work on the World. "I would have bartered ten years of my life for the chance," he wrote later. "It was the realization of my fondest dream."

The following day Chapin went to work as a reporter, and his upward spiral began. As prosperity engulfed the Chapins they took a suite at the Hotel Plaza, the most magnificent of New York hotels. The magnificence may or may not have pleased Nellie, but it did continue the day-by-day barrenness of her Chicago years. Living in a hotel, with Chapin constantly on the job, Nellie had none of things which supposedly make life worth while for a woman. She was childless, always alone. Says one account: "They never owned a stick of furniture and Mrs. Chapin never cooked a meal. She had a maid named Katie, and while her husband worked she and Katie used to take walks and go to the theatre. Mrs. Chapin would tell Katie what a fine man Chapin was and how much she loved him."

It is no wonder that, living such a stagnant existence, Nellie Chapin began to fade rapidly, growing old and drab. On the other hand, Chapin, while his gray hair and gray skin always made him look far older than his years, seemed to grow more lively and spruce. He carried through on this by becoming one of the most dandified of contemporary dressers. He wore natty tweeds and her-ringbones, always with a calendula, gardenia, or bachelor's button in the buttonhole. His winter overcoats sported caracal collars, and he derived great pride from an enviable collection of watch fobs, tie pins, studs and flaming ascot ties. His hair was cut daily, and he always gave off the odor of bay rum or other pungent male perfumes. Yet, in conversation at least, he did not let his enormous vanity turn him from the fading Nellie. He praised her to all and sundry as "such a great little pal." More than one of his colleagues was mystified by the incongruous but apparently sincere devotion he seemed to have for the delicate wisp of a woman who was his wife.

When the new century started to unroll, Chapin increasingly found a rich life ahead of him. As city editor, he was entitled to a certain entree in high places, for he could—and did—kill unflattering stories, and devote much space to dinner parties, debuts and other social functions. But Chapin's real weapon was Russell Sage. No sooner had he arrived in New York than Chapin set about ingratiating himself with his multimillionaire uncle. This was not hard to do, since Sage liked people around to take financial advantage of them. Now a septuagenarian, he still saved money by refusing to wear underwear. When in time the subways opened, Sage liked someone as a companion who would pay his five-cent fare. Usually this companion was Chapin, for early in their new relationship Sage had cemented the younger man to him by assuring him that he, Chapin, would be his sole heir.

"Love of luxury was my besetting sin," a sadder, wiser Chapin wrote in his autobiography. For though he never made more than twenty thousand dollars a year, he began living like a millionaire. He had a team of fast horses and owned one of the first automobiles in New York City. Leaving Nellie at home, he took grand tours of Europe, passing weeks as Mr. Pulitzer's honored guest. He was seen at the race track, ball games and social events. He was able to do this because of his expectancy from Russell Sage. Chapin made no secret of the fact that he would inherit most of his uncle's eighty million, and on this prospect alone borrowed more than fifty thousand dollars. There were other ways in which he made money. Chapin played the stock market, acting on inside tips from his Evening World financial editor. It was also a day of flexible newspaper ethics, and all Park Row knew that Chapin—no less than other city editors —did journalistic favors for the robber barons, in return for which he received tips, considerations, or outright cash.

So while Chapin was known to Park Row as a demon and a scourge, he was something of a benign figure in the sporting and social circles uptown. He also had political influence, and once insisted that Mayor John Purroy Mitchel appoint one of his friends to a judgeship. "Is he a Republican or a Democrat," Mitchel asked plaintively. "I don't know and don't care," Chapin snapped. "I just want to get him the job." Mitchel, who already had his own choice for the post, was forced to accede.

Thus Chapin appeared to have ascended the heights . . . but his first indication that heights can crumble came when news flashed into the city room that Russell Sage had died. Before the knowing eyes of his staff, Chapin tried to manifest suitable sorrow, but he could not resist an occasional anticipatory rubbing of hands. He attended the financier's funeral and bounced through the days following in happy expectation of coming millions. Then he was called to a private phone in the World executive offices. He returned a broken man. Uncle Russell, to whom he had devoted so much attention and time, had left him a mere fifty thousand dollars, not even enough to pay back the sums he had borrowed as Sage's heir.

The next day he rallied and, in an illumination of contemporary newspaper ethics as well as his own, ordered Cobb to write a series of articles calling Sage incompetent when he drew up the will. "There's no doubt," he instructed his star reporter, "that the miserable old ingrate was doddering, senile, and in no shape to dispose of his affairs. He was putty in the hands of any unscrupulous scoundrels who wanted to enrich themselves at the expense of those who are really entitled to a suitable share of his fortune!" It seemed to be Chapin's intention to rally the other neglected heirs to break the will, and some believe that the Sage estate, after reading the first of Cobb's articles, actually bought Chapin off with another fifty thousand. But the luxury-loving man never got his millions, and life seemed empty with the dream of them gone.

From the Evening World dais Chapin continued his pitiless firings, though one incident shows that some seeds of doubt must have entered his soul. There came an afternoon when Chapin salved himself with a particularly brutal dismissal. It was done so cruelly that "Wurra-Wurra" McLaughlin, his assistant city editor, found himself boiling with Irish rage and did the unprecedented by striding to Chapin's desk to remonstrate. Chapin heard him through in wintry silence, then waited until McLaughlin returned to his desk.

Once he was seated Chapin began to lecture him from the eminence of the throne. "McLaughlin," he rasped, "you are too mush-hearted, too sentimental for your own good. You'll never get ahead in this game, never get an inch past where you are now. And when you die, you won't leave a red cent to bury you with."

Such lectures were usually accepted in lip-gnawing silence by his frightened staff, but McLaughlin was still seething. He jumped to his feet and shouted back. "True for you, Chapin, but when I die there'll be a hell of a lot of people who will come to the funeral."

Chapin reacted as if struck by an invisible sledgehammer. He slumped in his chair, the gray face going milk-white, and he winced as if suffering excruciating pain. He made no effort to reply, nor display his usual reflex action of firing the offender. All afternoon he sat hunched and motionless in the chair, eating no candy, staring straight ahead, chewing the dead stub of his cigar to a sodden pulp. Irvin Cobb, already convinced that Chapin was psychic, came to believe that while suffering through this afternoon Chapin tore aside the veil of the future to see clearly the appalling fate that lay before him. "I was sorry for Chapin that day," Cobb later wrote, "and I'm sorry for him now."

When finally he got to his feet, the demon city editor was a broken, dragging figure. But next morning he was his pouter-pigeon self again. He stepped jauntily into the city room wearing a bright orange ascot tie, with a matching calendula in his buttonhole. On the way to his dais he stopped at McLaughlin's desk. "When I got uptown last evening," he informed him, "I told Mrs. Chapin what you told me here in the afternoon. And do you know what Mrs. Chapin said? She said, 'How Irish!'" Giving his harsh, grating, "Ho, ho!" Chapin proceeded on to the dais and with great satisfaction established himself behind the throne-like desk.

As one of his contemporaries said, no one ever fooled Chapin for long—except Chapin himself.

CHAPTER FIFTEEN

Pulitzer Passes

Early in the year 1904, Joseph Pulitzer, still the absentee overlord of the New York World, as well as of the Evening and Sunday Worlds, sat at a dinner table together with the secretaries whose responsibility it was to keep him constantly stimulated, entertained and informed. Usually they did this by talking quickly on many subjects until Pulitzer's restless attention was caught by one. He would immediately signify interest by a provocative disagreement. A lively argument would result, with secretaries leaping up from the table to run to Pulitzer's ever-present reference library for proof of their points.

Such dinners customarily ran from seven p.m. to eleven or midnight, providing the highlight of the blind man's day. But Pulitzer was also capable of moods of melancholy which could turn dinners into depressing occasions. At such times he would lower his forehead to the triangle made by his thumb and a long sensitive forefinger. From this morose position he would complain that his life was "a story of unceasing work and worry, of misery and decrepitude, of years of humble invalidism and absenteeism."

Yet in early 1904 Pulitzer had a reason for worry and its concomitant self-pity. William Henry Merrill, the only man he could trust to turn his terse memos into crusading editorials for the New York World, was nearing the age of sixty. By the peculiar grapevine through which Pulitzer always seemed able to keep abreast of matters at 63 Park Row, he had learned that members of the World staff had begun calling Merrill "Pop." What was worse, they had begun to make fun of him. It was a serious matter, for where could Pulitzer ever find a man to replace Merrill? Through the years many had been tried, and no other found possible. Pulitzer dictated many World editorials himself, but inevitably there came moments when he did not feel like doing so. Then a few jerky, indignant phrases could be sent to Merrill. An adequate, if not a truly Pulitzer, editorial would always be the result.

Usually when Pulitzer bemoaned his lot in life, his secretaries kept carefully quiet for fear of attracting their explosive employer's sudden wrath. But one night, as Pulitzer continued to lament the physical decline of W. H. Merrill, a new young secretary named Samuel R. Williams made bold enough to speak. "There must be lots of editorial writers who could be trained to meet your standards," he said.

Pulitzer, momentarily shocked out of his black mood, found this optimism interesting. "If you think so, Williams," he answered tersely, "why don't you find him for me?" Williams nodded, and announced that he would set off that afternoon on his search. He would tour American cities, in each carefully reading the press and conferring with local editors. Pulitzer was impressed by this plan and agreed to pay his expenses for the trip. But he warned, "Don't tell anyone of your mission, and above all don't make commitments."

So Williams journeyed from city to city, yet his search did not pay off until he reached Detroit. Only there, in the Free Press, did he find a particularly pungent, intelligent editorial. He investigated, to discover that it had been written by a thirty-four-year-old newspaperman named Frank I. Cobb. Williams arranged to spend an evening with Cobb and found him a brilliant conversationalist, an omnivorous reader, a shrewd observer and a keen analyst of men and affairs, with great vitality of brain and body. All this he wrote to Pulitzer, concluding, "I knew immediately that I had found the Ideal Editor."

Pulitzer, however, was far from impressed. In a characteristic, telegraphed response, he demanded:

What has Cobb read in American History, Rhodes, McMaster, Trevelyan? What works on the constitution and

constitutional law? Has he read Buckle's History of Civilization? Where did he stand during Bryan's Free Silver Campaigns? What about the state of his health? How tall is he?
Is his voice harsh or agreeable? My ears are very sensitive.
Take him to dinner and note his table manners. Is his dispo-
sition cheerful? Sound out his ambitions—whether satisfied
or looking to a larger field. Be very careful to give no intimation I am interested. Describe minutely his appearance,
color of eyes, shape of forehead, mannerisms, how he
dresses. Search his brain for everything there is in it.

J. P.

Spurred on by this, Williams passed another evening with Cobb.
He found that the energetic newsman had read all the books mentioned in the Pulitzer wire. Then he discovered a dreadful flaw. Cobb
admired Theodore Roosevelt, the ebullient occupant of the White
House. This was directly contrary to Pulitzer's opinions, for not only
was Roosevelt a Republican at a time when the World had become
the only Democratic paper in New York, but in general, Pulitzer
had always professed to distrust men of such vigorous, undisciplined
energy. Long ago, he had said of Roosevelt, "Here is a child of
fortune who needs a strong curb." The World had, on numerous
occasions, attempted to provide precisely that curb.

In view of this, Williams wondered if Pulitzer would still consider Frank I. Cobb. Surprisingly, he would. Williams was called
to Bar Harbor for further cross-examination on the matter. Then
Cobb himself, who has been described as muscular, clear-eyed,
smooth-faced and buoyant, was invited for a weekend. Pulitzer was
enormously impressed. "Cobb will do," he dictated in a memo to
Williams. "He knows American history better than anyone I have
ever found. He has that damnable Roosevelt obsession and he must
learn to be brief. But in time, we can make an editor of him."

With a few lingering regrets over leaving Detroit, Cobb agreed
to become chief editorial writer—and, in a sense, editor—of the New
York World. With almost any publisher other than Pulitzer the story
would end at this point: if Cobb were successful he would keep the
job; if a failure, he would be fired. But Pulitzer worked by no
such black-and-white formula. Having tacitly admitted a man's po-

tential by hiring him, he believed in testing him additionally by goading him to the limit of his endurance. Nothing was more pleasing to Pulitzer than to make an important member of the staff shout back at him. He now began this curious procedure with Cobb. Daily he sent unflattering memos dissecting Cobb's editorials sentence by sentence. In personal interviews, he pricked him with cutting sarcasm. Finally Cobb exploded in anger. To Pulitzer all this had been enjoyable, with Cobb behaving exactly as he wished. But Cobb had been thinking longingly of Detroit. A few days before Easter, on a day which marked the end of his first year on the World, Cobb wrote out a letter of resignation and quit.

The letter was delivered to Pulitzer during a stopover in New York. It rocked him to the depths of his sensitive soul. In a voice choked with fury, he shouted at the emissary from Park Row, "Go back to the office and *tell that man I will not let him resign.*" This edict, which had been successful with David Graham Phillips and other favored employes, caused Cobb to pause briefly in his preparations for departure. Taking advantage of this, Pulitzer summoned him to a personal meeting. Expecting to be verbally castigated, Cobb was amazed when Pulitzer tweaked his ear affectionately and in the gentlest of voices said, "My dear boy, don't you realize you have quite spoiled my Easter?" In the same soothing tone, he informed Cobb that he had really been much impressed by his first year's work, and never again would criticize him so strongly. Under these terms, Cobb agreed to remain. When he had left, Pulitzer advanced still another reason for wishing to keep him on the job.

"You know," he mused, "I really like that young man. I like the way he swears."

So Joseph Pulitzer, fifty-seven years old in 1904 and a blind invalid for the past fifteen years, had undergone few personality changes. Tall, broad-shouldered, emaciated, with a soaring forehead, prominent nose and distinguished Van Dyke beard, he was still physically an impressive and awe-inspiring man. This was especially true because of his eyes. The one totally blind continued dull-looking and half closed. But the one in which the slight suffusion remained was of a startling brilliance. A deep purplish blue, it did not seem to be blind at all. Rather, it gave an impression of searching, eagle-like penetration.

As years had passed, Pulitzer's manner of living became increasingly extravagant. He traveled with an entourage comprising at least six secretaries, a personal physician, a combination valet-steward-majordomo and miscellaneous others. On occasion, wife and family accompanied him, but the intensity of his family feelings, together with the noises made by growing children, caused him such "sleepless nights, savage pain, and desperate weariness" that this did not often happen.

Also, Pulitzer had purchased several additional estates in the United States, England and France, so that no less than James Gordon Bennett, he had become a satrap. Yet there was ever a deep difference between the two men. Where Bennett was never more than a boorish eccentric, Pulitzer was a cultivated one. Beneath his moody behavior reposed a great erudition, with constant craving for more. Endlessly he picked the minds of his secretaries. When one of them suggested a few moments of reflective silence, Pulitzer burst out, "Never stop talking or reading. I must have something to occupy my mind all the time, no matter how exhausted I am." Restless, arrogant, caustic, he could at all times be rendered tractable by a fact which caught the interest of his flying mind.

To this end, Pulitzer surrounded himself with the most intelligent men—it may truthfully be said—his money could buy. Pulitzer's six (often more) secretaries were not callow youths with a gift for shorthand. Each was middle-aged, with a distinguished career behind him. Norman Graham Thwaites, for instance, had been a lieutenant-colonel in Her Britannic Majesty's service. William Romaine Paterson, a scholar of note, was known to other Pulitzer secretaries as the Walking Encyclopedia. Arthur H. Billing, the secretary Pulitzer liked best, was the son of a bishop, a naval architect and nautical expert. Alleyne Ireland, who became the best known of the secretaries by writing a book about Pulitzer called *An Adventure with a Genius*, was recognized as an authority on British colonization and political economy. Nor did Pulitzer ever relax his insistence that his secretaries be highly educated, soft-voiced Englishmen. The only exception to this remained Dr. Friederich Mann, the German-reader and player of soothing piano music.

Each morning Pulitzer rose about nine o'clock, to be assisted in dressing by Jabez E. Dunningham, his majordomo. After breakfast, he would summon the secretary whose duty it had become this day to take care of what might be called the first work shift. It was this man's responsibility to read aloud the New York World, from column one, page one, to the final column of the last page. As he read, Pulitzer expressed his emotions in the way he sat in his chair. If pleased, the black-clad figure would sit relaxed, stroking his long nose or the goatee with sensitive fingers. He expressed disapproval by writhing as if tormented. Frequently, the reading would be stopped while he explosively dictated such memos as this:

> Good lead on the Kaiser Wilhelm story—tell Cobb not to indulge in fancy guess-work—does he know situation between France and Germany getting worse? Get the facts. Rest of page weak—bank robber described as short—what is short? Four feet? Five feet? Be exact. Electric power utility scandal written too vague—I know the name of every man involved and so do you. Put them in. The World protects no one. Editorial on Philippines good—keep it up—the World favored war with Spain but should have given them independence immediately afterward—call it by right name—Teddy Roosevelt imperialism—women suffrage article very poor—ridicule not effective.

With this initial step of the day completed, another secretary would softly enter to take the place of the first. During the time Pulitzer had listened to the World, this man had been busy preparing a digest of all other New York newspapers, as well as those of the major cities of the United States and Europe. Now he read this digest to Pulitzer, who from it gained ideas which might be passed along to Park Row, or provocative statements that might lead to World editorials. Next another secretary took over, to read aloud Pulitzer's correspondence and take down the blind man's answers. On the surface, Pulitzer the invalid always seemed to be a calm man, but his letters indicated that inwardly he seethed with the old furies. Invariably he ended correspondence with such phrases as "In usual haste," "In great haste," or "Dictated as usual in a hurry." Sometimes he varied this by writing, "I am in a dreadful hurry with the usual headache."

With the correspondence done, Pulitzer usually took a walk—in his late fifties, he seldom rode horseback—with hand hooked in a secretary's elbow. In New York, he loved to promenade Fifth Avenue. In Maine, Surrey and the south of France, he showed a contrasting desire for rugged, hilly paths. After the walk came lunch, and with this meal appeared the second part of a secretary's function. All secretaries had to attend this meal, striving to keep Pulitzer entertained by their conversation. It was for this—far more important at dinner—that the six men spent spare time studying abstruse subjects and scoured whatever territory Pulitzer's travels might take them for new books to provide table talk. After lunch, it became the job of another secretary to read Pulitzer into his afternoon nap. This truly awesome responsibility has been described by Alleyne Ireland in *An Adventure with a Genius:*

> At a word from Mr. Pulitzer the secretary began to read in a clear, incisive voice. After a few minutes Mr. Pulitzer would say *Leise* (softly) and the secretary's voice was lowered until, though it was still audible, it assumed a monotonous and soothing quality. After a while the order came *Ganz leise* (more softly). At this point the reader ceased to form his words and commenced to murmur indistinctly, giving an effect such as might be produced by a person reading aloud in an adjoining room, but with the connecting door closed.
>
> If, after ten minutes of this murmuring, J.P. remained motionless it was to be assumed that he was asleep; and the secretary's duty was to go on murmuring until Mr. Pulitzer awoke and told him to stop or to commence actual reading again. This murmuring might last for two hours, and it was a very difficult art to acquire, for at the slightest change in the pitch of the voice, at a sneeze, or a cough, Mr. Pulitzer would wake with a start, and an unpleasant quarter of an hour followed.

After a nap of several hours, Pulitzer was led to his heavily draped library. There he demanded light reading: the plays of Shakespeare, a contemporary novel or play. Such reading should have been a pleasurable chore. It was not. The fussy man believed that no secretary could do justice to a novel or play until he had previously read it at least twice. Thus there were no enjoyable surprises for any reader of light material to Joseph Pulitzer.

Dinner provided the great challenge—and not always of an intellectual variety. First came what secretaries called The Soup Test. When anyone made gurgling or sucking sounds while disposing of soup, the keyed-up Pulitzer recoiled as if physically struck. "Soup should be eaten, not inhaled," he was fond of declaring. New secretaries who were clumsy at soup-eating were hastily disengaged from the Pulitzer payroll. Guests who made similar noises were seldom invited again.

But if the sound of soup ineptly eaten caused Pulitzer annoyance, the sound of a knife or fork scraped across a plate was torture which drove him to agonizing rage. He would leave the table in a state of trembling, nauseous fury, and hours of soothing reading and soft piano playing would be required to calm him down. On the whole Pulitzer manifested a hearty appetite for an invalid, yet he considered no dinner a success unless the food was forgotten in favor of hot intellectual argument. In these he was a formidable opponent. Not only did he have a background of imposing erudition—picked up, astoundingly, in the years when he seemed to be devoting all his teeming energies to the Post-Dispatch and World. But the manner in which, through his years of blindness, he had picked the minds of others made him an expert in a magnitude of subjects. "I'd like to take your brain apart and take a good look into it," he once said to a man whose knowledge awed him. "I'm glad you can't," the man replied fervently. "You'd mix the parts and never get them together again."

Pulitzer's greatest pleasure at dinner was to prove himself mentally superior to younger men whose eyesight had not failed them. On a morning after he had done this, one Pulitzer secretary was heard to groan, "I sat up until three o'clock reading Rousseau's *Confessions*. Last night I made the mistake of saying Rousseau left the

Hermitage because of a quarrel with Diderot. J.P. challenged me, and he was right. Now he's caught me in one mistake, and he'll go after me hammer and tongs on the rest of it." Sometimes at dinner Pulitzer dropped his careful guard to make frank admissions about himself. "Real troubles never bother me," he confessed in a rare moment. "It's only the small annoyances that upset me." Again a secretary asked why he always spoke harshly of editors and kindly of reporters. "I suppose," he said, "it is because every reporter is a hope and every editor a disappointment."

After the excitements of dinner, Pulitzer needed calming. Puffing a long cigar he was led to the music room, where Dr. Mann softly played the German *Lieder* he loved. Reminded by Jabez Dunningham that bedtime had arrived, he would retire to his room, undress, and call for still another secretary to read him to sleep. Often he would ask Dr. Mann to read to him in German, for this he found especially restful. Murmuring his *Leise, ganz leise,* he would then drift off. Or he might not. All too often one of the younger secretaries would be routed out of bed at four A.M. by Dunningham. The insomnia-ridden Pulitzer, having dozed for several hours, would be wide awake and in need of further reading.

One of the few sounds of the outer world which continued restful to the tormented man was water lapping against the side of a boat. By the same token, he loved the sound of running brooks. On Chatwold, his Bar Harbor estate, he erected a huge granite pile called The Tower of Silence. On it he constructed a small balcony overhanging a rock canyon through which a brook contentedly bubbled. This immediately became his favorite spot on the estate: "and there he would sit in the cool of the morning or in the grateful shade of the afternoon, gaining a tranquility denied him elsewhere in the clatter of life."

Yet a brook is never an ocean, and inevitably Pulitzer's thoughts turned to yachts. In 1906, the nautical-minded Arthur Billing was dispatched to Leith, Scotland, to supervise the construction of one of the largest private vessels ever built. This ship was not designed for speed, as was James Gordon Bennett's *Lysistrata*. Rather Pulitzer's yacht—christened *Liberty*—was constructed for comfort. It was a vessel 300 feet over-all, with a beam of 35.6 and an average cruising speed of 12 knots. Coal capacity would permit voyages of six thousand miles.

The *Liberty* was launched on December 5, 1907, and for once a new possession did not disappoint Pulitzer. It proved to be everything he dreamed it would be. In all, he cruised one hundred and thirty thousand miles on her, crossing the Atlantic at least nine times. On the *Liberty* he seemed able to conquer, for short periods at least, the demon of restlessness that beset him on land. "I love this boat," he once said, as he paced the deck accompanied by a secretary. "On it I am at home and comfortable. In a house I am lost in my blindness, always fearful of falling on stairs or over obstacles. Here the narrow companionways give me safe guidance and I can find my way about alone. Nothing in my life has given me so much pleasure."

If Pulitzer reveled in the *Liberty*, his staff of secretaries reacted somewhat differently. Among them the stately craft became known as the *Liberty, Ha! Ha!* "Find a breeze," was Pulitzer's most frequent order to his captain, and in response the ship would steam far out to sea. On land the secretaries could on occasion break loose from the relentless tyrant who was their employer. On the *Liberty*, they were trapped. Even Dr. Mann, who served Pulitzer so long and devotedly, found life aboard the *Liberty* a strain. "Always der cold gray sky, always der cold gray sea," he would mutter as he paced the deck. The peace of mind brought by cruises on the *Liberty* only increased Pulitzer's mental alertness, causing him to make greater demands than ever on his secretaries. Once, when the yacht had arrived in New York after a monotonous Atlantic crossing, Alleyne Ireland explained why Pulitzer insisted that his secretaries be Englishmen. "J.P. chooses Englishmen," he said, "because you Americans lack the temper control we have. One of you might accidentally shove him off the boat, push him off a cliff, or bash his head in when he gets in one of his abusive moods."

With the *Liberty* in his life, Pulitzer began spending some three hundred and fifty thousand dollars annually on his travels and comfort. It is not hard to see how he did this. Running expenses of the *Liberty* came to two hundred thousand dollars a year. Then he maintained at least four basic estates in the United States, England and France. Once, with his own establishment at Cap Martin, he rented a villa nearby which had once been occupied by Queen Victoria. Further, Pulitzer's restlessness sometimes caught up with him at sea. He would then order the ship into the nearest port, and on landing the secretaries would fan out to locate a grand hotel where Pulitzer could rent a large suite, together with those on all sides of it, as well as above and below. Thus he got the dead silence his nerves demanded.

Though he spent much time roaming Europe, New York remained Pulitzer's home and his favorite city. Early in the century his Fifty-fifth Street mansion was destroyed by fire, giving him an opportunity to make plans for a still more impressive home at 7-15 East 73 Street. For this he had taken the inevitable step of employing Stanford White as architect. But where Pulitzer was lucky with the yacht *Liberty*, he was unfortunate with the mansion. As his secretaries noted, the man so fiendishly sensitive to sound seemed dogged by a perverse fate where noise was concerned. Stanford White used all contemporary methods of soundproofing, adding ingenious new ones of his own. But when at last Pulitzer stretched out for a night's sleep in his East Side mansion, he heard a hollow, ghostly knocking that drove him almost frantic. It was almost as if the bedroom were haunted, and he furiously accused White of trying to drive him mad. White was baffled until the contractor admitted that a living spring had been discovered on the property during excavation. The contractor decided to keep this fact to himself and diverted the spring by feeding it into a sump pit, a process requiring an automatic pump. This he had placed under Pulitzer's bedroom in the belief that the extraordinary soundproofing would kill its sound. But the drum of a nearby heating system acted as a sounding board to the pump, sending its measured reverberations directly into Pulitzer's bedroom.

The pump was moved beyond the elegant, chateau-like courtyard and placed under the sidewalk. Even so, Pulitzer forevermore refused to sleep in the bedroom, which now joined a ballroom and a swimming pool as unused features of the Italianate mansion. Instead, he built a new sleeping annex, where further diligence was used to achieve silence. The double walls were packed with mineral wool, the windows plated with triple-glass. Three heavy doors stood between Pulitzer and the main mansion, and the floor of the passageway, as well as that of the annex, was built on ball bearings to prevent vibration. Ventilation was by the fireplace chimney only, and after his first night in the sleeping annex Pulitzer declared that the shrill sound of early morning factory whistles came down the chimney to assail him as he slept. Silk threads were then stretched across the opening to break this sound. "Now at last," writes one of his associates, "he found zero. The room was so still as to be uncanny."

With all his mania for peace and silence—together with the unusual faith he now found himself able to place in Frank I. Cobb—Pulitzer never lost his ability for attracting journalistic attention, not to say trouble. For in November, 1908, the New York World became the only American newspaper ever to be sued for libel by a President of the United States.

Not unexpectedly, the President was Theodore Roosevelt, who over the years had been continuously belittled by the World. The World had further earned the hatred of the President by filching a letter from the files of E. H. Harriman, in which the railroad magnate wrote his lawyer that Roosevelt had requested a donation in the campaign of 1904. This, the World claimed on its front page, only proved what the paper had loudly contended: that Roosevelt, far from being the champion of the ordinary man, was in reality another paid creature of the money barons.

The World's final challenge to Roosevelt had its roots in the abandoned De Lesseps attempt to build the Panama Canal, when rights for the land on which the canal was to be built lapsed back to the Republic of Colombia. From time to time American financiers talked of taking over the assets of the French company, then clearing the title with Colombia. By far the most energetic of these groups was led by William Nelson Cromwell, a New York attorney. One of his associates in the projected deal was Douglas Robinson, a brother-in-law of Roosevelt. Another was Charles P. Taft, a brother of the man eventually picked by Roosevelt as his successor.

When Roosevelt ascended to the Presidency, Cromwell easily got his ear to outline a project which vastly appealed to the Rough

Rider in Teddy. In 1903, while the energies of Roosevelt and Secretary of State John Hay were rather conspicuously directed elsewhere, a revolution was generated in the Colombian province of Panama. As a result the toy Republic of Panama was established. Almost instantly Roosevelt and Hay formally recognized it, without the approval of Congress or, by inference, the people of the United States. Roosevelt later put this action succinctly in a campaign speech: "I took the Isthmus, started the Canal, and then left Congress, not to debate the Canal, but to debate me."

To all this the New York World—ever the champion of the people, if not of Congress—took raucous exception. It did no good: "The ruthless outrage is complete," it admitted in an editorial. Congress easily agreed to pay stockholders in the French company the sum of forty million dollars for the seemingly worthless rights it still possessed. The Canal was begun, and in time successfully completed. But rumors of graft persisted. According to these, Cromwell and his group had paid only three and a half million to France, pocketing the juicy remainder themselves. Even the triumph of the Canal opening could not kill the rumors and from time to time the World undertook to agitate muddy waters by printing editorials demanding WHO GOT THE MONEY?

Yet the Panama scandal might possibly have died had not Roosevelt so ruthlessly pushed the nomination of William Howard Taft through the Republican Convention in 1908. In doing this, he enraged a man named Charles W. Fairbanks, who himself had nursed Presidential or Vice-Presidential ambitions. Fairbanks owned the Indianapolis News, and on November 2, 1908, his paper featured a front-page rerun of the World editorials which had demanded WHO GOT THE MONEY? This did little good, for Taft swept Indiana as well as the nation. But two men were wildly infuriated by the story. One of course, was Roosevelt, for the Indianapolis paper had not hesitated to stress the part played by Douglas Robinson and his White House influence. The other was William McM. Speer, the World editor who had made the Panama story his own personal project. Speer felt that the World's righteous thunder had been stolen in an unconscionable manner. For a month he stewed over this seeming injustice. Then, in December, he launched a campaign in

the World which demanded WHO GOT THE MONEY? in more vigorous
terms than ever. Among other things, he demanded a Congressional
investigation of the President. At this Roosevelt, who, though a lame-
duck President, was still in office until March 4, 1909, reacted with
every sign of fury—and perhaps of guilt. Immediately he issued a
ringing statement in the course of which he declared:

> It is idle to say that the known character of Mr. Pu-
> litzer and his newspaper are such that the statements in that
> paper will be believed by nobody; unfortunately, thousands
> of persons are ill-informed in this respect and believe the
> statements they see in print, even though they appear in a
> newspaper published by Mr. Pulitzer.

In his reaction to all this, Pulitzer exposed peculiarities of character. On the one (or editorial) hand, he wired Speer to continue asking WHO GOT THE MONEY? until a satisfactory answer was forthcoming. On the other (or personal) one, he manifested alarm, if not fear.
There was good reason. Others in the Cromwell group turned out to
be J. P. Morgan, Elihu Root and men of equally exalted stature. In
addition, Roosevelt himself was reported to have said that he was
"out to get old Pulitzer." Pulitzer, despite all his faith in freedom of
the press, was inclined to believe that Presidential powers made such
vengeance possible. Accordingly, he boarded the *Liberty* immediately on learning that Roosevelt, Robinson and Cromwell, together
with Morgan, Root and Charles Taft, had filed a suit for criminal
libel against the World, Pulitzer, Caleb Van Hamm (managing
editor), Robert Hunt Lyman (night city editor), and the Press Publishing Company. In the midst of an icy winter, he ordered the yacht
to sea, where it ploughed tirelessly between New York and Charleston, docking hastily at each city for fear a United States marshal
might be on the dock. None ever was, but still Pulitzer ordered discreet inquiries made as to what sort of jail he might be placed in if
convicted.

While the *Liberty* continued its unpleasurable cruising, another
figure appeared in the case. This was William Travers Jerome, the
pugnacious District Attorney who in 1906-7 gained world fame by
his role of prosecutor in the two Harry Thaw trials. If the Pulitzer

World had opposed Theodore Roosevelt with relentless determination, it had opposed Jerome with a virulence that today seems unsportsmanlike. Ever a tireless worker, Jerome late one night put head on arms at the desk to enjoy a few minutes' rest. In that posture he was seen by a World photographer, who snapped his picture. The paper used this repeatedly on the front page during the next city election, the implication being that no sensible citizenry would vote for a man who fell asleep on the job. Nonetheless, Jerome was elected. Even more anxious than Roosevelt to get old Pulitzer, Jerome requested a local indictment in the Panama libel case. This alarmed Pulitzer further. "My opinion is that if anything comes out of the Roosevelt-Panama matter, it will be through Jerome," he wrote Cobb.

Still, Pulitzer appeared to be getting the legal breaks. The Government attorney designated to try the case resigned rather than handle it. Following this a Grand Jury announced itself unable to find complicity on the part of Pulitzer himself. But Van Hamm and the New York World were indicted under an 1825 statute entitled "An act to Protect the Harbor Defense from Malicious Injury, and Other Offenses." This failed to reassure Pulitzer. At the moment the news reached him, the *Liberty* was cruising off Hampton Roads. He summoned the captain to ask, "Which way is the yacht heading?" "Due east, sir," the captain told him. Pulitzer then inquired, "If we keep east, where will we fetch up?" "Lisbon, sir." "Then keep on, due east."

So began the *Liberty's* unhappiest voyage. Almost immediately the yacht encountered a violent storm, followed by heavy swells which caused it to roll at 45 degrees. In the midst of this already uncomfortable situation, Pulitzer was taken ill with a bronchial infection. After the honorable retirement of Dr. Hosmer, Pulitzer had difficulty in finding a medical man who would put up with his unceasing demands, not to mention life afloat on the *Liberty*. The result was that the doctor aboard was usually a young man just out of medical school. Now one such found himself unable to diagnose Pulitzer's condition. When at last the *Liberty* reached Lisbon, a doctor recognized Pulitzer's malady as whooping cough, which in an adult is both uncomfortable and serious. While Pulitzer coughed in his four-poster, the *Liberty* took off for the south of France. En route a new affliction struck. William Romaine Paterson, the Walking Encyclopedia, had boarded the yacht at Lisbon. Now he broke out in spots which the young physician had no difficulty in diagnosing as smallpox. Paterson was isolated, and at Gibraltar rushed ashore. Then the entire ship had to be fumigated, while Pulitzer, his entourage, and all crew members endured vaccinations. In time, the *Liberty* reached Marseille, from whence Pulitzer traveled to Aix-les-Bains to mend his shattered constitution.

In time, Roosevelt's libel case against the New York World reached the Supreme Court, where by unanimous consent it was dismissed. No one ever discovered the true fate of the forty million, and finally even the New York World ceased asking. Pulitzer, recovered in health, had in the meantime returned to the United States, temporarily fed up with the *Liberty*. But seemingly he had forgotten the tenacious William Travers Jerome. Egged on by Roosevelt and Robinson, Jerome announced that he planned to ask an indictment under the state law governing malicious misstatements. Or was the astute Jerome merely enjoying a cat-and-mouse revenge? If such was the intention, he succeeded far beyond any dreams he may have had. In his East Seventy-third Street mansion, Pulitzer fell into panic. He insisted on knowing whether Jerome was going to draw up an indictment, and to this end hired new private detectives and firms of lawyers, and offered inducements to friends and assistants of Jerome himself. Through all this hysterical activity, Jerome infuriatingly did nothing, though on occasion he did prolong the agony by stating that the matter was occupying his mind.

Then, after several months of excruciating suspense, a bit of World gossip percolated up to Pulitzer. He learned that the Evening World's star reporter, Irvin Cobb, was a close friend of Jerome. Next morning, when Cobb reported for work, he was met by Don Carlos Seitz, who by that time had become business manager of the World papers. Seitz, whom Cobb considered bluff and assertive, demanded to know whether Cobb was indeed a friend of Jerome. Cobb admitted that he was, adding that the District Attorney affectionately called him Kentuck. Seitz was delighted. "You know,

Cobb," he said, "Mr. Pulitzer is in a very depressed, very harassed state. The possible consequences to his health are dangerous, most dangerous. So as a last resort we are asking your co-operation. Can we count on you for immediate action?"

The homely, drawling Cobb allowed that he would try to do all he could. Whereupon he was requested to visit Jerome and ask, man to man, whether he planned to follow through on the case. Cobb did so. At Jerome's office, he invited the District Attorney out for a drink and the two seasoned drinkers thereupon adjourned, appallingly to enjoy an early morning cocktail. Finally Cobb put his question. Jerome replied by stating that he hated Pulitzer, whom he called His Imperial and Sacred Majesty, Pulitzer the First. But, he continued, he had no intention of needlessly harassing a sick man, even when pressured to do so by a former President of the United States. With this choice information, Cobb returned to Park Row where he paused at his desk to make out an expense account reading

Special assignment W.T.J. matter
To carfare up Center Street .... 5 cents
To carfare down Center Street .... 5 cents
Total   10 cents

This he ceremoniously presented to Seitz, to whom he also reported that Jerome had no intention of prosecuting. Overjoyed, Seitz propelled Cobb to a telephone which appeared to have been kept open all the time he was gone. "Quick," he ordered. "Get on that wire. One of Mr. Pulitzer's staff is on the other end, at the mansion uptown, waiting for developments."

Cobb repeated his story to Norman Thwaites, the best-liked of the Pulitzer secretaries. When he finished there came a pause while Thwaites relayed the information to Pulitzer. Then Thwaites said, "Cobb, Mr. Pulitzer is desirous of knowing how this most gratifying result was achieved so speedily."

It was a great moment for Cobb, who all his life detested sham. In his slowest, Judge Priest manner, he drawled, "Well, it was like this. I got on a surface car and I went up to Canal Street and I went up to the Criminal Courts and I sent word in to Mr. Jerome that a reporter from the World wanted to see him and he came out to where I was, and I asked him—and he told me."

This, too, was repeated to Pulitzer, and now for the first and only time in his World career Cobb heard the voice of his Olympian employer. It seemed, he recalled, both high-pitched and guttural, with a slight accent. It also showed that, for all his years, Pulitzer still had not become thoroughly familiar with the English language. For what he said was:

"Well, I wish I might be God damned."

At approximately noon on the morning of Monday, January 23, 1911, David Graham Phillips, at forty-three established as a top-selling American novelist and presently considered one of the important literary figures of all time, awoke after a night's sleep following his customary stint of nighttime writing. Wrapping his six-foot-three frame in an elaborate, colored dressing gown, he sauntered to the spacious living room of his duplex apartment at 119 East 19th Street, around the corner from Gramercy Park. There breakfast was immediately served him by his devoted sister, Mrs. Frevert. At a more normal hour, Mrs. Frevert herself had risen. As usual she found outside her bedroom door a small pile of meticulously handwritten manuscript which Phillips had finished the night before. This she had carried to a nearby typist, who in return had given her the completed typescript of an elongated short story called "Enid," which was destined both for serialization in the *Saturday Evening Post* and publication in book form by Appleton & Company as part of a collection of three Phillips short novels titled *Degarmo's Wife*.

Phillips's few hours of daily leisure were as carefully regulated as his long hours of work. After breakfast, he shaved and donned one of the ornate and expensive suits for which he was famed. In winter, he always covered his imposing frame with a rich-looking raglan overcoat. Then he went out for a walk. This was his only form of exercise and it was his habit to leave the Nineteenth Street apartment alone. He then walked around Gramercy Park to the Princeton Club, at the corner of Lexington Avenue and the Park. There he paused to pick up his mail. After glancing through it, he again returned to the sidewalk, where he would find Mrs. Frevert waiting. The two would take the rest of his constitutional together.

On the morning of January twenty-third, Phillips was in a state of particular contentment. His epic work, *Susan Lenox: Her Fall and Rise*, had been completed three weeks before. Phillips had labored off and on for over ten years on this realistic novel, which was of such bulk that even when edited down it still filled two large volumes. There was a special satisfaction in finishing *Susan Lenox*, for if Phillips lived under a premonition of sudden death he had at least completed what he considered his great work. Not even the fact that Joseph H. Sears, the president of Appleton, had expressed himself as shocked after reading the manuscript could dampen Phillips's feelings. The novelist was an intelligent man and, as such, aware that the moral climate was showing signs of changing. If Appleton would not publish *Susan Lenox*, someone else would. But it was more likely that Appleton would change its mind.

The completion of his epic had not changed Phillips's habits. He was still the highly successful author who did not dare to be lazy. He worked all night, seven nights a week, and the hour of his walk was keyed to his night work. At one thirty on this January twenty-third, as on all other afternoons, he called to his sister that he was commencing the walk and would meet her outside the Princeton Club. Big, erect, conspicuously attired, he walked around the west end of the Park and turned right, in the direction of the club. As he did so, a pale young man who had been waiting on the corner started toward him. Phillips, who had never seen him before, paid no attention, though the young man seemed to regard him with unusual intensity as the distance between the two men closed. At the moment they were all but face to face, the young man suddenly shouted, "Now I've got you!" Drawing a revolver from his pocket he fired six shots straight at Phillips. Three of these crashed through the folded copy of "Enid" which Phillips had placed in his breast pocket, intending to deliver it to the Appleton office in the course of the walk. One of the bullets entered his lung, and as he fell to the sidewalk, the young man pulled a second revolver from his overcoat pocket. This he pointed at his own temple and pulled the trigger. He fell dead.

At Bellevue Hospital, Phillips grimly clung to life through two long days. Then he died. The entire country was stunned, for if nothing else this was one of the more pointless murders of all time. The pale young man was discovered to have been Fitzhugh Coyle Goldsborough, son of a wealthy Washington family. Physically frail, mentally neurotic, Goldsborough was supported by his family, a fact which left him with nothing to do but brood over the moral state of the nation. Like everyone else at the turn of the century he read the novels of David Graham Phillips, and doing so became outraged by the cynical remarks certain Phillips characters made about women.

Then came publication of *The Fashionable Adventures of Joshua Craig*, one of Phillips's most successful novels. The locale was Washington and a main character was Margaret Severence, a beautiful young society girl at whom many of the author's tart observations were directed. The brooding Goldsborough instantly became convinced that Margaret Severence had been patterned after his own social-butterfly sister. It made no difference that Phillips did not know the Goldsborough family, or that the sister firmly denied ever meeting the author at any of the many social functions she attended. By the summer of 1910, Goldsborough was in the grip of such an obsession that he began writing Phillips anonymous letters threatening his life. Phillips, however, had just published a journalistic exposé called *The Shame of the Senate*. In this, with material furnished by Gustavus Myers, who later wrote *History of the Great American Fortunes*, he systematically tore to shreds the reputations of many United States Senators. As a result, his mail abounded in threatening letters, and one more in the pile he daily leafed through at the Princeton Club made no impression.

At last, weary of writing, Goldsborough came to New York. He rented a small room on East Nineteenth Street, from which he could see Phillips leave his apartment at precisely the same moment each day. At one fifteen on January twenty-third, Goldsborough crammed two revolvers in his overcoat pocket. Only a few moments later, he had stationed himself in a position to see David Graham Phillips as he approached along the Gramercy Square sidewalk. . . .

Ten months later Pulitzer, too, was dead—at the age of sixty-four. His weak constitution battered by the tensions of the libel suit, as well as by the incongruous siege of whooping cough, he had spent the summer of 1911 quietly at Bar Harbor, with occasional find-a-breeze cruises as far south as New York. On July fifth, he listened intently as a secretary read an Independence Day address made by Woodrow Wilson, then Governor of New Jersey. The speech had a ring Pulitzer liked, and he telegraphed Park Row for other Wilson speeches, especially those indicating the Governor's opinions on Standard Oil and other monopoly matters. "Should prefer essence to verbosity," he ended the wire. Then, as if this were not enough for a staff fully accustomed to his whims, he added, *"But brevity, brevity!"*

In late September he returned to the Seventy-third Street mansion, but as always, "wherever he settled a demon of restlessness always evicted him." He next boarded the *Liberty* to resume the coast-wide cruising that he had discovered during the Roosevelt libel suit. Several times, he sailed to Maine, then cruises south to Charleston began. On October eighteenth, the *Liberty* set out from New York on a southern voyage. Aboard were Pulitzer's son Herbert, aged sixteen; his tutor; and the usual complement of secretaries, among them Dr. Mann, Norman Thwaites, Alleyne Ireland and Harold S. Pollard. On the second day out, Pulitzer fell ill. He took to his four-poster bed, and again a young doctor newly added to the staff was unable to diagnose the ailment. Yet Pulitzer was only slightly uncomfortable and it was decided to continue to Charleston. There an experienced physician was called in. According to his verdict, Pulitzer's illness was simple indigestion.

With that, Pulitzer rallied to entertain at lunch the editor of the Charleston Courier. After which he lay down while Alleyne Ireland read aloud Macaulay's "Essay on Hallam." As the reading proceeded, Pulitzer complained of new pains. He was given veronal but continued uncomfortable through the next day, in the course of which Mrs. Pulitzer arrived by train from New York. On Sunday, October twenty-ninth, the sick man seemed to have rallied once more. After an early lunch, Dr. Mann read to him in German from

the *Life of Louis XI*. Muttering his usual *Leise, ganz leise*, he soon
fell asleep. As he did, Mrs. Pulitzer took Dr. Mann's place at his bedside. At one forty she realized that Pulitzer had whispered *Leise,
ganz leise* for the last time. In the words of Don Carlos Seitz: "He
who all his life had ridden upon the storm, had left it as gently as
the dying of the wind."

Perhaps the true measure of Pulitzer is to be found in his will,
which remains one of the most farseeing and public-spirited testa-
ments ever left by a prominent man.

The will was first drawn up in 1904. Clarifying codicils were
added in 1909. Shortly before he died, Pulitzer was engaged in adding codicils to clarify the clarifications. Arrangements for the School
of Journalism at Columbia—the first school of its kind—had largely
been completed during Pulitzer's last years. With the two-million-
dollar bequest for this went the famous Pulitzer awards to encourage
journalism, literature, art and music. These are the annual Pulitzer
Prizes so well known to us today. In addition, he left five hundred
thousand dollars (later increased to nearly a million) to the Metropolitan Museum of Art. Another five hundred thousand (similarly
increased) went to the Philharmonic Symphony, part of which was
to be used for supplementary concerts in New York. Of these Pulitzer plaintively wrote, "I hope they will not be too severely classical
[but will] recognize my favorite composers, Beethoven, Wagner and
Liszt." Among other bequests, he left various scholarships for worthy
high-school students, funds for a statue of Thomas Jefferson, whom
he had always admired, and fifty thousand dollars for a fountain at
the Plaza Hotel entrance to Central Park. This last still stands, and
is often cited as the most beautiful fountain-statue in New York.

The remainder of the twenty-million-dollar estate went to his
widow, three sons, two daughters and two grandsons. He left the
newspapers to the trust of the family, with the stipulation that none
could ever be sold unless it began to lose money. But, seemingly,
this did not pertain to the World. It appeared to be his wish that in
the unlikely event that such a mighty paper ever encountered financial
trouble, the lucrative St. Louis Post-Dispatch was to be sold in order
to gain money to set the World back on its feet. In one paragraph,
especially, the dead man spoke:

I particularly enjoin upon my descendants the duty of preserving, perfecting and perpetuating the World newspaper (to the maintenance and upbuilding of which I have sacrificed my health and strength) in the same spirit in which I have striven to create and conduct it as a public institution, from motives higher than mere gain, it having been my desire that it should be at all times conducted in a spirit of independence and with a view to inculcating high standards and public spirit among the people and their official representatives, and it is my earnest wish that said newspaper shall hereafter be conducted upon the same principles.

At other points in the lengthy document, Pulitzer harked back to the World, making plain that he expected the paper to keep his name alive in perpetuity. However, a straw in the wind immediately appeared. For reasons never made crystal clear, Pulitzer appointed his youngest son, Herbert, a trustee of the estate in 1904. Then in 1909 he added a codicil which failed to include him, though the names of Joseph, Jr., and Ralph remained. After the will had been made public, the absence of Herbert's name was deemed by the family "an unfortunate omission." It was neatly rectified only a month later when Harrington Putnam, one of the trustees, resigned. Herbert was solemnly elected by the others to fill the vacancy: thus creating perhaps the first instance where the letter of Pulitzer's will may have been violated.

But at the moment this seemed minor. Pulitzer's paramount desire was obvious. He wished his beloved World to continue forever. It seemed eminently possible. In 1911, nothing appeared likely ever to arise which would stand in the way of the dead man's most cherished wish. . . .

CHAPTER SIXTEEN

Farewell to Park Row

AT the time of Joseph Pulitzer's death, New York City was the proud possessor of fourteen daily newspapers. All but two were still located in the Park Row area. The seven papers published in the morning were: The World, The Times, The Tribune, The Herald, The Sun, The American, and The Press. Evening papers were: the Evening World, Evening Sun, Evening Journal, The Post, The Mail, The Telegram, and The Globe.

Slow changes in the coverage of news by all these papers were becoming apparent. The Age of the Reporter, glowingly saluted by Irvin Cobb in 1904, had receded under the impact of such world-shaking stories as the Thaw Case and the sinking of the *Titanic*. Now the story was king. Having progressed from the Age of the Great Editor to the Great Reporter, Park Row had settled into the Age of the Great Story.

In part this was a result of the speed-up of contemporary life. With improvements in travel and communications, numerous reporters could be dispatched from many cities to cover a story. Single talents no longer stood out as they had when only a few rich newspapers sent reporters on distant coverage. Another cause of change was the New York Times. Times reportage was studiously impartial, with the personality of the writer carefully edited out. The continued prosperity of the Times made this seem the most satisfactory way of presenting news. Then, on Park Row as elsewhere, newspapers were making increasing use of the so-called legman who, after getting the details of a story, phoned them back to a rewrite man in the city room. In every city American journalism was departing the personal for the impersonal.

Other factors contributed. Not the least was that the price of newsprint, machinery, labor and all else connected with the mechanical production of newspapers, was beginning to rise so that newspapers no longer made money from circulation alone. The voice of the business department, until then largely neglected in the counsels of newspapers, began to carry weight. A few years before, a department-store advertiser had begged the World to kill the story of an accident in his store. It was such an insulting suggestion that in retaliation the accident was splashed across the front page. From 1912 on, such things would not happen.

Even the lowly reporter was aware that a portion of his salary came from advertising, and a seemly caution began to pervade all city rooms. Soon the hammering and tearing down of partitions in many Park Row offices also showed that business and advertising offices were being enlarged at the expense of editorial. It all made an unhappy Charles Edward Russell sum up: "Newspapers have come to a point where manufacture at a loss is necessary. Under this, advertising in great quantities is necessary to a paper's existence."

However, a more menacing shadow was lengthening across Park Row. It was cast by the figure of a ruthless, glacial man named Frank A. Munsey. Eventually, Munsey would earn the withering hatred of nearly every working journalist of his time. "Newspapermen as a class hated Munsey's name when he lived and were glad when he died," states his biographer, George Britt. This was no exaggeration. On Munsey's death, William Allen White composed perhaps the most scathing obituary of all time:

> Frank Munsey, the great publisher is dead.
>
> Frank Munsey contributed to the journalism of his day the talent of a meat packer, the morals of a money changer, and the manners of an undertaker. He and his kind have about succeeded in transforming a once-noble profession into an 8 per cent security.
>
> May he rest in trust.

Munsey was born in 1854 on a small Maine farm. In later years he would buttonhole total strangers to recount in detail the story of his rags-to-riches life. "I've earned my living since I was seven years old," he would begin. This was almost true. As an Alger-like teenage youth, Munsey found himself in charge of the Western Union office in Augusta, Maine. Looking around this pleasant city, he reached two conclusions. One was that he wished to leave the state of Maine. The other stemmed from the fact that Augusta possessed a thriving, if small, publishing house. From this he concluded that in publishing lay the road to inevitable wealth. On a few later occasions he admitted seeing a fallacy in this. "If I had gone into real estate, I would have made more money and made it faster," he would say at such times.

In 1882, aged twenty-eight, Munsey arrived in New York with forty dollars in his pocket—a fact which would be commemorated in 1922 when he uttered his famous "Forty dollars, forty years, forty millions." But at first the forty millions seemed far distant. Munsey had plans for a children's magazine to be called *Golden Argosy*. He established this and, despite vicissitudes that seem unbelievable today, was able to keep it going. Lacking even the small sums to pay contributors, the seemingly talentless man sat down and wrote his own serials. For ten years he worked eighteen hours a day and spent money personally only for food and an eight-dollar-a-week room. At one time he survived in business only because his accounts were kept in three different banks. "I kept thousands of dollars in the air between those banks," he later gloated. "It was a dizzy, dazzling, daring game; a game to live for, a game to die for; a royal, glorious game."

Munsey's first sniff of success came when, at the urging of Charles A. Dana, he advertised in the Sun. As subscriptions began returning he paid a visit to Dana, whom he gratefully told, "Someday I'm going to own the Sun." With the first real profits from *Golden Argosy* (soon to be called *Argosy*), Munsey branched out. He started a magazine which, with characteristic modesty, he called *Munsey's*. In this era most magazines cost twenty-five to thirty-five cents. *McClure's*, the popular, muckraking publication, was priced at fifteen. Munsey astutely sold his new magazine for ten cents. Even so, another innovation assisted him more in his climb to forty millions. He was the first publisher to make a steady policy of putting a picture of a pretty girl on the front cover of his magazine. Munsey never married, but he never forgot this debt to pretty girls. On becoming the most important publisher in the United States, he issued orders that only the prettiest possible girls were to be hired as secretaries and receptionists in his organization.

Munsey's contribution to publishing—if it can be called that—was to see it as big business. He vastly admired Commodore Vanderbilt, who had seized ownership of most American railroads by process of merging, buying out rivals, scrapping, consolidating, eliminating duplication and ruthlessly killing off the weak. With money coming in, the newly successful publisher began doing the same. "I keep on experimenting, creating and killing, till I happen to hit the public's taste," he explained at the time. Over a characteristic, sample period he did this by buying a failing magazine named *Scrap Book* and combining it with another called *Live Wire*. Turning his eyes from these two, which continued under the name *Live Wire*, he bought *Godey's* and merged it with *Puritan*. Then he incorporated the better features of these two into *Junior Argosy*, which shortly merged with *Argosy*. He then bought *Peterson's Magazine* which, after a few months on its own, was also thrown into *Argosy*. *Ocean*, *Live Wire*, *Cavalier*, *Railroad Man's*, *Woman*, and *All-Story* were then shuffled about until a successful pattern evolved. If the proper solution could not be found, the magazines would all be killed. Munsey, says Britt, was a publisher not squeamish about death sentences.

As he made fast millions, Munsey began to dream of becoming a power in Republican politics. This, he decided, could best be achieved by the ownership of newspapers, since popular magazines carried no political weight. To intimates he confided plans for a chain of five hundred newspapers. In 1901, he started toward this by buying the Washington Times for two hundred thousand dollars; the New York Daily News for four hundred thousand; and the Boston Journal and Evening Journal for five hundred thousand. His methods with big-city newspapers proved no different from those he used with minuscule magazines. Munsey experimented, created and killed just as before. In Boston, he first streamlined both Journals in a manner to reflect credit on his ability. But this was not enough. He killed the Evening Journal, then three days later created the Boston Evening News, published from the same shop, with the same equipment, by the same men. Two weeks later he reduced the price of this paper by a penny. Nine months later he stopped the Sunday Journal and started an enlarged Saturday Evening News. Seven weeks later he revived the Sunday Journal again. A year after creating it, he killed off the Evening News, after which he raised the price of the Journal. Then, on September 11, 1904, he killed the Sunday Journal.

Temporarily fatigued by such labors, he set off for New York by way of New London, where he paused long enough to establish a chain of department stores which operated under the slogan, "More for a dollar than a dollar will buy elsewhere." These proceeded to flourish, promising more millions. Arriving in New York, he irritably killed the Daily News, which had failed to show a profit during his stay in Boston. Then he moved on to Philadelphia, Baltimore and Washington, buying further papers in each. Shortly, however, he realized that newspapers in such cities failed to carry the national political weight of a Park Row paper. Returning to New York, he paid one million dollars for the New York Press, still edited by the Ervin Wardman, who had coined the phrase Yellow Journalism.

As soon as Munsey purchased a newspaper, he ordered all fat men on the staff fired, for he considered them lazy as a breed. Then the gaunt, sour-looking figure would stalk into the busy city room, to state loudly, "I want NO SMOKING signs put up all around here. Do you know why? Because smoking means loss of time. Whenever men stop to puff a cigarette or light a pipe, time is wasted. And God hates a waster."

Yet even with these infuriating idiosyncrasies, Munsey's worst offense in the eyes of newsmen was that he never seemed able to realize that a newspaper had a soul. To him the papers he acquired were in no way different from public utilities, steel companies, or chains of Munsey stores. By Munsey's tried and true formula, a newspaper existed only to make money. If it failed to do so, it was killed. But before this another paper would be purchased, so that any good features from the first could be incorporated into the second. And now, convinced that New York City was his true pro-

vince, Munsey disposed of most of his papers in other cities. At that
a chill wind seemed to whistle through Park Row. For word was
circulating that he wanted to buy another newspaper into which to
incorporate the ailing Press.

But for months no further word was forthcoming, and in city
rooms editors and reporters forgot the bleak shadow of Frank A. Munsey. Then, suddenly, on June 30, 1916, news came of what—far
more than the departure of the Times and the Herald—presaged the
finish of Park Row as Newspaper Row. Exactly as he had predicted
to Dana in 1893, Munsey had bought the Sun, at a price of four and
a half million dollars. It was a stunning blow to the city room of
that proud newspaper, where benumbed reporters could only sit
reminiscing of Dana, puffing the last pipes and cigarettes they would
be able to enjoy during work hours. Soon the NO SMOKING signs
would be put up, with Munsey himself darting unexpectedly in and
out to make sure his rule was enforced.

Munsey also disliked the careless, picturesque atmosphere of city
rooms, and as soon as possible would no doubt remodel the Sun's
along the clean lines of a real-estate office (actually he moved the
Sun to new quarters at 280 Broadway). But there was little the unhappy staff members could do. With the folding of the News, and
the now-inevitable disappearance of the Press, newspaper jobs on
Park Row would be hard to get. Further, the pressures of a European war had cut into advertising revenues, so that most newspapers were wary of added expense. The staff could only await the
coming of the Munsey regime with the hope that it would not be as
bad as painted. It was a situation neatly summed up by Frank Ward
O'Malley. "The slaves," he said, "go with the plantation."

Yet, if new forces were gathering to hasten the end of the Park
Row era, a few old forces could still demonstrate that they were not
spent. One such was Richard Harding Davis, who, early in 1914, was
south of the border, covering uprisings in Vera Cruz for the New
York Tribune. By summer, he was back, spending relaxing days
with Bessie McCoy Davis at Crossroads Farm, Mt. Kisco, the con-
tented couple's home. Then, at the end of July, newspaper headlines
told of threatened mobilization and war in Europe. This was the

sixth war in Davis's exciting lifetime, and plainly it would be the
biggest. He immediately received an offer to cover it for the Wheeler
Syndicate and on August 4, 1914, caught an emergency sailing of
the *Lusitania*: "Lights out, her wireless crackling out the momentous
message that Great Britain would stand with the Allies, the great
ship steamed across the sea which ten months later would sweep on
through a torpedo gash in her hull and engulf her."

After five wars the vaunted Davis luck still held. As anxious as
ever to be close to the front, Davis hastened to Brussels, taking quarters near the American legation. Shortly came the day that was, perhaps, the high point of his great journalistic career. As the German
armies marched into Brussels, Davis watched. Afterward he wrote
what many considered the finest dispatch of World War I. His colleague Arno Dosch-Fleurot called it "a picture of imperialism itself
coming down the road," but Park Row did not need to indulge in
such phrases. There the Davis story merely proved that there is no
pro like an old pro. For, in sentences that almost echoed the heavy
tread of marching feet, Dick Davis wrote:

> The change came at ten in the morning. It was as
> though a wand had waved and from a fête-day on the Con-
> tinent we had been wafted to London on a rainy Sunday.
> The boulevards fell suddenly empty. There was not a house
> that was not closely shuttered. Along the route by which we
> now knew the Germans were advancing, it was as though the
> plague stalked. That no one should fire from a window, that
> to the conquerors no one should offer insult, Burgomaster
> Max sent out as special constables men he trusted. Their
> badge of authority was a walking-stick and a piece of paper
> fluttering from a buttonhole. These, the police, and the
> servants and caretakers of the houses that lined the boule-
> vards alone were visible. At eleven o'clock, unobserved but
> by this official audience, down the Boulevard Waterloo
> came the advance-guard of the German army. It consisted
> of three men, a captain and two privates on bicycles. Their
> rifles were slung across their shoulders, they rode unwarily,
> with as little concern as the members of a touring-club out
> for a holiday. Behind them so close upon each other that
> to cross from one sidewalk to the other was not possible,

came the Uhlans, infantry, and the guns. For two hours I
watched them, and then, bored with the monotony of it,
returned to the hotel. After an hour, from beneath my window, I still could hear them; another hour and another went
by. They still were passing. Boredom gave way to wonder.
The thing fascinated you, against your will, dragged you
back to the sidewalk and held you there open-eyed. No
longer was it regiments of men marching, but something
uncanny, inhuman, a force of nature like a landslide, a tidal
wave, or lava sweeping down a mountain. It was not of this
earth, but mysterious, ghostlike. It carried all the mystery
and menace of a fog rolling toward you across the sea. The
uniform aided this impression. In it each man moved under
a cloak of invisibility. Only after the most numerous and
severe tests at all distances, with all materials and combinations of colors that give forth no color, could this gray have
been discovered. That it was selected to clothe and disguise
the German when he fights is typical of the General Staff,
in striving for efficiency, to leave nothing to chance, to neglect no detail.

After you have seen this service uniform under conditions entirely opposite you are convinced that for the German soldier it is one of his strongest weapons. Even the
most expert marksman cannot hit a target he cannot see. It
is not the blue-gray of our Confederates, but a green-gray. It
is the gray of the hour just before daybreak, the gray of un-
polished steel, of mist among green trees.

I saw it first in the Grand Place in front of the Hotel de
Ville. It was impossible to tell if in that noble square there
was a regiment or a brigade. You saw only a fog that melted
into the stones, blended with the ancient house fronts, that
shifted and drifted, but left you nothing at which to point.

Later, as the army passed under the trees of the Botan-
ical Park, it merged and was lost against the green leaves.
It is no exaggeration to say that at a few hundred yards you
can see the horses on which the Uhlans ride but cannot see
the men who ride them.

If I appear to overemphasize this disguising uniform it
is because, of all the details of the German outfit, it appealed to me as one of the most remarkable. When I was

near Namur with the rear-guard of the French Dragoons and Cuirassiers, and they threw out pickets, we could distinguish them against the yellow wheat or green gorse at half a mile, while these men passing in the street, when they have reached the next crossing, become merged into the gray of the paving-stones and the earth swallowed them. In comparison the yellow khaki of our own American army is about as invisible as the flag of Spain.

Major-General von Jarotsky, the German military governor of Brussels, had assured Burgomaster Max that the German army would not occupy the city but would pass through it. He told the truth. For three days and three nights it passed. In six campaigns I have followed other armies, but, excepting not even our own, the Japanese, or the British, I have not seen one so thoroughly equipped. I am not speaking of the fighting qualities of any army, only of the equipment and organization. The German army moved into Brussels as smoothly and as compactly as an Empire State express. There were no halts, no open places, no stragglers. For the gray automobiles and the gray motor-cycles bearing messengers one side of the street always was kept clear; and so compact was the column, so rigid the vigilance of the file-closers, that at the rate of forty miles an hour a car could race the length of the column and need not for a single horse or man once swerve from its course.

All through the night, like a tumult of a river when it races between the cliffs of a canyon, in my sleep I could hear the steady roar of the passing army. And when early in the morning I went to the window the chain of steel was still unbroken. It was like the torrent that swept down the Connemaugh Valley and destroyed Johnstown. As a correspondent I have seen all the great armies and the military processions at the coronations in Russia, England, and Spain, and our own inaugural parades down Pennsylvania Avenue, but those armies and processions were made up of men. This was a machine, endless, tireless, with the delicate organization of a watch and the brute power of a steam roller. And for three days and three nights through Brussels it roared and rumbled, a cataract of molten lead. The infantry marched singing, with their iron-shod boots beating out the time.

They sang "Fatherland, My Fatherland." Between each line of song they took three steps. At times 2000 men were singing together in absolute rhythm and beat. It was like blows from giant pile-drivers. When the melody gave way the silence was broken only by the stamp of iron-shod boots, and then again the song rose. When the singing ceased the bands played marches. They were followed by the rumble of the howitzers, the creaking of wheels and of chains clanking against the cobblestones, and the sharp, bell-like voices of the bugles.

More Uhlans followed, the hoofs of their magnificent horses ringing like thousands of steel hammers breaking stones in a road; and after them the giant siege-guns rumbling, growling, the mitrailleuses with drag-chains ringing, the field-pieces with creaking axles, complaining brakes, the grinding of the steel-rimmed wheels against the stones echoing and re-echoing from the house front. When at night for an instant the machine halted, the silence awoke you, as at sea you wake when the screw stops.

For three days and three nights the column of gray, with hundreds of thousands of bayonets and hundreds of thousands of lances, with gray transport wagons, gray ammunition carts, gray ambulances, gray cannon, like a river of steel, cut Brussels in two.

For three weeks the men had been on the march, and there was not a single straggler, not a strap out of place, not a pennant missing. Along the route, without for a minute halting the machine, the post-office carts fell out of the column, and as the men marched mounted postmen collected post-cards and delivered letters. Also, as they marched, the cooks prepared soup, coffee, and tea, walking beside their stoves on wheels, tending the fires, distributing the smoking food. Seated in the motor-trucks cobblers mended boots and broken harness; farriers on tiny anvils beat out horseshoes. No officer followed a wrong turning, no officer asked his way. He followed the map strapped to his side and on which for his guidance in red ink his route was marked. At night he read this map by the light of an electric torch buckled to his chest.

To perfect this monstrous engine, with its pontoon

bridges, its wireless, its hospitals, its aeroplanes that in rigid alignment sailed before it, its field telephones that, as it advanced, strung wires over which for miles the vanguard talked to the rear, all modern inventions had been prostituted. To feed it millions of men had been called from homes, offices, and workshops; to guide it, for years the minds of the high-born, with whom it is a religion and a disease, had been solely concerned.

It is, perhaps, the most efficient organization of modern times; and its purpose only is death. Those who cast it loose upon Europe are military-mad. And they are only a very small part of the German people. But to preserve their class they have in their own image created this terrible engine of destruction. For the present it is their servant. But, "though the mills of God grind slowly, yet they grind exceeding small." And, like Frankenstein's monster, this monster, to which they gave life, may turn and rend them.

Having finished this magnificent story, Davis, who was traveling on an American passport, found himself in a Belgium totally occupied by the Germans. He proceeded to evoke shades of the Spanish-American War by attiring himself in his best English tweeds and starting to walk to the faraway British lines. Inevitably, he was halted at gun-point and rudely arrested as an English spy.

All his life Davis had tried to appear the English gentleman, but it is possible that now he regretted it. For to the court-martial before which he was hauled, he looked every inch the English officer out of uniform, traveling with a false American passport. While Davis sweated, the court-martial debated whether to believe his story or put him before a firing squad. Finally, in the middle of the night, he was ordered to return to Brussels alone and on foot. It was a dangerous journey, during which Davis slept in haystacks. Arriving at the American legation, the ever-immaculate man looked, it was said, like a weary tramp. And from that moment on, Davis hated the Germans with a fury he had felt for nothing else in life.

Next Davis traveled to France and Greece, finding it increasingly difficult to understand why America hesitated over entering the war. The phrase "Too proud to fight" infuriated him and on returning to this country early in 1916, he announced, "If President Wilson had seen what I have seen, he never would ask the people of the United States to preserve the mental attitude of neutrals." At Crossroads Farm he paused briefly to enjoy the company of his newly born daughter, Hope Harding Davis. Then he began using his fame to draw attention to training camps at Plattsburg, N.Y., and elsewhere. Photos of him at these camps remain, showing him stern-faced as he demonstrated how to handle a gun. While doing this, Davis felt spasms of pain in the region of the heart, and at times his breath came in gasps. On long marches, he felt weak and his face reddened alarmingly. But the Davis code would permit no dropping out of line. In addition to these physical problems, he had mental ones. As America kept out of war, his wrath mounted. He was at Crossroads Farm on the day an American labor leader was reported as saying, "To hell with the Flag." Davis simmered about this all day long and after dinner sat down to write a letter to newspapers venting his wrath. From upstairs Bessie McCoy Davis, who had retired early, heard him make a phone call. It seemed to end abruptly and soon she went downstairs to investigate. Davis was crumpled at the phone, dead of a heart attack.

He was only fifty-two. Of him, his friend Gouverneur Morris wrote, "The gods loved him, and he had to die young."

Early in 1918, a correspondent for the New York Herald returned to the newspaper's New York office, still located in uptown Herald Square. "How's the Commodore?" he was inevitably asked. For though James Gordon Bennett had reached a ripe seventy-seven years, he still ruled from Paris with an iron hand. "The Commodore's dead," the man answered. "The old drunken, enterprising, money-spending Jimmy Bennett is dead. In his place has come a sober Scotch miser."

It was true. In the final years of his life the colorless Scotch side of Bennett—noted many years before by Dr. Hosmer—got the upper hand, pushing aside the mad Irishman. One indication of change was that at the age of seventy-three, crowning fifty years of roaring bachelorhood, Bennett married. His bride was Maud Parker, of Philadelphia, widow of Baron de Reuter, of the news-agency family. With her, he lived out his remaining years.

One thing Bennett never lost, however, was his capacity for fury. From 1914 he loathed the Germans with an intensity worthy of his prime. It was he who coined the word *Boche* to describe the enemy. Conspicuously hung in the office of the Paris Herald was a map of Europe, into which he daily stuck pins to show the position of the warring armies. As the pins of the German armies moved dangerously close to Paris, the staff of the Herald fled. Not so the doughty Commodore—no Boche armies could ever dislodge him. Standing alone in the Paris Herald city room, he soon had the extreme pleasure of moving his German pins gradually back, back, back. . . .

It was his final, splendid triumph. Shortly, he took to bed in his Villa Namouna, at Beaulieu. On May 10, 1918, he suffered a severe stroke. The next morning he was dead. Fittingly, the owner of the New York Herald was buried in the outskirts of Paris.

So the titans who gave Park Row its great vigor seemed to be passing. But it was not to cease being Newspaper Row without a last grim, theatrical stroke of high melodrama.

This was furnished by Charles Chapin, the by-now-legendary Hardboiled Charlie of the Evening World city room. Despite the shattering blow of his paltry Russell Sage inheritance, Chapin had continued his reckless, millionaire-type living. He had done it by continued speculation in stocks. For years, he operated on tips given him by World financial editors and Wall Street friends. Doing this, he had thrived. But then the supreme egoist decided that he knew more about stocks and bonds than any of those advising him. He started to plunge heavily on his own erratic hunches. Results were disastrous. By the summer of 1918 Chapin was so hopelessly deep in a financial morass that extrication seemed impossible.

Chapin was above all a proud man. He had been forced to borrow heavily and now could see only one way out of his self-inflicted disaster. This was suicide. But before killing himself, he planned to murder his wife. This grisly decision had been reached after he inquired of his relatives if they would take care of his faded, frail Nellie if he should die penniless. Response to the idea had been lukewarm, to say the least. That night, tossing in bed, Chapin decided, "I could not die like a coward and leave her to bear all the poverty and disgrace that was sure to follow. I cried all night, sickened at the thought of what I would have to do."

Chapin's financial reverses had been such that the couple could no longer afford to live at the Hotel Plaza, where Chapin owed a bill of three thousand dollars. Accordingly, they had been forced to take a suite in a much humbler hotel, the Cumberland, at Broadway and Fifty-fourth Street. Early in the summer of 1918, the pair began leaving the Cumberland on short trips. Nellie Chapin considered these vacations, but on each Chapin carried a police revolver, given him by his close friend, Police Commissioner Rhinelander Waldo. It was his intention to shoot Nellie with this formidable instrument, then turn it on himself.

On the first out-of-town trip the pair made he had almost done this. Ostensibly he had taken Nellie to Washington to celebrate their thirty-ninth wedding anniversary. But on the night after their anniversary dinner, Chapin waited until Nellie fell asleep. Reaching under the bed for the revolver, he lifted it to point at the back of Nellie's head. But suddenly, he always said, the ghost of his mother appeared:

> She stood in the room but a few feet from the bed, not the white-haired old woman, wasted with disease, that I had come to see a few days before she died, but the beautiful mother I had idolized when I was a child. She looked at me with the same sweet smile and gently shook her head, just as she had done in childhood days when reproving me for something I shouldn't have done. Then she faded away. . . . I do not know if it was my mother's spirit or a figment of my fevered brain. But there was no murder that night. Instead, I took my sleeping wife in my arms and kissed her, at the same time breathing a silent prayer of gratitude that she was still alive.

Unhappily, this mood did not last. Chapin soon took Nellie to Atlantic City. The ghost of his mother failed to appear, but when the moment came to fire, he could not summon the nerve. Next morning, however, as the couple hastened to the railroad station, they passed an old woman selling pencils. Seeing her, Nellie Chapin

uttered the words that sealed her doom. "Poor old soul," she whispered to Hardboiled Charlie. "How awful if that should ever happen
to me." On the train Chapin found that his mind had vividly retained the image of the pencil woman—"then her face would fade
and my wife's face would take its place. I would see her, sick and
trembling, and wan and feeble, stretching out her hand to chance
passers-by. There was only one way I could save her from such a
fate."

By the time the couple arrived in New York, Chapin found himself able to view with equanimity the act of killing Nellie and turning the pistol on himself—and those curious about the twisted
thoughts of a murderer shortly before his crime will be interested in
Chapin's later interpretation of his state:

> My mind at this time was perfectly clear. I had come to
> myself and I knew what I was doing. I had scarcely slept for
> more than a week. My nerves were unstrung and there was
> a prickling sensation as if my brain was being tortured with
> red hot needles. I felt that I was going mad and I was fear-
> ful that insanity might so twist my brain that I would be
> unable to carry out what I had planned to do. What if I
> became insane and killed myself and left my wife alone
> in the world, without relatives or friends, to suffer and
> starve, after all her loving devotion through our long mar-
> ried life? This thought was a constant torment. I wonder
> now how I ever remained sane.

Still, Chapin was the man whose first love was the newspaper
business. At Penn Station, he dispatched Nellie home to the Cumberland while he went downtown to Park Row to crack his whip over
the city room. He labored normally—which is to say, tirelessly and
sadistically—through the afternoon of Friday, September 14, 1918.
Before leaving the Pulitzer Building he cashed a check for one hundred dollars at the cigar stand in the lobby. Chapin's once-towering
finances had fallen to such a sorry state that he did not have this
amount in the bank, and he knew it. Yet it did not deter him. Over
the weekend the Chapins hardly left the Cumberland suite, and on
Sunday afternoon, September sixteenth, Chapin sat down at the desk

in his suite to write a letter to the World business manager, Don Carlos Seitz:

> I am conscious of being on the verge of a nervous breakdown and it is apparent that the moment is close when I will completely collapse. When you get this I will be dead. My wife has been such a good pal. I cannot leave her alone in the world.

Late Sunday evening Chapin descended to the lobby of the hotel, where he posted the letter to Seitz. He also ordered dinner to be sent to the Chapin suite on the eleventh floor. Neither touched the food: Nellie may have been upset by some of Chapin's actions and Chapin, if his letter of the afternoon is to be believed, was hardly in a mood to eat. In time, they began preparing to retire and Chapin placed the revolver in the now-familiar position within reaching distance underneath the bed. By the time the two settled for sleep it was nearly midnight. Chapin was determined to fire his shot into the back of Nellie's skull, so that her features would not be marred. For six seemingly interminable hours, Nellie slumbered peacefully on her back, thus thwarting this noble intention. But shortly before six A.M. the frail little woman turned over on her left side. It was the precise moment Chapin had waited for. In the course of the long night he had moved the revolver up under his pillow. He now groped for it and, when his fingers had it, lifted himself up on an elbow. Raising the revolver, he pointed the long muzzle at a spot slightly above Nellie's right ear. This time he experienced no difficulty in exerting the pressure that would make the gun fire.

Once he had sent the bullet crashing into his sleeping wife's skull, the time had come for Chapin to turn the revolver on himself and finish his own life. But he failed to do so.

At first there was an extenuating circumstance. Nellie Chapin did not die instantly from the shot—and a curious aspect of the murder is that no guest of the Cumberland seems to have been awakened by the sound made by the shot. For two hours Nellie writhed unconscious in whimpering death throes while Chapin attempted to comfort her. "He cradled her in his arms and talked of love and joy and other beautiful things," states an account sympathetic to Chapin. At last, shortly after seven thirty A.M., the wisp of a woman gave a shuddering gasp and went limp in his arms. Chapin knew she was dead. "He got down on his knees beside the bed and held her hand and prayed that God would understand."

Now—if ever—came the real moment for Hardboiled Charlie to turn the revolver on himself and complete the planned tragedy. But if the idea occurred to him, he never said so in voluminous confessions. Instead, he proceeded to act as if Monday the seventeenth were just another day. Half an hour later—at eight A.M.—a Cumberland bellboy appeared at the door of the suite with the usual morning newspapers, for in recent years Chapin, who at sixty looked over seventy, had relaxed his rigid seven A.M. arrival at the Evening World city room. When the bellboy knocked, Chapin was up and about, attired nattily in a gray summer suit with a bright orange tie. The tortoise-shell pince-nez with its distinguished silk cord was firmly affixed to his nose and in his buttonhole reposed a gay calendula. He accepted the newspapers wordlessly, but seeing a maid in the hall called out, "Mrs. Chapin was up late last night, I want her to sleep late this morning."

After closing the door, he roughly lettered a DO NOT DISTURB sign on a piece of brown wrapping paper and with one of Nellie's hatpins pinned it on the outside of the door. Then he put the revolver in his pocket and clapped a black derby on his head. From a humidor he extracted his morning Corona-Corona which, after puffing down to a butt, he habitually kept clamped in his teeth between mouthfuls of candy.

In the lobby he encountered the advertising manager of the World, who also lived at the Cumberland. Chapin asked him to carry word downtown that he would be late for work that morning. "I have business matters to attend to," he explained. But he seemed in no hurry to discharge them, for his first stop was the hotel barbershop, where he got a shave. Though his confession later said, "My brain was dead, I felt numb and insensate," he gave every outward appearance of spruce normality to his favorite barber. At nine A.M., erect and freshly shaved, he was on the Broadway sidewalk outside the Cumberland, hailing a passing cab. He did not order this to go full speed to Park Row, as was his custom. Instead he directed the driver to take him to Grand Central. There, in what he apparently considered a mystifying maneuver, he leaped into another and was driven to Central Park.

In later writings, Chapin declared it his purpose to put a bullet into his brain in the Park. Yet he still did not. He walked for hours and "it seemed to me that wherever I walked there were hundreds of outstretched hands waiting to snatch my weapon and prevent me from carrying out my purpose." Though his mind was filled with such fancies, he was capable of reasoning. At some point during the afternoon he realized that he might become a conspicuous figure wandering dazedly through Central Park with a big revolver in his pocket. He also knew that Nellie Chapin's body would soon be discovered and the hunt for him on. Indeed, at just about the same moment Don Seitz was handed Chapin's letter. He read it, and in great alarm phoned the manager of the Cumberland. The manager in turn summoned a policeman and the two entered the Chapin suite with a house key. In the first room they found a piano with sheet music open on its stand. In the second was the untouched dinner from the night before. In the bedroom lay the body of Nellie Chapin, dead.

Soon the Extras came out with headlines screaming CHARLES CHAPIN WANTED FOR MURDER! At the time Chapin was riding the city's subways, for he had decided that in the depths of the transit system he would be less conspicuous than in the Park.

> All day (he wrote later) I rode about the city on elevated trains and subways. Crouching in a corner. Riding on and on, like a dead man might. I went to Prospect Park and waited for the crowds to go away and give me a chance to die. Night came, and I fled from the shadows of trees. It was raining. I sat on a bench and fancied myself dead. My hands were ice. My blood was frozen. I could not think or move.

Chapin's stay in Prospect Park is interesting, for sitting on a bench there the strength to lift the pistol to his temple seemed at last to come to him. Then, just as he did so, a policeman sauntered along and a terrified Chapin dashed from the Park to the nearest subway. Boarding a train, he rode to the opposite end of the line, to discover himself standing before the locked gate of Bronx Park. Once more the appearance of a policeman frightened him away and he rushed back to the safety of the subway. Shortly he felt a natural urge and in the subway lavatory of the West Sixty-sixth Street station found a newspaper delivery boy arranging a pile of early morning editions. Chapin bought one and found himself staring at his own name in an eight-column headline. The story under it declared—not unexpectedly, in view of his letter to Seitz—that the police considered Chapin dead. This acted on the distracted man like the proverbial dash of cold water. He mounted the subway stairs to the sidewalk and proceeded to the nearest station house. There, for the last time in his life, he made full use of his importance as Hard-boiled Charlie, the terrible newspaperman. He was on familiar terms with every police captain in the city and now he would surrender himself to no one less. "Call Captain Tierney and get him down here right away," he snarled at the man on the desk. "I won't talk to anyone else."

An hour later, at Police Headquarters, Chapin was confessing to the district attorney and a group of high police officials. He was in control of himself and in good spirits. "Today is the first happy day I have known since falling into financial difficulties," he astonished his hearers by saying. With that he signed his confession with a flourish and allowed himself to be led to cell 1116 of the Tombs where, as he well knew, Harry Thaw had once been incarcerated. Here a guard perpetually paced the corridor and lights shone in each cell throughout the night. Chapin was on Murderer's Row, but his spirits did not appear to swoop downward. He lay down on the iron cot and slept the sleep of exhaustion for nearly twelve hours. Then he rose and characteristically demanded a supply of candy bars, a cigar and all New York newspapers. He munched candy as he read the accounts of his crime and confession, and the relentless editor in him was far from pleased by what he saw. From Murderer's Row, he issued a Chapinesque statement: "As well as I know newspapermen, I cannot understand how the reporters managed to distort my story as much as they did."

It is said that when news of Chapin's arrest reached the Evening World, city-room men reacted jubilantly. They pounded each other on the back and shouted, "I always told you the Boss was crazy." Some danced jigs of gloating happiness atop desks, and a bottle passed from hand to hand, tilting from lip to lip.

But there were others who did not join the jubilation. Those with some comprehension of human nature kept out of the celebration, out of sympathy for the city-room tyrant. A few actually visited Chapin in his cell, bringing with them precious bits of Evening World gossip. This kindness paid off in an odd way, for all those who visited Chapin in Murderer's Row slowly began to notice what can only be called a phenomenon. In his damp, gloomy cell, Chapin actually began to change. It was not a change for the worse, but for the better. His gray, color-of-ashes skin began to take on a healthy, human glow. The whining snarl of a voice seemed deeper, beginning a change that eventually made it deep and resonant. The shallow snake eyes, which had seemed only to reflect the light from without, now seemed to shine from within, becoming a bright, deep blue.

In every way Chapin, who should have been a beaten man, appeared to take on the look of a happy one—or at least a man from whose life a terrible weight had been lifted. This inevitably leads to speculation as to the real forces which drove him to kill his wife of forty years. Chapin, instead of loving Nellie as he so persistently declared, may really have felt for her an undying hatred. Hardboiled Charlie had always been known as a connoisseur of female flesh. Despite his lavish protestations of love for Nellie, he was an accomplished girl-watcher, a seasoned ogler of women. Along Park Row and elsewhere, the gnarled genius was always one to stop a conversation while a pretty girl passed by. Then he would swivel around to follow her with his eyes, at the same time favoring any male companion with an expert analysis of her fine points.

Thus it is possible to visualize Chapin as similar to the Reverend Davidson in *Rain:* of high moral principles and in seeming control of himself, but inside burning with sexual frustration. Deeply unhappy people try to blame someone for their unhappiness. It is possible that over the years Chapin came to hate Nellie for standing in the way of an inner, life-loving man. He may in time have come to focus all the blame for his misfortunes on her frail, color-less person. If she could only be removed from his life—it may have seemed to his frantic inner self—all his problems (including the financial) would evaporate and the world would be sweet again.

Or perhaps Chapin—instead of losing heavily in stocks, as he al-ways said—was being blackmailed. Certainly, a Reverend Davidson type would have had a difficult time in the New York of Chapin's prime. The vice-ridden Tenderloin lay in the heart of midtown and no newspaperman, city editor or cub, could avoid entering it at some time or other in line of duty. It could be that Chapin was solicited by exactly the type of girl he liked to ogle, and succumbed. He may have done this only once, or perhaps returned to start a liaison. Ei-ther would be enough to make a man in his position vulnerable. A photograph may have been taken, or an affidavit signed. With it, a blackmailer could bleed Chapin white, threatening the proud, stern man with loss of job, social position, or even his wife. But, after killing Nellie, Chapin may have realized that he had perpetrated a deed so awful that he was forever beyond the reach of a blackmailer. There was no need to kill himself now. He was free at last, and even prison may have seemed preferable to what he had gone through over the years.

At this early point Chapin seemed convinced that his stay in Murderer's Row, and in any subsequent prison, was only an interim period on the way to a full pardon. Already his political influence had become manifest, for the court ruled that, if he would plead guilty, he could do so to second-degree murder. This was satisfactory to Chapin, since it eliminated a public trial and removed the pos-sibility of death in the electric chair. On a chilly morning in mid-January, 1919, while newsboys outside shouted headlines about Pro-hibition and the forthcoming Paris Peace Conference, he was taken into court for sentencing. There the still-rejuvenating man's eager voice cut in ahead of his lawyer's, "quick as lightning and piercing shrill," to plead for himself "Guilty of muder in the *second* degree."

From the bench Judge Weeks sentenced him to twenty years to life in Sing Sing. It was not until arrival at the gloomy prison on the Hudson that Chapin seemed to feel a twinge of fear that he might remain behind bars for the rest of his life. He was assigned

the number 69690 and the superstitious man in him immediately
added these individual numbers in his head. The total came—dreadfully—to 30. In every newspaper city room the number 30 was
traditionally typed at the end of a story to indicate its end. To the
intensely impressionable Chapin, it suddenly seemed that Sing Sing
Prison might be his journey's end.

CHAPTER SEVENTEEN

End of the World

O N January 17, 1920, the sale of the New York Herald to Frank A. Munsey was announced. The price was four million, and included in the sale were the Paris Herald and the Evening Telegram, the latter of which Bennett had started in 1867 and always treated like a poor relation of the mighty Herald. But in 1920 the Telegram was making money where the Herald was not, since it had never been able to recover from the indecency charges brought by William Randolph Hearst. Even so, the Telegram was still considered a neglected relation. Yet the Telegram could afford to wait. Its great days were soon to come.

The purchase of the old and honorable Herald was a great moment for Munsey. Ordinarily impervious to sentiment, he allowed himself briefly to dwell on the fine tradition of the paper he had bought. Visiting the Herald office, he shut himself in Commodore Bennett's office, which was still kept spick and span, with the latest edition of the Herald on the desk, even though Bennett would never again visit the premises. As visualized by George Britt in this rare moment, Munsey

> . . . sat up straight in James Gordon Bennett's chair, at Bennett's small old-fashioned desk, beside the fire burning cosily in the hearth in Bennett's office in the lovely old Herald Building, and he permitted himself to sip temperately of that heady draught, the pride of ambition achieved.

It was hoped that Munsey, impressed at last by the heritage of a newspaper he had bought, would use his money to build the Herald to its previous eminence. But Munsey was ever Munsey. Two weeks after his sensational purchase, he announced the merger of his two great newspapers. Thus for a short—and seemingly forgotten—period, New York boasted a morning paper clumsily called The Sun and the New York Herald. It was a shock, for though Munsey had played his peculiar game with small papers he had not been thought capable of merging two such giants. Yet, of course, he was. According to one source: "He took the Herald and the Sun and stuck them together as easily as if he were moving the canned vegetables, soda crackers, and prunes of one grocery to the enlarged shelves of another."

Munsey, naturally, saw his act only in terms of money. "Pride has no place in economics," he stated. "To have continued the Herald as an independent entity would have been in opposition to all the laws of economics, all the laws of sound business." As always, behind these cold words lay much human suffering, for when Munsey amalgamated, people lost jobs. By the hundreds, men and women from the Herald and Sun were turned into the street. "They were bitter and helpless," it was said. "For they had leaned on the Herald and Sun for support. It was a blow to pride and affection, no less than a way of life."

Even so, the staff of the Herald bade farewell to the paper in a manner that might have warmed the erratic emotions of the formidable old Commodore. On January 30, 1920, Herald men from all over the city returned for a combination reunion and farewell. They greeted each other, sang songs, opened bottles and shed tears. At midnight a bugler in the uniform of the 71st Regiment blew a melancholy Taps. When the last form was locked up in the composing room, a bouquet of flowers was placed upon it, and as it rolled to the stereotyper there was dead silence in the room.

Even the plans of ice-blooded multimillionaires sometimes go awry. Having acquired the Herald, Munsey found himself in competition with the Times and the World. He had not the imagination, perspective, or skill to put the Herald back to a position to do battle with such titans. This would have involved comprehension of the hu-

man factor, and Munsey only noted dollars and cents. In a sense he
had become the victim of his own greed. In his determination to
own a major Park Row morning paper, he had failed fully to absorb
the fact that the Herald was a money-loser. Nor had the Morning
Sun ever matched the Evening in earning power. At the same time,
to follow his usual policy of killing the Sun-Herald, or just the Herald, would have been an admission of terrible defeat, especially so
soon after his display of un-Munsey-like pride of purchase. There
was also the four million he had paid for the Herald.

Usually Munsey bought papers for the negative purpose of getting rid of them, so that properties he owned would face less competition. This was the only forward step he could see now. There is no
record that he ever made overtures to the Times or World, but by
1923 he had fixed his gimlet eye on the Tribune, which under
Horace Greeley and Whitelaw Reid had always catered to conservative, property-owning readers, yet managed to maintain considerable
journalistic importance at the same time. Munsey made up his mind
to buy the Tribune, and made an appointment to see Ogden Reid,
the paper's publisher. At this, he received an astonishing jolt. Reid
listened silently to his offer, then replied, "The Tribune is not for
sale, but we will buy the Herald."

It was the sharpest setback Frank Munsey had ever suffered,
and he could not accept it. Over succeeding months he repeated the
offer frequently, only to receive the same flat answer. In time, the
Reid clan grew tired of his persistence and contrived in March, 1924,
to get him invited to dinner by the dowager Mrs. Whitelaw Reid,
who lived in a massive Florentine mansion behind St. Patrick's
Cathedral. From the Ritz-Carlton, where he dwelt in ever-solitary
state, Munsey walked the few steps up Madison Avenue: "A bustling,
dry man within a few months of seventy, his step quick, but his hair
white, a tired man, depressed in spirit, stubbornly delayed in getting
a very big thing he wanted."

After dinner, Munsey broached the sale of the Tribune to Mrs.
Whitelaw Reid, using the argument that there were too many morning newspapers in New York. The imposing dowager wholeheartedly
agreed and when she informed him the Tribune was not for sale,
Munsey at last believed it. On the spot, he agreed to sell the Herald

to the Reids for five million. He mentioned the stipulation in Commodore Bennett's will that the name New York Herald never be changed. Mrs. Reid pleasantly agreed to call the new paper the New York Herald Tribune.

To Munsey, who in the name of cold business efficiency had brought so much hardship to others, this was a bitter draught. "It hurts me more than anything I ever did in my life," he mourned when he signed the papers of sale. As if unable fully to comprehend what had happened, he kept describing to friends his precise emotions as he finally became convinced that the Reid family would not sell. "That old woman is a good businessman," he would declare. "The earth seemed to dissolve under me. It was not what I wanted."

Munsey died in December, 1925, after ten days of excruciating pain from an attack of appendicitis. Inexplicably, his multimillions were left to the Metropolitan Museum of Art, an institution in which he had never showed the slightest interest during life. Indeed, it is doubtful that he ever set foot in the Museum's marble halls.

During his period as publisher of New York newspapers, the gray wolf who was Munsey reduced the number of city papers from fourteen to nine. Not only had he eliminated the Herald and the Press, but the Globe and the Mail had been sacrificed to clear the path to profits of the Evening Sun. With his sale of the Herald, the Morning Sun also disappeared. After Munsey, only the World papers in the still-proud Pulitzer Building remained on Park Row, for the Herald Tribune, like the Times, was being published uptown, near Times Square.

But if Park Row had changed, so had the World—and all New York journalism. The Roaring Twenties had combined with the Jazz Age to produce the tabloid: the Daily News, Daily Mirror and the egregious Graphic. These especially menaced the World papers, which had ever attempted to appeal to all segments of the population. Readers looking for the terse and exciting in news coverage found the sensational, photo-crammed tabloids more to their liking.

The World had another reason for resenting tabloids. On December 31, 1899, Joseph Pulitzer had made a courtly gesture. He gave editorship of the new century's first edition of the World to Alfred Harmsworth, later Lord Northcliff, who was visiting this country. In a ceremony not likely to be repeated anywhere on December 31, 1999, all World reporters that night appeared in the office in evening clothes. Still more remarkable was that for January 1, 1900, Harmsworth produced a paper amazingly like the tabloid of the future. It was such a change that he felt called upon to apologize. "Let me explain at once," he wrote in an editorial, "that this is merely a twentieth century suggestion on my part . . . closely resembling the newspaper of the future." With the newspaper of the future thus charted, the World had never done anything about it. When the Daily News profitably appeared, the editors may well have wondered if they had not neglected a golden opportunity reposing in their laps.

Other problems beset the World, to gradually change its character. Prominent among these were the three Pulitzer heirs, of whom it was said that Ralph inherited his father's idealism, Joseph his tough qualities and Herbert his stubbornness. None, unfortunately, had inherited all three. Nor had any of the three seemed to inherit Pulitzer's great strength of spirit.

For ten years after Pulitzer's death, the World proceeded under his momentum. In part, this was due to the presence on the staff of Herbert Bayard Swope, who, like Pulitzer, had come to New York by way of the St. Louis Post-Dispatch. Swope was (and is) one of the most energetic men of our time, and one of the best reporters. "Swope," writes James W. Barrett, the last city editor of the World, "was probably the best reporter not only on the World but in the whole wide world. His personality could break down almost any barrier. He had a tremendous fund of background information for any story that came along and could see further ahead in the development of a story than any newspaperman I ever met." Some fail to share this rapturous view, pointing out that Swope was admired by those above him on the ladder of success but not always by those below. Donald Henderson Clarke recalls entering the World men's room one day to find Swope grimacing attractively before the mirror. "What in hell are you doing, Herb?" he demanded. Swope explained, without shame, that in a few minutes he would be meeting Ralph Pulitzer for the first time and wished to put his most agreeable self forward. "Don't worry," Clarke said drily, "you'll put yourself over." Swope paid no attention. He was carefully arranging his thatch of reddish hair.

Walter Lippmann—who on the death of Frank Cobb succeeded to the World editorial page—once said to Swope, "Herbert, you are a lucky, fascinating devil." With all his obvious ambition, Swope was truly dedicated to the New York World, and remained so until he began to find race tracks more stimulating. It was he who, in 1916, received the first Pulitzer Prize for reporting. Such a dynamo of a man could never remain a reporter long. He became city editor, managing editor and (in the 1920's) executive editor, a title fashioned to fit himself. But Swope's determined newsgathering never received full support from the Pulitzer family. By now Joseph had discovered that he preferred life in St. Louis, where he happily ran the Post-Dispatch. In 1919, Herbert went abroad to live, becoming the owner of a famous shoot in Scotland. This left Ralph, who had inherited his father's idealism but not his strength, to run the World. It was not an enviable position, especially since the three Pulitzers were in the odd spot of serving as trustees of the estate, and at the same time were officers of the newspapers which were the main assets of the estate. It became their duty as trustees to see that, as publishers, they made as much money as possible for the trustees.

Not surprisingly, Ralph Pulitzer began lending a willing ear to strenuous business-department demands for economies in newsgathering expense. So the second generation of Pulitzers began presiding over a strange twist in the life of the World. The World had always been a fighting newspaper. Now it ceased to fight. Instead of news the paper began to stress the editorial by-products of news. Its main contribution to the teeming journalism of the Twenties was the Op Ed —or Opposite Editorial—page. There a group of writing luminaries, led by Heywood Broun, F.P.A., Frank Sullivan, Harry Hansen and cartoonist Rollin Kirby, held forth daily. This brought great intellectual prestige to the paper, but having succeeded in this the World deemed it permissible to cut down on straight news. It began calling itself a "selective" newspaper—in which only the *best* news was offered!

A graver misstep came in 1925 when the price of the Morning

World was raised to three cents. Efforts had been made to persuade
the Times and Herald Tribune to go along on this. They had refused, and the World disastrously proceeded alone. At the time, its
circulation was one hundred thousand ahead of its competition. In
slightly over a year the hundred-thousand advantage had disappeared.
Desperately the selective newspaper cut pages, so that in a three-
cent World the reader got only thirty to thirty-two pages, while in
two-cent competition he found fifty-six to sixty-four. In 1927, the
price of the World was again reduced to two cents. But the damage,
irreparably, had been done.

At one point, it was suggested to Ralph Pulitzer that the Morning World be streamlined into a condensed, highly selective, brightly
edited paper which would sell at one cent, aiming at a million circulation. Pulitzer brushed the idea aside with the remark, in effect,
that such drastic changes were impossible in both newspapers and
people.

Yet if Pulitzer—or anyone—wished an example of drastic personal change, it was only necessary to look at Sing Sing Prison, where
the incredible saga of Charles Chapin was playing itself out.

On arrival in prison, Chapin had been clothed in prison gray.
His clipped, military-looking moustache had been shaved off, baldly
exposing the look of facial weakness which it had successfully hidden.
Even so, Chapin continued to look better. His eyes, once a palish,
shallow gray, became bright, deep blue. The voice lost its whine and
sounded deep and resonant. His complexion continued to take on a
healthier glow. Prison authorities, warned to watch Chapin because
of his past ideas of suicide, gradually relaxed. Hardboiled Charlie
seemed on the way to becoming a model prisoner.

Almost immediately Chapin uncovered the fact that Sing Sing's
recent past included a newspaper called Star of Hope. It had been
started by a group of inmates and lapsed largely because of their in-
experience. However, the Star of Hope had been regarded as a potential morale builder and Chapin had little difficulty in obtaining
permission to activate it. The sprightly oldster acted as if this were
a huge shot in the arm. Given an empty cell for an office, a typewriter
and four of the better-behaved and more literate prisoners as staff,

he applied himself to the Star of Hope with the zeal he would have applied to reviving a moribund newspaper outside prison walls. He himself began writing a series of articles on his exploits as a reporter, and, realizing that Sing Sing was a fertile field for human-interest crime stories, he invited the more accomplished inmates to set down the unvarnished stories of their crimes.

Outside newspapers saluted Sing Sing's lively new Star of Hope. Then Chapin, accustomed to being rewarded for his successes in life, was dealt a blow which cruelly reminded him that he now lived outside the law. State penal authorities were outraged at the publicity and ordered the publication ended. "Chapin," says one wry account, "made his prison paper so popular that it choked to death on its own popularity."

Newly installed as Sing Sing's warden was Lewis E. Lawes, later to become famous as author of such best-selling books as *20,000 Years in Sing Sing*. Lawes took a liking to Chapin, whose continuing physical transformation made him less the aloof egoist and more the approachable human being. Warden Lawes urged Chapin to expand the reminiscences he had prepared for the Star of Hope into an autobiography. Chapin did this and *Charles Chapin's Story: Written in Sing Sing Prison* was published by G. P. Putnam's Sons in 1920. Today this 335-page volume more than holds its own as a model of spare, city-room prose. Yet the very clarity of writing brings coldness to the book, as if Chapin had used only his mind and none of his emotions in its preparation. This fact was noted by one reviewer who called it, "mostly alibis and extenuating circumstances." Aside from the few contradictions in fact between it and his post-crime confessions, the book told a story with which the newspaper-reading public was already familiar. This and emotional emptiness kept it from creating much excitement when published. Nor had it taken Chapin long to write. The superficial style and lack of soul-searching allowed him to finish it in less than six months.

Newspaper gone, autobiography finished, 69690 began to grow listless and indifferent. As he did, a thought occurred to both Warden Lawes and the Catholic chaplain, Father Cashin. They urged Chapin to consider doing something with the prison yard, the patch of ground around which the prison buildings stood. Most cells looked out on it, and prisoners marched through it daily. As part of any American college, it would have been an attractive campus, but Sing Sing had for the past hundred years used it as a dumping ground for cinders and rubble until it had become, in Warden Lawes's own words, barren to the eye, hopeless to the heart. "Maybe if you tried to plant some flowers around, Charlie . . ." the Warden suggested one day. Chapin's only answer was to shake his head and mutter, "What's the use?" Father Cashin pointedly left a lavishly illustrated seed catalog in 69690's cell. Chapin hardly picked it up.

Indeed, his only reading during these black days seemed to be his beloved Evening World, which came to him regularly by mail. Then one day a poem in praise of gardens appeared on the editorial page of the paper. It ignited his energies. With the same fiendish intensity he had given every edition of the paper, he read through the seed catalog. Then he announced himself ready. "Remember," Warden Lawes warned, "I can furnish you with all the rough labor you need, but no money." He created a Garden Squad, some of whom Chapin put to work digging up the rubbish which paved the filled-in yard. Others were set to fetch topsoil from nearby state property. As they worked, 69690 repaired to the typewriter in his cell where he hammered out letters detailing his plans for a Sing Sing garden. He sent one to garden magazines, requesting bone meal for fertilizer. A manufacturer immediately donated a ton. Another sent a second. Soon Chapin had enough.

At this early stage of his garden plans, Chapin polled Sing Sing occupants to learn their favorite flower. Almost unanimously, it was roses. Chapin dispatched another of his letters to the American Rose Society, which responded by sending hundreds of plants to the prison. The roses flourished, and prisoners stopped Hardboiled Charlie to wring his hand and express thanks for bringing color into their drab lives. But roses, appreciated though they might be, were merely the cornerstone of Chapin's soaring plans for his prison gardens. There still remained considerable space in the yard, much more along walks and around and between the numerous buildings. Chapin went to his typewriter again to write local nurserymen asking for surplus stock. One sent iris, another delphiniums, a third petunias.

As such offerings poured in, Chapin labored like the city editor of old. By this time he had been allowed to move to a more spacious cell in what was called the Sing Sing Annex. There a green rug covered his floor, prints decorated the wall, and over the door hung John Gay's self-composed epitaph: "Life is a jest/And all things show it/I thought so once/And now I know it." In time, a twittering canary in a cage added to the comparative pleasantness of his quarters. Chapin left his cell at seven A.M. and seldom returned until ten P.M. He expected the men under him to labor every bit as hard as he did, and according to one story, Warden Lawes was forced to take his favored prisoner aside to admonish, "Look Charlie, these men working for you are wards of the state. You can't treat them like men on the Evening World."

The Sing Sing gardens, of course, were not Chapin's creation alone. Warden Lawes was sagacious enough to make the Garden Squad an honor detail to which prisoners were assigned as a reward for good behavior. But no matter how many men labored at the gardens, no matter how well they worked or how hard Chapin drove them, the most remarkable feature of the Sing Sing gardens will always be Charles Chapin himself. The man who had lived in hotels, never fingering anything but newsprint, turned out to possess the greenest of green thumbs. After brief study, the mysteries of gardening seemed to become as clear to him as the mysteries of the city room. With large areas of the prison grounds sprouting roses, tulips and delphiniums, Chapin began to yearn to conquer more difficult fields. He now wrote his millionaire friends of former years who possessed greenhouses. Adolph Lewisohn was the first to respond, sending Chapin a crate of rare orchids. Another sent red lilies from Jamaica.

One day Chapin removed John Gay's bitter epitaph to put up a quotation from Samuel Smiles: "There are natures which blossom and ripen amidst trials that would only wither and decay in an atmosphere of ease and comfort." But despite his switch in mental attitude, he retained some of the grisly humor of his past. When the priceless orchids from Adolph Lewisohn reached Sing Sing, he appropriated for them the old morgue, adjoining the execution chamber. It brought macabre pleasure to him to grow his fairest flowers on the slabs where the charred bodies of murderers once lay. "See those orchids on that slab," he would say to visitors, "That's where they used to cut up the bodies."

As word of Chapin's transformation spread beyond the Sing Sing walls, his former star reporter Irvin Cobb paid him a visit. Cobb, become one of the top article and humor writers in the United States, then wrote an article on Chapin called "The Convict Who Made a Garden on the Road to Hell." It was published in Cosmopolitan, and

> . . . told how the bleak compound, covered with smelly garbage cans that had been the last sight on which a condemned man's wistful eyes rested as he was led into the Death House was a glorious dahlia bed; how the specimen roses, the gifts of rich men, now by hundreds lined the walkways; how the glass-roofed hut where formerly autopsies were performed on the scorched bodies of those who died in the Chair had been converted into a conservatory.

One result of the widely read Cobb article was that Chapin received a deluge of further plants, including rare and exotic specimens from Australia and South Africa. Another came when Chapin received a letter from a girl named Constance, who wrote that she worked on a trade paper in Cleveland and confided to him her hopes of a writing career. Chapin answered all the mail that came to him in prison, and doing so spent long night hours hunched over a typewriter in his work-cell with only the twittering of a canary to keep him company. He answered Constance, saying that his favorite rose bore her name. She replied and the correspondence continued matter-of-factly until she sent her picture.

Then the old girl-ogler sat up. Constance was in her early twenties and a real beauty, precisely the type he had eyed with such extreme relish in City Hall Park. He began writing her in more intimate fashion, while Constance replied in kind. Chapin's motives in this are easy to follow, for any lonely man, in jail or out, would be flattered at having a lovely young girl as a pen pal. Why Constance opened up such a correspondence with a sixty-six-year-old convict is more difficult to fathom. It was not love of flowers, for her interest in the horticultural aspect of Chapin appeared nonexistent. For some reason she seemed interested in the personality of Hardboiled Charlie himself, and in 1924 the two embarked on an increasingly ardent correspondence which eventually was published in book form as *The Constance Letters of Charles Chapin*.

In time, Constance journeyed to Sing Sing to visit Chapin and the meeting showed that in the elderly man still lurked the flamboyant spirit that had worshipped luxury, worn orange ties to work—and whose innate love of the dramatic may have been stifled over forty years by Nellie Beebie Chapin. He entered the visitor's room at Sing Sing carrying a beautiful, yellow Constance rose. "They shook hands," says an account in *The Constance Letters*,

> . . . and he drew her to him and kissed her. They both cried a little and he gave her the rose. Then they sat down side by side and Constance pinned the rose on her dress. Chapin said that he had not slept all night, and was nervous. He was like a schoolboy embarrassed and happy. But after that they did not talk, for there were no words for their emotion.

The years 1924-5 became Chapin's best in Sing Sing. Constance wrote him daily, and visited often. His health seemed excellent, despite age and the tragedy he had survived. Magazines and newspapers wrote about him, and he received quantities of mail and Christmas cards. He lived in a comfortable cell, and worked in still another equipped with roll-top desk, typewriter and files. He was the boss of a work gang and enjoyed the esteem of most of his fellow prisoners, who called him "Boss," as had the men on the Evening World. He had his meals in a greenhouse room named the Rosarie.

Assisting him at all times was a good-looking young convict named Larry who was serving a term for forgery. Larry became Chapin's devoted man of all work, tending the precious orchids, feeding the birds, opening Chapin's correspondence, and cooking him delicacies he liked, especially roast chicken, deep-dish berry pie, frosted cake, soufflés and, most importantly, crêpes suzette. In return Chapin gave him lists of books to read and discovered in his young protégé a liking for esoteric philosophy and the poetry of Shelley. . . . In all, Chapin's prison life resembled the gentlemanly incarcerations of European political prisoners of past centuries—with one difference.

Where time hangs heavy on the hands of even the most comfortable prisoner, Chapin was cheerfully and fiendishly busy.

Yet despite this outward appearance of well-adjusted industry, the old demons of self-destruction lurked in the curious man. In 1926 the handsome Larry came up for release from Sing Sing. Why Chapin, with his social and political connections, failed to assist the young man's return to civilian life remains another of the mysteries of the Chapin case. Larry was a sensitive sort, who in the outer world soon felt that everyone he passed on the street recognized him as a jailbird. Unhappy, desperate, he searched his mind for an understanding person to talk to. Finally, he thought of Constance. He telephoned her and for Chapin's sake the girl offered help. She found him a room in Cleveland and began efforts to locate a congenial job. Then she happily wrote Sing Sing, describing her Good Samaritan activities to Chapin. It was a colossal mistake. The thought of young, handsome Larry seeing his adored Constance at will caused 69690 to erupt into a volcano of jealousy. Constance made a hurried trip to the prison, but Chapin flatly refused to see her. She enlisted the help of Mrs. Lawes, who persuaded her husband to have Chapin brought to the Warden's office. There Chapin, hard as granite, would not speak to her. He only reviled Larry, shouting, "I'll have his ears cut off."

Constance retired to send a note to the prison saying that unless she heard from Chapin within twenty-four hours she would return home. No reply came and she again consulted Mrs. Lawes. "Is he still obdurate?" she asked. "Hard as nails," Mrs. Lawes replied. "He won't eat his food or look at his flowers, and I think he cried all night. But there's nothing to be done. He's beside himself and there's no use talking to him."

Constance never again set eyes on Chapin. From time to time the two exchanged letters, but where the correspondence had been ardent it was now cool and impersonal. "The old fire and the beautiful enthusiasm were gone," writes Eleanor Early in her introduction to *The Constance Letters*.

Chapin's entire life and personality changed after the break with Constance. He asked Warden Lawes to move him from the comfortable quarters in the Annex to less pleasant quarters on the second floor of the Death House. Now he seemed to feel a desire to bring solace to the prisoners who were under sentence to die. This might have stemmed from the feeling that he, too, should have been elec- trocuted for the murder of Nellie, or from the realization that to one terrible crime he had added another by killing the love given by Constance. Whatever the reason, he became a valued comforter to Death House inmates and their families, feeling especially drawn to Ruth Snyder and Judd Gray. "Society has no right to execute poor creatures like these," he wrote after their execution.

"I have found religion in my flowers," he told Father Cashin. As his seventieth birthday approached, he worked with the furious energy of yore. Horticulturists and ladies' garden clubs visited the prison to look at the wonders he had wrought. In 1928 he turned seventy, then came his seventy-first birthday, and his seventy-second. In 1933 he would qualify for parole and there was no doubt that this model prisoner would be set free the moment his minimum sen- tence was served.

But in the fall of 1930 Warden Lawes carried unhappy news to 69690. The State had appropriated money for much-needed improve- ments in the century-old Sing Sing cell blocks. In order for the work to be completed the prison yard would have to revert to its former status as a dumping ground. Chapin's glorious blooms would have to be ploughed under, his fountain carted away, his precious walks torn up. In vain did the Warden assure Chapin that once the new construction was over the gardens could be re-created in all their splendor. On the day tractors began tearing through his priceless flowers, Hardboiled Charlie took to his bed. Warden Lawes and Father Cashin urged him to begin writing the gardening guide he had been pondering for years. Chapin only shook his head. "Is there anything I can do for you, Charlie, anything you want?" War- den Lawes asked. "Yes," Chapin answered. "I want to die, I want to get it over with."

On December 16, 1930, he did. His will read: "I especially ask that there be no services in New York or Washington. I wish the casket to be the least expensive obtainable, enclosed in a box and sealed, the box never to be opened."

There were no mourners when, a few days later, the body of

the greatest city editor Park Row had ever known was lowered into a grave next to that of the wife he killed.

The World papers survived Chapin by a little more than two months. The end had begun in 1928 with the resignation of Ralph Pulitzer, for reasons of health. This made it necessary for Herbert Pulitzer to leave his Scotch shoot and return to the United States to take over responsibility for the World newspapers.

Rightly or wrongly, Herbert Pulitzer has been named the villain in the hundreds of thousands of words written about the demise of the World. At best, he appears to have had little heart for his job, doing nothing to win the friendship or loyalty of the staff. Indeed, Herbert had been out of the country for so long that he knew almost no one on the papers. Further, he failed to speak to those he did know, among them William H. Laurence (later the distinguished science editor of the Times), who had been his tutor at Harvard. Herbert vastly compounded these offenses by smoking perfumed cigarettes and wearing clothes of distinct English cut. His voice was also explosively British, so that as uttered by him his family name sounded to some like "Pollitzah." To others, it resembled "Pork Chop."

All this might have been overlooked by a dedicated staff, however, had not Herbert committed the unpardonable by preferring the Evening World, a paper his father had treated almost with scorn. Without looking right or left Herbert would walk rapidly through the World city room, to establish himself at an Evening World desk where John F. Tennant, the managing editor, pondered the paper's daily make-up. At other times he joined Tennant and Evening World men in a glass of beer at Rackey's, behind the World Building. The only member of the World staff to whom he ever spoke was Swope, who was rapidly becoming fed up. Ralph Pulitzer still paid occasional visits to the office and in October, 1928, he summoned Swope to compliment him on an exposé of radium poisoning in New Jersey factories, one of the last great crusades carried on by the World. Swope thanked him for the praise, then suddenly said, "Ralph, suppose we make that my exit line." That night he left the Pulitzer Building forever.

The World's last big scoop was the disappearance of Judge Crater. Early in August, 1930, an anonymous female voice phoned the city desk to report that the Judge had disappeared into a limbo from which he has not yet returned. It was the kind of story that had always been a World specialty, and for a week the city room was galvanized into exciting, old-time activity. At the same time rumors were spreading that the World papers were for sale. In the Depression year of 1930 the papers which had made over twenty-five million dollars profit since the death of Joseph Pulitzer would earn only thirteen million, which meant a loss of more than one and a half million.

When this became known, an appalling fact came to light. Unlike most successful corporations, the Press Publishing Company had set aside no funds to cover such setbacks. In his angry book, *The World, the Flesh, and Messrs. Pulitzer*, James W. Barrett writes: "The World did not fail at all. It was the ownership of the World that failed. The Pulitzers had got into the habit of taking the profits at the expense of the maintenance of the institution. Luxurious living had become more important than the kind of devoted journalism indicated by their father's will." Whatever the cause, management had never saved for a rainy day. When the rains came, the Worlds had no umbrella.

But they did have a gross annual business of thirteen million, with circulations of three hundred and twenty thousand for the Morning; five hundred thousand for the Sunday; and two hundred eighty-four thousand for the Evening. Many newsmen have expressed the belief that if somewhere—say, in the person of Swope—a strong guiding hand could have been found, the World papers could have survived. This however, would have required that the Pulitzers abandon authority over their own properties, or sell the properties intact. Apparently they never considered either.

The privileged John Tennant tipped the news of sale early in 1931. When James Barrett made some remark about the future, Tennant said, "There won't be any next year. The show is over. Scripps-

Howard has bought the whole thing." Scripps-Howard now owned the Telegram, but it did not own the World—yet. In view of this, it is hard to understand the inertia of the World staff, which only at the last possible moment began frantic efforts to buy the paper. Still, the World had been alive longer than most staff members and—as later with the Sun—a New York without the three Worlds seemed an utter impossibility. Some staff members hoped for the best, some prayed—all thought that somehow the Worlds would manage to survive.

They did not. The fact that the papers had lost money in 1930 provided the loophole to break Joseph Pulitzer's will. Late in February hearings were held before the Surrogate. At them, Herbert Pulitzer declared that several offers had been received for the World papers, the Scripps-Howard bid of five million for the Evening World being the best. This was questioned on some sides, but a telling factor in favor of Scripps-Howard was the Pulitzer contract with the International Paper Company for the purchase of three to four million dollars' worth of newsprint annually. Only a thriving newspaper chain could absorb this. During court hearings Paul Block futilely tried to place a bid; Swope (backed by Averell Harriman, Bernard Baruch and Owen Young) attempted to gain a stay; and World employees held mass meetings to raise funds. It was too little, too late. The sale to Scripps-Howard, which would combine the Evening World with the Telegram, apparently was a *fait accompli*, agreed to behind the scenes. Perhaps the Pulitzer family considered that a continuing New York World would be a Banquo's Ghost, capable of haunting them even in St. Louis. Whatever the case, with the Surrogate's blessing the Evening World was sold to Scripps-Howard. The World and the Sunday World expired.

On February 27, 1931, the last New York World went to press. Lindesay Parrott wrote out the final story, while women cried and men took to drink. Since the advent of Frank Munsey, death-of-newspaper scenes had become familiar to New York, but the World was given an unprecedented tribute by the metropolis it had so long served. As news of the sale became known, a pall of sadness appeared to spread over the entire city. The death of the World appeared to have taken a fragment of the soul of New York City along with it. . . .

Now no newspapers were printed on Newspaper Row, a fact lamented by the Sun from its Munsey-bought headquarters on Broadway beyond City Hall. On February twenty-eighth, a nostalgic article in the Sun took readers on this flight of fancy:

> Night after night and year after year, until last night hale old ghosts foregathered in Park Row to marvel at these new times and sometimes curse them roundly. They were grand marvelers and grand swearers, too, those great old boys who came flitting out of the hereafter—Dana of The Sun, the elder Bennett of the old Herald, Greeley of The Tribune, Henry Raymond of The Times, and Pulitzer of The World. Night after night through a long parade of years they came back to their old battleground —until last night.
>
> For last night there was nothing left for them to come back to. Their last link with the living world had been broken. The golden tower of the New York World was dark and silent. Throughout the whole World Building—the Pulitzer Building—there was silence and darkness. Not one echo of that restless life which is so peculiarly a newspaper's could have reached these deathless gentlemen. In all Park Row, from the Brooklyn Bridge to the St. Paul Building and Broadway, and in all of the side streets adjacent, there was left not one single throb of newspaper life. With the passing of the New York World went the last newspaper of Park Row.

Shortly the once-famous stretch of street was given over to quick, Depression businesses, bowling alleys, legal offices and movie theatres. The World Building remained and next to it the old Tribune Building with its clock tower, but no longer did the street resound with the excitements of daily newspapers. Newspaper Row was gone. Park Row was just another commercial street.

The great reporters went, too. Through the Thirties and Forties,

Irvin Cobb, Frank Ward O'Malley, Albert Payson Terhune, Martin Green and numberless others died. At times, the new age even appeared to be trying to wreak a terrible vengeance on the old, as if jealous of its tradition of more leisurely days. An especially grievous blow was dealt the shade of David Graham Phillips. In 1944 his biographer, Isaac F. Marcosson, decided to present a bust of Phillips to DePauw University, which the novelist attended before going to Princeton. Marcosson carefully collected every known photograph of Phillips. These he gave to the sculptor Henry Hering, from whom he commissioned a bust of the handsome Phillips.

Hering's studio lay atop 10 West 33rd Street, across the street from the Empire State Building, erected on the site of the Waldorf-Astoria of the Park Row era. Hering modelled the bust through the summer of 1945. Then, on a foggy Saturday, an airplane crashed into the Empire State Building. Hering had wisely decided to play golf that day, but in the center of his studio sat the bust, surrounded by the valuable Phillips pictures. Hurtling through the steel structure, an engine of the plane landed on the roof of 10 West 33rd. Nearly all Hering's sculpture was smashed, including the bust of Phillips. As the wreckage was sifted only one charred photograph of Phillips remained.

In January, 1950, the Sun went the way of the World. On Frank Munsey's death the paper had been bought by W. T. Dewart, who quickly sold the Evening Telegram to Scripps-Howard. Dewart had been Munsey's right-hand man, and his interest in the editorial side of newspapers was slight. Under him, however, the excellent Sun staff kept alive the paper's notable tradition. But with Dewart's death, his two sons were found to be even less interested in newspapers than the Pulitzer heirs. In retrospect the Sun staff—no less than the World—seemingly should have known what was coming. But again they did not. At the last awful moment they began a scramble to raise money to prevent the paper's sale to Scripps-Howard. Again the effort was too late.

So the once-lowly Telegram became the New York World-Telegram and Sun. Old newspapermen today say that, though it absorbed the two most individual newspapers in New York, the Telegram remains the Telegram. In St. Louis, ironically, the Post-Dispatch continues as an excellent crusading newspaper, in the best Joseph Pulitzer tradition.

The Pulitzer Building fell next. Plans for a sweeping esplanade leading to Brooklyn Bridge doomed the gold-domed building in the early 1950's. But the plans of municipalities move slowly and before wreckers arrived the Building enjoyed a last moment of glory. During a period when City Hall was remodeled, the Mayor of New York and his staff occupied the sixth floor of the World Building. On May 1, 1955, they moved out, and demolition promptly began. As always, the wreckers built a protective wooden fence around the job and, following custom, took the finest door in the Building to make an entrance to the wooden fence. Thus the paneled door to Joseph Pulitzer's Tower office performed its last function along Park Row. Shortly after, a nighttime fire was discovered on the eleventh floor, where the two World city rooms had once been. It was as if the assorted spirits of Colonel Cockerill, Charles Edward Russell, Charles Chapin, Frank I. Cobb and other memorable editors had returned to protest. It did no good. The blaze was quickly discovered and put out.

Today only the Tribune Building remains, with its red-brick clock tower recalling the flavor of old Park Row. That is all, but it is perhaps a tribute to the old Newspaper Row that three of New York's seven daily newspapers are still published within a long stone's throw of Park Row. The World-Telegram and Sun on Barclay Street, the Post on West Street, and the Journal-American on South Street still bring a newspaper flavor to downtown New York.

As this book is completed, the Wall Street Journal solemnly announces a survey to find out why young men are no longer attracted to journalism. The grandeur that was Park Row is gone. Today the street's splendid era is no more than a memory—or, at best, a footnote to history. But no less than the turn-of-the-century newspapermen cited by Ned Brown, Park Row was a citizen of no mean state.

BIBLIOGRAPHY

THE AUTHOR is especially indebted to Isaac F. Marcosson, Rube Goldberg, Walter Marshall and others mentioned in the text. He is also indebted to Harry Hershfield, whose reminiscences of Park Row helped kindle interest in the subject. Also to Professor Edwin Arthur Hill, of the College of the City of New York, for advice; and to his publisher for encouragement and support.

Aside from the verbal, sources of the book are these:

Barrett, James W.: *Joseph Pulitzer and His World*
———— *The World, The Flesh and Messrs. Pulitzer*
Beer, Thomas: *The Mauve Decade*
———— *Stephen Crane*
Berger, Meyer: *The Story of the New York Times*
Britt, George: *Forty Years, Forty Millions*—The Career of Frank Munsey
Brooks, Van Wyck: *John Sloan*
Carlson, Oliver: *Brisbane*
———— (with Ernest Sutherland Bates) *Hearst*
Chapin, Charles: *Charles Chapin's Story*
———— *The Constance Letters*, edited by Eleanor Early
Clarke, Donald Henderson: *Man of the World*
Clarke, Selah F.: *Frivolous Recollections of Newspaperdom*
Cobb, Irvin: *Exit Laughing*
Collins, Frederick L.: *Glamorous Sinners*
Crane, Stephen: *Maggie, A Girl of the Streets*
———— *Stories and Tales*, edited by Robert Wooster Stallman
———— *The Red Badge of Courage*

Creelman, James: *On the Great Highway*

Crockett, Albert Stevens: *When James Gordon Bennett was Caliph of Bagdad*

Davis, Elmer: *History of the New York Times*

Davis, Richard Harding: *Van Bibber and Other Stories*

Downey, Fairfax: *Richard Harding Davis*

Ford, James L.: *Forty Years in the Literary Shop*

Golding, Louis T.: *Memories of Old Park Row*

Ireland, Alleyne: *An Adventure with a Genius*

Lundberg, Ferdinand: *Imperial Hearst*

Lynn, Kenneth S.: *The Dream of Success*

McDougall, Walt: *It's a Great Life*

Marcosson, Isaac F.: *David Graham Phillips*

————— "Marse Henry"—A Biography of Henry Watterson

Millis, Walter: *The Martial Spirit*

Morris, Lloyd: *Incredible New York*

————— *Postscript to Yesterday*

Noble, Iris: *Joseph Pulitzer*

O'Brien, Frank M.: *The Story of the Sun*

O. Henry: *Collected Stories*

Phillips, David Graham: *The Fashionable Adventures of Joshua Craig*

————— *The Great God Success*

————— *Susan Lenox: Her Fall and Rise*

Pringle, Henry F.: *Theodore Roosevelt*

Ralph, Julian: *The Making of a Journalist*

Riis, Jacob: *How the Other Half Lives*

————— *The Making of an American*

Rosebault, Charles J.: *When Dana was The Sun*

Rovere, Richard: *Howe and Hummel*

Russell, Charles Edward: *Bare Hands and Stone Walls*

————— *These Shifting Scenes*

Samuels, Charles: *The Girl on the Red Velvet Swing*

Seitz, Don Carlos: *The James Gordon Bennetts*

————— *Joseph Pulitzer—His Life and Letters*

Steffens, Lincoln: *Autobiography*

Sullivan, Mark: *Our Times—The Turn of the Century*

Tebbel, John: *The Life and Good Times of William Randolph Hearst*

Terhune, Albert Payson: *To the Best of My Memory*

Walker, Stanley: *City Editor*

Winkler, John K.: *William Randolph Hearst*

MAGAZINES
American Mercury
The Bookman
The Independent
The New Yorker

NEWSPAPERS
Evening World
New York Journal
New York Sun
New York Times
New York World
. . . and others of the era

INDEX

338   Index

White, Stanford, 165, 209-10, 226, 230, 241-5, 277
White, William Allen, 291
White (Stanford) Murder. *See* Thaw (Harry K.) Case
Whitney, Caspar, 116
Wilcox, Ella Wheeler, 52, 80
Wild Rose, 226
Williams, Jesse Lynch, 223
Williams, Samuel R., 268
Wilson, Woodrow, 63, 287, 300
Winkler, John K., 334
Within the Law, 52
Woman magazine, 293
Wood, General Leonard, 119, 125, 130
Woollcott, Alexander, 232
World, the Evening. *See* Evening World, the
World, the New York (Morning), 9, 10, 11, 27-44, 45, 46, 47, 49, 50, 51-7, 60, 61, 62, 63, 64, 65, 66, 67, 70, 71, 72, 75, 76, 77, 79, 81, 82, 83, 86, 87-90, 92-7, 99, 100, 102, 106, 107, 111, 114-5, 116, 120-1,

128-9, 133, 134, 137, 167, 176, 177, 186, 188, 189, 190, 216, 223, 224, 225, 233, 236, 239, 243, 245, 246, 248, 252, 255, 267-70, 272, 274, 278-82, 288-9, 290, 291, 305, 313, 314, 315, 316, 317-8, 326, 327, 328, 329
World, the Sunday. *See* Sunday World, the
World Building, the, 43-4
World, the Flesh, and Messrs. Pulitzer, The, 327

"Yama Yama Girl." *See* Davis, Mrs. Richard Harding
"Yellow Kid, the," 81-2
Young, Brigadier General B. S. M., 124, 129
Young, Caesar, 232
Young, Owen, 328
Yucatan, the, 121, 123

Ziegfeld, Florenz, 212
Zogbaum, Rufus, 117
Zola, Emile, 202